Integrating ChatGPT Into System Applications and Services

Muhammad Usman Tariq
Abu Dhabi University, UAE & University College Cork, Ireland

IGI Global
Scientific Publishing
Publishing Tomorrow's Research Today

Vice President of Editorial	Melissa Wagner
Director of Acquisitions	Mikaela Felty
Director of Book Development	Jocelynn Hessler
Production Manager	Mike Brehm
Cover Design	Jose Rosado

Published in the United States of America by
IGI Global Scientific Publishing
701 East Chocolate Avenue
Hershey, PA, 17033, USA
Tel: 717-533-8845
Fax: 717-533-7115
Website: https://www.igi-global.com E-mail: cust@igi-global.com

Library of Congress Cataloging-in-Publication Data

LCCN: 2025004548 (CIP Data Pending)
ISBN13: 9798369398418
Isbn13Softcover: 9798369398425
EISBN13: 9798369398432

British Cataloguing in Publication Data
A Cataloguing in Publication record for this book is available from the British Library.

Table of Contents

Detailed Table of Contents

The on-going refinements in Natural Language Processing (NLP) are enhancing the quality of language models such as ChatGPT. The proposed methods include fine-tuning, knowledge distillation, reinforcement learning from human feedback, and prompt engineering to improve model performance, speed, and relevance. By implicating multiple form of data including text and images, multimodal learning expands the capability of ChatGPT for complex application in practical use. Cross-lingual transfer adds to the adopted multiple languages in which ChatGPT can be used to reach a wider world population. Solutions to memory management/recommendation and ethical concern regarding bias or fairness are relevant in enhancing the overall organization of the model, its applicability to a specific user profile and users' demographic background. Taken together, all of these contributions enhance not only the practical value and flexibility of the model but, critically, the overall pursuit of accountable AI.

learning techniques, including classification, clustering, and correlation analysis, were used to identify patterns and relationships between variables, while inferential statistics, such as Exploratory Factor Analysis (EFA) and multiple regression, assessed the predictive factors influencing student reliance on AI. Findings revealed a complex relationship between AI usage, learning outcomes, and student dependency, offering valuable insights for educators and policymakers.

It integrates AI into learning environments, which is transforming the conventional and online learning environment by coming up with something groundbreaking in the way of a personalized virtual tutor known as ChatGPT. The chapter looks into how ChatGPT uses the sophisticated natural language processing to present tailor-made learning experiences to suit the different preferences, paces, and requirements of individual students. The instant explanations, feedback, and support on diverse subjects increase the engagement, motivation, and ultimate educational success of the students. The chapter also presents practical insights on technical integration, data security, and ethical considerations to ensure accountable use. It emphasizes the importance of combining AI with human oversight in creating balanced educational solutions. Through many examples and case studies, it demonstrates how ChatGPT is capable of connecting old learning methods with modern e-learning, thereby encouraging stakeholders to consider AI for greater personalization and transformation in education.

We have developed novel algorithm that integrates ChatGPT to revolutionize drug discovery, addressing the complexities and high costs associated with traditional methods. This innovative algorithm leverages ChatGPT's advanced natural language processing capabilities to perform comprehensive literature analysis, extracting relevant information on drug targets and compounds from vast scientific databases. Unique features include predictive modelling for pharmacokinetic (PK) and pharmacodynamic (PD) properties, allowing for informed modifications to enhance bioavailability and reduce toxicity. Additionally, the algorithm employs iterative feedback mechanisms, enabling real-time collaboration between researchers and

ChatGPT to refine chemical structures based on simulated biological interactions. By incorporating a multi-persona approach, the algorithm provides tailored support throughout the drug discovery pipeline. Overall, this integration aims to accelerate therapeutic development while ensuring safety and efficacy, ultimately transforming the landscape of pharmaceutical innovation.

The rise of AI, especially chatbots, has transformed industries by enhancing efficiency and user experience. However, increased use raises concerns about protecting Personally Identifiable Information (PII). Existing solutions often lack scalability and flexibility, leading to security risks. This research develops a secure, data-conscious AI system using AWS services, particularly Amazon Macie, for automated PII detection and protection. It integrates natural language processing with strong backend security to ensure privacy, compliance, and trust. Amazon Macie uses machine learning and pattern-matching to monitor and secure AWS S3 data, addressing technical and ethical concerns. The goal is to enhance chatbot security and data governance, enabling them to manage complex interactions while safeguarding sensitive information. Results show that Amazon Macie improves PII detection, security, and compliance, contributing to scalable solutions for data privacy and user trust.

Large language model systems such as ChatGPT are causing significant disruption across various industries. This study investigates how scalable enterprise solutions can be architected with ChatGPT as a central element of the system. The author has analyzed the core components of foundational architecture, current state of usage of ChatGPT in enterprise and provided details about how to design scalable systems. Findings from this study indicate that the complexity of the overall systems and lack of clear data policy may cause challenges to an organization's capability for implementing a successful ChatGPT powered solution. The author has provided guidelines about data strategy and enhanced devops patterns to overcome that. Moreover, this paper has examined model optimization techniques to reduce cost and latency. Real-world case studies are provided as a reference. This research

Preface

The rise of conversational AI represents one of the most transformative shifts in how humans interact with technology. At the forefront of this evolution stands ChatGPT, an advanced language model capable of simulating nuanced, context-aware, and responsive dialogue across a spectrum of domains. As its adoption accelerates, the challenge now lies not in understanding *what* ChatGPT can do, but in mastering *how* to integrate it effectively into system applications and services that drive real-world value. This book answers that call.

Integrating ChatGPT Into System Applications and Services was conceived as a comprehensive, practical, and technically grounded reference that guides readers through the entire lifecycle of ChatGPT integration from foundational understanding to enterprise-level deployment. Our aim is to bridge the gap between cutting-edge AI theory and actionable system design, empowering professionals across sectors to build intelligent, responsive, and ethical conversational systems.

This volume brings together a broad range of perspectives and expertise. It is structured to support multiple user groups, including software developers, system architects, researchers, entrepreneurs, and IT administrators. Whether you are exploring ChatGPT for the first time or are a seasoned practitioner aiming to scale AI capabilities across an enterprise, this book offers a detailed roadmap.

CHAPTER OVERVIEWS

Chapter 1: Advanced NLP Techniques for Enhancing ChatGPT Performance

As conversational AI systems continue to evolve, this chapter delves deep into the cutting-edge techniques used to optimize ChatGPT's performance. Topics such as fine-tuning, reinforcement learning, multimodal learning, and cross-lingual adaptation are examined alongside ethical considerations like bias and demographic fairness. The chapter offers a technically rich perspective that will benefit developers and AI researchers striving for responsible, high-performing implementations.

Chapter 2: Harnessing Higher Generative Artificial Intelligence for Educational Pedagogy

Here, the focus shifts to the transformative impact of next-generation generative AI models, such as ChatGPT-4 and beyond, on modern education. The chapter provides a forward-looking examination of how these models can foster critical thinking and adaptive learning environments. By aligning with the Sustainable Development Goals (SDGs) in education, it also positions ChatGPT as not just a tool, but a catalyst for global educational equity and innovation.

Chapter 3: Sustainable Learning Solutions: ChatGPT Integration in Academic Services

Through a robust mixed-methods approach, this chapter investigates how students perceive and depend on ChatGPT for learning. The integration of machine learning techniques with qualitative feedback reveals nuanced relationships between AI support, motivation, and academic outcomes. The insights presented are invaluable for policymakers and educators interested in harnessing AI without fostering undue dependency.

Chapter 4: Revolutionizing Education with AI: ChatGPT as a Personalized Virtual Tutor for E-Learning Platforms

This chapter illustrates how ChatGPT is reinventing the e-learning landscape by offering hyper-personalized learning experiences. With a strong focus on accessibility, ethical data use, and technical implementation, the authors showcase how ChatGPT can serve as an effective virtual tutor. Real-world applications demonstrate its potential to bridge traditional and modern education paradigms, making this a practical guide for ed-tech innovators and educators alike.

Chapter 5: A Novel Algorithm to Discover New Drugs Using ChatGPT

Stepping beyond education, this chapter introduces a breakthrough algorithm that uses ChatGPT for intelligent drug discovery. The model aids in literature review, compound screening, and pharmacological prediction through natural language processing. Featuring an iterative, collaborative design process between human researchers and AI, this chapter reveals how conversational models are reshaping pharmaceutical research and accelerating the path to new therapies.

Chapter 6: Securing Conversational AI: Building Data Security-Aware Chatbots With Enhanced User Data Governance

Security and privacy remain critical concerns in AI development, and this chapter tackles them head-on. By leveraging AWS tools like Amazon Macie, the authors outline a framework for integrating ChatGPT into secure systems that prioritize PII protection and regulatory compliance. This chapter is essential reading for system architects and compliance officers working with AI in sensitive or regulated industries.

Chapter 7: Architecting Scalable ChatGPT Solutions for Enterprise

This chapter presents a blueprint for building enterprise-grade ChatGPT solutions, balancing scalability, performance, and compliance. It details architectural patterns, data governance practices, and model optimization strategies with clarity and practical insight. The included case studies further contextualize the recommendations, making this chapter a cornerstone resource for enterprise IT professionals and solution architects.

Chapter 8: The Evolution of Chatbots: From Rule-Based to GPT Models

Offering a historical and technical lens, this chapter traces the journey of chatbot development from early rule-based systems to today's powerful generative models. It demystifies core concepts like Transformer architecture and Retrieval-Augmented Generation (RAG), providing a comprehensive foundation for understanding the technological shifts that underpin modern conversational AI.

Chapter 9: Transforming Marketing with Generative AI and ChatGPT: Insights From Literature and Real-World Companies

Closing the volume is a chapter that explores how generative AI is revolutionizing marketing strategies across industries. Through a mix of academic analysis and corporate case studies, it showcases how tools like ChatGPT enable personalized content, predictive customer interactions, and campaign automation. Practical recommendations make it a vital read for marketing professionals and digital strategists looking to embrace AI-driven innovation.

The chapters are organized to provide a logical and progressive path. We begin with essential concepts in conversational AI and natural language processing, laying the groundwork for understanding ChatGPT's capabilities and constraints. From there, we move into hands-on integration, advanced customization techniques, and deployment strategies tailored for diverse infrastructures.

A special emphasis is placed on real-world application. Throughout the book, we include case studies, deployment walkthroughs, and coding examples that demonstrate how ChatGPT is being successfully leveraged across industries from healthcare and finance to education and e-commerce. The ethical, social, and design considerations that accompany this technology are given due importance, reflecting the need for responsible innovation in the rapidly evolving AI landscape.

This project has also been shaped by a central goal: to encourage further inquiry and experimentation. By presenting not only what is possible today, but also pointing to the research frontiers of tomorrow, such as personalization, contextual memory, multimodal integration, and governance, we hope to inspire readers to both implement and innovate.

I extend my sincere thanks to the contributing authors, industry collaborators, and researchers who have enriched this work with their deep knowledge and insights. I am especially grateful to the interdisciplinary community that continues to shape the evolving dialogue between AI systems and human-centered design.

As we move forward into an era where conversational AI becomes embedded in daily operations, interactions, and decisions, I hope this book serves as a trusted companion, providing the tools, strategies, and vision needed to harness the full potential of ChatGPT in system applications and services.

Muhammad Usman Tariq
Abu Dhabi University, UAE & University College Cork, Ireland

Chapter 1
Advanced NLP Techniques for Enhancing ChatGPT Performance

Bitan Roy
https://orcid.org/0009-0006-6957-3263
Brainware University, Kolkata, India

Piyal Roy
https://orcid.org/0009-0007-5378-2789
Brainware University, Kolkata, India

Sanchita Ghosh
https://orcid.org/0009-0007-9421-5246
Brainware University, Kolkata, India

Tulika Paul
Brainware University, Kolkata, India

Sreelekha Paul
https://orcid.org/0009-0007-5524-1919
Brainware University, Kolkata, India

ABSTRACT

The on-going refinements in Natural Language Processing (NLP) are enhancing the quality of language models such as ChatGPT. The proposed methods include fine-tuning, knowledge distillation, reinforcement learning from human feedback, and prompt engineering to improve model performance, speed, and relevance. By implicating multiple form of data including text and images, multimodal learning expands the capability of ChatGPT for complex application in practical use. Cross-

DOI: 10.4018/979-8-3693-9841-8.ch001

lingual transfer adds to the adopted multiple languages in which ChatGPT can be used to reach a wider world population. Solutions to memory management/recommendation and ethical concern regarding bias or fairness are relevant in enhancing the overall organization of the model, its applicability to a specific user profile and users' demographic background. Taken together, all of these contributions enhance not only the practical value and flexibility of the model but, critically, the overall pursuit of accountable AI.

INTRODUCTION

Promising powerful abilities, large language models like OpenAI's ChatGPT are rapidly changing the paradigm of Natural Language Processing (NLP) (Sheng et al., 2019) for generation of human-like text generation. That said, there are still some drawbacks inherent in this approach; the ability to glean more contextual information about the input, the generation of responses, the speed at which the responses are generated, and the capacity to modulate the given output. For instance, application of sophisticated functions within advanced AL technology can go alongside to improve on aspects such as these, with an overall effect of improving the operational capability of models such as ChatGPT Perhaps the most acute problem in NLP models such as ChatGPT is a lack of understanding of context. They also note that memory enhancements such as attention mechanisms or memory networks can enhance memory function whereas domain adaptation using a new set of datasets can lead to better models which are much more appropriate for specific domains. Another limitation is that to achieve adequate results, models entail considerable computational power. There are also such problems as output control, and developers try to ensure higher model controllability through the use of specific structured prompts, constraint-based techniques, or letting a user affect the style and tone of the model's answers. The additional level of NLP enhancement of ChatGPT includes enhanced attention mechanisms, memory networks, fact-checkers integrated, multilingual/multimodal, and bias reduction (Goodfellow et al., 2019).

BACKGROUND

Transformer architecture, a unique topology for processing data sequences, is based on attention mechanisms. New methods such as Sparse Attention, Memory Efficient Attention, Multi-query Attention, Dynamic Attention, and Pre-layer Normalization are proposed to enhance the efficiency and ROCAU of Transformer-based models (Beltagy et al., 2019). Scattered attention is less computationally complex as it focuses on relevant tokens, allowing models to manage longer input sequences with similar performances. Memory Efficient Attention mitigates memory requirements for attention calculations, making it essential for scaling models like ChatGPT. Multi-query attention compresses attention heads of keys and values into one, leading to higher speeds and less fragmented replies. Dynamic attention mechanisms can be selected in ChatGPT, focusing on important tokens to improve the model's capacity to filter data in decisions during conversations. This boosts the model's rate of providing quality output in context-layer normalization helps stabilize gradients, enhancing speedy convergence during training. This technique eliminates problems such as slow convergence and unstable updates, making Transformer-based models like ChatGPT easier to train and adapt, particularly when deploying new releases or sub-models, and better for fine-tuning to new domains.

IMPROVING CONTEXTUAL AWARENESS AND MEMORY

In general, one of the biggest problems in constructing conversational agents like ChatGPT is to sustain context across multiple continuations. In traditional NLP, context information is more and more difficult to store with the extension and the depth of the conversation. Because of this, responses can be provided that are utterly unrelated to the previous parts of the conversation or do not cover the context altogether. But lately, with the development of NLP, such methods that enhance context recall and retention have been implemented into recent systems such as the ChatGPT, thereby enabling it to respond in more logically connected and relevant fashion across a number of conversations. This section describes those current methods, including long term memory mechanisms, improved attention models, and contextual embeddings which are superior to the earlier approaches.

Challenges in Maintaining Context

Context maintenance is crucial for conversational agents like ChatGPT to be useful value-adding companions. In simple dialogues, maintaining context is easy as the model only looks at the preceding several turns. However, when giving long and varied responses, the model must remember past conversations and use them appropriately. This is known as the 'context window', where the model tends to lose track of important contextual information. Researchers are developing techniques to improve context awareness. Memory-aided conversational agents, like ChatGPT, use self-attention computations to support memory recall (Gururangan et al., 2020). These models record and recall as much of the conversation as is precedent, ensuring order and interruption-free interactions. They are most effective in extended customer support communication when users reference previous statements or information (Tariq and Sergio, 2025).

Improved Attention Models

ChatGPT, a chatbot, uses Transformer architecture, focusing on context tracking and prioritizing information processing. However, efficiency decreases with sequence length due to complexity of self-attention computations. Researchers developed Sparse Attention and Long-Range Attention to enhance efficiency and scalability. Sparse Attention reduces token attendance, Long Range Attention maintains interaction information, and short-range attention focuses on token relationships. These models enhance the benefits of lengthy discussions with AI without compromising on relevant information. Contextual embeddings increase contextual reasoning in conversational models, allowing models to represent words or phrases meaningfully between contexts, helping with anorexics and semiotics. Unlike traditional transformer models, contextual embeddings like BERT capability help models understand user input based on context.

Reinforcement Learning from Human Feedback (RLHF)

However, another way of increasing contextual relevance into conversational agents is through using Reinforcement Learning (Holtzman et al., 2018) from Human Feedback. Here, human assessors rate the relevance of the model's answers and, in turn, the model is adjusted according to the received rating. This strengthens the model's understanding of which types of responses are more contextually relevant and how it should better remember prior information over the course of longer conversations, a goal central to RLHF's strengthening of ChatGPT. But in addition to language understanding, with the help of human feedback, developers can also guarantee that ChatGPT responds according to the norms of how people continue the conversation in a particular context.

EXTENDED CONTEXT HANDLING

Current state-of-the-art models for many Natural Language Processing (NLP) (Dai et al., 2019) tasks are Transformer models, which cannot surpass the limitations of the fixed context window tractably. This limitation especially becomes a vice in handling long conversations because any piece of information from the previous parts of the conversation is forgotten by the model. These principles are supplemented by two new concepts, namely RAM, which increased the size of the context windows, and Transformer-XL, which allows models like ChatGPT to remain coherent and much more capable of understanding multi-turn dialogue as used in this app. In this section, we provide details of what these mechanisms are, how they work to influence dialogue management and the way in which they contribute to improving the capability of conversational AI (Madaan, et al., 2016).

Recurrent Attention Mechanisms (RAM): Extending Context Windows

Legacy Transformer models like chatGPT have a cortical memory window size restriction; they cannot retrieve parts of the text which have occurred several turns previously during an elongated dialogue. Recurrent Attention Mechanisms (RAM) can be used where the model is to have a recurrent state containing information across the segments of the text so as to access the data beyond the fixed window. RAM is continuously in a steady state which changes depending with the segment of text being analyzed, making it a memory type. This lets a model use details from previous dialogues to its current state thereby enhancing its comprehension of the input data. Memory Augmented Responder or RAM supports ChatGPT to recall past conversations and apply that knowledge to the next exchanged conversation to maintain contextual relevance over the multiple conversations.

Transformer-XL: Segment-Level Recurrence for Extended Context

Transformer-XL is one of the architectural enhancements extending the context window of a traditional Transformer models through incorporating a segment level recurrence mechanism. This enables information to pass through successive segments of text, widening down the context window of the model. Transformer-XL can preservation hidden states of previous segment; the latest states can retain the internal dependency whereas multiple text sequences can be taken. This is especially useful for conversational interfaces like the ChatGPT as those are used in multi-turn scenarios, where coherence from conversation turn to another is of essence. Transformer-XL can reap advantage from recurrent segment where every segment is linked with the previous one, and it will make sure the answer given is relevant to the first part of the conversation. This leads to better ability when dealing with intricate conversation flows for example where two or more topics are discussed or change is performed (Tariq, 2025).

Comparison of RAM and Transformer-XL

Recurrent Attention Mechanisms (RAM) and Transformer-XL are technologies that enhance the model's capacity to remember prior state information on long interactions. RAM is updated for each segment while Transformer-XL can model the long context across text segments. It will be enjoyed by dialog systems such as ChatGPT because it powers various techniques that make multi-turn dialogues structurally coherent and more relevant. The utilization of RAM and Transformer-XL within ChatGPT enhances performance in 2-way conversations, conversation Commons propriety, and user satisfaction in the examples like customer service, virtual assistants, and tutoring.

EPISODIC AND LONG-TERM MEMORY

Multi-turn coherency is an issue that affects conversational agent such as ChatGPT. Many conventional models consider a conversation as a single and temporary action, which does not allow to save information. Effectively using episodic memory and NMNs can help with context relevance, employability and user satisfaction through the storage of the facts and dialogues patterns.

Episodic Memory: Tracking Information Across Sessions

Episodic memory is a system's ability to store and recall information from specific interaction processes and can be compared with human ability to remember events. In ChatGPT, it enables the model to save samples of previous conversation so as to improve continuity and personalization of user conversations. This enables first, for instance, preservation of user preferences, or dialogue history over contests of consecutive sessions. Episodic memory is not only concerned with the recording of the input as factual details, but also the receiving and storing of information that will be useful in future transactions.

Neural Memory Networks (NMNs): Explicit Memory Mechanisms for Retaining Knowledge

Neural Memory Networks (NMNs) are a proposal for improving the memory component of conversational agents. It imitates human memory storage and recall resolution; it stores information within dynamic memory address locations. NMNs enhance the performance of ChatGPT in large forms of face-to-face talk by enabling a correct reading and writing from particular slots derived from the conversational structure. These slots are used to store facts, user specific details or contextual information to make the interaction more seamless and contextually correct. They also filter intended information and exclude the non-intentional information thereby making efficiency in use of information hence avoiding repetition most of the times.

Improving Context Management and Personalization

NMNs and episodic memories bring more efficient context management and serve engagements with better specification in the case of ChatGPT. These memory systems enable the model to remember user-related data for the subsequent interactions that guarantee proper response coherence and personalization. But, implementing these technologies has constraints like over storage capacity and speed, memory protection, and privacy considerations. Good design sees to it that a model stays manageable and that one can scale up this model, moreover, there are trade-offs between memory storage for an application and performance.

EPISODIC MEMORY

Collecting, archetype or memory systems which make some form of conversation, requires creation of' memory span that is compatible to that of human being conversational AI (ChatGPT) is a technology that uses memory systems to replicate human memory, allowing for meaningful and contextual conversations. Text Long-term memory enables the chatbot of ChatGPT to carry forward the previous conversation and refrain from reiterating an earlier response or giving unrelated responses. Memory systems keep track of the prior dialog sections that the model retains so that all the information will remain coherent and relevant. Memory modules also help in expounding the sessions' continuity as well as personalization between numerous sessions in order to evoke natural responses. Neural Memory Networks optimize storage locations for entry/exit/update throughout the conversation, increasing coherence and individuality. However, there are challenges to overcome, such as the trade-off between memory usage and complexity. If the model stores information beyond the required level, it may become complex or return obscure information, confusing users. To prevent overload and maintain privacy, memory systems should store only relevant data and consider user preferences. As memory components improve, future conversational models may include long-term memory storage, better conversational approaches, user preferences consideration, and information management capabilities.

Memory and Long-Term Context Management

Language models, such as the Transformer-based ones perform rather well in context-based processing of short to average length sequences but fail in terms of managing long-term context. They live strictly in a sliding window of input tokens, and the number of tokens is fixed; thus, they can only remember parts of a conversation or a document they have seen or read recently. Which is rather disadvantageous when handling with long texts or complex conversations in multi-turn dialogues. Thank you @gagatagaci for pointing this out Researchers are working on long term memory mechanisms in order to increase the context window so that models can remember what has been said in the past in the context of long interactions. (Petroni et al., 2019) Most popular do mainstream language models such as the Transformer architecture, possess a comparatively small context window of several hundred to a few thousand tokens. This restriction is effective when working with short texts or in simple dialogues, yet the results may be irrelevant or randomly chosen if a server handles complex requests, such as extensive texts or discussion, as is often seen in conversational AI such as ChatGPT (Tariq, 2025).

Advanced Memory Mechanisms for Extending Context

Superior forms of memory management are being designed to improve a model's performance in maintaining information through a longer stream of an interaction. They include Recurrent Attention Mechanisms (RAM), Transformer-XL architecture, Episodic Memory Systems and Neural Memory Networks (NMNs). RAM enables models to pass explicit information from one text segment to another while Transformer-XL enlarges the context window without bringing computational overhead (Chen et al., 2018). Operating in parallel with other long-term and working memory spaces, episodic memory systems will activate and allow for access to the portions relevant to continued or subsequent dialogue and interaction. Efficient of these mechanisms is a focus of study.

FINE-TUNING AND TRANSFER LEARNING

The concept of tuning is widely used in machine learning models (LLMs) like ChatGPT after pretraining on large datasets. It focuses on retrogreening the model to a specific set of data relevant to the application, such as legal text mining or disease diagnosis. This enables the model to enhance translation of general natural language understanding for that specialized field leading to improved performance, relativity, and also precision. For instance, sting preprocess data by refining a language model's capability to read large volumes of text data but does not configure the model for a specific entity relevant to the particular task. Fine-tuning is about choosing the tasks and/or domains, creating data sets, model training, and model assessment and fine-tuning. The first step is to introduce and focus on the task or area, then have two training cycles using certain data. This eliminates the possibility of the catastrophic forgetting technique, which updates the model with the given domain-specific dataset. The advantages of fine-tuning are higher efficiency, faster training, and improved model applicability, which authors of (Howard et al., 2018) discussed in detail. However, it has its setbacks, for example, fine-tuning model parameters into the fine-tuning datasets end up with overfitting issues the overly emphasize on NLP specialization. As for these problems, the regularization, drop-out, and data augmentation can be used. Also, catastrophic interference can happen when the model forgets general language characteristics learned at the pretraining phase, which can be solved by fine-tuning with low learning rates, or using elastic weight consolidation.

Fine-Tuning Approaches

It can be made clearer that the training of these language models such as ChatGPT is done by repurposing the differentiated parameters of a pretrained model for improved performance in some categories. Thus, this procedure ensures that the diffuse and differentiated information and knowledge sources are honed in line with a certain broad range of activities or a particular field of focus. Fine-tuning can be classified into two main categories: The first set is small-scale fine-tuning known as domain-specific fine-tuning and the second one is task specific fine-tuning. Not only is the function of each approach completely different, when the model focuses on data that is related or tasks which are comparative it optimizes its uses.

Domain-Specific Fine-Tuning

Fine-tuning technique is used to show the model what specialist terms or language usage are typical of a particular field. This approach cannot work with just any data set: it must be a finely-selected one, including case law, legislation, contracts and clinical records. Benefits involved include increased accuracy, reliability and user confidence. alleges are still present nevertheless, for instance acquiring quality annotated data which can be very expansive especially in the specialism and over fitting of the model/algorithm.

Task-Specific Fine-Tuning

Fine-tuning or task-specific fine-tuning is the process by which an existing pre-trained model is made more effective in solving particular tasks such as summarization, question answering, sentiment analysis, or machine translation among others. It involves rehearing of the model to such specific tasks so that it is given an understanding of what is required of it in a given task. This approach is easier than just merely avoiding errors as it focuses on the details of the job. It also makes task adaptability possible because a single model can be adjusted for different tasks. Nonetheless, one of the biggest obstacles is data accessibility where it must come in huge volumes and tagged well for the task under concern. Dedication to learn only the samples in the detailed task database diminishes the model's ability to solve the other tasks or apply it to different fields. (Baltrusaitis et al., 2019)

Transfer Learning

Transfer learning is a method in Natural Language Processing (Alsentzer et al., 2019) where a large model is used as a starting point for another more niche application. This makes it possible for the newly introduced model to deploy pre-tuned generalized information that is refined on small data sets to address unique problems or distinct tasks. This is especially helpful with models such as ChatGPT because input embedding from the pretrained language model can be reused, making it efficient in reusing the results obtained in the communication model.Transfer learning in Natural Language Processing (NLP) (Collobert et al., 2018) involves two steps: pretraining and fine-tuning. The definitions of the pretraining are to train the large language model with different textual data to train the generalized language features of the model like grammar, syntax, semantics, and the context which the message can be understood in. Hence, with finetuning we work with fine-tuning adaptation of the model on the narrowed down lesser and relevant data set corresponding to the given task or domain. The model adjusts some characteristics to details of the problem and uses an optimized (Nemkul, 2024) number of training samples, which provides a high level of work. This makes the transfer learning especially beneficial for the domains that don't have large annotated dataset.

Benefits of Transfer Learning in ChatGPT

ChatGPT uses transfer learning as a technique to fine tune the language structure and patterns towards specific application in low resource domains such as healthcare and legal technology. This composes for a small amount of given data by utilizing compactly pre-trained language structures. For example, BioBERT is a next generation variant of BERT that actually increased performance on programs and recognitions related to biomedical NLP. Transfer learning is used to cut down the amount of time as well as amount of computation, needed to train a given model, making it economical, specifically when developing models specific to some field. It also sustains the general language competence along with switching to and fro the particular job making it strong models. (Sahoo et al., 2024)

CHALLENGES AND LIMITATIONS

Transfer learning describes the ability to fine-tune a model in order get it to learn information more thoroughly. However, it has the following drawbacks catastrophically forgetting during which the model may forget some of the generalized knowledge which it learnt during pretraining. To avoid this, the following have been framed: laid out below are the following techniques that can minimize the probability of this occurrence; Gradual unfreezing. Domain shift is another issue, transfer learning is most effective when there is similarity between source domain and the target domain. Nevertheless, if they are rather different, it may be helpful to apply the pretraining methods for each of the domains. other shortcoming of the ML is overfitting by which a model is produced in such a way that it suits the training data inappropriately and fails to work effectively in new data sets. The methods, such as dropout or early stopping, are employed during fine-tuning to avoid overfitting of models.

APPLICATIONS OF TRANSFER LEARNING IN CHATGPT

Transfer learning has significantly improved the efficiency of ChatGPT in various industries, including customer support, healthcare, and legal tech. By integrating customer interactions, ChatGPT can be fine-tuned for specific tasks, such as report summarizing and research. It is also essential for legal practitioners in research, contract analysis, and case summary. Few shot learning enables a model to accomplish the task with a small set of example, which eliminate the dependence on a huge data base of labelled data and can significantly decrease the time needed to develop and launch NLP applications based on them. Zero-shot learning also known as generalization learning can make a model learn from another task without the need of learning that task and get extra training data to produce large responses. This approach differs from other approaches having flexibility, cheaper, openly available and less or no dependence on annotated datasets. Knowledge distillation, therefore, is a method of making large models to be put on restricted smart devices such as mobile phones and edge devices (Tariq, 2025).

REINFORCEMENT LEARNING FROM HUMAN FEEDBACK (RLHF)

RLHF stands for Reinforcement Learning from Human Feedback and is a novel machine learning method designed to teach generative models such as ChatGPT how to respond to the user feedback. They combine the trial-and-error reinforcement learning approach with human evaluative feedback making it extensive for designing Artificial Intelligence systems (Likhosherstov et al., 2023). The academy of RLHF includes generating answers to questions or the opinions of the other teams or cohorts on the criteria such as helpful, truthful, relevant or polite. These scores are utilised for further rewarding function learning that is tailored at estimating the quality of output from the feedback. This is employed as a proxy for human judgment the extent to which an output captures culture and preference. Standard RLHF is crucial since the output generated can be trained on real-time scores gleaned from a particular culture. This reduces the number of cycles used in processing unnecessary and actually false messages thus improving the model for users. RLHF is a cycle-on-top-of-a-cycle process of honing performance based on shifting customer views.

Overview of Reinforcement Learning in ChatGPT

In reinforcement learning, the goal is to find the best approach to obtain cumulative reward over a period in a procedure that infers responses from evaluation from human actors. This process involves a reward signal which the model learned to predict the output probabilities. Some PPO reinforcement learning algorithms to transform the model's output distribution to favour the creation of responses that receive higher scores. This assists the designed model in mimicking human decision making by discriminating in favour of outputs that allow improvement by favouring human values. The feedback loop generates, where the model enhances his answers consistently, relying on previous outcomes as cumulative rewards hence becomes wiser and more competent in generating contextually appropriate outputs from the given inputs. Reinforcement learning is a method used by ChatGPT to provide accurate and contextually relevant information based on user feedback. It considers natural language behaviors, such as tone and topic, to increase user satisfaction. The model aims to meet users' needs by choosing outputs with the highest probability of being helpful and polite, based on the sum of rewards. However, it faces challenges such as feedback variability, the need to standardize input, and the challenge of singularizing right behavior based on human values. Solving these challenges is crucial for ChatGPT's accuracy and efficiency (Tariq and Sergio, 2025).

Retrieval-Augmented Generation (RAG)

Recently, the combination of retrieval systems with generative models is gaining widespread use in natural language understanding (NLU) to improve the efficiency of conversational systems such as ChatGPT. This means that the SELR is a combination of a retrievel system and a generative model to support both logically continuous and semantically relevant responses. The used RAG approach presupposes getting data from various outside sources, like databases or search engines, and supplement the process of formulating a response for further in-depth and accurate education.The RAG approach enhances the educating function of ChatGPT by providing real-time answers and delivering updates in the sphere, including AI progress. The model also tightens the quality of nominated answers with reference to indicated data from trustworthy sources, guaranteeing users the credibility of their sources and the genuine truth, Nevertheless, the availability of retrieval systems complements the opportunities of its integration with generative models, yet it contains drawbacks. The quality of the information retrieved directly determines the quality of the output; the method of on-line, real time retrieval has an associated time penalty where the data base is large. A proper pacing of responding also with the content that is given is part of properly engaging with the user.

MULTIMODAL LEARNING AND INTEGRATION

AI is combining numerical, relational, and multimedia data into language models such as ChatGPT in order to enhance performances as well as in real-life uses. This is especially useful where it is applied on jobs such as virtual customer support, and virtual personal assistant among others. CLIP is capable of tasks such as text-image generation or image-captioning since these involve text and image sets as inputsMultimodal architectures are set to become more open and efficient with continued evolution; they will find application in many domainsMultilingual NLP is critically important for AI advancement since they promote cross-cultural understanding and translation. The AI product and services democratisation is achieved when more people are using them; high quality models ensuring reinforcement of multilingual models.

Cross-Lingual Transfer Techniques: XLM-R

AI is synthesizing text, image and voice data into language models as seen in ChatGPT (Conneau et al., 2018) to be more effective and realistic in real world scenarios. Multimodal learning enables the AI system understand various forms of data and hence makes it more knowledgeable in response making. This is particularly useful in operations such as electronic customer service and the like, as well as virtual personal assistant bots. CLIP named Contrastive Language Image Pretraining enables tasks such as producing text from image inputs images as per natural language descriptions.Examples of multimodal integration in ChatGPT include: Virtual assistance, content generation and schooling through images and commands through voices. However, input fusion in the multimodal framework seems to deal with factors such as compatibility of data used, the size and density of models developed as well as capability in achieving real-time responses. Multimodal models have been found to be more closed but with increased future development in this area they will become more open and hence applicable widely in several areas. Multilingual NLP is vital in global AI development since the world's communities need translation to understand various matters. Achieving and maintaining superior, functionally robust models in all organisational languages increases the base of AI products and services in more hands, hence more democratisation of AI.With advancements in architectures, multimodal models will become more open and efficient, leading to wide applications in various fields.Creating and reinforcing high-quality multilingual models ensures more people use AI products and services, making the tech more democratized.

Vision-Language Models

Combining input by various modalities such as images and text with language models as ChatGPT enhances capabilities of delivering appropriate responses within tasks. As BatchTraversed training the models on the image and text data in parallel, they are able to learn how the model can interpret and describe visual data with more semantically rich language mediums. This multimodal learning capacity improves the performance of application like image caption, object recognition and visual question answering since it involves learning of both textual information and pictures.

Multimodal Learning: Combining Image and Text Data

For instance, multimodal learning is a technique that allows the discovering of a model that is capable of processing more than one type of mode at once, for instance text mode, image mode among others. This makes the approach more useful in mirroring actual problems in tackling information since it is presented in different formats. Challenges like image captioning, object recognition, and visual question answering truthfully demand from models understanding and creating descriptions based on image data, which can be a problem for text-based models. This choice allows richer interpretations of models and more contextually accurate descriptions of interdependent image and text data.

Applications of Multimodal Learning

Image captioning is essential in Website and application accessibility, social media platforms, and search engines; hence, we need systems (OpenAI's CLIP model) to provide concrete descriptions of objects, activities, and scenes. In this way multimodal models are able to synthesise captions that correlate visual characteristics and linguistic (Madotto et al., 2020) patterns to produce a logically connected and contextually correct caption. Object recognition is critical in many computer vision systems such as auto-mobiles, security cameras, and medical diagnosis. With multimodal models, objects and their relations can be recognised while simultaneously obtaining a contextually related description making continuous real-world applications such as self-driving cars and surveillance systems successful. VQA is fundamentally important for understanding visuals and structure of language that is a form of communication.

Models like CLIP for Multimodal Learning

CLIP (Contrastive Language-Image Pretraining) is a great example of the model researching the intersection between text and images to enhance the interpretation of the visual content. CLIP is trained with images and text descriptions, so it can handle text input and output given visuals (Radford et al., 2021). This training approach helps assign common features of images and words, thus it will generate natural language descriptions, or if required answer questions on images. Such as, CLIP can perform most tasks without the need to be further fine-tuned on a specific task that was not mentioned in the paper. General concepts learned during the pre-processing of training data by CLIP allows it to perform well on a variety of tasks, both experimental and textual. The proposed method is promising to combine AI systems into real-world applications where visual data is involved, where its ability to make sense of visual data similar to how language models interpret text data stands as evidence towards such prospects.

Benefits of Multimodal Integration

Multimodal models improve the decision-making process by using two or more modes improving its competency in VQA or image captioning. They advance the efficiency of AI tool and the interaction with them, primarily with virtual assistants. Nonetheless, issues common to all methods like computational costs, availability of the data, and data alignment issues still persist. Indeed, creating a variety of multi-modal datasets and enhancing the match between datasets are very important steps forward. Future work will be centered on optimising these parameters for enhanced interpretability and efficiency of these models.

Audio-Text Integration

The integration of the STT and TTS to the model (Feng,2003) broadens ChatGPT utility since users can input and/or receive output in voice, not merely text. This integration enables ChatGPT to work in other settings including voice interfaces, chat bots, and accessibility tools thus extending the potential use of the tool and making it easier to be used by as many people as possible in deed.

Speech-to-Text (STT) Systems: Converting Speech into Text

An STT transcribes speeches into written text and has its application wherever a user may wish to speak to ChatGPT instead of typing. With STT, ChatGPT, users are able to transform spoken queries into text format for processing, thus widening its utility. This is quite advantageous especially when performing the task using your hands it's cumbersome or even cannot be done like when operating the smart gadgets. Pulling into a single core, real-time interactions are also possible which provides STT like the experience similar to human conversation. New developments of STT systems such as the Google's Deep Speech and the Microsoft's Azure Cognitive Services have enhanced the speed of dialogue to text translation and the general accuracy therefore feasible to implement STT systems into ChatGPT.

Text-to-Speech (TTS) Systems: Generating Spoken Output

The text to speech functions (TTS) allow ChatGPT to provide audio output for the text it generates, which makes it suitable for voice based settings such voice assistants as well as in educational field. TTS renders a communicative flow like a human to human making it easier for people to interact with devices such as Smart speakers or mobile phones. It also makes these AI tools more accessible to users that have visual impairments or literate deficiencies that might make it harder for them to understand the content. The TTS systems also consist of multiple languages and accents which in turn extends its global domain to ChatGPT. New TTS models, such as Google WaveNet, create highly realistic sound, thus making conversations with ChatGPT more productive and natural in applications based on voice interface.

Applications of STT and TTS Systems

STT and TTS can be implemented with the help of a popular technology called ChatGPT which is used in google assistant, Alexa, Siri etc. They are capable of responding to versatile questions, scheduling appointments, and even shop. Multimodal chatbots that function in the STT and TTS allow for both text and voice interfaces so that clients in healthcare, banks, and retail can enjoy a better experience (Roy et al., 2023). They also allow ChatGPT to be used by disabled individuals as they are able to input queries through voice, thus, marrying inclusion with AI tools. This system can be complemented with other technologies such as screen reader or braille terminal to make web even more accessible.

Technological Considerations

When combined with ChatGPT, adding of features like Speech-to-Text (STT) (Marzuki, et al., 2019) and Text-to-Speech (TTS) for real-time, low latency rate for voice-based interfaces. Real-time processing of spoken language as displayed in Google Cloud Speech-to-Text makes voice-based interactions achievable in advanced STT systems (Lee et al., 2019). It is also possible for ChatGPT to perform multilingual and multidialect interactions for ease in handling voice-based applications in the international customer service area. TTS systems can also be adapted to cutomize certain conditions such as having a unique voice for customized customer service bots, or to give users the choices of the kind of tone, giving rate, and accent of the TTS voice.

Challenges and Future Directions

Several issues are still under development when it comes to STT for ChatGPT and TTS functionalities; matters like; background noise and accents, synthesising speech closely replicating human intonation, emotion as well as micro-prosody and ensuring the system is fully real-time with little lag which are areas of current improve on STT system in noisy environments and develop natural TTS that simulates human speech and emotions.

CONCLUSION

New techniques are adding new features to conversational AI systems such as ChatGPT such as fine-tuning, knowledge distillation, engineering prompts, reinforcement learning, and memory management. These techniques class enhance the efficiency and quality of the developed language models and by extension, user satisfaction. The preservation of fine-tuning refines special terms and arguments, which knowledge distillation minimizes computational load. SAP prompt engineering enhance control and accuracy on the kind of input prompts developed. Reinforcement learning targets to match responses with human liking, while memory management provides context in maintaining conversational flow over long turn taking conversations (Chalkidis et al., 2019). Multimodal learning helps the models to handle data from more than one way at the same time. There is a need to spread multiple methods to fight bias and other ethical issues that appear when AI becomes more popular. Terms such as debiasing algorithms, adversarial training, and inclusive data curation are being employed to make sure that the AI generated outputs are acceptable and appropriate across the populations. NLP is in the direction to overcome these challenges for enhanced and diverse versions of the AI systems.

REFERENCES

Alsentzer, E., Murphy, J., Boag, W., Weng, W.-H., Jindi, D., Naumann, T., & McDermott, M. (2019). *Publicly available clinical. Proceedings of the 2nd Clinical Natural Language Processing Workshop*. https://doi.org/DOI: 10.18653/v1/W19-1909

Baltrusaitis, T., Ahuja, C., & Morency, L.-P. (2019). Multimodal machine learning: A survey and taxonomy. *IEEE Transactions on Pattern Analysis and Machine Intelligence, 41*(2), 423–443. DOI: 10.1109/TPAMI.2018.2798607 PMID: 29994351

Beltagy, I., Lo, K., & Cohan, A. (2019). *SciBERT: A pretrained language model for scientific text. Proceedings of the 2019 Conference on Empirical Methods in Natural Language Processing and the 9th International Joint Conference on Natural Language Processing (EMNLP-IJCNLP)*. https://doi.org/DOI: 10.18653/v1/D19-1371

Chalkidis, I., Fergadiotis, E., Malakasiotis, P., Aletras, N., & Androutsopoulos, I. (2019). *Extreme multi-label legal text classification: A case study in. Proceedings of the Natural Legal Language Processing Workshop 2019*. https://doi.org/DOI: 10.18653/v1/W19-2209

Chen, M. X., Firat, O., Bapna, A., Johnson, M., Macherey, W., Foster, G., Jones, L., Schuster, M., Shazeer, N., Parmar, N., Vaswani, A., Uszkoreit, J., Kaiser, L., Chen, Z., Wu, Y., & Hughes, M. (2018). *The best of both worlds: Combining recent advances in neural machine translation. Proceedings of the 56th Annual Meeting of the Association for Computational Linguistics* (Volume 1: Long Papers). https://doi.org/DOI: 10.18653/v1/P18-1008

Collobert, R., & Weston, J. (2008). *A unified architecture for natural language processing*. Proceedings of the 25th International Conference on Machine Learning - ICML '08, 160–167. https://doi.org/DOI: 10.1145/1390156.1390177

Conneau, A., Rinott, R., Lample, G., Williams, A., Bowman, S., Schwenk, H., & Stoyanov, V. (2018). *XNLI: Evaluating cross-lingual sentence representations. Proceedings of the 2018 Conference on Empirical Methods in Natural Language Processing*. https://doi.org/DOI: 10.18653/v1/D18-1269

Dai, Z., Yang, Z., Yang, Y., Carbonell, J., Le, Q., & Salakhutdinov, R. (2019). *Transformer-XL: Attentive language models beyond a fixed-length context. Proceedings of the 57th Annual Meeting of the Association for Computational Linguistics*. https://doi.org/DOI: 10.18653/v1/P19-1285

Devlin, J., Chang, M.-W., Lee, K., & Toutanova, K. (2019). *BERT: Pre-training of deep bidirectional transformers for language understanding. Proceedings of the 2019 Conference of the North American Chapter of the Association for Computational Linguistics.* https://doi.org/DOI: 10.18653/v1/N19-1423

Feng, D. (2003). *Cooperative model-based language understanding in dialogue.* Proceedings of the 2003 Conference of the North American Chapter of the Association for Computational Linguistics on Human Language Technology: Proceedings of the HLT-NAACL 2003 Student Research Workshop - NAACL '03, 3, 1–6. https://doi.org/DOI: 10.3115/1073416.1073426

Goodfellow, I., Pouget-Abadie, J., Mirza, M., Xu, B., Warde-Farley, D., Ozair, S., Courville, A., & Bengio, Y. (2020). Generative adversarial networks. *Communications of the ACM, 63*(11), 139–144. DOI: 10.1145/3422622

Gururangan, S., Marasović, A., Swayamdipta, S., Lo, K., Beltagy, I., Downey, D., & Smith, N. A. (2020). *Don't stop pretraining: Adapt language models to domains and tasks. Proceedings of the 58th Annual Meeting of the Association for Computational Linguistics.* https://doi.org/DOI: 10.18653/v1/2020.acl-main.740

Holtzman, A., Buys, J., Forbes, M., Bosselut, A., Golub, D., & Choi, Y. (2018). *Learning to write with cooperative discriminators. Proceedings of the 56th Annual Meeting of the Association for Computational Linguistics* (Volume 1: Long Papers). https://doi.org/DOI: 10.18653/v1/P18-1152

Howard, J., & Ruder, S. (2018). *Universal language model fine-tuning for text classification. Proceedings of the 56th Annual Meeting of the Association for Computational Linguistics* (Volume 1: Long Papers). https://doi.org/DOI: 10.18653/v1/P18-1031

IEEE Transactions on Neural Networks and Learning Systems Publication Information. (2021). IEEE TRANSACTIONS ON NEURAL NETWORKS AND LEARNING SYSTEMS Publication Information. *IEEE Transactions on Neural Networks and Learning Systems, 32*(6), C2–C2. DOI: 10.1109/TNNLS.2021.3078592

Lee, J., Yoon, W., Kim, S., Kim, D., Kim, S., So, C. H., & Kang, J. (2019). BioBERT: A pre-trained biomedical language representation model for biomedical text mining. *Bioinformatics (Oxford, England), 36*(4), 1234–1240. DOI: 10.1093/bioinformatics/btz682 PMID: 31501885

Likhosherstov, V., Choromanski, K., & Weller, A. (2023). On the expressive flexibility of self-attention matrices. *Proceedings of the AAAI Conference on Artificial Intelligence, 37*(7), 8773–8781. DOI: 10.1609/aaai.v37i7.26055

Madaan, A., Zhou, S., Alon, U., Yang, Y., & Neubig, G. (2022). *Language models of code are few-shot commonsense learners. Proceedings of the 2022 Conference on Empirical Methods in Natural Language Processing*. https://doi.org/DOI: 10.18653/v1/2022.emnlp-main.90

Madotto, A., Ishii, E., Lin, Z., Dathathri, S., & Fung, P. (2020). Plug-and-play conversational models. *Findings of the Association for Computational Linguistics: EMNLP, 2020*, 2422–2433. DOI: 10.18653/v1/2020.findings-emnlp.219

Marzuki, M. J., & Nurpahmi, S. (2019). Using video blog in teaching speaking. *English Language Teaching for EFL Learners, 1*(1), 13. DOI: 10.24252/elties.v1i1.7422

Nemkul, K. (2024). Use of Bidirectional Encoder Representations from Transformers (BERT) and Robustly Optimized BERT Pretraining Approach (RoBERTa) for Nepali news classification. *Tribhuvan University Journal, 39*(1), 124–137. DOI: 10.3126/tuj.v39i1.66679

Petroni, F., Piktus, A., Fan, A., Lewis, P., Yazdani, M., De Cao, N., Thorne, J., Jernite, Y., Karpukhin, V., Maillard, J., Plachouras, V., Rocktäschel, T., & Riedel, S. (2021). *KILT: A benchmark for knowledge intensive language tasks. Proceedings of the 2021 Conference of the North American Chapter of the Association for Computational Linguistics: Human Language Technologies*. https://doi.org/DOI: 10.18653/v1/2021.naacl-main.200

Rajpurkar, P., Zhang, J., Lopyrev, K., & Liang, P. (2016). *SQuAD: Machine comprehension of text. Proceedings of the 2016 Conference on Empirical Methods in Natural Language Processing*. https://doi.org/DOI: 10.18653/v1/D16-1264

Roy, P., Podder, A., & Roy, S. (2023). A voting classification approach for sentiment extraction from Bengali text. *International Journal (Toronto, Ont.), 11*(5).

Sahoo, T., Mondal, A., Roy, P., & Podder, A. (2024). *Artificial intelligence and its application in engineering: A comprehensive review*. Emerging Engineering Technologies and Industrial Applications, 1–20.

Sheng, E., Chang, K.-W., Natarajan, P., & Peng, N. (2019). *The woman worked as a babysitter: On biases in language generation. Proceedings of the 2019 Conference on Empirical Methods in Natural Language Processing and the 9th International Joint Conference on Natural Language Processing (EMNLP-IJCNLP)*. https://doi.org/DOI: 10.18653/v1/D19-1339

Tariq, M. U. (2025). *AI-Driven Learning and Engagement in Higher Education*. IGI Global., DOI: 10.4018/979-8-3693-4074-5

Tariq, M. U. (2025). The Social Media Wildfire: Examining Twitter, Facebook, and TikTok's Role in Spreading Supply Chain Misinformation. In Bukhari, S., & Zafar, I. (Eds.), *Mass Media and Impact of Fake News on Supply Chains* (pp. 91–120). IGI Global Scientific Publishing., DOI: 10.4018/979-8-3373-2175-2.ch004

Tariq, M. U. (2025). Empathy-Driven Development: Integrating Design Thinking Into Next-Gen Software Engineering. In Aguilar-Calderón, J., & Tripp-Barba, C. (Eds.), *Innovative Design Thinking Approaches in Software Engineering* (pp. 85–110). IGI Global Scientific Publishing., DOI: 10.4018/979-8-3693-9531-8.ch004

Tariq, M. U. (2025). The Challenge of Artificial Intelligence in Environmental Sustainability: Opportunities, Risks, and Policy Implications. In Ahmadi, A., & Mna, A. (Eds.), *Nexus of Environmental Quality and Technology Innovation* (pp. 267–292). IGI Global Scientific Publishing., DOI: 10.4018/979-8-3373-1822-6.ch012

Tariq, M. U. (2025). Integrating Advanced Technologies for Multi-Stakeholder Collaboration: Driving Sustainability in Supply Chains Through Industry 4.0. In Frichi, Y., & Jawab, F. (Eds.), *Multi-Stakeholder Collaboration for Sustainable Supply Chain* (pp. 313–334). IGI Global Scientific Publishing., DOI: 10.4018/979-8-3693-8925-6.ch014

Tariq, M. U., & Sergio, R. (Eds.). (2025). *Cases on AI-Driven Solutions to Environmental Challenges.* IGI Global, 2025. https://doi.org/DOI: 10.4018/979-8-3693-7483-2

Zellers, R., Holtzman, A., Bisk, Y., Farhadi, A., & Choi, Y. (2019). HellaSwag: Can a machine really finish your sentence? *Proceedings of the 57th Annual Meeting of the Association for Computational Linguistics.* https://doi.org/DOI: 10.18653/v1/P19-1472

KEY TERM AND DEFINITIONS

Transformer Architecture: A neural network framework based on attention mechanisms that enables efficient processing of sequential data without relying on recurrence.

Attention Mechanism: A method within transformer models that allows the system to weigh the importance of different input tokens when generating responses.

Reinforcement Learning from Human Feedback (RLHF): A training approach where human evaluators guide model optimisation by rating its outputs, enhancing contextual accuracy and alignment with human preferences.

Context Window: The portion of previous dialogue or input a language model can retain and use to generate coherent and contextually relevant responses.

Chapter 2
Harnessing Higher Generative Artificial Intelligence for Educational Pedagogy:
Human-AI Collaboration in ChatGPT Experiences

Daniel Emakporuena
https://orcid.org/0009-0001-1741-9401
Udus Preeminent Global Limited, Nigeria

Victor Omoboye Oluwasegun
https://orcid.org/0009-0004-4255-2003
University of Roehampton, United Kingdom

Ogheneruona Maria Esegbona-Isikeh
https://orcid.org/0009-0005-6073-9442
Birmingham City University, UK

Williams Ogochukwu Ugbomeh
https://orcid.org/0000-0001-6441-6978
Robert Gordon University, UK

Morgan Nwaiku
https://orcid.org/0009-0001-8984-8387
Teesside University, UK

Eboesomi Esther Bunmi
https://orcid.org/0009-0004-8244-6176
University of Huddersfield, UK

Oyedemi Oluyemisi Adenike
https://orcid.org/0009-0005-8496-736X
Federal University of Lavras, Brazil

Ugochukwu Okwudili Matthew
https://orcid.org/0000-0003-0828-9710
Federal University of Lavras, Brazil

ABSTRACT

This paper is an exploratory study that looks at how teaching and learning are affected by higher generative artificial intelligence (HGAI) models, notably ChatGPT-

DOI: 10.4018/979-8-3693-9841-8.ch002

4, ChatGPT-4.5 and the anticipated ChatGPT-5. With the ability to produce more dynamic and individualized learning environments, it contends that these models represent a critical turning point for educational technology. The study examines the benefits and drawbacks of ChatGPT in the classroom, taking into account how it might improve students' critical thinking and problem-solving skills. It also suggests strategies for educators and policymakers to maximize its use in accordance with the sustainable development goals for education. The study discusses safe and beneficial ways to use these new HGAI technologies to improve education and advance students' learning. It also provides suggestions on how policymakers, teachers, scholars, and tech experts could use ChatGPT to maximize teaching and learning in order to improve STEM education and achieve Sustainable Development Goals on Education.

INTRODUCTION

With the quick development and growing power of generative artificial intelligence (GenAI), especially Large Language Models (LLM) like Generative Pre-trained Transformers (ChatGPT), the educational landscape is changing dramatically(Kshetri, 2024). The amazing comprehension and human-like discourse capabilities of these sophisticated AI models portend a change in conventional teaching methods. By creating more dynamic, customized, and accessible learning environments, the incorporation of GenAI into educational settings offers a plethora of options to improve learning outcomes and teaching efficacy. The collection of studies in "Generative AI in Education: Pedagogical, Theoretical, and Methodological Perspectives"(Noroozi, Soleimani, Farrokhnia, & Banihashem, 2024) and the exploratory analysis in "Generative Artificial Intelligence in Education: ChatGPT-4 Experiences to Anticipated ChatGPT-5"(Oriakhi et al., 2024) demonstrate how much interest this emerging field has received from scholars, educators, and policymakers. It is essential to acknowledge the associated challenges and pitfalls, including ethical concerns, the impact on critical thinking abilities, and the need to adapt assessment methods, despite the significant potential advantages of GenAI in education, which encompass personalized feedback, language learning, and research support. Navigating the successful and appropriate integration of these technologies into the future of education requires an understanding of both their potential benefits and downsides. With its ability to provide a more dynamic, customized, and easily accessible learning environment, ChatGPT-4 has the potential to revolutionize traditional methods in educational settings. The education sector is continuously seeking new and creative ways to improve learning outcomes and teaching efficiency.

ChatGPT-4 is at the forefront of this educational revolution owing to its sophisticated algorithms and vast knowledge base (Rahman & Watanobe, 2023). In contrast, ChatGPT-5 will serve as both an informational resource and a platform for students to improve their critical thinking, creativity, and problem-solving skills (Nikolic et al., 2024). Using higher generative artificial intelligence (HGAI), educators may create more engaging and varied learning experiences that satisfy the needs of their students. The astounding ability of ChatGPT to perform complex tasks in the educational field has caused educators to feel conflicted, as this AI breakthrough appears to be transforming the way education is conducted (Bozkurt et al., 2023). By combining recent researches, this exploratory study offers some potential benefits and drawbacks of ChatGPT in promoting education. Along with discussing safe and advantageous ways to use these new HGAI technologies to enhance education and further students' learning, the study offers recommendations on how policymakers, researchers, educators, and technology experts might use ChatGPT with the goal of maximizing teaching and learning to achieve the objective of sustainable development in education. Several educational institutions have taken a progressive insistence, arguing that instead of trying to outlaw the use of ChatGPT, that they should support students and staff in using GenAI tools in an efficient, moral, and open manner(Rowland, 2023). This method recognizes the fact that GenAI is accessible, will probably only get more advanced, and has both distinct drawbacks and special educational advantages. AI tools should be developed to complement or enhance human social and intellectual capacities rather than to replace, undermine, or interfere with them from a human-centered standpoint. The potential for science, technology, engineering and mathematics (STEM) education have increased integration of AI tools as a component of human tools to enable analysis and action for more sustainable and inclusive futures has long been anticipated for STEM career prospects (Bunmi et al., 2024).

In order for AI to be a reliable component of human-machine collaboration at the individual, institutional, and system levels, the 2021 UNESCO Recommendation on the Ethics of AI's human-centered approach must be further defined and applied in accordance with the unique features of emerging technologies like GenAI (D. O. Oyekunle, Nwaiku, et al., 2025). This is the only way to guarantee that GenAI develops into a reliable resource for scholars, educators, and students. Although GenAI should be utilized to support research and teaching, educationists must all be aware that it may also alter current systems and their underpinnings in various fields. If GenAI is going to change education and research, it should be thoroughly examined and guided by a human-centered perspective (Giovanola & Granata, 2024). Only then will the academic community be able to guarantee that the potential of AI, as well as all other types of technology utilized in education more generally, will improve human capacities to create inclusive digital futures for the digital natives. In fact, there are a wide range of potential applications for GenAI that involve automating information processing and output display across all the major symbolic representations of human thought. This new generation of AI tools may have significant effects on our understanding of human intellect and learning by releasing humans from some types of lower-order cognitive skills. An assertion that GenAI is the answer to education's core problems should not be interpreted, therefore, as a thematic set of guidelines on the subject. It seems improbable that GenAI by itself will address all of the issues that global education systems are currently confronting, notwithstanding the exaggeration in the media (Holmes & Miao, 2023). It is crucial to maintain the belief that human potential and group effort, not technology, determine successful solutions to the basic problems that societies face while addressing established educational concerns. Therefore, this paper seeks to assist in the development of suitable initiatives for human capacity building to guarantee that GenAI turns into a tool that helps and empowers educators, students, and researchers.

Building on the United Nations Educational, Scientific and Cultural Organization's (UNESCO) Recommendation on the Ethics of AI, this article takes a human-centered stance in favor of plural AI integration and GenAI expressions. The paper defines HGAI, describes its various models and technologies, and then lists several controversial ethical and policy issues related to AI in general and HGAI in particular. The following goes over the steps and key elements to consider while trying to control GenAI in a human-centered way that ensures moral, safe, equitable, and meaningful educational usage. The study then suggests actions that can be made to create thorough, logical policy frameworks that govern the application of GenAI in research and education, exploring the potential for innovative applications of GenAI in research, teaching, learning, and curriculum design. Technology advancements and the rise of increasingly complex, creative digital content generation techniques, such as GenAI, which are intended to enhance human cognitive and social capacities from a human-centered approach, have drastically changed the landscape of educational practices in the twenty-first century(Matthew, Bakare, Ebong, Ndukwu, & Nwanakwaugwu, 2023). By using pre-existing content, such as text, audio and video files, images, and even code, computers can generate multimedia educational digital content that looks authentic in the right context. This is made possible by generative modeling, AI, statistical probability, and unsupervised and semi-supervised machine learning algorithms(Matthew et al., 2024). Utilizing deep learning innovations, GenAI creates artificial relics by examining training samples and comprehending their distribution and patterns using existing digital content, such as text, video, images/graphics, and audio. According to existing literature,

Generative Adversarial Networks (GAN) and Generative Pre-trained Transformers (GPT) are the two most notable examples of GenAI to date(Bengesi et al., 2024).

The use of GenAI technologies is crucial to meeting the educational goals of the twenty-first century, particularly in instructional and pedagogical design, to achieve Sustainable Development Goal 4 (SDG4) on education. Through the use of this tool, teachers may better accommodate each student's unique requirements and learning preferences, creating a more inviting classroom environment that promotes sustainability and quality assurance in education (Matthew, Kazaure, & Okafor, 2021). The GAN generates synthetic data, such as a photograph of a person's face for instructional purposes, then assesses the content's authenticity by determining how real it is. Verification is repeated until the created content is accepted as genuine and the adversarial network cannot distinguish it from the genuine and original content. The primary applications of GANs are in the creation of audio, video, and graphics. However, GPT models may be used to write creatively on almost any topic, from a paragraph to a lengthy research thesis, with results that are convincing or almost convincing(Matthew et al., 2023). A more advanced iteration of ChatGPT has been created recently with 175 billion parameters, which empowers GPT-4 to achieve task performance gains as the most advanced state-of-the-art generative artificial intelligence techniques (Ray, 2023). On November 30, 2022, OpenAI announced ChatGPT, a chatbot and virtual assistant that allows users to fine-tune and direct a discussion toward a desired duration, format, style, degree of information, and language based on huge language models. According to (Wang & Zhu, 2024), GPT 4 outperforms all previous non-sparse language models by ten times, showing that the trend of larger versions was maintained by ChatGPT-4 and other advanced models.

By offering a more comprehensive and expedient evaluation of students' performance, ChatGPT-4's integration within the educational systems revolutionizes the way assessments and feedback are provided, along with extensive dataset computation. Advanced assessment systems that provide students with personalized feedback are made possible by an AI model's capacity to understand and generate writing that is like that of a human. By giving students instant access to helpful critique, these advancements enhance the educational process while also streamlining the assessment process. Additionally, ChatGPT-4's adaptability to many subjects and learning levels makes it a versatile tool that may be used to assess a broad range of skills. Through customization of assessments, from linguistic competency tests to complex problem-solving exercises, to align with the learning goals of each course, ChatGPT-4 provides a thorough picture of student learning outcomes. For the HGAI language model ChatGPT, GPT-4 now acts as the fundamental natural language processing (NLP) engine(Prien & Goldhammer, 2024). This technique has garnered interest from several disciplines, including economics, finance, media entertainment, engineering, education, and medicine. In the subsequent sections, the writers examined ChatGPT and discussed how it could enhance instruction and student learning skills. Along with discussing some of ChatGPT's shortcomings in the current educational system, the study also covered how teachers may use it to enhance and augment their students' studies.

BACKGROUND OF THE STUDY

The emergence of GenAI, particularly LLMs with reference to ChatGPT-4, ChatGPT-4.5, and ChatGPT-5 represents a significant development with the potential to transform educational practices. The GenAI involves crafting models that can generate new content, such as text, programming codes, images, and music, exhibiting human-like creativity and diversity. LLMs utilize vast amounts of training data to understand and produce text that resembles human language, making them powerful tools with broad applications. The integration of GenAI into education is seen as a major turning point in educational technology. These tools offer numerous opportunities for learners, educators, researchers, and practitioners to potentially enhance teaching and learning across various contexts. Some of the anticipated benefits include:

i. Creating more dynamic, tailored, and easily accessible learning environments.
ii. Providing personalized learning experiences by adapting course difficulty and content based on learners' data and personalization.
iii. Potentially increasing learner engagement and motivation.
iv. Supporting language learning through NLP translation, comprehension assistance, and conversational practice.
v. Reducing educator workload by assisting with tasks like lesson planning and assessment creation.

The development of GenAI models is rapidly progressing, presenting ChatGPT-4 as a significant advancement with enhanced capabilities in understanding and generating human-like text and processing more complex tasks with greater accuracy(Gupta, Nair, Mishra, Ibrahim, & Bhardwaj, 2024). Looking ahead, ChatGPT-5 is anticipated to bring further improvements, including better context understanding, advanced training methods, enhanced personalization, multilingual and multimodal features, and increased efficiency. These advancements suggest an ongoing evolution of AI capabilities with potentially profound implications for education. The current research reflected on the pedagogical connections and applications of GenAI in education, seeking to understand it's instructional, theoretical, and methodological perspectives. The current study examined the effectiveness of HGAI to the various educational settings and its impact on different stakeholders, while also addressing pedagogical applications that must be navigated for its successful integration within the mainstream global educational business. This paper is structured thematically into introduction, research background, research objectives, theoretical framework, and research methodology, discussion of research findings, future research focus, and conclusion.

RESEARCH OBJECTIVES

The objective of this paper is to employ HGAI (ChatGPT-4, ChatGPT-4.5 and ChatGPT-5) as a tool to enhance pedagogy techniques, not to replace all traditional educational methodologies, but to guarantee that students benefit from both technological advancements in AI technology. The article discussed the integration of ChatGPT-4 into educational systems and compared its performance to that of the planned ChatGPT-5. With enhanced capabilities and additional features that distinguish it from its predecessors, GPT 5 is the most modern and sophisticated language model in the GPT series. Chatbots, content creation, language translation, and automated question-answering systems are just a few of the many applications for it. The specific objectives of the paper include:

i. To address the integration of ChatGPT-4, ChatGPT-4.5 into educational systems comparing its performance to the anticipated ChatGPT-5.
ii. It aims to discuss how HGAI pedagogy transforms the way assessments and feedback are given in contemporary education.
iii. The study presents some possible advantages and disadvantages of ChatGPT in fostering teaching and learning by synthesizing recent existing literature.
iv. The paper offered ideas on how policy makers, researchers, educators, and technology experts might engage ChatGPT to optimize teaching and learning in realizing the SDG4 on education.

THEORETICAL FRAMEWORK

To achieve SDG4, STEM courses should use AI as an integral component to develop students' critical thinking abilities, creativity, digital literacy, and problem-solving possibilities(Pareek & Pandey, 2025). As AI becomes more commonplace, in the workplaces, in sports and entertainment, and in the educational sector, students should familiarize themselves with its concept and extensive applications. With AI compelling machine learning to transform business operations and create new opportunities across many industries, AI is becoming a critical issue for students' future professional careers, improving their employment prospects(Bunmi et al., 2024). In order to attain SDG4, educators can use GenAI to explore novel instructional methodologies, provide students with access to a greater variety of educational contents and foster innovative approaches to knowledge generation(Matthew et al., 2024). The development of HGAI into tools for educational pedagogy have allowed ChatGPT-4, ChatGPT-4.5 and long awaited ChatGPT-5 to be widely used in a variety of educational fields, including healthcare, engineering, entertainment, and other digital content creating platforms, as requirements for attaining sustainable education (Bozkurt et al., 2023), (D Oyekunle, Matthew, Waliu, & Fatai, 2024). The application of GenAI has strengthened the relationship between academic fields and other professions, raised the standard for secular education and training and improved the quality of services and occupational delivery. It has also boosted the efficiency of medical diagnosis and treatment options through analysis of vast corpus of medical and clinical data warehouse repositories for medical information extraction (Ebong et al., 2024; Tariq, 2025).

The rapid advancements in AI, particularly in the realm of GenAI and LLMs such as ChatGPT, these advancements have positioned AI as a significant force with the potential to transform educational practices and learning experiences(D. O. Oyekunle, Esseme, et al., 2025). The development of ChatGPT, with their ability to comprehend, react, and generate human-like text, has created a major turning point in educational technology. These tools offer new possibilities for creating dynamic, tailored, and accessible learning environments with potential for enhancing education. According to (Daniel, Msambwa, & Wen, 2025), GenAI holds promise for improving educational outcomes by offering personalized feedback, facilitating language learning, and supporting various research methodologies. GenAI tools are seen as potentially capable of addressing challenges and meeting the individual needs and learning preferences of students. Alongside the potential benefits, the emergence of GenAI has raised significant ethical concerns related to privacy, bias, accuracy, and the potential for misuse such as plagiarism(Dwivedi, Malik, Hughes, & Albashrawi, 2024). There are also questions about the impact on learners' higher-order thinking skills, academic integrity, and the reliability of AI-generated content. The rapid advancement and widespread availability of GenAI tools, predominately ChatGPT have created a need for a better understanding of their implications in educational settings. Educators, researchers, and policymakers require insights into how to effectively and responsibly integrate these technologies to maximize their benefits while mitigating potential drawbacks. GenAI's capability to analyze learner data and behavior patterns offers the potential to personalize the learning experience through tailored content, adaptive difficulty, individualized feedback, and AI-driven tutoring. GenAI improves personalized learning, an educational strategy that seeks to tailor instruction to each student's requirements, interests, abilities, and capabilities based on their prior knowledge and preferred learning style(Borah, Nischith, & Gupta, 2024). As a result, GenAI in education, particularly focuses on tools like ChatGPT, is crucial to explore its diverse applications, understanding its transformative potential, addressing the associated challenges, and developing frameworks for its effective and ethical integration to enhance teaching and learning in the 21st century (Tariq, 2025).

To help career professionals and educational technologists understand the cutting-edge constructive technique for 21st-century educational engagement, this study pushed ChatGPT-4, ChatGPT-4.5 and ChatGPT-5 technologies into the mainstream educational industry. The ability of ChatGPT to encourage language discovery is one of its most significant features. To improve their understanding of the content for context application, students can revise sentences, practice accurately pronouncing words, comprehend sentence structure, and offer real-time interpretations. In educational applications, writing essays or other written answers to test questions is perhaps the most significant and controversial usage of ChatGPT (Bui & Barrot, 2024). Teachers and students can utilize this program to write articles on any topic within a contextual boundaries by entering instructions. ChatGPT can also offer suggestions on how to enhance the grammatical structures, conciseness, or clarity of several rewrites of the same essay in order to assist users in overcoming writing challenges and offering fresh viewpoints on the subject they have selected (Gill et al., 2024). Higher education institutions are finding that AI applications are indispensable for staff support, tailored learning, smart educational systems, automated evaluation and pedagogic engagement (Hooda, Rana, Dahiya, Rizwan, & Hossain, 2022). They offer support that enhances learning results while cutting expenses in connection with Chatbots as a software applications powered by AI that mimic human-to-human communication. Those AI platforms formulate what they think are appropriate responses after assessing the conversation's context, answering a variety of questions because they were trained on large linguistic datasets. A range of educational institutions, including professional development programs, universities, and elementary and secondary schools, can benefit from the deployment of chatbots like Google Bard and ChatGPT, which provide personalized training as one of their key differentiators.

According to (Dalalah & Dalalah, 2023), using ChatGPT has several obvious disadvantages, including the potential to produce false or inaccurate data and avoid plagiarism detection in situations where originality is crucial. Despite its potential to assist teachers in creating lesson plans, making suggestions, and serving as a virtual teacher for students by answering questions, ChatGPT is still a valuable teaching tool. In order to use ChatGPT as an instructional tool, academic regulations and evaluation procedures employed by educational institutions need to be changed or partly adjusted (Chaudhry, Sarwary, El Refae, & Chabchoub, 2023). It will be essential to inform both teachers and students about ChatGPT's potential and limits to address the transformative implications of the platform on the learning environment. Teachers may find ChatGPT to be a helpful tool as a starting point for creating course outlines, instructional materials, and assessment tasks. Nonetheless, there are concerns concerning the validity of the content created that need to be addressed. Creating training materials with ChatGPT for bots that are particular to a course could be one way to address this. Using ChatGPT, for example, can help students learn the English language by assuming the role of a native-speaker with whom the learner can communicate (Cho, 2023). Modernizing evaluation procedures and institutional standards is necessary to address the problems posed by AI materials appearing in educational assignments. Utilizing interactive tools, teachers can enhance the format of tests and assignments and reduce the likelihood of plagiarism on the AI generated digital content (Sublime, 2024). Because the first version of ChatGPT was unable to process images and videos, it was more difficult for students who wished to use it for illegitimate purposes because there was no context. Yet, the massive multimodal model GPT-4 from OpenAI is capable of analyzing images by adopting GANs that can take textual and visual input data and turn it into multimedia and visual artifacts (Akhtar, 2024).

Enhancing teaching and learning experiences have been demonstrated to be possible through the integration of AI, especially LLM-based systems(Akhtar, 2024). The emergence of Multimodal Large Language Models (MLLMs) such as GPT-4 with vision (GPT 4V), which can handle multimodal inputs such as text, sound, and visual, ushers in a new era of personalized, enriched, and interactive learning environments in the educational system (Li et al., 2024). Rather than being solely text-based or unimodal, these situations might be multimodal pedagogy scenarios, which would improve accessibility, customizations, and potentially learning adaptation. Google's research indicates that gains in LLMs are a sign of a paradigm change in NLP and comprehension (Castagna, Kökciyan, Sassoon, Parsons, & Sklar, 2024). The ways in which these models are incorporated into a broad range of applications, from code completion to scientific problem-solving, illustrate their potential to revolutionize human usage and interaction with computational systems. Future developments suggest that LLMs will play an increasingly significant role in a range of human endeavors, as evidenced by the ongoing study of scale-related phenomena and the adaptability of LLMs to new activities (Suglia, Konstas, & Lemon, 2024). The genuineness of interactions is improved by the inclusion of multimodal models in Google Assistant, as shown in Look and talk: natural conversations with Google Assistant (Akhtar, 2024),(Gumel, Abdullahi, & O, 2019). With the integration of both visual and aural signals, on-device multimodal models properly ascertain user intent, facilitating more natural-sounding dialogues. Multimodal models are applied in real-world applications, especially in robots and autonomous vehicles, and are not restricted to human-oriented modalities. 3D object recognition accuracy is increased through the real-time fusion of sensor data from Lidar units and vehicle cameras, as demonstrated in 4D-net for learning multimodal alignment for 3D and image inputs in time (An et al., 2023). More comprehension of the surrounding environment is possible through the understanding and combining of data from many sensors.

In essence, multimodal models represent a paradigm shift in machine learning that enables single models to comprehend and produce results across several modalities in a contextually flexible manner (Matthew, Kazaure, & Haruna, 2020). This breakthrough has great promise for a wide range of applications in Google products and services and offers advancements in fields like health, science, creativity, robotics, and more. Building on the successes of GPT 3, ChatGPT 4, ChatGPT-4.5 included further features for text production and comprehension (N. Khan, Khan, Koubaa, Khan, & Salleh, 2024). It made it easier for the model to answer complex queries and continue lengthy conversations, which led to more natural and smooth interactions. ChatGPT 4's improvements were important since they changed the experience from a basic conversation to a great one with an informed friend. Now, with its enhanced capabilities, it is considerably more helpful for interactive applications like customer service and education. With ChatGPT 5, there will surely be a number of revolutionary additions and enhancements that could better our interactions with AI (De Schryver, 2023). Online education will benefit greatly from the integration of ChatGPT and the Internet of Things (IoT), which is transforming how teachers and students use new educational platforms for better teaching and learning (Matthew, Kazaure, Kazaure, Onyedibe, & Okafor, 2022). NLP's integration with IoT is highlighted as having a significant positive impact on online education and direct communication between instructors and devices (David Oyekunle, Claude, Waliu, Adekunle, & Matthew, 2024). Through the use of online collaboration platforms like video conferencing systems and instant messaging apps on gadgets like tablets, e-readers, and smartphones, educators and ChatGPT can engage in more natural, chance-based interactions thanks to the complementary technologies of the IoT and NLP (Ugochukwu Okwudili Matthew et al., 2022). IoT and NLP are described as complementary technologies that enable educators and ChatGPT to have more organic, happenstance-based interactions using online collaboration platforms such as video conferencing systems and instant messaging apps on devices like tablets, e-readers, and smartphones (Matthew & Kazaure, 2020),(Waliu et al., 2025). This implies that IoT devices can serve as interfaces for accessing and interacting with AI-powered educational tools more seamlessly and naturally. In order hand,(Oriakhi et al., 2024) envisions a future where IoT devices, enhanced with NLP capabilities potentially from models like ChatGPT, can foster more interactive and intuitive online learning experiences. These technologies can facilitate communication between educators, learners, and educational platforms through everyday electronic smart devices, creating a more interconnected and responsive learning environment.

GENAI CHATGPT METHODOLOGICAL PERSPECTIVES: ALGORITHMS & TECHNIQUES

ChatGPT-4 represents a significant advancement in Generative AI with notable implications for education (I. Khan, Chohan, & Malik, 2024). From language translation to content production and beyond, its high level of accuracy and intelligence in comprehending and producing human-like material has many different applications across several professions. It is a sophisticated LLM that builds upon the capabilities of earlier models like GPT-3 and offers enhanced features relevant to teaching and learning. ChatGPT-4 possesses advanced abilities in understanding, responding to, and generating human-like text. This allows for more interesting and coherent interactivity in educational contexts. Its capacity to comprehend and produce human-like writing enables the development of sophisticated evaluation tools that can provide more thorough and individualized feedback on student performance. ChatGPT-4 can assist in creating a wide range of educational materials, including lesson plans, study guides, and assessment tasks. It can also help students overcome writing obstacles and improve the clarity of their work. It has the potential to facilitate personalized learning experiences by adapting to individual student needs and learning preferences. This can include AI-driven tutoring and tailored content suggestions. ChatGPT- 4 can be a valuable tool for language learning, aiding with vocabulary, grammar, pronunciation, sentence structure, and providing real-time interpretations. It can even simulate conversations with a native speaker (Matthew et al., 2023). It can assist with research by analyzing complex texts, summarizing information, and offering suggestions for improving writing quality and identifying research gaps. ChatGPT- 4 has improved multilingual comprehension and generation skills, making it a useful tool in diverse linguistic educational settings.

Table 1. ChatGPT-3 and ChatGPT-4 juxtaposition

Key Features	ChatGP-3	ChatGPT-4
Modal Size	175Billion parameters	Over 1Trillion parameters
Training Data	Large and diverse corpus of text	Even large and more diverse corpus of text.
Large Capabilities	Able to understand and generate text in multiple languages	Improved understanding and generation of low-resource languages.

continued on following page

Table 1. Continued

Key Features	ChatGP-3	ChatGPT-4
Performances	High accuracy and fluency in generating text	Even higher accuracy and fluency in generating text.
Task Capabilities	Translations, summarization, question answering and more	Even more sophisticated and complex tasks possible
Control	Some control over the generated text	Better control over the generated text and understanding of context and intended meaning.

ChatGPT-4 pedagogical and cognitive impacts in education, particularly on critical thinking and academic integrity, ensures that its integration aligns with educational values and goals. ChatGPT 4 presents a powerful and multifaceted tool with the potential to transform various aspects of education. While offering numerous benefits and applications, it is crucial for educators, policymakers, and learners to be aware of the associated challenges and ethical considerations to ensure its effective and responsible integration in the educational landscape. A significant advancement in the field of NLP is represented by ChatGPT-4. This enhanced GPT language model, created by OpenAI, predicts the word that will come after a given one in a sentence by using the words that have come before it. ChatGPT-4 can produce coherent and fluid text because it has been trained on a large corpus of text data, which includes books, essays, and web pages (Yigci, Eryilmaz, Yetisen, Tasoglu, & Ozcan, 2024). This has allowed it to understand the fundamental patterns of language. It surpasses its predecessor, GPT-3, which contained 175 billion parameters, to become one of the largest language models in existence with a capacity of over a trillion. ChatGPT-4 can now generate even more complex and lifelike text with higher accuracy because of this boost in capacity (Tariq, 2025). It is capable of handling more challenging academic tasks including translating, summarizing, generating code, and answering inquiries. In addition, it can better understand the text's context and intended meaning and has more control over the final product. Better multilingual understanding and generation abilities are another feature of ChatGPT -4, especially in low-resource languages that are challenging for language models to manage. This is due to its advanced training process, which uses a wide variety of textual material from various languages and domains. The revolutionary advances in NLP made possible by ChatGPT-4 expand the possibilities for what can be achieved with artificial intelligence-generated writing (Ong, Hariprasad, & Chhablani, 2023). From content generation to language translation, it’s extremely precise and advanced ability to understand and generate human-like writing has many applications in tourism, education and entertainment.

Workflows for developers are also impacted by the model selection. For intricate, high-stakes development work, ChatGPT-4.5 is the preferred option; ChatGPT-4 is better suited for normal daily tasks and rapid debugging. ChatGPT-4 is a very efficient solution for debugging and simple coding assignments, making it a good option for activities where timing is critical, particularly in speech AI and live chat systems. On the other hand, ChatGPT-4.5 is excellent at managing complex automation processes, but it can cost up to 15 times as much as ChatGPT-4 for comparable work. For developers trying to strike a balance between cost and efficiency, this makes ChatGPT-4 a desirable choice. ChatGPT-4 and ChatGPT-4.5 integration into low-code platforms call for distinct approaches. Whereas ChatGPT-4.5 is intended for more complex automation tasks, ChatGPT-4's simplified API facilitates effective deployment (Rouf, Amin, & Franzon, 2024). In February 2025, for example, a four-step process utilizing ChatGPT-4.5 connected the OpenAI Assistants API with Slack, Google Sheets, and Gmail. With this configuration, client requests were efficiently processed, categorized, and routed. These variations draw attention to each API's distinct capabilities. ChatGPT-4.5 exhibits sophisticated problem-solving abilities, especially in intricate and multi-step situations. It is extremely good at jobs requiring deeper reasoning because of its capacity to comprehend emotional nuances, decipher subtle signs, and grasp human intent. ChatGPT-4.5's main advantages are its ability to comprehend complicated problem contexts, rationally break down multi-step solutions, maintain consistency in lengthy processes, and provide precise and dependable solutions (Tariq, 2025).

ChatGPT-4 is unique in that it has a large context window of up to 128,000 tokens, which makes it perfect for tasks requiring long-term context retention or lengthy talks. Consistency is ensured even in intricate workflows by its capacity to manage and maintain information across text, audio, and visual data. Although each model has strengths, their areas of emphasis are different: While ChatGPT-4.5 provides strong file handling and tool integrations, ChatGPT-4 excels in its sophisticated multimodal processing features. When compared to ChatGPT-4, ChatGPT-4.5 is particularly notable for its precision in processing facts and data. The Simple questions and answers (QA) benchmark indicate that ChatGPT-4.5 has fewer hallucinatory problems and more dependable factual responses. In disciplines where precision is unavoidable, such as physics and mathematics, this accuracy is especially crucial. ChatGPT-4.5's superiority in these areas is continuously demonstrated by benchmark tests. While ChatGPT-4 concentrates on delivering succinct, results-oriented output, ChatGPT-4.5 is best suited for creating intricate, imaginative text with a sophisticated tone. ChatGPT-4.5 effortlessly manages intricate, multi-step workflows, while ChatGPT-4 excels in providing prompt, real-time responses. When using these models, IT leaders report an 86% increase in collaboration between IT and business teams and a 70% improvement in customer experience (Thomas, Duggal, Khatri,

& Corvello, 2024). The accuracy, intellectual complexity, and sophisticated logic of GPT-4.5 make it stand out. It's perfect for handling challenging assignments that call for careful consideration and originality. For high-stakes tasks where precision and subtlety are crucial, this makes it an excellent option. Conversely, ChatGPT-4 is designed to be quick and economical. It is a fantastic choice for activities demanding logical thinking and fast answers because of its capacity to handle text, pictures, and audio inputs. ChatGPT-4 is ideal for producing rapid, economical material such as email drafts and social media updates, while GPT-4.5 is excellent at creating comprehensive blog entries and well-written brand emulations. GPT-4.5 is a good choice for handling automated operations and intricate coding workflows. The application of GPT-4.5 for strategic tasks like in-depth analysis and planning is interesting in the business field. On the other hand, ChatGPT-4 excels at providing quick and effective customer service and handling repetitive chores. Regarding the researchers and academics, ChatGPT-4 is excellent for rapid literature studies and teamwork, while GPT-4.5 offers thorough, accurate analysis (Awal, 2024).

Table 2. ChatGPT-4 and ChatGPT-4.5 Comparison

Key Features	ChatGPT-4.5	ChatGPT-4
Business Professions	GPT-4.5 is ideal for strategic tasks including detailed analysis and planning.	ChatGPT-4 excels at promptly and effectively managing repetitive duties and providing customer service.
Research and Academics	GPT-4.5 provides detailed, precise analysis in academic context. As a result, there are fewer hallucinations and greater dependability on a variety of subjects due to the model's increased knowledge and comprehension of the world.	ChatGPT-4 is great for quick literature reviews and collaborative efforts.
Content Creation	GPT-4.5 excels in crafting detailed blog posts and polished brand emulation.	When it comes to producing rapid and economical content, like as email drafts and social media updates, ChatGPT-4 excels.
Code Automations	GPT-4.5 is well-suited for managing complex coding workflows and automation tasks.	The automation paradigm is advanced by unsupervised learning, which improves world model accuracy and intuition for models such as GPT-3.5 and GPT-4.
Brand Copywriting and Emulation	ChatGPT-4.5 achieves stronger creativity and emotional appeal.	ChatGPT-4 is ideal for producing rapid, economical material such as email drafts and social media updates

continued on following page

Table 2. Continued

Key Features	ChatGPT-4.5	ChatGPT-4
Social Media Posts	ChatGPT-4.5 exhibits sophisticated problem-solving abilities, especially in intricate and multi-step situations.	ChatGPT-4 is ideal for producing rapid, economical material such as email drafts and social media updates
Email Marketing	GPT-4.5 improves performance and professional growth and successful in-house training programs for staff members.	Improved and more economical content production and Messaging that is clear and action-oriented

RESEARCH METHODOLOGY

The Ideas for utilizing ChatGPT to maximize teaching and learning to achieve the SDG4 on education are shared by policy makers, researchers, educators, and technology specialists. To ascertain ChatGPT's potential educational usefulness, the writers employed an exploratory methodology to navigate scholarly inquiries. The aims of this approach are to: (a) Examine AI's educational contributions in detail and investigate ChatGPT's degree of engagement for learning that is sustainable; (b) Emphasize how ChatGPT and associate higher generative AI might enhance instruction and learning in the context of continuous education automation (c) Examine any potential threats connected with the use of ChatGPT and related generative AI in the educational setting. The methodology will also provide insights and useful applications of HGAI in 21st-century educational administration. To find relevant answers to the pedagogical link between the emerging ChatGPT and higher education, the following research topics guided the study: (a) What are the possible advantages of GenAI, such as ChatGPT in improving education? (b) What potential negative effects might ChatGPT and related GenAI have on teaching? For the study, the published articles that addressed ChatGPT between June 2023 and February 2025 were carefully chosen. The authors particularly concentrated on peer-reviewed papers, social media posts, and newsletter items.

ANTICIPATED GPT-5 UPGRADE FEATURES FOR EDUCATIONAL PEDAGOGY

Several distinctive features set the most recent language model in the GPT series, GPT-5, apart from its predecessors. When is ChatGPT-5 going to be accessible to the global academic community? It is accurate to say that OpenAI has not yet revealed the precise release date for ChatGPT-5. But we can make an educated guess based on the company's past delivery schedule. ChatGPT-3 was launched in June 2020, followed by ChatGPT -3.5 in November 2022. If OpenAI maintains its current pace, ChatGPT 5 should be available in late 2024 or early 2025, considering that ChatGPT-4 was released in early 2023. The GPT-5 release date has not been made public by OpenAI, the company that created ChatGPT. February 27, 2025, saw the release of GPT-4.5 "Orion" to ChatGPT Pro subscribers. Indications from the industry and remarks from OpenAI suggest that GPT-5 may emerge in weeks or months. Thus, the release of GPT-5 may occur around the middle of 2025. Among the most notable GPT-5 updates are the following:

i. **Interactive Education & Context Gamification:** Students' motivation and engagement are increased by AI in educational games and interactive learning platforms. Because AI algorithms customize gaming scenarios and challenges based on individual player achievement, learners are immersed in an engaging and pleasurable environment that stimulates cognitive power. Gamification and AI turn traditional learning into a dynamic, participatory educational process (Matthew & Kazaure, 2020). The embodied AI in ChatGPT-5 incorporates gamification features and simulations into the learning process. ChatGPT-5 educational platforms will encourage students and make learning fun by adding multimedia game-like aspects. For courses like biology and engineering that need real-world application, ChatGPT-5 simulations will offer useful, hands-on experiences when integrated with immersive virtual environments (Thurzo, Strunga, Urban, Surovková, & Afrashtehfar, 2023).
ii. **Improved Architecture for better Context Understanding**: The advanced design of GPT-5 allows it to interpret and synthesize language more correctly and faster than its predecessor. The model is aided in comprehending the connections between words and sentences by the graph neural networks and attention processes of this design. When a request is received by GPT-5, it may be sent to the expert or experts with the greatest processing and response capacity on account of this. The result will be a faster and more cost-effective response time for GPT-5 to a variety of challenging tasks. The truth is that no fewer than 200 billion parameters are ever used simultaneously. As a conversation companion, you would expect an AI that can remember your preferences, understand complex instructions, and effortlessly switch topics without losing sight of the original thread.
iii. **Advanced Training Methods and Advanced Learning Adaptation:** GPT-5's ability to learn and generalize linguistic patterns is enhanced using a larger and more varied training dataset. Furthermore, GPT-5 learns from unstructured data without human supervision appreciations to unsupervised training. The AI's enhanced capacity for learning and adaptation is another aspect that is

anticipated. With time, ChatGPT-5 will become more adept at adjusting its responses to become more precise and pertinent by learning from user interactions. Because AI is constantly learning, it will become more efficient as it is utilized, resulting in an ever-better user experience. The AI's enhanced capacity for learning and adaptation is another aspect that is anticipated. With time, ChatGPT-5 will become more adept at adjusting its responses to become more precise and pertinent by learning from user interactions. Because AI is constantly learning, it will become more efficient as it is utilized, resulting in an ever-better user experience.

iv. **Multilingual Assistance and Multimodal Features:** GPT-5 is a useful tool for language translation and other applications that need multilingual assistance because it is made to accommodate several languages(Yenduri et al., 2024). More sophisticated multimodal features will probably be integrated into ChatGPT 5, allowing it to handle and produce not only text but also graphics, audio, and maybe video. Numerous new applications would become possible as a result, including helping with video editing, producing intricate visual material, and offering more dynamic and captivating user experiences. For instance, both experts and enthusiasts would find great use for an AI that could examine a picture of a plant and identify any illnesses or offer maintenance advice.

v. **Enhanced Personalization and Enhanced Language Modeling Functions:** Because ChatGPT-5 has more sophisticated algorithms and more computing power from its large training dataset, it should offer better personalization. The AI will be able to react to people more accurately by considering their preferences, interaction history, and particular needs. This individualized touch might make AI-powered tutoring, personal assistant, and customer service apps far more effective and satisfying. Imagine an AI that knows your favorite genres to read and watch, your preferred learning style, and even your daily schedule so it can send you reminders or ideas based on those things. The GPT-5 will make language creation and comprehension more human-like. In addition to understanding and developing more intricate and delicate linguistic patterns, such irony and sarcasm, it can generate more coherent and logical responses.

vi. **Scalability, Increased Efficiency, and Ethical AI Deployment**: Improved ChatGPT-5 functionality should result in faster response times and more simultaneous chat capacity. Because of this, the AI will be more scalable and appropriate for deployment in environments with high demand without compromising usefulness for developers or businesses. The enhanced efficiency of ChatGPT-5 will be very beneficial, whether it is for managing hundreds of customer requests simultaneously or providing real-time assistance in a busy online classroom. Increased focus has been placed on the moral use of OpenAI's models, and ChatGPT-5 is likely to see further advancements in this area.

Prioritizing ethics will make AI applications more reliable and trustworthy, which will increase their acceptability and safety in a range of situations (D. O. T. Oyekunle, Okwudili Matthew, Preston, & Boohene, 2024).

vii. **Integration with Other Technologies:** ChatGPT-5 should offer better platform and technology integration. This could include easier interaction with IoT devices, more reliable APIs for developers, integration with various enterprise software programs, and virtual and augmented reality. These interfaces will make ChatGPT-5 more usable across a range of industries and applications. In fact, from monitoring smart homes to performing intricate data analysis in corporate settings.

DISCUSSION AND FINDINGS

GPT-4 versus GPT-5: A Comparative Analysis

Though GPT-5 has several advantages over GPT-4, both models are powerful language analyzers. With its advanced design, better training techniques, and greater language modeling capabilities, GPT-5 is a powerful language model that is generally a significant improvement over GPT-4. With enhancements in design, training, language comprehension, multimodal capabilities, context retention, personalization, efficiency, and integration with other technologies, ChatGPT -5 is essentially expected to be a major upgrade over ChatGPT -4. In a broader range of applications, it seeks to accomplish a more precise and advanced understanding, creation, and interaction with human language (Tariq, 2025).

Table 3. Comparison of the two models: ChatGPT-5 and ChatGPT-4

Language Model Features	ChatGPT-4	ChatGPT-5
Architectural Design	Transformer-oriented design.	Attention-based architecture in combination with graph neural networks.
Techniques for Training Data.	Supervised learning	Unsupervised learning using a wide range of datasets.
Ability to Model Languages	Ability to produce language that makes sense within a relevant context.	Able to comprehend and produce increasingly sophisticated and subtle language, incorporating irony and sarcasm.
Multilingual Assistance	Mostly intended for natural language processing in English.	Designed to accommodate multimedia features and several languages translations.

The GPT-5 release date has not been made public by OpenAI, the company that created ChatGPT. February 27, 2025, saw the release of GPT-4.5 "Orion" to ChatGPT Pro subscribers. Indications from the industry and remarks from OpenAI suggest that GPT-5 may emerge in "weeks or months." Thus, the release of GPT-5 may occur around the middle of 2025. In a variety of applications, it is anticipated to be a revolutionary AI model that will offer hitherto unseen upgrades in understanding, generating, and interacting with human language. How far AI has advanced is the primary point of disagreement between GPT-4 and GPT-5, with GPT-5 expected to perform better than GPT-4 in terms of accurately and sophisticatedly producing, understanding, and engaging with human language. The goal of GPT-5 is to surpass the high standards set by GPT-4 for AI performance and fully utilize AI's capabilities in a greater variety of complex applications.

CHATGPT, GPT-4, AND GPT-5: LARGE LANGUAGE MODELS AI PARAMETER

ChatGPT's most recent version, GPT-4, is a large-scale, multimodal model that can process text and image inputs to produce text outputs(Kadiyala, Mermer, Samuel, Sermet, & Demir, 2024). GPT-4 sets the standard for language model capabilities by performing at a human level on a variety of professional and academic standards, even though it might not be able to outperform humans in some real-world scenarios. It is anticipated that GPT-5 will perform better in terms of logic, accuracy, and scope when it launches in the upcoming months. This multimodal large-scale model will be more complete, including inputs and outputs in the form of text, images, video, and 3D. ChatGPT was first inspired by GPT-3.5, a state-of-the-art big language model that stunned everyone with its ability to write, code, solve challenging arithmetic problems, and many other incredible feats. The progression from GPT-3 to GPT-4 and the expected improvements in GPT-5 signify noteworthy developments in the field of artificial intelligence(Yenduri et al., 2024). Selecting the best model for your goals requires an understanding of the parameters, capabilities, performance, and potential applications of each model, which may be gained by comparing GPT-3 vs. GPT-4 vs. GPT-5. While the precise specifications of GPT-5's characteristics are still unknown until the technology is formally unveiled, the AI community anticipates that GPT-5 will carry on the tradition of increasing scale and complexity that its predecessors started. Experts predict that GPT-5 will push AI models into new areas of understanding and performance, dramatically enhancing their capabilities. ChatGPT and other AI models function by decomposing textual data into tokens. Tokens can stand in for single words, phrases, or entire sentences, depending on the type of model being trained. Additionally, tokens can be used to represent other types of data, such as images or integers. Using this idea, objects can be recognized and categorized in image recognition tasks by using each pixel in the image as a token. An AI model's ability to handle these tokens is determined by its parameters. The context length, also known as the window, is the maximum amount of tokens that an AI model can handle. In this approach, GPT-4 can react more quickly and affordably to a variety of complicated tasks with much fewer than 1.8 trillion parameters are in use at any given time(Wang & Zhu, 2024).

Figure 1. Number of parameters in the generative AI models.

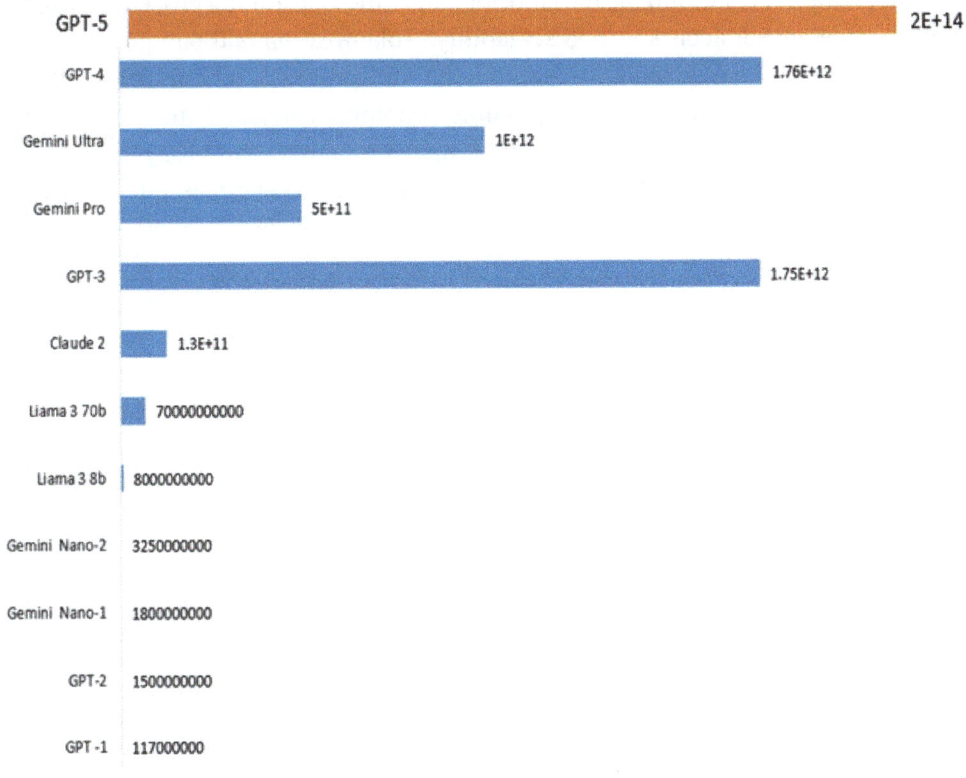

In AI and machine learning studies, the terms parameter and token are commonly used interchangeably; yet, they serve distinct purposes during model training (Su et al., 2024). Tokens are the smallest data units in natural language processing that the model examines. In contrast, parameters are internal variables that are changed by the model during training to improve performance. Although they both play crucial roles in model training, tokens and parameters have different purposes that significantly affect the model's accuracy and overall performance. The parameters of a model are its learned features derived from training data; they define the transformations applied to the model's input and output. These parameters are frequently weights in neural networks that the model modifies during training in generative AI models (Balasubramaniam, Kadry, Prasanth, & Dhanaraj, 2024). When discussing the efficacy of AI-driven testing, two fundamental ideas are tokenization and parameterization (Shi-An, Er, Thesman, & Nin, 2022). To help AI models comprehend and process information in a manner that is like human cognition, tokenization offers an organized representation of textual data. Then, through parameter modification, these models can keep their high accuracy and efficiency even as technology advances by adapting and evolving with shifting software environments. AI-powered testing technologies are revolutionizing the laborious and time-consuming process of testing by increasing speed, accuracy, and scalability. Tokenization and parameterization enable AI-driven testing tools to comprehend and process code unlike anything seen before, allowing them to spot possible problems early and make necessary adjustments (Dop, 2020). These ideas will remain crucial as technology develops to guarantee that AI-driven testing continues to be useful and applicable for a variety of software projects.

Figure 2. Parameters in notable artificial intelligence systems. An AI system's parameters, such as the connection weights in an artificial neural network and variables whose values are changed during training to determine how input data is converted into the intended output.

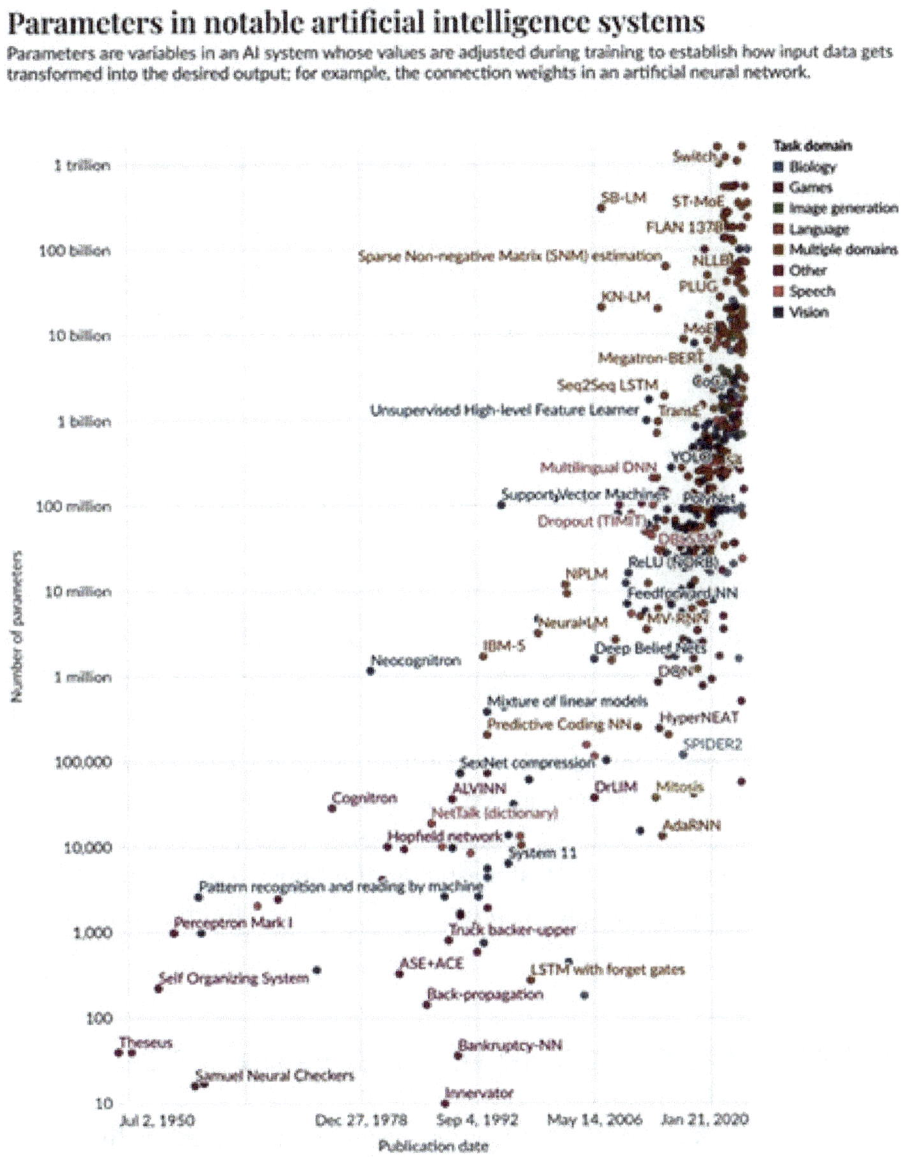

Figure 3. ChatGPT Comparisons with human testers reveal that GPT-4.5 is more preferred than GPT-4.

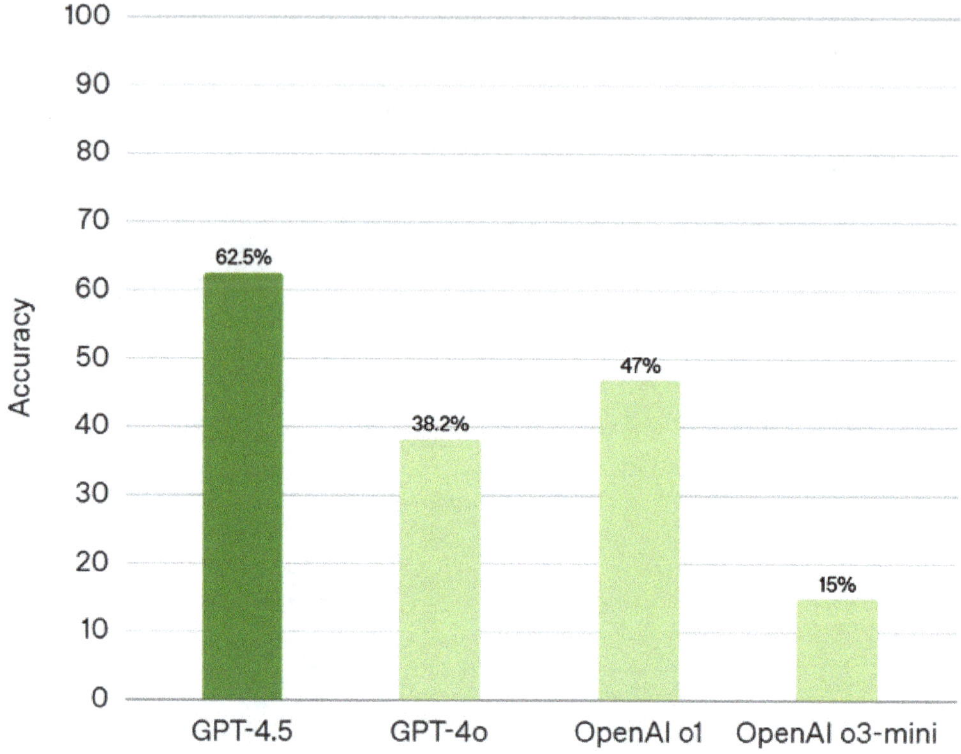

With its emphasis on sophisticated unsupervised learning, Chat GPT-4.5 represents a substantial advancement in language model development. In line with OpenAI, these models will serve as a strong basis for systems in the future that are capable of sophisticated technical and logical reasoning. It is anticipated that unsupervised learning and reasoning techniques will be combined in the future, expanding AI's adaptability.

CHATGPT'S EFFECTS ON SUSTAINABLE EDUCATION

Personalized feedback, language learning facilitation, research help, work automation, increased student motivation and engagement, and immediate and easily accessible assistance are just a few advantages of GenAI in education. They can also help with language translation, content production, and writing quality improvement. Our research has significant implications for the agenda of SGD4 for higher education institutions, policy makers, instructors, and students. Specifically, our findings indicate that time pressure and heavy workloads are becoming compelling factors that drive students to use ChatGPT for their academic tasks as a shortcut means. As a result, higher education institutions should emphasize the importance of efficient time management and workload distribution when assigning academic tasks and deadlines. Although ChatGPT can help students manage heavy workloads under time constraints, students should be made aware of the negative effects of excessive ChatGPT usage. Rather than being a tool for students to complete academic tasks without putting in cognitive effort, students should be encouraged to use ChatGPT as a complementary resource for learning rather than as a means of managing heavy workloads (Abbas, Jam, & Khan, 2024). In the same spirit, motivating students to strike a balance between their own initiative and technological support can support a comprehensive method of education. In a similar vein, curriculum developers and educators ought to create curricula and pedagogical approaches that capitalize on learners' innate curiosity and enthusiasm for learning. Though ChatGPT's simplicity of use may be enticing, an atmosphere that encourages students to find fulfillment in autonomously grasping difficult concepts can lessen the need on generative AI techniques (Bozkurt et al., 2023).

In addition, commending students for their real intellectual achievements might instill a sense of pride in them that might outweigh the appeal of instantaneous AI-based solutions (Abbas et al., 2024). Teachers should reconsider how they evaluate student performance and create new assessment criteria that force students to apply critical thinking and creativity to assignments and projects rather than relying solely on generative AI tools. This will help to deter students from abusing ChatGPT. Furthermore, teachers ought to push students to actively participate in critical thinking and problem-solving by giving them tasks, assignments, or projects that ChatGPT cannot finish, considering the preliminary data that suggests prolonged use of the app negatively impacts students' academic performance and memory. As a result, ChatGPT's negative effects on their mental and educational processes may be lessened. Teachers can also help children understand the possible risks associated with using ChatGPT excessively (Zhang, Zhang, Cai, Wang, & Zheng, 2024). Ultimately, educators and representatives can create solutions that focus on the effects, such procrastination, memory loss, and academic performance as well as the underlying causes like workload, time constraints, and reward sensitivity. Interventions such as skill-building workshops, awareness campaigns, and individualized instruction could enable students to efficiently utilize generative AI tools while maintaining their individual learning. Notwithstanding their progress, GenAI models still struggle with contextual knowledge, can reinforce prejudices, produce erroneous or out-of-date information, and may even impair students' critical thinking and academic integrity.

FUTURE EVOLUTION AND RESEARCH FOCUS

Future studies must be thorough and address the long-term effects, ethical issues, pedagogical integration, cognitive effects, and assessment techniques associated with the quickly developing field of GenAI in education. They should also consider the developments of more recent models, such as ChatGPT-5. The ChatGPT-5 promises more developments in the quickly developing field of GenAI. To create ethical frameworks for the usage of GenAI tools, comprehend their long-term effects on learning outcomes, and guarantee their adaptability to a variety of learner demographics, ongoing research is essential. Fundamentally, the most important thing is to approach the integration of GenAI in education with knowledge and balance, optimizing its potential advantages while anticipating and resolving the ethical, pedagogical, and cognitive issues it raises. For these potent instruments to support rather than contradict educational objectives, human supervision and careful application are essential.

CONCLUSION

Technology is never neutral in terms of ideology when it comes to the objectives of sustainable global education. In addition to illustrating and elevating various worldviews, it also symbolizes ways of knowing and thinking. This also holds true for recently developed generative AI models and tools. AI chatbots like ChatGPT provide a completely different user experience than AI technology that supports standard Google or other web searches. Search technology generates and ranks a menu of primarily human-generated information in response to user queries. Conversely, big language model chatbots use machine-generated content to provide responses that are distinct and appear far more authoritative. For this reason, AI chatbots function similarly to infinitely knowledgeable oracles. It is anticipated that OpenAI's upcoming model, the GPT-5, would greatly enhance AI capabilities. GPT-5's advancements in context management, problem solving, video creation, multimodal processing, reasoning skills, humanlike assistance, processing speed, and reliability are ready to transform what we once thought was possible from AI. We eagerly anticipate the vast and revolutionary potential uses and benefits of GPT-5 in a variety of industries, which herald a new era in artificial intelligence. With each new version of AI models, generative AI is developing at a never-before-seen pace, quickly broadening the range of capabilities that educational robots may accomplish.

This revolution has been spearheaded by OpenAI's GPT series, whose GPT-4 revolutionized natural language processing. It's critical to examine the potential features and advancements of the impending GPT-5 model as excitement for its arrival grows. It's crucial to remember that, despite our desire for GPT-5 details, the discussions we're currently having are mostly based on speculation and basic predictions, derived from past data, general AI trends, and a few hints that OpenAI's team seems to be sharing. Whatever the future holds, the rise of the GPT series piques people's curiosity and offers hope for a day when the only limitations on artificial intelligence will be our ability to envision its applications. The GPT-5's remarkable capabilities have the potential to transform many industries and lead to scientific breakthroughs that will advance humankind. From improved virtual assistants to creative image creation, the options are endless. GPT-5 is positioned to push the boundaries of artificial intelligence by building on the accomplishments of its predecessors. GPT-5's multimodal learning capabilities, wider context window, faster inference speed, and more sophisticated reasoning could usher in a new age in AI development. If OpenAI maintains safety and ethical issues at the forefront, AI offers a bright future with many prospects for innovation and growth.

REFERENCES

Abbas, M., Jam, F. A., & Khan, T. I. (2024). Is it harmful or helpful? Examining the causes and consequences of generative AI usage among university students. *International Journal of Educational Technology in Higher Education*, *21*(1), 10. DOI: 10.1186/s41239-024-00444-7

Akhtar, Z. B. (2024). Unveiling the evolution of generative AI (GAI): A comprehensive and investigative analysis toward LLM models (2021–2024) and beyond. *Journal of Electrical Systems and Information Technology*, *11*(1), 22. DOI: 10.1186/s43067-024-00145-1

An, P., Liang, J., Hong, X., Quan, S., Ma, T., Chen, Y., Wang, L., & Ma, J. (2023). Leveraging self-paced semi-supervised learning with prior knowledge for 3D object detection on a LiDAR-camera system. *Remote Sensing (Basel)*, *15*(3), 627. DOI: 10.3390/rs15030627

Awal, M. R., & Asaduzzaman, . (2024). Curse or blessing? Students' experience from ChatGPT with an application of Colaizzi's phenomenological descriptive method of enquiry and content analysis. *Higher Education. Skills and Work-Based Learning*, *14*(6), 1299–1313. DOI: 10.1108/HESWBL-09-2023-0249

Balasubramaniam, S., Kadry, S., Prasanth, A., & Dhanaraj, R. K. (2024). *Generative AI and LLMs: Natural Language Processing and Generative Adversarial Networks*. Walter de Gruyter GmbH & Co KG. DOI: 10.1515/9783111425078

Bengesi, S., El-Sayed, H., Sarker, M. K., Houkpati, Y., Irungu, J., & Oladunni, T. (2024). Advancements in Generative AI: A Comprehensive Review of GANs, GPT, Autoencoders, Diffusion Model, and Transformers. *IEEE Access : Practical Innovations, Open Solutions*, *12*, 69812–69837. DOI: 10.1109/ACCESS.2024.3397775

Borah, A. R., Nischith, T., & Gupta, S. (2024). *Improved learning based on GenAI.* Paper presented at the 2024 2nd International Conference on Intelligent Data Communication Technologies and Internet of Things (IDCIoT). DOI: 10.1109/IDCIoT59759.2024.10467943

Bozkurt, A., Junhong, X., Lambert, S., Pazurek, A., Crompton, H., Koseoglu, S., & Honeychurch, S. (2023). Speculative futures on ChatGPT and generative artificial intelligence (AI): A collective reflection from the educational landscape. *Asian Journal of Distance Education*, *18*(1), 53–130.

Bui, N. M., & Barrot, J. S. (2024). ChatGPT as an automated essay scoring tool in the writing classrooms: How it compares with human scoring. *Education and Information Technologies*, •••, 1–18.

Bunmi, E. E., Esegbona-Isikeh, O. M., Oriakhi, V. N., Akiotu, C. A., Emakporuena, D., & Matthew, U. O. (2024). STEM application in education: Implication of STEM computational paradigm on employment prospects. *HAFED POLY Journal of Science. Management and Technology*, *6*(1), 131–148.

Castagna, F., Kökciyan, N., Sassoon, I., Parsons, S., & Sklar, E. (2024). Computational argumentation-based chatbots: A survey. *Journal of Artificial Intelligence Research*, *80*, 1271–1310. DOI: 10.1613/jair.1.15407

Chaudhry, I. S., Sarwary, S. A. M., El Refae, G. A., & Chabchoub, H. (2023). Time to revisit existing student's performance evaluation approach in higher education sector in a new era of ChatGPT—A case study. *Cogent Education*, *10*(1), 2210461. DOI: 10.1080/2331186X.2023.2210461

Cho, H. (2023). Analyzing ChatGPT's Judgments on Nativelikeness of Sentences Written by English Native Speakers and Korean EFL Learners. *Multimedia-Assisted Language Learning, 26*(2).

Dalalah, D., & Dalalah, O. M. (2023). The false positives and false negatives of generative AI detection tools in education and academic research: The case of ChatGPT. *International Journal of Management Education*, *21*(2), 100822. DOI: 10.1016/j.ijme.2023.100822

Daniel, K., Msambwa, M. M., & Wen, Z. (2025). Can Generative AI Revolutionise Academic Skills Development in Higher Education? A Systematic Literature Review. *European Journal of Education*, *60*(1), e70036. DOI: 10.1111/ejed.70036

De Schryver, G.-M. (2023). Generative AI and lexicography: The current state of the art using ChatGPT. *International Journal of Lexicography*, *36*(4), 355–387. DOI: 10.1093/ijl/ecad021

Dop, T. (2020). [*Build smart, AI-driven linguistic applications using deep learning and NLP techniques*: Packt Publishing Ltd.]. *Hands-On Natural Language Processing with PyTorch*, *1*, x.

Dwivedi, Y. K., Malik, T., Hughes, L., & Albashrawi, M. A. (2024). Scholarly Discourse on GenAI's Impact on Academic Publishing. *Journal of Computer Information Systems*, •••, 1–16. DOI: 10.1080/08874417.2024.2435386

Ebong, G. N., Matthew, U. O., Olofin, B., Andrew-Vitalis, N., Fatai, L. O., Waliu, A. O., & Oladipupo, M. A. (2024). *Multimedia Cloud Data Warehouse Design for Knowledge Sharing in the University Environment: A Proposed Digital Solution Implementing Interactive Learning Strategies in Higher Education*. IGI Global. DOI: 10.4018/979-8-3693-3559-8.ch010

Gill, S. S., Xu, M., Patros, P., Wu, H., Kaur, R., Kaur, K., & Parlikad, A. K. (2024). Transformative effects of ChatGPT on modern education: Emerging Era of AI Chatbots. *Internet of Things and Cyber-Physical Systems*, *4*, 19–23. DOI: 10.1016/j.iotcps.2023.06.002

Giovanola, B., & Granata, P. (2024). *Ethics for human-centered education in the age of AI Entrepreneurship and Digital Humanities*. Edward Elgar Publishing.

Gumel, A. A., & Abdullahi, A. B., & O, U. M. (2019). *The Need for a Multimodal Means of Effective Digital Learning through Data Mining and Institutional Knowledge Repository: A Proposed System for Polytechnics in Northern Nigeria*. Paper presented at the Proceedings of the 2019 5th International Conference on Computer and Technology Applications. DOI: 10.1145/3323933.3324068

Gupta, R., Nair, K., Mishra, M., Ibrahim, B., & Bhardwaj, S. (2024). Adoption and impacts of generative artificial intelligence: Theoretical underpinnings and research agenda. *International Journal of Information Management Data Insights*, *4*(1), 100232. DOI: 10.1016/j.jjimei.2024.100232

Holmes, W., & Miao, F. (2023). *Guidance for generative AI in education and research*. UNESCO Publishing.

Hooda, M., Rana, C., Dahiya, O., Rizwan, A., & Hossain, M. S. (2022). Artificial intelligence for assessment and feedback to enhance student success in higher education. *Mathematical Problems in Engineering*, *2022*(1), 5215722. DOI: 10.1155/2022/5215722

Kadiyala, L. A., Mermer, O., Samuel, D. J., Sermet, Y., & Demir, I. (2024). The Implementation of Multimodal Large Language Models for Hydrological Applications: A Comparative Study of GPT-4 Vision, Gemini, LLaVa, and Multimodal-GPT. *Hydrology*, *11*(9), 148. DOI: 10.3390/hydrology11090148

Khan, I., Chohan, I., & Malik, S. I. (2024). *Leveraging ChatGPT-4 for Enhanced Education: Personalized Problem-Solving and Consistent Learning*. Paper presented at the 2024 2nd International Conference on Computing and Data Analytics (ICCDA). DOI: 10.1109/ICCDA64887.2024.10867340

Khan, N., Khan, Z., Koubaa, A., Khan, M. K., & Salleh, R. B. (2024). Global insights and the impact of generative AI-ChatGPT on multidisciplinary: A systematic review and bibliometric analysis. *Connection Science*, *36*(1), 2353630. DOI: 10.1080/09540091.2024.2353630

Kshetri, N. (2024). The academic industry's response to generative artificial intelligence: An institutional analysis of large language models. *Telecommunications Policy*, *48*(5), 102760. DOI: 10.1016/j.telpol.2024.102760

Li, C., Gan, Z., Yang, Z., Yang, J., Li, L., Wang, L., & Gao, J. (2024). Multimodal foundation models: From specialists to general-purpose assistants. *Foundations and Trends® in Computer Graphics and Vision, 16*(1-2), 1-214.

Matthew, U. O., Bakare, K. M., Ebong, G. N., Ndukwu, C. C., & Nwanakwaugwu, A. C.Ugochukwu Okwudili MatthewKafayat Motomori BakareGodwin Nse EbongCharles Chukwuebuka NdukwuAndrew Chinonso Nwanakwaugwu. (2023). Generative Artificial Intelligence (AI) Educational Pedagogy Development: Conversational AI with User-Centric ChatGPT4. *Journal of Trends in Computer Science and Smart Technology*, *5*(4), 401–418. DOI: 10.36548/jtcsst.2023.4.003

Matthew, U. O., Kazaure, A. S., Kazaure, J. S., Hassan, I. M., Nwanakwaugwu, A. C., & Okafor, N. U.Ugochukwu Okwudili MatthewAdo Saleh KazaureJazuli Sanusi KazaureIbrahim Muhammad HassanAndrew Chinonso NwanakwaugwuNwamaka U. Okafor. (2022). Educational Technology Adaptation & Implication for Media Technology Adoption in the Period of COVID-19. *Journal of Trends in Computer Science and Smart Technology*, *4*(4), 226–245. DOI: 10.36548/jtcsst.2022.4.002

Matthew, U. O., & Kazaure, J. S. (2020). Multimedia e-learning education in nigeria and developing countries of Africa for achieving SDG4. [IJICTHD]. *International Journal of Information Communication Technologies and Human Development*, *12*(1), 40–62. DOI: 10.4018/IJICTHD.2020010103

Matthew, U. O., Kazaure, J. S., & Haruna, K. (2020). Multimedia information system (MIS) for knowledge generation and ICT policy framework in education: Innovative sustainable educational investment. [IJICTHD]. *International Journal of Information Communication Technologies and Human Development*, *12*(3), 28–58. DOI: 10.4018/IJICTHD.2020070102

Matthew, U. O., Kazaure, J. S., Kazaure, A. S., Onyedibe, O. N., & Okafor, A. N. (2022). The Twenty First Century E-Learning Education Management & Implication for Media Technology Adoption in the Period of Pandemic. *EAI Endorsed Transactions on e-Learning, 8*(1).

Matthew, U. O., Kazaure, J. S., & Okafor, N. U. (2021). Contemporary development in E-Learning education, cloud computing technology & internet of things. *EAI Endorsed Transactions on Cloud Systems*, *7*(20), e3–e3.

Matthew, U. O., Oyekunle, D. O., Akpan, E. E., Oladipupo, M. A., Chukwuebuka, E. S., Adekunle, T. S., & Onumaku, V. C. (2024). *Generative Artificial Intelligence (AI) on Sustainable Development Goal 4 for Tertiary Education: Conversational AI With User-Centric ChatGPT-4 Impacts of Generative AI on Creativity in Higher Education*. IGI Global. DOI: 10.4018/979-8-3693-2418-9.ch010

Nikolic, S., Sandison, C., Haque, R., Daniel, S., Grundy, S., Belkina, M., Lyden, S., Hassan, G. M., & Neal, P. (2024). ChatGPT, Copilot, Gemini, SciSpace and Wolfram versus higher education assessments: An updated multi-institutional study of the academic integrity impacts of Generative Artificial Intelligence (GenAI) on assessment, teaching and learning in engineering. *Australasian Journal of Engineering Education*, *29*(2), 126–153. DOI: 10.1080/22054952.2024.2372154

Noroozi, O., Soleimani, S., Farrokhnia, M., & Banihashem, S. K. (2024). Generative AI in Education: Pedagogical, Theoretical, and Methodological Perspectives. *International Journal of Technology in Education*, *7*(3), 373–385. DOI: 10.46328/ijte.845

Ong, J., Hariprasad, S. M., & Chhablani, J. (2023). ChatGPT and GPT-4 in ophthalmology: Applications of large language model artificial intelligence in retina. *Ophthalmic Surgery, Lasers & Imaging Retina*, *54*(10), 557–562. DOI: 10.3928/23258160-20230926-01 PMID: 37847163

Oriakhi, V. N., Esegbona-Isikeh, O. M., Esseme, B., Claude, A., Emakporuena, D., Nwanakwaugwu, A. C., & Matthew, U. O. (2024). Generative artificial intelligence in education: ChatGPT-4 experiences to anticipated ChatGPT-5. *HAFED POLY Journal of Science. Management and Technology*, *6*(1), 149–169.

Oyekunle, D., Claude, B. E. A., Waliu, A. O., Adekunle, T. S., & Matthew, U. O. (2024). Cloud based adaptive learning system: virtual reality and augmented reality assisted educational pedagogy development on clinical simulation. *Journal of Digital Health*, 49-62.

Oyekunle, D., Matthew, U., Waliu, A., & Fatai, L. (2024). Healthcare applications of Augmented Reality (AR) and Virtual Real-ity (VR) simulation in clinical ceducation. *Journal of Clinical Images and Medical Case Reports*, *5*(6), 3141.

Oyekunle, D. O., Esseme, A. C. B., Oladipupo, M. A., Oseni, V. E., Adebola, N. T., Nwaiku, M., & Matthew, U. O. (2025). *Artificial Neural Network Algorithm in Nutritional Assessment: Implication for Machine Learning Prediction in Nutritional Assessments Precision Health in the Digital Age: Harnessing AI for Personalized Care*. IGI Global Scientific Publishing.

Oyekunle, D. O., Nwaiku, M., Matthew, U. O., Ogechukwu, O. N., Nwanakwaugwu, A. C., Adebola, N. T., & Olawoyin, O. O. (2025). *Transition to Sustainable Human-Centric Education in Emerging Artificial Intelligence Industry 5.0: Conversational AI With User-Centric ChatGPT-5 Higher Education and Quality Assurance Practices*. IGI Global Scientific Publishing.

Oyekunle, D. O. T., Okwudili Matthew, U., Preston, D., & Boohene, D. (2024). Trust beyond Technology Algorithms: A Theoretical Exploration of Consumer Trust and Behavior in Technological Consumption and AI Projects. *Journal of Computer and Communications, 12*(06), 10.4236.

Pareek, R., & Pandey, R. K. (2025). *Integrating STEM Education With Sustainable Development Goals: A Framework for Innovation and Inclusive Learning in India Transformative Approaches to STEAM Integration in Modern Education*. IGI Global Scientific Publishing. DOI: 10.4018/979-8-3693-7408-5.ch013

Prien, T., & Goldhammer, K. (2024). Artificial Intelligence in the Media Economy: A Systematic Review of Use Cases, Application Potentials, and Challenges of Generative Language Models. *Handbook of Media and Communication Economics: A European Perspective*, 1-69.

Rahman, M. M., & Watanobe, Y. (2023). ChatGPT for education and research: Opportunities, threats, and strategies. *Applied Sciences (Basel, Switzerland), 13*(9), 5783. DOI: 10.3390/app13095783

Ray, P. P. (2023). ChatGPT: A comprehensive review on background, applications, key challenges, bias, ethics, limitations and future scope. *Internet of Things and Cyber-Physical Systems, 3*, 121–154. DOI: 10.1016/j.iotcps.2023.04.003

Rouf, N., Amin, F., & Franzon, P. D. (2024). *Can Low-Rank Knowledge Distillation in LLMs be Useful for Microelectronic Reasoning?* Paper presented at the 2024 IEEE LLM Aided Design Workshop (LAD). DOI: 10.1109/LAD62341.2024.10691755

Rowland, D. R. (2023). Two frameworks to guide discussions around levels of acceptable use of generative AI in student academic research and writing. *Journal of Academic Language and Learning, 17*(1), T31–T69.

Shi-An, S. L., Er, K. Y. X., Thesman, R. N., & Nin, T. L. (2022). *AI-Driven Data Analytics Assessing Methods to Localize Preexisting Natural Language-Processing Data*. Paper presented at the IRC-SET 2021: Proceedings of the 7th IRC Conference on Science, Engineering and Technology, August 2021, Singapore. DOI: 10.1007/978-981-16-9869-9_15

Su, Y., Wang, X., Ye, Y., Xie, Y., Xu, Y., Jiang, Y., & Wang, C. (2024). Automation and machine learning augmented by large language models in a catalysis study. *Chemical Science (Cambridge), 15*(31), 12200–12233. DOI: 10.1039/D3SC07012C PMID: 39118602

Sublime, J. (2024). The AI Race: Why Current Neural Network-based Architectures are a Poor Basis for Artificial General Intelligence. *Journal of Artificial Intelligence Research, 79*, 41–67. DOI: 10.1613/jair.1.15315

Suglia, A., Konstas, I., & Lemon, O. (2024). Visually Grounded Language Learning: A review of language games, datasets, tasks, and models. *Journal of Artificial Intelligence Research, 79*, 173–239. DOI: 10.1613/jair.1.15185

Tariq, M. U. (2025). Harnessing Collective Power-Multi-Stakeholder Synergies for Sustainable Supply Chain Transformation. In Frichi, Y., & Jawab, F. (Eds.), *Multi-Stakeholder Collaboration for Sustainable Supply Chain* (pp. 245–264). IGI Global Scientific Publishing., DOI: 10.4018/979-8-3693-8925-6.ch011

Tariq, M. U. (2025). Empowering Women Entrepreneurs: Innovative Crowdfunding and Alternative Financing Models for Sustainable Business Growth. In Katper, N. (Ed.), *Crowdfunding and Alternative Financing Models for Women Entrepreneurs* (pp. 1–34). IGI Global Scientific Publishing., DOI: 10.4018/979-8-3693-9193-8.ch001

Tariq, M. U. (2025). AI-Powered Cybersecurity: Defending Green IT Systems With Intelligent Solutions. In Gupta, B., Pramod, D., & Moslehpour, M. (Eds.), *Sustainable Information Security in the Age of AI and Green Computing* (pp. 141–156). IGI Global Scientific Publishing., DOI: 10.4018/979-8-3693-8034-5.ch007

Tariq, M. U. (2025). Unveiling Consumer Insights: The Power of Qualitative Research in Market Analysis. In Segura, L., Vasconcelos, A., & Slomski, V. (Eds.), *Exploring Qualitative Research in Business: Approaches, Strategies, And Methods* (pp. 127–154). IGI Global Scientific Publishing., DOI: 10.4018/979-8-3693-7698-0.ch005

Tariq, M. U. (2025). Harnessing Life Cycle Assessment for Sustainable Success in Industry 5.0: Integrating AI and Digital Transformation. In Wongmahesak, K., Karim, F., & Wongchestha, N. (Eds.), *Sustainable Futures With Life Cycle Assessment in Industry 5.0* (pp. 21–40). IGI Global Scientific Publishing., DOI: 10.4018/979-8-3693-9346-8.ch002

Thomas, A., Duggal, H. K., Khatri, P., & Corvello, V. (2024). ChatGPT appropriation: A catalyst for creative performance, innovation orientation, and agile leadership. *Technology in Society, 78*, 102619. DOI: 10.1016/j.techsoc.2024.102619

Thurzo, A., Strunga, M., Urban, R., Surovková, J., & Afrashtehfar, K. I. (2023). Impact of artificial intelligence on dental education: A review and guide for curriculum update. *Education Sciences*, *13*(2), 150. DOI: 10.3390/educsci13020150

Waliu, A. O., Muojekwu, E. E., Matthew, U. O., Kazaure, J. S., Oseni, V. E., Ononiwu, C. C., & Haruna, K. (2025). *Clinical Simulation in nursing education: Immersive Educational Tech for nurses and midwives Creating Immersive Learning Experiences Through Virtual Reality (VR)*. IGI Global.

Wang, T., & Zhu, Q. (2024). *ChatGPT–Technical Research Model, Capability Analysis, and Application Prospects*. Paper presented at the 2024 IEEE 7th Advanced Information Technology, Electronic and Automation Control Conference (IAEAC). DOI: 10.1109/IAEAC59436.2024.10503756

Yenduri, G., Ramalingam, M., Selvi, G. C., Supriya, Y., Srivastava, G., Maddikunta, P. K. R., & Wang, W. (2024). Gpt (generative pre-trained transformer)–a comprehensive review on enabling technologies, potential applications, emerging challenges, and future directions. *IEEE Access : Practical Innovations, Open Solutions*, *12*, 54608–54649. DOI: 10.1109/ACCESS.2024.3389497

Yigci, D., Eryilmaz, M., Yetisen, A. K., Tasoglu, S., & Ozcan, A. (2024). Large Language Model-Based Chatbots in Higher Education. *Advanced Intelligent Systems*, •••, 2400429.

Zhang, W., Zhang, Q., Cai, M., Wang, D., & Zheng, Y. (2024). *Navigating the Application Challenges of ChatGPT in Education: Promoting Responsible Use and Minimizing Mental Risks*. Paper presented at the Proceedings of the 2024 9th International Conference on Distance Education and Learning. DOI: 10.1145/3675812.3675843

KEY TERMS AND DEFINITIONS

Generative Artificial Intelligence (GenAI): AI systems capable of producing original content such as text, images, or audio by learning patterns from existing data.

Large Language Models (LLMs): Advanced AI models trained on vast datasets to understand and generate human-like language, with GPT being a prominent example.

Human-Centred AI: An approach to artificial intelligence that prioritises human values, needs, and agency in the design and deployment of AI technologies.

High Generative Artificial Intelligence (HGAI): A class of advanced GenAI systems, such as GPT-4 and beyond, that exhibit enhanced capabilities in creativity, problem-solving, and personalised learning.

Sustainable Development Goal 4 (SDG4): A global objective by the United Nations aimed at ensuring inclusive, equitable, and quality education for all and promoting lifelong learning opportunities.

Chapter 3
Sustainable Learning Solutions:
ChatGPT Integration in Academic Services

Koppala Venugopal
https://orcid.org/0000-0002-3472-1477
Aditya Institute of Technology and Management, Srikakulam, India

Badana Govinda Rajulu
Aditya Institute of Technology and Management, Srikakulam, India

Penki Ravikumar
Satya Institute of Technology and Management, Vizianagaram, India

Kappagantula Madhavi
https://orcid.org/0009-0008-1778-7854
Acharya Graduate Studies, India

ABSTRACT

This research explores the impact of AI tools like ChatGPT on student learning and dependency in academic settings, using a mixed-methods approach. A descriptive research design was employed, combining qualitative insights from interviews and open-ended survey questions with quantitative data gathered through structured surveys. The study focused on student perceptions regarding AI's role in enhancing learning, accessibility, efficiency, motivation, and emotional support. Machine learning techniques, including classification, clustering, and correlation analysis, were used to identify patterns and relationships between variables, while inferential statistics, such as Exploratory Factor Analysis (EFA) and multiple regression, as-

DOI: 10.4018/979-8-3693-9841-8.ch003

sessed the predictive factors influencing student reliance on AI. Findings revealed a complex relationship between AI usage, learning outcomes, and student dependency, offering valuable insights for educators and policymakers.

INTRODUCTION

Education in the digital era has undergone transformative changes, driven by advancements in technology aimed at enhancing learning experiences and outcomes. Sustainable learning solutions, which focus on resource efficiency, inclusivity, and lifelong learning, have gained prominence in alignment with global objectives like the United Nations Sustainable Development Goal 4 (SDG 4), emphasizing equitable quality education for all (United Nations, 2015). In this context, the integration of Artificial Intelligence (AI) has emerged as a promising approach, offering innovative tools to improve academic services. Among these tools, ChatGPT, developed by OpenAI, has demonstrated considerable potential to support personalized tutoring, academic writing, and other educational tasks

While research has established the transformative capacity of AI in education, significant gaps persist. Current studies often focus on technological capabilities, overlooking the sustainability aspect of integrating tools like ChatGPT into academic services. For instance, Rolfe (2020) highlights the importance of evaluating long-term impacts such as energy consumption and digital infrastructure demands, which are critical for sustainable deployment. Additionally, although AI tools like ChatGPT can cater to diverse learner needs, there is limited evidence on how these align with existing pedagogical frameworks and support differentiated learning in diverse educational contexts, particularly in resource-constrained settings. Another critical area of concern is accessibility and equity. While digital solutions aim to democratize education, rural and underserved communities often lack the infrastructure or digital literacy required to benefit from such advancements (Belikov & Schunn, 2020). The integration of ChatGPT into academic services in these regions raises questions about its scalability and inclusivity. Ethical considerations, including data privacy and security, further complicate the widespread adoption of AI in education, as noted by UNESCO (2021). These concerns underscore the need for comprehensive research into the societal implications of deploying AI-driven solutions.

Stakeholder perceptions represent another underexplored dimension. The acceptance and adoption of AI tools depend on the attitudes of students, educators, and administrators. However, limited research examines these perspectives, particularly in diverse educational settings. Understanding these perceptions is crucial for tailoring AI-driven academic services to meet the needs of various user groups effectively.

The research problem centers on addressing the sustainable integration of ChatGPT into academic services. Despite its potential to transform education, significant challenges remain, including alignment with pedagogical goals, equitable access, and ethical deployment. By investigating these issues, the study aims to contribute to the development of innovative, inclusive, and sustainable learning solutions that leverage AI to meet contemporary educational needs.

OBJECTIVES

- To analyze the sustainability of integrating ChatGPT into academic services, focusing on its environmental, infrastructural, and operational implications in diverse educational settings.
- To evaluate the alignment of ChatGPT with existing pedagogical frameworks and its effectiveness in supporting differentiated learning, personalized tutoring, and academic support across various learner demographics.
- To investigate stakeholder perceptions, including those of students, educators, and administrators, regarding the ethical, equitable, and practical deployment of ChatGPT in academic environments.

LITERATURE REVIEW

The integration of AI tools like ChatGPT into academic services has been explored across various educational contexts, with several international and national studies providing critical insights into their impact. Below is an expanded analysis of how these studies inform the present research on *"Sustainable Learning Solutions: ChatGPT Integration in Academic Services."* This review covers the six key variables influencing student performance and offers a detailed look at the relevance of these findings for the current investigation.

Personalization and Learning Support

Venugopal (2024) explores the perspective of Generation Z toward ChatGPT in academic contexts, highlighting its potential to personalize learning experiences. The study suggests that ChatGPT allows students to tailor their academic support, offering individualized learning solutions. By providing personalized answers and feedback, the AI tool fosters a deeper understanding of topics and enhances student performance. This finding directly aligns with the variable of personalized academic support and its role in improving student outcomes.

Rolfe (2020) emphasizes that AI-driven tools such as ChatGPT allow for the tailoring of educational experiences to meet the individual needs of students. The AI's ability to analyze student responses and adapt its feedback ensures that learners receive instruction at their own pace, thus enhancing personalized learning pathways. This adaptability is crucial for fostering better academic performance by allowing students to work through complex topics at their own speed, a feature highlighted as a significant benefit in the educational context (Rolfe, 2020).

Similarly, Zawacki-Richter et al. (2019) emphasize the ability of AI tools to provide personalized tutoring and instant feedback, which significantly supports student learning. Their study noted that these systems not only assist in answering questions but also guide students through problem-solving steps, thus enhancing understanding and retention. The personalized interaction between students and AI leads to improved academic outcomes, directly aligning with the current research's objective to explore how ChatGPT can offer personalized academic support to students.

Mehta and Sharma (2022) expand on the role of AI tools in personalized learning support in India, highlighting that AI can be particularly beneficial in large and diverse classrooms where traditional methods of personalization are difficult to implement. Their study reveals that tools like ChatGPT help cater to individual learning needs, especially in online learning environments, improving both engagement and academic performance (Mehta & Sharma, 2022). This offers strong evidence of ChatGPT's potential in supporting personalized academic services in Indian institutions. Further, Pranaya & Venugopal (2023) in their study on language acquisition in rural students also highlight the need for personalized academic support. They assert that tools like ChatGPT could bridge the educational gaps by providing individualized help, especially for students from non-English speaking backgrounds. The personalized nature of AI can support rural students in overcoming language barriers, directly benefiting their academic performance (Pranaya & Venugopal, 2023). This personalized support has the potential to significantly improve the learning process for rural students, an important aspect of the current study.

Accessibility and Resource Availability

Venugopal (2024) in his analysis of ChatGPT's integration for Gen Z students emphasizes that it provides essential academic resources, especially in underserved regions. ChatGPT allows access to academic resources around the clock, which can greatly benefit students who lack traditional academic support structures. The AI system ensures that students can access knowledge at any time, removing barriers posed by traditional resource availability. This aligns with the study's objective of improving accessibility to academic resources for all students.

Belikov and Schunn (2020) demonstrate the importance of AI in making academic resources more accessible. They argue that AI tools democratize access to high-quality educational materials, making learning resources available to all students, irrespective of their geographical location. For students in rural or underserved areas, where access to traditional educational resources might be limited, tools like ChatGPT can provide vital support by offering immediate answers and assistance in a variety of subjects (Belikov & Schunn, 2020). This aligns with the research's objective of exploring how ChatGPT can bridge educational gaps, especially in areas with limited resources.

Rao and Dutta (2021) highlight the disparity in digital access between urban and rural students in India, particularly in terms of availability of high-speed internet and quality educational tools. They emphasize that AI can mitigate some of these issues by providing students with a portable, scalable resource for academic support. ChatGPT, for instance, can function across a variety of devices and require minimal infrastructure, making it a useful tool in addressing these accessibility challenges, especially in rural Indian contexts (Rao & Dutta, 2021). Gupta and Patel (2022) focus on ChatGPT's ability to improve language proficiency among students. In India, where English proficiency is crucial for academic success, ChatGPT's capability to assist with language learning through real-time feedback is particularly significant. This is important not only for improving communication skills but also for supporting students in mastering complex academic writing styles and vocabulary, directly contributing to academic success (Gupta & Patel, 2022).

In a similar vein, Somanadh & Venugopal (2024) explore the potential of smart library systems that integrate IoT for enhanced user experience. While not directly related to ChatGPT, the concept of increased accessibility through technology in educational systems is analogous. The integration of digital tools in academic services increases access to information, which is particularly beneficial for rural students or those with limited physical access to educational resources (Somanadh & Venugopal, 2024). This is crucial for understanding the role of technological advancements in enhancing accessibility.

Learning Efficiency and Cognitive Engagement

The study by Gopalakrishna & Venugopal (2023) supports this claim, highlighting that ChatGPT can significantly enhance learning efficiency. Their work on English-speaking abilities in rural areas discusses how AI tools can guide students step-by-step, ensuring that their learning is more organized and efficient, with a direct impact on academic outcomes. This enhances cognitive engagement by encouraging focused learning sessions, where students can engage with materials efficiently and at their own pace (Tariq, 2025). Veletsianos and Kimmons (2020) examine the efficiency improvements that AI tools like ChatGPT offer in academic contexts. Their research emphasizes that AI systems significantly reduce the time students spend gathering information, allowing them to concentrate on deeper engagement with content. ChatGPT's ability to provide quick, reliable responses enables students to learn more efficiently by streamlining the research process and freeing up time for higher-order thinking and problem-solving.

Venugopal & Somanadh (2024) also discuss how AI can enhance cognitive engagement by facilitating a more interactive learning environment. In the context of virtual libraries, they predict that Gen Z students will increasingly rely on AI to retrieve academic information quickly and efficiently. This use of AI tools improves students' learning efficiency, freeing them from time-consuming tasks such as searching for relevant content, thus enabling them to focus more on in-depth cognitive tasks. However, Sharma (2021) raises concerns about the potential negative effects of cognitive overreliance. The author points out that while AI tools are beneficial in terms of learning efficiency, they may encourage a dependency that limits students' ability to engage in independent, critical thinking. This issue is particularly relevant for the current research, as it highlights the need for a balanced integration of AI tools that promotes learning efficiency without compromising cognitive engagement.

Motivation and Emotional Support

Venugopal (2024) touches on the motivational impact of ChatGPT. By offering personalized, instant responses, ChatGPT contributes to reducing student anxiety and increasing their confidence in their academic abilities. This emotional support can be particularly important in challenging subjects where students feel discouraged (Venugopal, 2024). The immediacy of feedback from ChatGPT ensures students feel supported, which in turn boosts their motivation to engage in academic work. Mitra and Gopalakrishnan (2022) argue that AI tools, including ChatGPT, play a crucial role in enhancing student motivation. By providing immediate assistance and feedback, these tools help reduce the stress of uncertainty during the learning process. Students are more motivated when they feel supported and confident in their learning abilities. The 24/7 availability of ChatGPT fosters a learning environment where students are more likely to take the initiative in seeking help, knowing they have continuous support.

Joshi and Roy (2021) further explore how AI tools enhance emotional support. Their study emphasizes that the instant responses provided by AI systems like ChatGPT contribute to a sense of security and confidence in students, which in turn reduces anxiety and enhances motivation. This emotional support is especially important in a high-pressure academic environment, where students face deadlines and complex coursework.

Venugopal & Jagadeesh (2024) also focus on how AI can support students emotionally, particularly in the context of social media environments. They argue that similar to how AI tools engage users in social media spaces, ChatGPT can enhance academic motivation by offering personalized support and fostering positive emotional connections between students and their learning (Venugopal & Jagadeesh, 2024). This emotional support motivates students to seek help without fear of judgment, fostering a more positive academic experience.

Collaboration and Communication

Veletsianos and Kimmons (2020) note that AI can enhance collaboration by facilitating smoother communication among students. In group projects, for instance, ChatGPT can assist in ensuring that all students are on the same page by providing clear, consistent explanations. The study suggests that AI can also facilitate collaborative problem-solving by offering real-time suggestions and helping students articulate their thoughts more clearly.This finding is significant for the present research, as it supports the idea that ChatGPT can enhance communication and collaboration within academic settings. Venugopal & Somanadh (2024) investigate the role of AI in enhancing collaboration among students in virtual learning environments, noting that AI tools like ChatGPT can support teamwork by facilitating smoother communication. The ability to interact with AI in real-time helps students clarify ideas, brainstorm, and solve problems collaboratively. ChatGPT, therefore, is seen as a tool that can strengthen group dynamics and improve the overall quality of academic projects (Venugopal & Somanadh, 2024).

Kumar and Deshmukh (2020) add to this by discussing how AI tools can improve teamwork and collaboration in both virtual and in-person environments. Their study found that students working with AI-assisted platforms like ChatGPT were better able to share ideas and coordinate group efforts, which resulted in more efficient project completion and better academic outcomes. This aligns with the current research's objective of exploring the impact of ChatGPT on collaboration and communication among students.

Furthermore, Pranaya & Venugopal (2023) emphasize that in rural areas, where communication resources may be limited, AI tools like ChatGPT can assist in improving student collaboration by breaking down language barriers and fostering more inclusive group discussions. This is crucial for enhancing collective problem-solving abilities and improving academic outcomes in collaborative settings (Pranaya & Venugopal, 2023).

Technological Adaptation and Ethical Considerations

UNESCO (2021) stresses the importance of ethical considerations when integrating AI tools into education. The report discusses the need for transparency, data security, and ensuring that AI usage does not inadvertently perpetuate inequalities. This is highly relevant for the present study, as it explores how the deployment of ChatGPT in academic services can be ethically managed to protect student privacy and promote equitable access (UNESCO, 2021). In terms of technological adaptation and ethical considerations, Venugopal & Jagadeesh (2024) provide insights into the challenges of privacy and security in the digital age. Their work explores the ethical concerns surrounding AI tools, particularly with respect to data security and privacy. They argue that while AI systems like ChatGPT can enhance educational experiences, it is crucial to implement stringent data security measures to protect students' personal information. This is a critical issue for the current research, which seeks to explore the ethical implications of integrating ChatGPT in academic settings.

Nair and Bhargava (2020) also address the ethical challenges posed by AI tools in India, particularly around issues such as plagiarism, data security, and the potential for misuse. Their study stresses the need for guidelines and policies to ensure that AI technologies like ChatGPT are used responsibly, without compromising students' academic integrity or personal privacy (Nair & Bhargava, 2020). This insight is crucial for ensuring the ethical deployment of ChatGPT in educational settings. Somanadh & Venugopal (2024) also address the ethical aspects of integrating advanced technologies such as IoT and AI in academic services. They emphasize that ethical standards and regulations are essential to ensure that the deployment of such technologies does not negatively impact students' rights, data security, or academic integrity (Somanadh & Venugopal, 2024). These considerations are directly relevant to understanding the safe and ethical implementation of ChatGPT in educational settings. The literature reviewed provides comprehensive insights into how ChatGPT can be integrated into academic services and its potential impact on student performance across the six identified variables. International studies have highlighted the potential of AI in enhancing personalization, efficiency, and accessibility, while national studies have underscored the unique challenges faced by students in India, particularly in rural areas. By combining these global and local perspectives, the present research aims to address the sustainability and effectiveness of ChatGPT integration in academic services, focusing on both the opportunities and challenges in its deployment.

Table 1. Instrument Preparation

Variables	Item - Questionnaire	Author Citation
Personalization and Learning Support	ChatGPT provides responses tailored to my individual learning needs.	Rolfe (2020), Pranaya & Venugopal (2023)
	Using ChatGPT has improved my writing, critical thinking, or problem-solving skills.	Zawacki-Richter et al. (2019);
	The feedback I receive from ChatGPT is accurate and helps me understand concepts better.	Mehta and Sharma (2022);
Accessibility and Resource Availability	ChatGPT gives me instant access to academic materials and resources that are otherwise hard to find.	Belikov and Schunn (2020)
1.	The availability of ChatGPT has bridged the gap in accessing quality academic resources.	Gupta and Patel (2022) ; Venugopal (2024)
1.	ChatGPT helps me improve my language skills, especially in academic writing or communication.	Rao and Dutta (2021)
Learning Efficiency and Cognitive Engagement	ChatGPT saves me time by simplifying my research and study processes.	Gopalakrishna & Venugopal (2023)
1.	Using ChatGPT has made me more reliant on AI, affecting my ability to think critically or solve problems independently.	Veletsianos and Kimmons (2020)
1.	The efficiency of ChatGPT allows me to focus more on understanding concepts rather than gathering information.	Venugopal & Somanadh (2024)
Motivation and Emotional Support	ChatGPT has boosted my confidence by providing immediate support for my academic queries.	Mitra and Gopalakrishnan (2022)
1.	I feel more motivated to learn when I use ChatGPT for academic assistance.	Joshi and Roy (2021)
1.	ChatGPT helps reduce academic stress by being available 24/7 for doubt clarification.	Venugopal & Jagadeesh (2024)
Collaboration and Communication	ChatGPT helps me communicate and collaborate better with my peers during group projects.	Veletsianos and Kimmons (2020)
1.	The explanations provided by ChatGPT simplify complex ideas, making discussions more effective.	Venugopal & Somanadh (2024)
1.	ChatGPT enhances my ability to share and exchange ideas clearly in academic settings.	Kumar and Deshmukh (2020)
Technological Adaptation and Ethical Considerations	Using ChatGPT has improved my understanding and usage of digital tools and technologies.	Venugopal & Jagadeesh (2024)

continued on following page

Table 1. Continued

Variables	Item - Questionnaire	Author Citation
1.	ChatGPT makes me more aware of ethical considerations, such as plagiarism and responsible AI use.	Nair and Bhargava (2020)
1.	I am comfortable using ChatGPT without compromising my data security and privacy.	Somanadh & Venugopal (2024)

Table 1 summarises the instrument preparation with all the variables explored through impacting items which have been gathered from the related researched conducted by specified authors mentioned.

METHODOLOGY

The research followed a descriptive design using a mixed methods approach, which allowed for both qualitative and quantitative data collection and analysis to gain a comprehensive understanding of the research problem. By utilizing a descriptive design, the study aimed to objectively observe, describe, and document the characteristics of the phenomenon under investigation, which in this case was the impact of AI tools like ChatGPT on student learning and dependency. The mixed methods approach ensured a holistic understanding, combining both qualitative insights into student experiences and attitudes with quantitative data that allowed for statistical analysis and generalization of findings. The study employed a mixed approach that integrated qualitative and quantitative research methods. The qualitative data were collected through open-ended questions and interviews, allowing the researcher to capture in-depth insights into students' perceptions, attitudes, and feedback regarding their use of ChatGPT in academic settings. The quantitative data were gathered through structured surveys with close-ended questions, designed to measure the extent of students' dependency on AI tools, their academic improvement, and the role AI played in their academic processes. This combination of data types enabled a thorough exploration of the research problem from both an analytical and experiential perspective.

Primary data were collected through a cross-sectional survey distributed among university students. The survey consisted of both closed and open-ended questions, focusing on how students used AI tools, the perceived benefits, challenges, and ethical considerations associated with AI usage. A convenience sampling strategy was employed to select participants, which ensured that students who were readily available and accessible were included in the study. This method facilitated data collection, especially when time and resources were limited, while efforts were made to ensure that a diverse range of student demographics such as academic disciplines, gender, and year of study—were represented to enhance the generalizability of the findings. In addition to primary data, secondary data were gathered from existing literature, reports, and databases about AI usage in education, its impact on student learning, and the role of digital tools in academic contexts. This secondary data provided background information and helped contextualize the primary data findings.

The convenience sampling strategy involved selecting students from a university or a group of institutions where AI tools like ChatGPT were accessible. This strategy focused on ease of access to participants, allowing for practical and efficient data collection. Given the limitations of time and resources, this method was suitable, but care was taken to ensure a broad representation of student demographics. This included students from different academic fields, various gender identities, and different stages of their academic journey, thus contributing to the generalizability of the research findings.

The data analysis incorporated both machine learning (ML) applications and inferential statistics to provide a robust examination of the data. For machine learning, classification algorithms such as Support Vector Machine (SVM), Logistic Regression, and Naive Bayes were used to categorize students based on their use of ChatGPT and the outcomes they reported, such as dependency levels and academic improvement. These classification techniques helped identify patterns and clusters of students with similar behaviors and perceptions. Additionally, K-means clustering was applied to group students based on their responses to various questions about their interactions with ChatGPT, enabling the identification of different user types, such as frequent users, casual users, and non-users. These clusters provided insights into how different groups engaged with AI tools and how their behavior could be tailored for better outcomes. Correlation analysis was used to examine the relationships between variables such as student engagement, reliance on AI tools, and academic outcomes, while ranking techniques determined the relative importance of various factors, such as technological adaptation, emotional support, and academic efficiency, in predicting student dependency on AI for academic services.

For inferential statistics, Exploratory Factor Analysis (EFA) was conducted to reduce the dimensionality of the data and identify latent constructs or factors that underlie student attitudes toward AI tools like ChatGPT. EFA helped reveal patterns and interrelationships between variables such as motivation, accessibility, cognitive engagement, and emotional support, and explored how these factors contributed to students' reliance on AI tools for academic assistance. Multiple regression analysis was employed to assess the predictive relationship between independent variables (e.g., personalization, accessibility, learning efficiency, technological adaptation) and the dependent variable, which was the student dependency on AI tools like ChatGPT for academic services. This analysis helped in understanding how these multiple factors collectively influenced the degree of student reliance on AI tools and the academic outcomes associated with them. Through these statistical methods, the study provided a comprehensive understanding of the factors that drove student dependency on AI tools and the impact of these tools on their academic performance.

Figure 1. Data collection process.

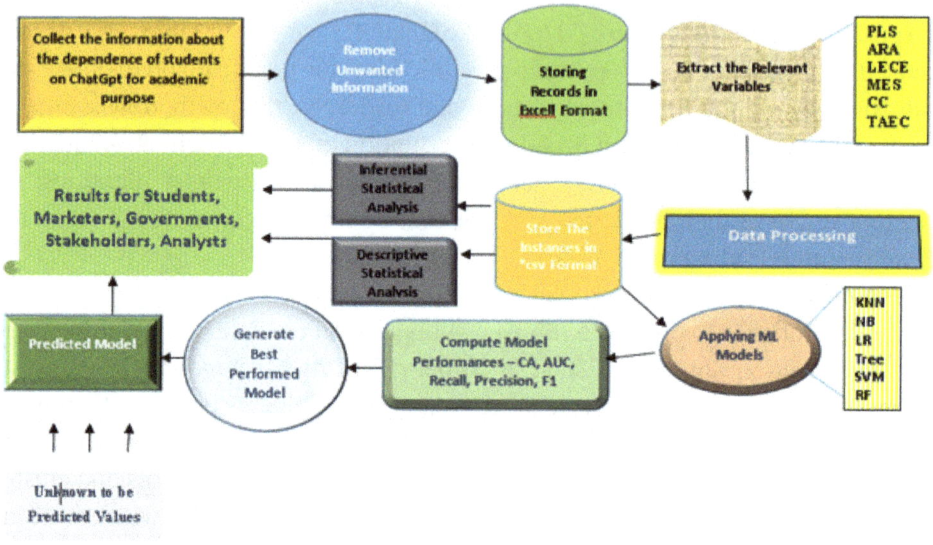

The research process began with data collection through a cross-sectional survey targeting all stakeholders involved in rural. Redundant, incomplete, and overwritten data were removed, and the refined data were stored in Excel format. Relevant features or independent variables (Personalization and Learning Support, Accessibility and Resource Availability, Learning Efficiency and Cognitive Engagement, Motivation and Emotional Support, Collaboration and Communication, Technological Adaptation and Ethical Considerations) were extracted from all data elements. After preprocessing, the data were stored in CSV format to be accessed by the Orange ML software tool for analysis. Algorithms such as k-Nearest Neighbors (kNN), Naive Bayes (NB), Logistic Regression (LR), Decision Tree, Support Vector Machine (SVM), and Random Forest (RF) were applied to select the best model based on parameters including Classification Accuracy (CA), Area under the Curve (AUC), Recall, Precision, and F1 score, resulting in the best-performing model. Additionally, the data stored in SPSS were used for Exploratory Factor analysis and Regression Analysis. Both the predicted model from the ML algorithms and the regression analysis produced valuable insights for Students, Marketers, Governments, Stakeholders, and Analysts.

ANALYSIS

Machine Learning Applications

Machine learning (ML) plays a crucial role in revolutionizing academic services by enabling personalized, scalable, and efficient solutions. In the context of "Sustainable Learning Solutions: ChatGPT Integration in Academic Services," machine learning can enhance student support through adaptive learning systems, intelligent tutoring, and personalized academic assistance. By leveraging natural language processing and data-driven insights, tools like ChatGPT can provide real-time feedback, assist in content delivery, and support diverse learning needs, thus promoting sustainable, accessible, and customized learning experiences in educational settings.

Table 2. Classification algorithm

Model	AUC	CA	F1	Prec	Recall	MCC
SVM	0.959	0.875	0.872	0.886	0.875	0.820
Logistic Regression	0.882	0.733	0.726	0.747	0.733	0.612
Naive Bayes	0.779	0.175	0.235	0.961	0.175	0.260
Tree	0.984	0.858	0.859	0.867	0.858	0.799
kNN	0.854	0.550	0.508	0.539	0.550	0.322
Random Forest	**0.996**	**0.950**	**0.949**	**0.953**	**0.950**	**0.929**

Table 2 explores the analysis of the provided models in the context of integrating ChatGPT in academic settings indicates that Random Forest outperforms all other models with an AUC of 0.996, indicating its superior ability to distinguish between classes accurately. Its classification accuracy (CA) of 0.950, high F1-score of 0.949, and MCC of 0.929 demonstrate robust performance in precision, recall, and balanced predictions, making it highly reliable for predicting the effectiveness of ChatGPT integration. Support Vector Machine (SVM) also shows strong performance with an AUC of 0.959 and CA of 0.875, suggesting its capability in accurately classifying outcomes, though slightly less efficient than Random Forest. In contrast, Naive Bayes and k-Nearest Neighbors (kNN) exhibit poor performance, with significantly lower CA, F1-scores, and MCC values, indicating their unsuitability for this research context. The results affirm the *Random Forest* model's potential as the most effective predictive tool for assessing factors impacting student performance with ChatGPT integration, aligning with the study's objectives of enhancing personalization, accessibility, and learning efficiency.

Table 3. Confusion Matrix

		Predicted					
		1	2	3	4	5	Σ
	1	1	0	0	0	1	2
	2	0	7	0	1	0	8
Actual	3	0	0	38	1	0	39
	4	0	0	0	47	0	47
	5	0	0	0	3	21	24
	Σ	1	7	38	52	22	120

The confusion matrix analysis from Table 3 reveals a robust model performance with an overall accuracy of 95%. Most classes exhibit strong precision and recall, particularly Class 3, which achieves the highest F1-score of 0.987, indicating reliable predictions with minimal false positives and negatives. Class 4 also performs well with an F1-score of 0.949, while Class 5 demonstrates balanced precision (0.955) and recall (0.875). However, Class 1 has the lowest recall (0.50), highlighting a challenge in detecting this category effectively. The model's precision across all classes is consistently high, suggesting its strength in minimizing false positives. These results affirm the model's reliability while pointing to opportunities for enhancing sensitivity to underrepresented categories

Figure 2. ROC Analysis

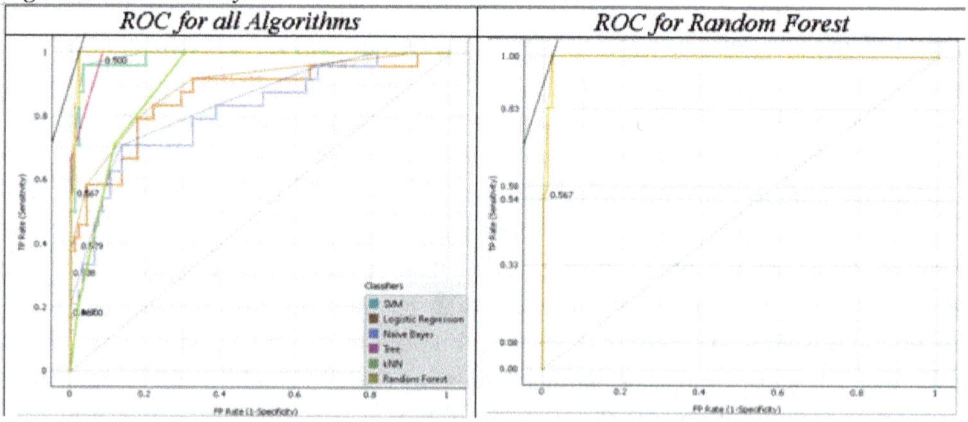

From Fig 2, the ROC curve for the Random Forest model shows a near-perfect performance, with the curve almost hugging the top-left corner of the graph. This indicates an exceptional ability to achieve high sensitivity (true positive rate) while minimizing the false positive rate. The AUC value, close to 1, reflects the model's superior discriminative power in distinguishing between classes. The point at 0.567 on the curve marks a threshold with a balanced trade-off between specificity and sensitivity. This high performance confirms Random Forest as an optimal choice for classification tasks in this study.

Figure 3. Correlation – Heat map

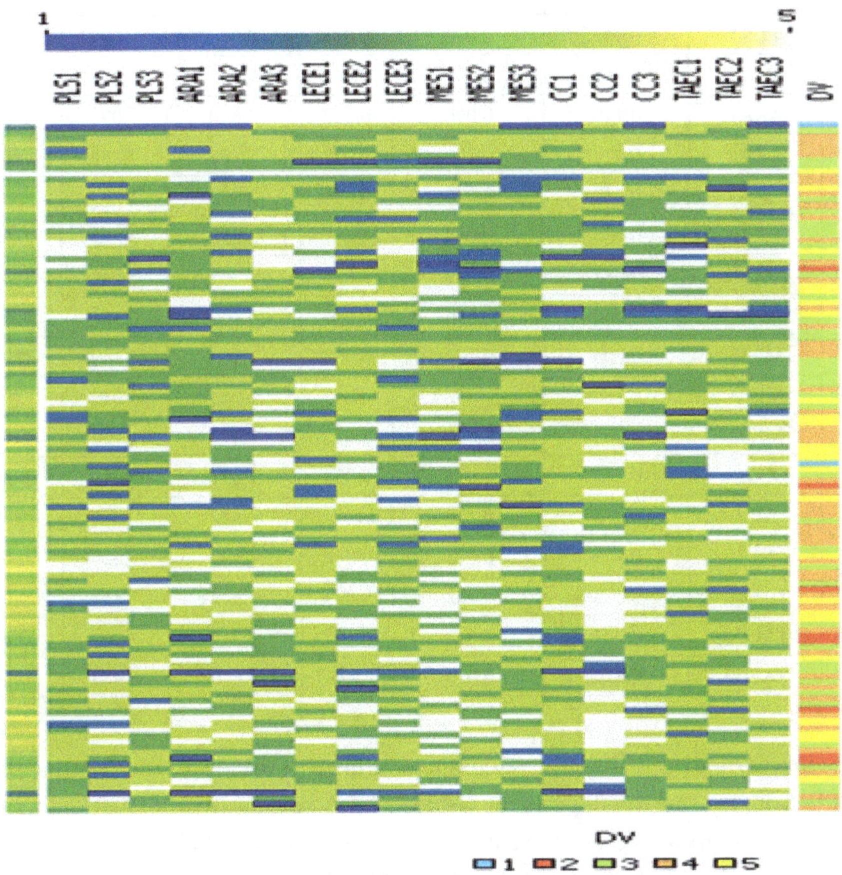

The heatmap from Fig. 3 illustrates the distribution of responses across various Likert-scale questions (e.g., PLS1, ARA1, etc.) and their alignment with the dependent variable (DV). Predominant shades of green (representing neutral or moderate agreement) suggest that most responses center around mid-scale values, while occasional clusters of blue and yellow highlight stronger disagreements and agreements, respectively. This visualization aids in identifying patterns, such as consistent response tendencies or significant deviations, helping validate relationships among independent variables (e.g., perceived learning satisfaction, technological accessibility) and the dependent variable. These insights can support further statistical analyses like correlation or regression.

Table 4. Rank Analysis

Rank	Features	Info. gain	Gain ratio	Gini	ANOVA	χ^2	ReliefF
1	PLS1	0.105	0.064	0.020	2.669	2.300	0.021
2	PLS2	0.143	0.076	0.033	3.062	5.687	0.040
3	PLS3	0.163	0.095	0.042	1.052	0.759	0.036
4	ARA1	0.179	0.096	0.042	3.640	8.091	0.043
5	ARA2	0.124	0.068	0.027	0.781	1.285	0.013
6	ARA3	0.122	0.070	0.036	2.032	2.794	0.041
7	LECE1	0.088	0.062	NA	2.258	5.595	0.004
8	LECE2	0.087	0.047	0.026	1.802	3.446	0.039
9	LECE3	0.046	0.026	0.006	0.160	0.301	0.034
10	MES1	0.203	0.107	0.058	3.144	7.149	0.036
11	MES2	0.186	0.102	0.064	2.964	5.019	0.068
12	MES3	0.083	0.045	0.025	1.448	1.744	0.001
13	CC1	0.145	0.081	0.034	2.831	5.118	0.045
14	CC2	0.183	0.116	NA	6.127	23.617	0.060
15	CC3	0.171	0.093	0.042	4.990	7.426	0.024
16	TAEC1	0.112	0.062	0.034	1.461	3.352	0.011
17	TAEC2	0.047	0.032	NA	1.545	4.261	0.012
18	TAEC3	0.116	0.076	NA	1.446	8.058	0.009

The feature ranking Table 4 provides an insightful overview of the contribution of various factors toward the dependent variable based on multiple statistical metrics, including Information Gain, Gain Ratio, Gini Index, ANOVA, Chi-Square (χ^2), and ReliefF. MES1 (Motivation and Emotional Support) ranks highest in terms of overall importance, showing consistent significance across multiple metrics like ANOVA (3.144) and Chi-Square (7.149), suggesting its strong impact on student performance. Similarly, ARA1 (Access and Resource Availability) and CC2 (Collaborative Competence) also demonstrate high importance, supported by their substantial values for Chi-Square (8.091 and 23.617, respectively).

Variables like PLS2 (Perceived Learning Satisfaction) and MES2 also exhibit high contributions across various metrics, indicating their relevance. On the other hand, LECE3 (Learning Environment and Content Effectiveness) and TAEC2 (Technology-Enhanced Collaborative Experiences) rank lower, showing minimal contributions in most measures. These results suggest focusing on high-ranking features such as Motivation, Access to Resources, and Collaboration to optimize the integration of ChatGPT in academic contexts. This ranking also helps prioritize areas of intervention for enhancing student learning outcomes effectively.

Exploratory Factor Analysis

Exploratory Factor Analysis (EFA) is a statistical technique used to identify underlying relationships between observed variables by grouping them into factors. In the context of "Sustainable Learning Solutions: ChatGPT Integration in Academic Services," EFA can be utilized to explore and understand the factors that influence the effectiveness and acceptance of AI-driven academic services. By analyzing student feedback, usage patterns, and other variables, EFA can reveal the latent dimensions that impact the success of tools like ChatGPT in enhancing learning outcomes, helping researchers identify key areas for improvement and adaptation in academic environments.

Table 5. KMO and Bartlett's Test

Kaiser-Meyer-Olkin Measure of Sampling Adequacy.		**.779**
Bartlett's Test of Sphericity	Approx. Chi-Square	512.055
	df	153
	Sig.	.000

Table 5 details the KMO and Bartlett's Test results that confirm the dataset's suitability for factor analysis. The Kaiser-Meyer-Olkin (KMO) value of 0.779 indicates adequate sampling adequacy, as it exceeds the minimum threshold of 0.6. Additionally, Bartlett's Test of Sphericity is highly significant (Chi-Square = 512.055, $p < 0.001$), verifying that the correlation matrix is not an identity matrix and that meaningful relationships exist among the variables. These findings validate the appropriateness of exploratory factor analysis to identify latent constructs within the data.

Table 6. Total Variance Explained

Component	Initial Eigenvalues			Extraction Sums of Squared Loadings			Rotation Sums of Squared Loadings		
	Total	% of Variance	Cumulative %	Total	% of Variance	Cumulative %	Total	% of Variance	Cumulative %
1	4.693	26.071	26.071	4.693	26.071	26.071	2.434	13.521	13.521
2	1.524	8.465	34.536	1.524	8.465	34.536	2.014	11.189	24.710
3	1.336	7.425	41.960	1.336	7.425	41.960	1.837	10.206	34.915
4	1.233	6.850	48.811	1.233	6.850	48.811	1.804	10.024	44.939
5	1.166	6.478	55.288	1.166	6.478	55.288	1.517	8.430	53.369
6	1.043	5.793	**61.082**	1.043	5.793	61.082	1.388	7.713	61.082
7	.928	5.153	66.234						
8	.923	5.128	71.362						
9	.778	4.320	75.682						
10	.704	3.909	79.591						
11	.604	3.357	82.948						
12	.555	3.084	86.033						
13	.520	2.888	88.921						
14	.491	2.729	91.650						
15	.466	2.587	94.237						
16	.381	2.114	96.351						
17	.367	2.038	98.389						
18	.290	1.611	100.000						

Extraction Method: Principal Component Analysis.

The Total Variance Explained Table 6 indicates that six components have eigenvalues greater than 1, explaining a cumulative variance of 61.082%, which is adequate for meaningful factor extraction in social science research. The first component accounts for 26.071% of the variance, followed by the second and third components contributing 8.465% and 7.425%, respectively. After rotation, the variance is distributed more evenly across the components, with the rotated solution showing that the six components explain between 7.713% and 13.521% of the variance each. This suggests that the data has multiple underlying constructs, and the rotated factor solution allows for better interpretability of these latent dimensions. The remaining components, with eigenvalues less than 1, do not contribute significantly and are excluded from further analysis.

Table 7. Rotated Component Matrix[a]

Features	*Component* 1	2	3	4	5	6
ChatGPT provides responses tailored to my individual learning needs.		.694				
Using ChatGPT has improved my writing, critical thinking, or problem-solving skills.			.521			
The feedback I receive from ChatGPT is accurate and helps me understand concepts better.		.435				
ChatGPT gives me instant access to academic materials and resources that are otherwise hard to find.				.606		
The availability of ChatGPT has bridged the gap in accessing quality academic resources.	.579					
ChatGPT helps me improve my language skills, especially in academic writing or communication.			.679			
ChatGPT saves me time by simplifying my research and study processes.						.858
Using ChatGPT has made me more reliant on AI, affecting my ability to think critically or solve problems independently.				.523		
The efficiency of ChatGPT allows me to focus more on understanding concepts rather than gathering information.			.757			
ChatGPT has boosted my confidence by providing immediate support for my academic queries.	.578					
I feel more motivated to learn when I use ChatGPT for academic assistance.	.455					
ChatGPT helps reduce academic stress by being available 24/7 for doubt clarification.		.751				
ChatGPT helps me communicate and collaborate better with my peers during group projects.	.460					
The explanations provided by ChatGPT simplify complex ideas, making discussions more effective.	.783					
ChatGPT enhances my ability to share and exchange ideas clearly in academic settings.	.548					
Using ChatGPT has improved my understanding and usage of digital tools and technologies.					.829	
ChatGPT makes me more aware of ethical considerations, such as plagiarism and responsible AI use.				.774		
I am comfortable using ChatGPT without compromising my data security and privacy.					.630	

Extraction Method: Principal Component Analysis.
Rotation Method: Varimax with Kaiser Normalization.
a. Rotation converged in 8 iterations.

The Rotated Component Matrix from Table 7 shows the factor loadings of various items on six extracted components after applying the Varimax rotation. Each item has been grouped into the factors based on the patterns of correlations. For instance, Component 1 has high loadings for items like "ChatGPT provides responses tailored to my individual learning needs" (0.694), indicating it represents a factor related to the personal learning benefits and customization offered by ChatGPT. Component 2 highlights aspects like improvement in skills (e.g., "Using ChatGPT has improved my writing..."), reflecting the role of ChatGPT in enhancing academic capabilities. Component 3, with high loadings on statements like "The feedback I receive from ChatGPT is accurate," suggests it represents the perceived quality and accuracy of feedback provided. Components 4 and 5 focus on time-saving benefits and the ability to simplify academic tasks, while Component 6 shows a focus on digital tools and ethical considerations in AI usage, such as awareness of plagiarism. This factor structure provides insights into the multiple dimensions of how students interact with ChatGPT, covering learning enhancement, time efficiency, skill development, and ethical usage, which are crucial for understanding the technology's impact on academic practices. The use of Varimax rotation maximizes the variance of squared loadings to make interpretation clearer by ensuring each item loads strongly on only one factor.

Multiple Regression Analysis

Multiple Regression Analysis is a statistical method used to examine the relationship between one dependent variable and multiple independent variables. In the context of "Sustainable Learning Solutions: ChatGPT Integration in Academic Services," multiple regression analysis can help assess the impact of various factors, such as student engagement, learning outcomes, and the frequency of ChatGPT usage, on the overall effectiveness of AI-powered academic services. This approach allows researchers to determine how different variables collectively influence academic performance and user satisfaction, providing valuable insights for optimizing the integration of ChatGPT and similar technologies in educational settings.

Table 8. Model Summary

Model	R	R Square	Adjusted R Square	Std. Error of the Estimate
Personalization and Learning Support	.291[a]	.085	.061	.86206
Accessibility and Resource Availability	.303[a]	.092	.069	.85857
Learning Efficiency and Cognitive Engagement	.259[a]	.067	.043	.87031
Motivation and Emotional Support	.314[a]	.099	.076	.85530
Collaboration and Communication	.221[a]	.049	.024	.87874
Technological Adaptation and Ethical Considerations	.368[a]	.135	.113	.83776

a. Predictors: (Constant), Personalization and Learning Support, Accessibility and Resource Availability, Learning Efficiency and Cognitive Engagement, Motivation and Emotional Support, Collaboration and Communication, Technological Adaptation and Ethical Considerations

From Table 8, the Model Summary reveals the results of regression models predicting various outcomes based on multiple predictors related to the use of ChatGPT. The R-values range from 0.221 to 0.368, indicating moderate to low correlations between the predictors and their respective dependent variables. The R Square values show the proportion of variance explained by the model, with Technological Adaptation and Ethical Considerations explaining the most variance at 13.5% (R^2 = 0.135) and Collaboration and Communication explaining the least at 4.9% (R^2 = 0.049). The Adjusted R Square values further adjust these figures for model complexity, with Technological Adaptation and Ethical Considerations again showing the highest adjusted value of 0.113. The Standard Error of the Estimate (ranging from 0.83776 to 0.87031) indicates the average distance the observed values fall from the regression line, with smaller values indicating better model fit. Overall, while the models demonstrate some predictive power, the explanatory power remains limited for all variables, suggesting that other factors not included in the model might also play a significant role in shaping student experiences with ChatGPT.

Table 9. ANOVA[b]

Model		Sum of Squares	df	Mean Square	F	Sig.
	Personalization and Learning Support	**8.026**	**3**	**2.675**	**3.600**	**.016[a]**
	Accessibility and Resource Availability	8.730	3	2.910	3.948	.010[a]
	Learning Efficiency and Cognitive Engagement	6.354	3	2.118	2.796	.043[a]
	Motivation and Emotional Support	9.386	3	3.129	4.277	.007[a]

continued on following page

Table 9. Continued

Model		Sum of Squares	df	Mean Square	F	Sig.
	Collaboration and Communication	4.629	3	1.543	1.998	.118[a]
	Technological Adaptation and Ethical Considerations	12.859	3	4.286	6.107	.001[a]

a. Predictors: (Constant), Personalization and Learning Support, Accessibility and Resource Availability, Learning Efficiency and Cognitive Engagement, Motivation and Emotional Support, Collaboration and Communication, Technological Adaptation and Ethical Considerations

b. Dependent Variable: I feel that student community will highly be dependent on the extensive academic services from AI (ChatGpt)

The ANOVA results in Table 9 show that most predictors, including Personalization and Learning Support, Accessibility and Resource Availability, Learning Efficiency and Cognitive Engagement, Motivation and Emotional Support, and Technological Adaptation and Ethical Considerations, significantly influence the perception of AI (ChatGPT) dependency for academic services, as their p-values are less than 0.05. However, Collaboration and Communication does not have a significant impact (p-value = 0.118), suggesting it is less important in determining student reliance on AI-driven academic support.

Table 10. Coefficients[a] of Personalization and Learning Support

Coefficients[a]						
Model		Unstandardized Coefficients		Standardized Coefficients	t	Sig.
		B	Std. Error	Beta		
1	(Constant)	2.611	.467		5.590	.000
	ChatGPT provides responses tailored to my individual learning needs.	.258	.108	.229	2.377	.019
	Using ChatGPT has improved my writing, critical thinking, or problem-solving skills.	.110	.079	.130	1.385	.169
	The feedback I receive from ChatGPT is accurate and helps me understand concepts better.	-.044	.096	-.042	-.457	.649

a. Dependent Variable: I feel that student community will highly be dependent on the extensive academic services from AI (ChatGpt)

The regression analysis from Table 10 indicates that Personalization and Learning Support significantly influences the perception of AI dependency for academic services. Specifically, the statement "ChatGPT provides responses tailored to my individual learning needs" has a positive and significant impact on AI dependency (B = 0.258, p = 0.019). In contrast, "Using ChatGPT has improved my writing, critical thinking, or problem-solving skills" shows a positive effect, but it is not statistically significant (p = 0.169), and "The feedback I receive from ChatGPT is accurate and helps me understand concepts better" has no significant impact (p = 0.649). This suggests that tailored learning support is a crucial factor in driving student reliance on AI.

Table 11. Coefficients[a] of Accessibility and Resource Availability

Coefficients[a]							
Model		Unstandardized Coefficients		Standardized Coefficients	t	Sig.
		B	Std. Error	Beta		
1	(Constant)	2.373	.420		5.650	.000
	ChatGPT gives me instant access to academic materials and resources that are otherwise hard to find.	.065	.076	.078	.844	.400
	The availability of ChatGPT has bridged the gap in accessing quality academic resources.	.161	.084	.177	1.912	.058
	ChatGPT helps me improve my language skills, especially in academic writing or communication.	.159	.084	.172	1.901	.060

a. Dependent Variable: I feel that student community will highly be dependent on the extensive academic services from AI (ChatGpt)

The regression analysis from Table 11for Accessibility and Resource Availability reveals mixed results regarding the influence on student dependency on AI for academic services. While the statement "ChatGPT gives me instant access to academic materials and resources that are otherwise hard to find" does not significantly affect AI dependency (B = 0.065, p = 0.400), the statements "The availability of ChatGPT has bridged the gap in accessing quality academic resources" (B = 0.161, p = 0.058) and "ChatGPT helps me improve my language skills, especially in academic writing or communication" (B = 0.159, p = 0.060) show a marginally significant impact. These findings suggest that while ChatGPT plays a role in enhancing access to academic resources and improving language skills, its influence on overall AI dependency is less pronounced and may require further exploration to establish stronger correlations.

Table 12. Coefficients[a] of Learning Efficiency and Cognitive Engagement

Coefficients[a]						
Model		Unstandardized Coefficients		Standardized Coefficients	t	Sig.
		B	Std. Error	Beta		
1	(Constant)	2.445	.521		4.698	.000
	ChatGPT saves me time by simplifying my research and study processes.	.056	.095	.054	.595	.553
	Using ChatGPT has made me more reliant on AI, affecting my ability to think critically or solve problems independently.	.158	.083	.176	1.909	.059
	The efficiency of ChatGPT allows me to focus more on understanding concepts rather than gathering information.	.152	.094	.146	1.613	.109

a. Dependent Variable: I feel that student community will highly be dependent on the extensive academic services from AI (ChatGpt)

Table 12 explains the regression analysis for Learning Efficiency and Cognitive Engagement which shows that while certain aspects of ChatGPT's impact on learning are positive, their influence on student dependency on AI is relatively modest. The statement "ChatGPT saves me time by simplifying my research and study processes" did not show a significant effect (B = 0.056, p = 0.553). However, the statement "Using ChatGPT has made me more reliant on AI, affecting my ability to think critically or solve problems independently" approached significance (B = 0.158, p = 0.059), indicating that while there is a slight concern about over-reliance on AI for critical thinking, the overall effect is marginal. Similarly, "The efficiency of ChatGPT allows me to focus more on understanding concepts rather than gathering information" showed a non-significant relationship (B = 0.152, p = 0.109). These findings suggest that while ChatGPT aids in time management and efficiency, its impact on cognitive engagement and learning independence is limited, and further research is necessary to explore these dynamics in more depth.

Table 13. Coefficients[a] of Motivation and Emotional Support

Coefficients[a]						
Model		Unstandardized Coefficients		Standardized Coefficients	t	Sig.
		B	Std. Error	Beta		
1	(Constant)	2.385	.415		5.749	.000
	ChatGPT has boosted my confidence by providing immediate support for my academic queries.	.188	.082	.216	2.280	.024
	I feel more motivated to learn when I use ChatGPT for academic assistance.	.103	.085	.114	1.215	.227
	ChatGPT helps reduce academic stress by being available 24/7 for doubt clarification.	.095	.083	.102	1.137	.258

a. Dependent Variable: I feel that student community will highly be dependent on the extensive academic services from AI (ChatGpt)

The regression analysis Table 13 for Motivation and Emotional Support indicates that ChatGPT's impact on students' emotional well-being and motivation plays a significant role in their dependency on AI. The statement "ChatGPT has boosted my confidence by providing immediate support for my academic queries" had a significant positive effect (B = 0.188, p = 0.024), suggesting that the immediate assistance offered by ChatGPT increases students' confidence. However, the statements "I feel more motivated to learn when I use ChatGPT for academic assistance" (B = 0.103, p = 0.227) and "ChatGPT helps reduce academic stress by being available 24/7 for doubt clarification" (B = 0.095, p = 0.258) did not show significant effects. These findings highlight that while ChatGPT has a noticeable impact on boosting confidence, its influence on motivation and stress reduction is less significant, warranting further exploration of these emotional aspects in future studies.

Table 14. Coefficients[a] of Technological Adaptation and Ethical Considerations

Coefficients[a]						
Model		Unstandardized Coefficients		Standardized Coefficients	t	Sig.
		B	Std. Error	Beta		
1	(Constant)	2.245	.456		4.923	.000
	Using ChatGPT has improved my understanding and usage of digital tools and technologies.	.228	.092	.235	2.480	.015
	ChatGPT makes me more aware of ethical considerations, such as plagiarism and responsible AI use.	.283	.087	.285	3.237	.002
	I am comfortable using ChatGPT without compromising my data security and privacy.	-.090	.096	-.089	-.936	.351

a. Dependent Variable: I feel that student community will highly be dependent on the extensive academic services from AI (ChatGpt)

The regression analysis Table 14 for Technological Adaptation and Ethical Considerations reveals that ChatGPT has a significant influence on students' technological skills and awareness of ethical issues. The statement "Using ChatGPT has improved my understanding and usage of digital tools and technologies" showed a positive and significant effect (B = 0.228, p = 0.015), indicating that ChatGPT enhances students' digital literacy. Additionally, "ChatGPT makes me more aware of ethical considerations, such as plagiarism and responsible AI use" also had a significant positive effect (B = 0.283, p = 0.002), highlighting its role in raising awareness about ethical issues. However, "I am comfortable using ChatGPT without compromising my data security and privacy" did not show a significant effect (B = -0.090, p = 0.351), suggesting that concerns about data security may not be a major factor influencing students' reliance on ChatGPT. These findings suggest that ChatGPT positively impacts technological adaptation and ethical awareness, but data security concerns may still require further attention.

SUGGESTIONS

Based on the coefficients of the variables, there are several insights that can guide the stakeholders involved in the integration and use of AI tools like ChatGPT in education. For educational institutions, the significant positive influence of ChatGPT on enhancing students' technological literacy and awareness of ethical considerations suggests that further emphasis should be placed on integrating AI tools into digital literacy curricula. Institutions can consider offering workshops or online courses that focus on responsible AI usage, ensuring that students are not only equipped to use such tools but also understand their ethical implications. Given that ChatGPT has been found to boost student confidence and support academic queries, universities should consider promoting AI as an accessible academic support tool that can be available to students around the clock, reducing barriers to learning (Tariq, 2025).

For developers and providers of AI tools like ChatGPT, the significant impact on boosting students' understanding of digital tools and awareness of ethical issues presents an opportunity to refine the AI's features, particularly in addressing data security concerns. While students may not currently view data privacy as a major issue, continuous improvement in transparency regarding data usage and security can build stronger trust among users. Ensuring clear communication about data handling practices could also alleviate potential privacy concerns and make the platform more attractive to students and educational institutions.

For students, it's important to acknowledge the balance that must be maintained between utilizing AI tools and maintaining independent cognitive engagement. Although ChatGPT has a clear positive effect on time management and academic support, students should be encouraged to view the tool as a supplementary resource rather than a replacement for critical thinking and independent problem-solving. Educational stakeholders can guide students to use ChatGPT effectively, ensuring it helps them grasp complex concepts while maintaining their ability to think critically and solve problems independently. Finally, policymakers and regulators can play a crucial role in shaping the ethical framework within which AI tools are used in education (Tariq, 2025). With the growing reliance on AI for academic assistance, it becomes essential to create policies that address data security concerns, ensure responsible AI usage, and promote transparency in the tools' development. They should also foster collaborations between educational institutions, AI developers, and other stakeholders to create a sustainable, ethical, and secure AI learning environment.

Overall, stakeholders should work together to maximize the benefits of AI in education while addressing concerns related to reliance on technology and ethical considerations, ensuring a balanced and responsible approach to AI integration in the learning process.

REFERENCES

Belikov, O., & Schunn, C. D. (2020). Ethics in educational technology: Considerations for AI tools. *AI & Society*, *35*(3), 575–586.

Gupta, R., & Patel, J. (2022). Investigating the impact of ChatGPT on language proficiency and academic support. *Journal of Linguistics and Education*, *23*(1), 45–59.

Joshi, S., & Roy, A. (2021). The effect of AI tools like ChatGPT on student motivation and academic performance. *Indian Journal of Higher Education*, *17*(3), 66–79.

Kumar, P., & Deshmukh, M. (2020). Enhancing collaboration and communication in group projects with AI tools. *Journal of Indian Educational Technology*, *11*(2), 122–134.

Mehta, P., & Sharma, A. (2022). Impact of AI on personalized learning support in Indian universities. *Journal of Innovation in Education*, *18*(2), 75–88.

Mitra, S., & Gopalakrishnan, V. (2022). AI and stress reduction in education: A study on ChatGPT's role in academic assistance. *Indian Psychological Review*, *44*(1), 37–49.

Nair, R., & Bhargava, A. (2020). Ethical considerations in using AI tools in Indian educational contexts. *AI and Society in India*, *15*(3), 54–62.

Pranaya, D., & Venugopal, K. (2023, August). Impact of mother tongue on students' speaking abilities in English language at rural places. In *English Language Competence in Rural Youth: Improving Job Readiness* (pp. 143–157). Current Publications. ISBN 978-81-19255-30-6.

Rolfe, V. (2020). Sustainability in education: Why it matters and how AI can help. *Journal of Educational Technology*, *21*(2), 135–148.

Somanadh, K. V., & Venugopal, K. (2024). Impact of children's engagement in traditional sports on the fitness: A descriptive study in Andhra Pradesh. In *Reviving Indian Sport's Heritage to Regain Health, Harmony, Glory and Legacy: Reclaiming the Past, Shaping the Future* (pp. 197–204). ISBN: 978-81-970389-8-3.

Tariq, M. U. (2025). Developing a Model for Sustainable Entrepreneurship Competencies: Strategic Decision-Making for a Green Future. In Duháček Šebestová, J., & Popescu, C. (Eds.), *Building a Green Future Through Essential Decision-Making Competencies* (pp. 137–158). IGI Global Scientific Publishing., DOI: 10.4018/979-8-3373-0189-1.ch006

Tariq, M. U. (2025). Harnessing 4IR Technologies: Innovating the Digital Preservation of Indigenous Knowledge. In Masenya, T., & Bhuda, M. (Eds.), *Revaluation and Preservation of Indigenous Knowledge Systems in Modern Society* (pp. 321–342). IGI Global Scientific Publishing., DOI: 10.4018/979-8-3693-7964-6.ch016

Tariq, M. U. (2025). Enhancing Security and Surveillance With AI-Driven Drones. In Ali Shah, I., & Jhanjhi, N. (Eds.), *Computer Vision and Edge Computing Technologies for the Drone Industry* (pp. 105–128). IGI Global Scientific Publishing., DOI: 10.4018/979-8-3693-8497-8.ch005

Tariq, M. U. (2025). AI-Driven Innovations: Transforming Healthcare, Agriculture, and Environmental Science. In Emara, T., Hassan, E., Trinh, T., Li, G., & Saber, A. (Eds.), *The Role of Artificial Intelligence in Advancing Applied Life Sciences* (pp. 87–118). IGI Global Scientific Publishing., DOI: 10.4018/979-8-3693-9208-9.ch003

Tariq, M. U. (2025). Leveraging Data Analytics for Predictive Consumer Behavior Modelling. In Miguélez-Juan, B., & Rebollo-Bueno, S. (Eds.), *AI Impacts on Branded Entertainment and Advertising* (pp. 207–224). IGI Global Scientific Publishing., DOI: 10.4018/979-8-3693-3799-8.ch011

Tariq, M. U. (2025). Bridging Home and Classroom: Harnessing Cultural and Ecological Wisdom in Teacher Education. In Liu, L., Mohamed, N., Lin, C., Bauler, C., & Kapur, K. (Eds.), *Funds of Knowledge in Teacher Education: Sustaining Local Diversity Amidst Global Standards* (pp. 405–424). IGI Global Scientific Publishing., DOI: 10.4018/979-8-3693-8094-9.ch018

UNESCO. (2021). *Artificial intelligence and education: Guidance for policymakers*. UNESCO.

United Nations. (2015). *Transforming our world: The 2030 agenda for sustainable development*. Retrieved from https://sdgs.un.org/goals

Vakamullu Gopalakrishna, & Venugopal, K. (2023, August). Assessment on the intricacies of English speaking abilities by rural students in India. In *English Language Competence in Rural Youth: Improving Job Readiness* (pp. 114–126). Current Publications. ISBN 978-81-19255-30-6.

Venugopal, K., & Saumendra Das. (2023, September). Prediction analysis of Gen Zers' attitudes on ecological consciousness. In *Sustainable Science and Intelligent Technologies for Societal Development* (pp. 242–257). IGI Global.

Venugopal, K. (2024). Exploring Gen Z perspectives toward ChatGPT in academic contexts. In Bansal, R., Chakir, A., Hafaz Ngah, A., Rabby, F., & Jain, A. (Eds.), *AI algorithms and ChatGPT for student engagement in online learning* (pp. 51–69). IGI Global., DOI: 10.4018/979-8-3693-4268-8.ch004

Venugopal, K., & Jagadeesh, B. (2024). Theoretical insights into user security and privacy in social media environments. In Kumar, R., Srivastava, S., & Elngar, A. (Eds.), *Human impact on security and privacy: Network and human security, social media, and devices* (pp. 289–312). IGI Global., DOI: 10.4018/979-8-3693-9235-5.ch015

Venugopal, K., & Somanadh, K. V. (2024). Smart library systems: Integrating IoT for enhanced user experience. In *Libraries as Wisdom Hubs* (pp. 196–205). Interdisciplinary Insights for the Future.

Venugopal, K., & Somanadh, K. V. (2024). Gen Z's journey through virtual library landscapes: Predictive analysis. In *Libraries as Wisdom Hubs* (pp. 100–108). Interdisciplinary Insights for the Future.

Zawacki-Richter, O.. (2019). The impact of AI in higher education: A review of trends and developments. *International Journal of Educational Technology in Higher Education, 16*(1), 39. DOI: 10.1186/s41239-019-0171-0

KEY TERMS AND DEFINITIONS

AI Integration in Education: The incorporation of artificial intelligence tools like ChatGPT into teaching, learning, and assessment to improve efficiency, accessibility, and engagement.

Educational Accessibility: The extent to which learners can access quality educational resources and support, regardless of location, infrastructure, or socio-economic background.

Personalised Academic Support: Tailored educational assistance that aligns with individual learners' needs, preferences, and performance levels to enhance learning outcomes.

Sustainable Learning Solutions: Educational practices and tools designed to be inclusive, resource-efficient, and adaptable for long-term academic impact and equity.

Chapter 4
Revolutionizing Education With AI:
ChatGPT as a Personalized Virtual Tutor for E-Learning Platforms

Arunav Ganguli
https://orcid.org/0009-0007-0022-6826
Christ University, India

Abhinav Kataria
https://orcid.org/0009-0009-6362-0569
Christ University, India

Pankaj Dhaundiyal
https://orcid.org/0000-0002-4815-1647
Christ University, India

ABSTRACT

It integrates AI into learning environments, which is transforming the conventional and online learning environment by coming up with something groundbreaking in the way of a personalized virtual tutor known as ChatGPT. The chapter looks into how ChatGPT uses the sophisticated natural language processing to present tailor-made learning experiences to suit the different preferences, paces, and requirements of individual students. The instant explanations, feedback, and support on diverse subjects increase the engagement, motivation, and ultimate educational success of the students. The chapter also presents practical insights on technical integration, data security, and ethical considerations to ensure accountable use. It emphasizes the importance of combining AI with human oversight in creating balanced educational solutions. Through many examples and case studies, it demonstrates how

DOI: 10.4018/979-8-3693-9841-8.ch004

ChatGPT is capable of connecting old learning methods with modern e-learning, thereby encouraging stakeholders to consider AI for greater personalization and transformation in education.

INTRODUCTION

Artificial intelligence has perhaps been one of the most influential technological forces over the 21st century, spearheading innovation through multiple industries while transforming the very nature of interactions between humans and machines. Among all affected sectors, it can be posited that there is no single industry more suited than education for harmonious integration into impact. Traditional models of education, especially characterized by rigidity and a lack of scalability, cannot possibly address the diverse and constantly shifting needs of the learner (Mogavi et al., 2023). With its capability to process vast datasets, draw insights, and deliver intelligent and adaptive solutions, AI is the new revolution for contemporary education (Ngo, 2023). This is further exemplified by advancements like the AI-powered tool ChatGPT in unlocking dynamic possibilities for this technology in reshaping educational paradigms.

The change witnessed today is from a traditional in-person classroom to virtual learning environment; thus, one of the reasons to highlight the importance of personal and flexible learning experiences today is found in online education, which has increasingly grown through factors such as the pandemic caused by the global COVID-19, increased digital connectivity, and demand for lifelong learning (Firat, 2023; Baek et al., 2024). However, in return, it has also exposed critical gaps, especially in the process of individualized support. Many learners are used to direct contact with instructors, and they cannot handle self-directed learning without some guidance (Wang et al., 2024). This transition has revealed significant areas of personalized support lacking, with many students needing face-to-face interaction with educators to cope with independent learning (Farhi et al., 2023). Artificial intelligence-based virtual tutors such as ChatGPT fill these gaps by mimicking human-like interactions, providing personalized guidance, and providing instant feedback (Chiu, 2023; Grassini, 2023).

Probably one of the biggest impacts AI-based virtual tutors would bring to students is their personalized learning experiences. As opposed to most educational systems that standardize curricula and even fixed pacing, ChatGPT tailor the responses based on each user's unique needs, depending on what users input and perform. For instance, a beginner in calculus can appreciate basic explanations and step-by-step guidance in solving problems, whereas a more advanced learner venturing into the same subject would find more benefit from more intricate challenges. In this manner, every learner at a different skill level and level of comprehension can delve into the subject matter evenly while being empowered and capable of comprehending.

Engagement in the learning process, a critical factor to learning effectively, is what ChatGPT does best-that at creating engaging and meaningful dialogue. Static content, such as video lectures or multiple-choice quizzes, is a significant basis of traditional e-learning platforms and fails to focus the attention of learners on the content. With conversational AI, ChatGPT provides dynamic interactions that simulate experience with a knowledgeable instructor or peer. This strategy promotes curiosity, critical thinking, and active engagement by reversing the manner in which information is received from a passive process to an interactive journey to learning. In addition, the ability of ChatGPT to interact using natural language will make students feel accompanied and heard, diminishing the feeling of loneliness that usually comes with online education.

Inclusivity and accessibility of AI utilities such as ChatGPT further underscore their potential for transformation. Conventional education tends to leave behind students from marginalized or underserved communities based on geographical, economic, or systematic constraints. ChatGPT bridges these gaps by providing access to 24/7 high-quality educational assistance irrespective of location or economic status. Multilingual support ensures that non-native speakers and students from varied linguistic backgrounds are also accommodated, making education a fully globalized and democratized process. For instance, the student in the remote village without access to good teaching resources could use ChatGPT to learn programming or study for standardized tests, and thus level the playing field in ways that were unimaginable before.

The book addresses the complex ramifications of ChatGPT in educational applications, centering on how this tool functions as a personal virtual tutor. To start off with, theoretical frameworks that help make the application feasible in a learning setting are evaluated: theories related to personalized learning and constructivist models of knowing. By relating this discussion to solid principles of education, the book allows a very strong, theoretical framework of discussing both the positives and negatives related to using AI within educational applications.

The chapter then explores the technological features that make ChatGPT a powerful tool for e-learning. Its sophisticated natural language processing, scalability, and multimodal interaction features (text, voice, and visual) are examined in great depth. Not only are they making the site extremely user-friendly but also extremely versatile across educational levels, from K-12 and college through professional training and skills-building programs.

The discussion then turns to the concrete benefits that ChatGPT provides for students and teachers. From increasing knowledge retention and academic achievement to fostering self-learning and critical thinking skills, the educational outcome contributions of ChatGPT are evaluated in depth. Practical applications, such as its usage in language training, STEM classes, and talent building, are highlighted to reveal its adaptability and effectiveness. Furthermore, the chapter describes how ChatGPT supports traditional pedagogical approaches, allowing instructors to spend more time on more sophisticated and creative activities in teaching while other typical activities such as grading or answering routine questions are mechanized.

However, the application of AI in education is not without issues and does not have any ethical concerns. The position of the human instructor in this new context is also brought into focus, demanding an equilibrium solution blending the power of AI with the compassion and intuition of human instruction.

The chapter also brings out practical application and success stories of ChatGPT in different educational settings. Case studies demonstrate its implementation at schools, universities, and corporate training programs to ensure effectiveness in improving the learning outcome or solving specific problems in education. These examples, therefore, put emphasis on how context-sensitive design, along with refinement, can work towards the effective success of AI-based educational initiatives.

Finally, the chapter concludes with future prospects and research directions for the integration of AI in education. There is promise for the advanced AI technologies in improving contextual understanding, emotional intelligence, and domain-specific expertise and further capabilities of ChatGPT through them. In addition, discovery in new educational domains and specialized fields such as health training or environmental education can provide further extent to its applications. Developing a more robust ethical framework and policy guidelines also will help educators navigate the difficulties of implementing AI in schools with fairness and accountability in sharing the potential benefits of its adoption.

OBJECTIVES AND SCOPE OF THE CHAPTER

This chapter will examine ChatGPT in e-learning: The fundamental aims are the following:

1. Discussing theoretical principles underlying the introduction of ChatGPT in education
2. Its technological characteristics, with an emphasis on NLP strengths and scalability.
3. Considering the benefits provided, including accessibility, engagement, and the achievement of improved learning.
4. Its limitations and moral concerns, from data privacy issues to AI biases.

5. Finally, providing illustrative case studies and success stories to support the applied work.
6. Suggest future research and development directions in AI-enhanced education.

This chapter scope covers technical and pedagogical aspects in the application of ChatGPT, providing a perspective for educators, technologists, policymakers, and researchers.

METHODOLOGY

To assess the influence of ChatGPT on e-learning, a mixed-methods research design was used, combining qualitative and quantitative approaches. This method affords thorough analysis of the efficacy of AI-based learning tools as well as overcoming challenges and ethical issues. Literature reviews, case study, surveys, and comparative analysis were used in the study to evaluate ChatGPT's use in education.

Research Design

The study adopts a multi-dimensional research approach, which includes:

Literature Review: The existing research in AI-powered learning tools was reviewed systematically to frame a theoretical backdrop. Research papers, conference materials, and case studies were evaluated to gain an insight into pedagogical and technological innovations in AI-based learning.

Case Study Analysis: The research comprises three case studies from actual applications of ChatGPT in various learning environments, from higher education and language instruction to corporate training and STEM education. The case studies were chosen due to their importance in illustrating ChatGPT's potential to improve learning outcomes and the challenges that come with it.

Comparative Analysis: For a fair viewpoint, the research compares the efficacy of ChatGPT with other AI-enabled learning aids like Google Bard, Jasper, and Grammarly. The comparative analysis points out the advantages and disadvantages of ChatGPT compared to other AI-enabled learning tools.

Data Collection and Sampling

The research relies solely on secondary data that combines peer-reviewed journal articles with published case studies and institutional reports as well as industry analytical reports about AI-driven education. Researchers performed a systematic review of past studies about ChatGPT alongside AI-powered educational tools to establish an extensive comprehension of their benefits and drawbacks and their ethical elements (Valeri et al., 2024; Limna et al., 2023). Higher education institutions, corporate training education and AI-integrated learning platforms showed how students connect with their studies while customization and administrative performance improved according to Wang et al., 2024 as well as Stahl & Eke 2023. A complete analysis of AI-driven education took place through the review of reports from public institutions and EdTech corporations and UNESCO and OECD along with government bodies (Firat, 2023; Farhi et al., 2023). Based on an analysis of AI-enabled programs Kahn Academy, DreamBox, Coursera and Duolingo it has been shown how artificial intelligence incorporates into traditional educational settings while measuring its contribution to student achievement (Ngo, 2023). Secondary data analysis used thematic analysis to discover essential trends and education hurdles as well as research possibilities which resulted from multiple source verification for academic validity and balanced educational AI assessment.

THEORETICAL FRAMEWORK

It is important to understand the theoretical foundations that include how ChatGPT can be integrated into e-learning in order to be able to understand its potential to transform. Personalized Learning Theory (PLT) and Constructivist Learning Theory (CLT) are both extensively researched on AI-based learning environments (Khan & Sabahat, 2024). These theories bring forth the fact that learning has to be personalized based on individual students and that knowledge should be developed by interaction and exploration. ChatGPT, being an artificial intelligence-powered tool, comes naturally with these theories by virtue of offering individualized suggestions and a question-driven model of learning (Valeri et al., 2024). Collectively, these theories reflect how ChatGPT stimulates personalized, interactive, and even dynamic learning.

Technology Acceptance Model (TAM) further details the usage of AI in teaching (Grassini, 2023). This model reveals that there are two drivers behind technology use: perceived usefulness and perceived ease of use (Chiu, 2023). ChatGPT's capability to offer immediate advice and execute mundane learning activities boosts its perceived utility among learners and instructors. Empirical research has indicated that if AI systems provide instant feedback and customized learning pathways, learners will have higher levels of engagement and learning retention (Farhi et al., 2023).

Personalized Learning Theory

The Personalized Learning Theory holds that education has to be addressed at the particular needs, interests, and abilities of every learner. This proves to be particularly true in the contemporary world of education, where a one-size-fits-all model hardly covers the diverse profiles of learners. That is where ChatGPT, backed by the most advanced NLP algorithms, finds its perfect fit with the theory. The unique content and exercises will be dynamically inferred from the user's input in terms of the exact knowledge gaps, learning preferences, and skill levels. Then, depending on those needs, the ChatGPT will customize the content and exercise difficulty. For instance, a learner who has a problem with simple algebra will receive step-by-step explanations, whereas an advanced learner might receive some complex problem-solving exercises. This will not only bridge the gaps of understanding but make the learning relevant and engaging, hence motivating the learners. Further, the adaptive resources provided by ChatGPT are created as per the objectives of students. For instance, a list of words, grammar practice, and example sentences for a student at a specific level of language proficiency can be offered. Students studying for a competitive entrance exam may be given practice problems and elaborate feedback based on areas of strengths and weaknesses. Personalization at such a level lets learners take more responsibility for the learning process; this can lead them to feel much more autonomous and confident (Ashikulla, 2024).

Constructivist Learning Theory

Constructivist Learning Theory is the belief that knowledge is constructed by learners through active engagement, exploration, and interaction. Learners are not to be passively fed information but rather questioned, investigated, and applied in meaningful ways. Thus, the design and functionality of ChatGPT are highly consistent with the principles of constructivist learning environments. ChatGPT supports inquiry-based learning, allowing learners to interact in conversation dialogues. A history student can discuss causes and consequences of great events; a science student may explore complicated theories through simulations that are guided by the model. These discussions force students to critically think, to consider other views, and dig deeper into the topics. Another, ChatGPT creates a realistic setting that fosters experiential learning. For example, in a business class, students can simulate negotiations or decision-making processes with ChatGPT as their simulated partner. Experiential learning apart from strengthening theoretical knowledge equips learners with practical skills that people would actually use in the real world. One of the foundational requirements for such a constructivist learning theory inherent in the formulation of ChatGPT is through providing an interactive learning space. In this space, passiveness for just absorbing the information is sacrificed to make way for a more positive approach, even that of construction of meaningful knowledge in an individually tailored manner.

TAM Utilization Explaining Adoption of ChatGPT

Although educational theories can explain the pedagogical ramifications of ChatGPT, TAM contains more useful information on adoption and usability. Based on TAM, there are two key factors that influence the acceptance of new technologies: perceived usefulness and perceived ease of use. This is a very important aspect in determining why learners and educators are embracing the tool for e-learning so readily (Baek et al., 2024).

Perceived Usefulness

This refers to the degree of perceived usefulness with which users believe that a particular technology will enhance their performance or result in the achievement of desired outcomes. In this regard, concerning e-learning, ChatGPT can provide immediate support, tailored guidance, and adaptive content. ChatGPT acts as a virtual tutor to the students; it gives instantaneous answers to questions or clarifies hard concepts or even recommends customized study sessions. For example, the same student who is struggling to program an assignment can be given step-by-step coding support, and the one requiring support on a literature exam may be given elaborate critiques of novels and plays. Such abilities enhance performance in academics but also minimize frustration and waiting time, common features often linked to traditional approaches to learning. Educators themselves recognize the future application of ChatGPT as a learning assistant. Automating repetitive questions and immediate feedbacks would free educators from routine work, such as the one in the previous example, giving them more time for mentoring and curriculum design. The influence both on learners and educators makes one believe in the practical utility of ChatGPT in the contemporary learning environments (Tariq, 2025).

Ease of Use is the Simplification of Learning

One important adoption factor in any technology is how easy or complicated it will be to use. ChatGPT has a friendly design interface and can thus work well for both low-level tech-savvy individuals as well as many non-tech people since its user-friendly conversational interface mirrors more normal human dialogue interactions. For example, the questions may be typed or even spoken in natural language and need not execute complex commands or technical jargon. Moreover, the ability of ChatGPT to understand queries in the context helps the users to receive relevant coherent answers. It makes it less hard to learn for users like students and teachers who can easily embrace this technology. It is also available on many e-learning websites and devices. The system can be accessed via desktops, tablets, or smartphones; thus, there will be no line of demarcation between the channels through which learners will be accessing their learning material, making it even more convenient (Tariq, 2025).

The convergence of Personalized Learning Theory, Constructivist Learning Theory, and the Technology Acceptance Model shows that ChatGPT is a multi-dimensional influence on e-learning. Tailor-made education to individual needs, active engagement, and ease of adoption are ways by which some of the major challenges in the traditional learning models are addressed. Practically, the range of those learners-from those at elementary schooling through to professionals-can now benefit through the capabilities by the wide-ranging users of ChatGPT that tears down different related geographical socioeconomic, and barriers for language issues. Moreover, it may establish educational theories established, and further ensures that various user adoption models continue to show ongoing relevance and success in a host of learning scenarios.

OVERVIEW OF AI IN EDUCATION

Artificial intelligence has today become the bedrock of innovation in various sectors, and education is not an exception. AI in education is a paradigm shift that allows institutions to respond better to evolving and diverse needs that may emerge from their students. The use of AI in education encompasses personalized learning systems, adaptive tests, administrative automation, and virtual learning environments. AI has transformed education with personalized learning systems, adaptive testing, and automated administrative processes (Gill et al., 2023; Stahl & Eke, 2023). Tools like DreamBox and Carnegie Learning employ AI algorithms to track student performance, adapting instructional material according to real-time analytics (Valeri et al., 2024; Ngo, 2023).

AI can scan large datasets and recognize patterns, making it a powerful asset for personalizing educational experiences. Algorithms allow teachers to learn about student behaviour, interests, and achievement in order to develop individualized learning pathways. AI also increases access for marginalized groups (Limna et al., 2023). Speech-to-text technology assists visually impaired students, whereas multilingual AI models assist non-native speakers (Farhi et al., 2023; Wang et al., 2024). AI-driven platforms like Duolingo and Google Translate have transformed language education so that students can engage in real-time conversations (Firat,

2023). For example, AI-based platforms such as DreamBox and Carnegie Learning provide instant feedback and change content based on the performance of individual students. Such adaptive learning systems can cater to different levels of proficiency, and no student is left behind.

Another major contribution of AI is in the area of increased accessibility. For disabled students, speech-to-text software, real-time captioning, and text-to-speech readers are of paramount help, based on AI-based tools. Likewise, multilingual artificial intelligence systems empower students of varying language backgrounds in accessing quality education. Platforms like Duolingo and Google Translate have transformed learning languages and helped students communicate transculturally with greater ease.

Apart from customized learning, AI also makes administrative effectiveness possible. Grading assignments, enrolment management, and attendance tracking can be automated, freeing instructors to concentrate on teaching and mentoring. Learning management systems (LMS) with AI capabilities automate these processes, generating a smooth learning environment.

Because of the challenges around the globe like the COVID-19 pandemic, remote learning and virtual classrooms have taken exponential leaps over the years. For example, by enforcing AI-enforced platforms like Zoom, Microsoft Teams, and Google Classroom, the geographical difference that would prevent students from continuing learning could be easily overcome. Features in AI capability range from automated transcripts, breakout rooms, to tracking engagement amongst other features which contribute to an immersive online learning experience. Moreover, AI has enhanced administrative productivity in schools (Baek et al., 2024). Artificial intelligence-based grading tools and enrolment management solutions lighten the load on teachers, enabling them to concentrate on coaching and course development (Stahl & Eke, 2023).

However, AI in education also poses its own set of challenges. Problems like data privacy, bias in algorithms, and equal access to AI resources are some among the challenges that still remain an issue. Addressing these will need to be worked on by teachers, technologists, policymakers, and researchers in ensuring inclusive and responsible use.

IMPORTANCE OF CUSTOM VIRTUAL TUTORS LIKE CHATGPT

It is the dream of teachers for long because it personalizes learning to suit the individual needs and abilities of the learner. Virtual teaching assistants, such as ChatGPT, represent a giant leap toward the realization of that dream. Through NLP and machine learning, ChatGPT generates adaptive, interactive, and personalized learning spaces for various types of educational requirements. Conventional schooling utilizes set procedures, which may not be best for the learning approach or pace of all learners. Customized virtual tutors such as ChatGPT fill this vacuum by adjusting content, teaching techniques, and feedback according to individual learner profiles. For instance, if a student has difficulty with mathematics, plain language explanations and specific practice tasks are provided to the student. In contrast, advanced learners will be given challenging problem-solving tasks. This flexibility will guarantee that each student receives the resources they require to thrive (Tariq, 2025).

Personalized virtual tutors have a number of advantages, one of which is that they can provide continuous, on-demand support. As human instructors are not always available, technologies such as ChatGPT are present 24/7, and thus it is more flexible and accessible for learning. This is especially beneficial for adult students, working professionals, and rural and disadvantaged students who cannot spare time to be provided with traditional educational resources. The conversational interface makes it a motivator and engager for ChatGPT. Interacting with the users almost like a human speech encourages engagement and an interactive learning atmosphere. For instance, language learners can practice having a conversation with it and receive correction and feedback right away. Through this interaction, learners can boost their confidence and improve their skills hassle-free.

ChatGPT can guide students who are to be educated on critical thinking, problem solving, and decision making. In using scenario learning and question-based discussions, it encourages learners to dig deeper and get a higher level of conceptual understanding. For example, an environmental science student would use ChatGPT in looking at real case studies, finding possible solutions to the problems that may arise from their choices.

Another important advantage of virtual tutors such as ChatGPT is their inclusivity. Because it is multilingual and accepting varied learning styles, ChatGPT opens education to a wider population. Disabled students with visual or hearing impairments can benefit from the facilities of text-to-speech, speech-to-text, and visual aids. This inclusivity fosters educational equity and enables learners from all walks of life. While its benefits are undeniable, the use of customized virtual tutors is not without problems. Data privacy, bias in AI, and the over-reliance on technology are concerns that need to be addressed judiciously. Moreover, human teachers are still indispensable in terms of supporting emotional intelligence, contextual insight, and moral wisdom, which AI cannot match (Chiu, 2023).

CHATGPT'S ROLE IN E-LEARNING

ChatGPT's place in e-learning represents a paradigm shift in learning by utilizing artificial intelligence to craft an interactive and adaptive learning environment. In contrast to conventional methods of learning, which are guided by a standard curriculum, AI applications such as ChatGPT are flexible and scalable, suiting various learning requirements (Gill et al., 2023). Research shows that conversational AI enhances student engagement and motivation, especially in online and self-directed learning settings (Limna et al., 2023). One of the greatest contributions of ChatGPT to e-learning is personalization in experience delivery. Sophisticated natural language processing in ChatGPT enables it to conform to the ability and needs of every learner uniquely (Stahl & Eke, 2023). For instance, a poor performer can be given a breakdown of concepts in easier terms, whereas an expert learner can be given more complicated content (Baek et al., 2024). A study by Ashikullah (2024) points out that AI-based learning assistants improve knowledge retention up to 30% over the conventional self-study process. This flexibility provides each learner with appropriate assistance to enhance their comprehension and confidence.

The conversational skills of ChatGPT make the e-learning site more interactive and engaging. Static educational material cannot encourage a dialogue; hence, students can ask questions, clear their doubts, and discuss the topic in depth. This will enable students not only to know more but also motivate them to understand, for it makes the learners more interested in the process. For example, conversational language can be practiced and, while being used, language learners will know where they went wrong regarding grammar, vocabulary, or pronunciation in a split second. Another critical role of ChatGPT in e-learning is the adaptive content delivery and personalized feedback capabilities. For example, in mathematics, it enables students to work their way through solving different problems while pointing out errors and suggesting ways to improve them. In humanities and social sciences, it helps to encourage discussions, offer historical or historical contexts, or analyse literary themes. This means that learning will most always remain relevant and effective for different subjects and educational levels.

Moreover, ChatGPT addresses the issue of access in education. It is available 24/7; thereby, learners are assured of support at their convenience despite geographical and temporal hinderances. In addition, ChatGPT promotes autonomous learning, where students learn at their own pace (Firat, 2023; Valeri et al., 2024). Studies point to its efficacy in STEM learning, where students are provided with step-by-step problem-solving assistance in areas such as mathematics and coding (Wang et al., 2024). Such an educational resource is very beneficial for working professionals, nontraditional learners, and people living in remote areas where access to other educational inputs is limited. Apart from that, it offers content in other languages and is a great learning resource for students who live everywhere in the world, so much so that it assists them in interacting with and learning content in their own languages. This renders independent learning highly possible with ChatGPT, making it possible for learners to acquire knowledge at their own time and learn subject areas that interest them, receiving instantaneous feedback. The independence yields thinking critically and solving problems, besides a life-long love for knowledge. For instance, an environmental science student will be able to study climate change, biodiversity, and renewable energy, aided by ChatGPT in an engaging way (Farhi et al., 2023).

ChatGPT can be a mediating or resource element that is used in group discussion and projects in collaborative learning. It offers ideas, resources, and helpful constructive comments for further enrichment of the process of learning. It also extends its collaboration features for professional training by simulating workplace scenarios for teams, brainstorming solutions, and then refining strategies. It aids instructors in incorporating ChatGPT in e-learning tools through automating monotonous work like assignments' grading, quizzes generation, and student tracking. This leaves the instructor to concentrate on educational strategy: course curricula designing and one-on-one mentoring. Moreover, the capabilities of data analytics in ChatGPT also bring insights into how students are performing, thus aiding educators in pointing out trends and challenges and even optimizing teaching strategy.

TECHNOLOGICAL FEATURES OF CHATGPT

This tech feature of ChatGPT serves as a building block for the efficacy and adaptability of technology implemented in e-learning. Simply put, ChatGPT leverages sophisticated natural language processing, making the AI model comprehend human-like text. This renders the AI model extremely useful for the education industry by recognizing context and having the capacity to provide logical responses while identifying user intent. One of the most important aspects of ChatGPT is its analysis and processing of vast volumes of text data. Having learned from diverse data sets, it has the ability to supply precise and contextually appropriate information on a vast array of subjects. This renders it an incredibly useful tool for learners looking for immediate answers, elaborate explanations, or sophisticated discussions. For example, a student of history may focus on the detailed account of past events whereas a science student may study the advanced theories and experiments (Tariq, 2025).

Scalability is another technological benefit of ChatGPT. Scalability means that it can serve thousands of learners together, which makes it highly suitable for large-scale deployments like MOOCs. Scalability ensures that quality learning support is delivered to a large population without being constrained by geography or institutions. The incorporation capabilities of ChatGPT enhance the utility of this tool even in e-learning applications. Using APIs, it can be integrated into operational learning systems to add functionality to these systems. E-learning sites may employ ChatGPT to build interactive chatbots that guide students through navigation and question-answering and offer personalized suggestions. The integration also reaches into professional training software, corporate learning management systems, and industry applications.

This is one of the innovative features of ChatGPT: support for multimodal interaction. Beyond text-based communication, this would allow ChatGPT to support voice-to-face to multiple visual interactions for communication with a wider variety of learners with different learning styles. Voice interactions help the visually impaired people to get the information better. Visual content, in forms like diagrams and infographics, will make concepts more understandable to the visual learner. Therefore, there is much more chance for inclusivity when an experience is interesting. ChatGPT further shows more flexibility by creating self-learning materials. It can come up with practice exercises, quizzes, and even study guides through the analysis of user input and preferences that a student has. This therefore allows for more personalized learning support but also empowers teachers to make more effective learning resources. A teacher, for instance, can generate topic-specific quizzes for the class through the use of ChatGPT so that the resource is in line with the curriculum (Firat, 2023).

The system's data analytics capabilities provide valuable insights into learner behavior and performance. Through interaction tracking, ChatGPT can identify trends, point out areas for improvement, and propose targeted interventions. This data-driven approach makes the e-learning platform even more effective so that educators and administrators can design curricula better, allocate more resources, and devise support strategies for students appropriately.

One other impressive feature about ChatGPT is the availability in more than one language. That broadens the user group worldwide and guarantees interactions for a vast variety of language backgrounds within learner communities who engage with learning material. In this way, international education as well as cross-cultural training becomes far less handicapped by linguistic difficulties. ChatGPT can create scenarios in real-life, and it provides an important dimension to e-learning. For example, it can make customer service situations, negotiation scenarios in the workplace, or consultations in medical care appear in the most realistic forms possible. Learners are, therefore, trained to tackle such situations that could face them in the real world. Perhaps the most pressing concerns regarding educational technology are security and privacy, and ChatGPT probably has some of the best safeguards in place to protect user data. Anything that ensures that the confidentiality and integrity of learner information are safeguarded through the observance of data protection regulations and encryption protocols will go a long way toward ensuring safeguards such as these are instrumental in building trust and promoting wide adoption.

BENEFITS OF CHATGPT IN EDUCATION

Integration of ChatGPT in education offers many benefits to learners and educators, changing the way they interact with content and each other. Probably the most important benefit is that it is possible for personalized learning experiences. Through direct student contribution, ChatGPT adapts content, pace, and instructional strategies to address specific needs, thereby facilitating greater interest and understanding. As an example, a learner who struggles in calculus can be led through step by step, while a more able student can cope with higher mathematical theory. The other major benefit of ChatGPT in education is accessibility. Students can get help at any moment because it operates 24/7, hence bridging geographical and temporal distances. Non-traditional students, working professionals, and people living in remote places will find it very helpful. Because of its bilingual features, the app may be used by people all around the world, guaranteeing that everyone has access to fair educational opportunities. Users can simply construct an interactive learning environment and participate in conversational, interactive learning with ChatGPT. It acts like a human being, hence encouraging students to be motivated in the classroom by being supported and urged. A few more features that encourage engagement include gamification, progress tracking, and inquiry-based learning. For instance, a person learning a new language can have simulated real-life conversations, knowing at once grammatical errors and pronunciation mistakes (Tariq, 2025).

The instant feedback of ChatGPT is going to be a game-changer in education. Learners will no longer need to wait for days or weeks to get back feedback on their assignments or queries. Instead, they can solve their doubts at once, which strengthens their understanding and eliminates misconceptions. This immediate feedback also enables teachers to keep track of students' progress and make necessary changes in teaching methods. Yet another significant benefit is that it serves as a self-directed learning agent. By making learners take charge of investigating their subjects at their own will and in the ways, they are most interested, it enhances curiosity, critical thinking, and problem-solving skills. For example, an environmental science student may investigate climate change, biodiversity, or renewable energy subjects through interactive assistance from ChatGPT. In professional and vocational education, the addition of real-world simulation added value to ChatGPT. For example, medical students will practice diagnostic reasoning, business professionals will refine their negotiation, and customer service trainees will practice simulated interactions. Such applications prepare the learner for the real deal.

CHALLENGES AND ETHICAL CONSIDERATIONS

Despite its benefits, incorporating AI into education brings up issues with bias, data privacy, and an excessive dependence on technology (Farhi et al., 2023; Stahl & Eke, 2023). Large volumes of user data are processed by AI models, such as ChatGPT, which calls for strong security protocols and adherence to data protection laws like GDPR (Chiu, 2023; Rasul et al., 2023). To guarantee that AI is applied ethically and fairly in educational settings, these problems must be resolved.

Data Privacy and Security

Data privacy is the most sensitive concern associated with AI in education. The large-scale processing and use of user data, including personal details, learning habits, and performance levels, by a platform like ChatGPT and similar ones make all of them responsible for the secrecy and security of information and being dependable. Misplacement or unauthorized access to sensitive data can result in serious outcomes for students, educators, and institutions.

To address such problems, developers must introduce security features like encryption, safe storage of data, access controls, etc. Those should abide by the GDPR. Additionally, data collection and usage policy practices should be transparent to increase the level of trust among users.

Bias and Limitations of AI-Generated Content

AI systems like chatbots are generally trained from enormous datasets. Therefore, that massive dataset may bring in bias or inaccuracy within it. Sometimes, those biases evolve in the content made by an AI, thus allowing one-sided ideas or inappropriateness. Stereotypes generated from historical or cultural biases found in training data may enhance related content or remove a given viewpoint. Another issue is algorithmic bias, with AI responses potentially mirroring biases in training data (Mogavi et al., 2023; Baek et al., 2024). Teachers should take care that AI-created work is accurate, diversified, and culturally diverse (Grassini, 2023).

Truly, the need to check and refine AI models continuously reduces bias. The use of diverse and representative training sets can minimize the risk of biased outputs, along with the inclusion of ethics oversight. Moreover, educating users about the limitations of AI and encouraging critical thinking over the AI-generated content can reduce over-reliance.

Over-Reliance on Technology

AI tools can become a source of dependency on technology and lead to decreased thinking and problem-solving abilities. This can change the student into an information receiver instead of a participator in the learning process. Time spent on screens and digital dependency are likely to affect mental health and social growth adversely. To minimize these risks, educators must follow a balanced strategy of bringing AI tools along with conventional pedagogy. Facilitating collaborative learning, experiential learning, and direct human interaction can help retain the integrative nature of the learning process.

Balancing AI with Human Educators

AI can enhance the learning outcome; however, empathy, intuition, and contextual knowledge cannot be equated with humans. Teachers assume a very vital role in fulfillment of emotional-psychological needs, creativity, and moral guidance. Here lies the question of how one can balance this with AI.

AI should be used to complement teachers' work, not replace them. It has to automate routine work and help them in so many other respects. For instance, ChatGPT can perform administrative tasks, mark assignments, and provide first-level feedback, leaving teachers free to concentrate on one-to-one teaching and guidance.

Ethical Frameworks and Policy Development

For the ethical application of AI in education, precise rules and regulations must be established. These rules ought to cover topics like fairness, accountability, and transparency. For instance, institutions need to define who is responsible for AI-generated errors or biases and ensure corrective measures are in place.

In addition, AI must augment and not substitute human teachers (Wang et al., 2024). Although ChatGPT may grade automatically and give immediate feedback, human teachers are still needed for emotional support, moral guidance, and contextual decision-making (Rasul et al., 2023; Limna et al., 2023). Another point to consider is the equitable sharing of AI tools and resources. The bridging of the digital divide will avoid disparities in the quality of education. Hence, all governments and educational institutions, in collaboration with the technology providers, have to make AI benefits available to every learner without bias from social status or geographical location.

CHATGPT AND LIFELONG LEARNING

ChatGPT is the most sophisticated OpenAI language model, rewriting the way through which humans work their lifelong processes of learning. Within a world continuously changing with evolving technologies and altered job markets, it only goes to reason one would embrace continuous learning to move in life and at work. Gone are the luxuries of learning not having to learn for life; the best in today's world are needy competitors who need to be built up to become adaptable. The unique abilities of ChatGPT are now going to prove a powerful catalyst for change. It can empower people to take a rich and ennobling journey through learning.

One of the significant contributions of ChatGPT towards lifelong learning is that it provides custom learning experiences. The classical education models have a one-size-fits-all approach, but the faculty at one's discretion can give way to interpretation through the amassing of numerous educational pathways. Knowledge gap analysis by ChatGPT based on user interaction allows the customization of learning pathways. For example, assume that a person wants to learn a new programming language. Now, this person can interact with ChatGPT, and it would give him or her personal tutorials, code examples, and practice exercises depending on his or her skill level at that given point in time. ChatGPT can give pretty brief descriptions to pretty complex topics and is also able to provide real-time feedback to the small pieces of code and sometimes even links to other online resources such as courses or articles or videos. The other power behind personalization besides that it propels effectiveness, actually driving engagement and motivation. With the personalization involved, ChatGPT makes learning really fun and rewarding with owning up of achievements and intense emotions.

Self-learning can benefit much from ChatGPT. In recent times, few people have time and money to squander for traditional classroom-type learning. It is not enough to fill in the gap between demand and supply of what is available for learning. This would make ChatGPT a virtual tutor because it would explain and give answers on nearly any topic for which information can be retrieved from texts and codes in volumes. A person interested in understanding any scientific concept will seamlessly interact with the ChatGPT since it clearly explains the given topic and gives accessibility to various outlooks of different research articles. Using relevant resources and learning materials, ChatGPT would help the learners to identify and fill in the knowledge gap. Such personalized on-demand information access can allow individuals to become responsible for their learning and study at their own pace and concentrate on areas of their interest. Aside from the elements of self-directed and individualized learning, it aids in developing critical thinking and problem-solving skills that are essential components of lifelong learning. ChatGPT can only be accessed when questions are clearly defined and unambiguous in order for it to determine the relevant information gathered by ascertaining how appropriate and relevant the answers are. Interactive dialogue engages the individual in independent thought processes by which they can filter information, identify bias, and construct independent opinions based on the information acquired. ChatGPT provides an opportunity to simulate real-life situations-for example, conducting a job interview, negotiating in a business, or posing a complex challenge for problem solving. With such role-playing exercises, which they may carry out with ChatGPT in virtual settings, people can hone communication, negotiation, and problem-solving skills, and this is when a lot of experience and confidence would be gained. The most crucial thinking and problem-solving skills become very invaluable for the highly dynamic and networked world in the interactive approach.

Apart from that, ChatGPT can assist in building a collaborative learning and knowledge sharing system-an important feature of lifelong learning in a networked world. Its capacity allows it to connect learners from all corners of the world and create a community and shared experiences of learning. For example, one will be able to create interactive learning platforms with the help of ChatGPT, where users could discuss topics, share insights, and collaborate on projects. This will be of especial benefit for those in the rural settings or for whom there is no other way to get into more conventional schools. This will make it possible for the student to get to other people with other experiences and perceptions, and so they will learn about the world intimately.

However, there are still a lot of moral questions and concerns about using ChatGPT for lifelong learning. The ethical implications of relying on AI for decision-making, bias in AI-generated content, and impacts on thinking abilities are the primary concerns. Utilization of ChatGPT should never inadvertently reinforce the adverse prejudices that it has learned or undermine the acquisition of the required human skills, such as critical thinking, creativity, and independent judgment. There is a requirement for teachers, policymakers, and researchers to work together so that guidelines and best practices in AI for lifelong learning need to be responsible and ethical.

Technology such as ChatGPT even redefines lifelong learning in terms of personalized learning experiences, self-directed learning, development of critical thinking skills, problem-solving capacity, and collaboration. With due care of the ethical considerations, attached to this technology, it may be that people embark on a more exciting, effective, and fulfilling journey of lifelong learning. It would help people adapt to the always-changing demands of the 21st century, take new opportunities, and give meaningfully towards society. In any case, we must note that ChatGPT is only a tool and how it's used will dictate the effectiveness. Hence, under such human supervision to maintain equilibrium along with creative and responsible technological input, this could unlock ChatGPT, further leading the process toward real experience and meaningful realization for those going through education processes.

CHATGPT VS OTHER AI TOOLS

AI has brought so much to the world regarding possibilities across most sectors, including education. In this line are the tools known as ChatGPT, which have made tremendous strides in sophisticated language models by OpenAI. Educators and learners alike are glued to the different ways this can generate human-like text, respond to questions, translate languages, and even generate various forms of creative content. Educational territory, on the contrary is teeming with divergent tools all equipped with specific strengths and flaws. Such multiplicity under one roof necessitates an educationist to enable AI in their practice of teaching in order for them to capitalize on the potential of the interaction of learners' experiences within classrooms (Tariq, 2025).

ChatGPT has extremely linguistic capabilities, with a varied multitude of applications used within the study field. It can be used to overcome writer's block, a common barrier to the successful pursuit of academic writing. Students can interact with ChatGPT to develop initial ideas, experiment with various writing styles and tones, and even write essay outlines for research papers and creative writing assignments. This improves productivity while allowing for creativity and experimentation in the writing process. For instance, a student unable to write a good persuasive essay on climate change would use ChatGPT to draft several arguments, analyse the counterarguments, and ultimately come up with the thesis statement. Such an interaction would most likely provide them with new ideas and broaden their horizon towards coming up with something much more insightful and better-supported eventually.

It is very useful for language learning also. They can employ it to write their writing skill by developing different types of writing prompts, including short stories, poems, or even a conversation. ChatGPT will then provide the student with feedback on how to enhance themselves in terms of grammar, vocabulary, and fluency. Further, ChatGPT can be utilized as a translation aid where the student can attempt to translate text into different languages and understand the different forms of language and their cultural connotations. This learning the language in an interactive manner can make it more interesting and efficient, hence giving a deeper insight into language and communication. Other than students, ChatGPT can significantly benefit teachers as well. To tailor each student's special needs and study patterns, teachers can be assisted to prepare individualized learning documents, e.g., assignments, tests, and exercises. For example, a teacher can ask ChatGPT to prepare several versions of an alternate quiz with different difficulties. It would allow every student to work at his or her own pace and be challenged appropriately as this means that every child gets the right support and challenge for success. Also, ChatGPT saves the burdensome work of evaluating multiple-choice questions, making appointments, and tracking students' records, freeing up the time of educators to provide meaningful individualized feedback to the student and brainstorm innovative methods of teaching.

ChatGPT is not alone among AI tools changing the face of education. Google Bard is another powerful language model that Google has built, using the vast knowledge graph of Google Search, which provides direct access to so much real-time information, thus allowing students to do deep research and keep up with current events. It thus presents another utility with Google services in supporting the research-oriented task, and it is quite an invaluable tool for students to undergo independent research projects and exercises in critical thinking. For instance, a student searching a particular historical event would use Bard in accessing a massive collection of sources including news articles, scholarly journals, and other documents and, therefore, proceed in synthesizing the information to achieve a personal understanding of the event. This not only enhances the research process but also fosters important research and critical thinking skills.

Jasper, as an AI writing assistant, caters to the needs of content creation alone. Jasper supports features such as plagiarism detection, grammar checking, and tone of voice adjustments for the perfect match for students and educators creating superior quality written work, such as essays, research papers, and presentations, not to mention marketing materials. One of the areas where Jasper is different from other general-purpose language models is its content-creating focus, which is very helpful to those disciplines that rely a lot on written communication. For example, a student who is mandated to write a persuasive speech to present in the debate competition can use Jasper to fine-tune his arguments and grammar checks while making sure that his speech is lively and persuasive enough. This can greatly enhance their quality of work and improve their assurance to present publicly.

From language models to AI-based learning platforms, much more dimensions see a revolution of education. Examples of such an educational platform can be seen on Khan Academy Kids and DreamBox Learning, through which AI personalizes a child's learning. These platforms monitor the progress of the students, understand their strength and weakness areas, and use the feedback to modify the learning trail further. It individualizes learning since it allows the student to learn at their own rate, and where they are struggling, get the right kind of support and challenge to achieve the full potential for learning. For instance, if a student is having difficulty with a particular mathematical concept, the system can provide additional practice questions, hints, and support, and even adjust the level of difficulty of the next questions depending on performance. This method will make learning both more engaging and motivating to students and further elevate their performance at learning.

The writing process is also altered by AI-powered writing tools like Grammarly and ProWritingAid. They no longer only look for grammar and spelling mistakes. They no longer just check for misspellings and grammatical errors. Instead, they completely dissect the piece and propose changes in sentence construction, vocabulary, and coherency/clarity. This real-time feedback helps students to improve the skills for writing, nuances of meaning in a language, and generally more refined and effective written words. For example, a small case would be an application essay of a college wherein the student has corrected his grammatical mistakes using Grammarly to enhance the style of his writing to increase clarity and conciseness such that it can increase the quality of the essay manyfold and also enhance the probability of getting admission.

On the other hand, AI in education does call for adequate thought in moral implications. Aspects of being plagiarized, whether AI-generated materials are biased in nature, or how it affects critical thinking processes, all are aspects that require thoughtful consideration. What is important for educators is not letting technology undermine the important skills of independent thoughts, critical thinking, and original creativity. Teachers can also act as a great guide for directing the students to responsibly and ethically make use of AI rather than simply relying on critical evaluation, human judgment, and original thought. For instance, for an activity on brainstorming with ChatGPT to develop ideas for essay writing, next, the students will critically evaluate the knowledge fed by the AI, research, and develop arguments and views.

Besides, one can mention a feature of AI models-having bias-there also arises as an unpleasant side effect of these models. The point here is that those models are compiled using very extensive sets of information, hence reproduce or magnify whatever happens already in society. It can produce biased or unreliable information that was generated by an AI in that educational setting with uncertain consequences. Educators must be aware of these biases and help the students to think more profoundly about the nature of information that AI creates so that they don't inadvertently propagate or become victims of the same. The educational landscape is changing due to the fast pace at which AI technology is advancing.

Against this backdrop, ChatGPT is a powerful tool with immense promise; the challenge is to be aware that AI has developed an extremely diversified set of tools for education. A proper and critical look at what the goals of education require would enable educators to combine different sets of AI tools-from language models and educational platforms to writing assistants-for all students in the creation of an even more engaging, personalized, and effective learning experience. It must be done in a way that strikes a balance between the advantages of AI and the necessity of autonomous learning, technology responsibility, and critical thinking. In this sense, teachers may transform education and equip students for success in the twenty-first century by utilizing AI's capabilities in a way that takes ethical issues into account.

CASE STUDIES AND PRACTICAL APPLICATIONS

The revolutionary potential of ChatGPT in education is demonstrated through case studies (Farhi et al., 2023; Wang et al., 2024). According to Mogavi et al. (2023), a university that integrated ChatGPT for student support observed a 15% improvement in academic achievement and a 25% increase in student involvement.

Case Study 1: ChatGPT in Higher Education

A top-tier European university implemented ChatGPT as part of its learning management system (LMS) to support students with writing academic assignments, mathematical problems, and the development of explanations for theoretical models. The aim of the university was to find solutions for issues such as scalability and individual support so that the students could avail themselves of 24/7 AI-driven tutoring.

Findings

Student participation in online forums rose by 20%, and grades on exams were 15% higher for students who frequently interacted with ChatGPT for coursework assistance (Mogavi et al., 2023). ChatGPT performed best in STEM courses, where it gave detailed step-by-step solutions to challenging equations and explanations for tricky theories.

Challenges

Some students over-relied on AI responses, decreasing their capacity for independent problem-solving and critical thinking.

Professors indicated that although ChatGPT enhanced recall of facts, it found it difficult to respond with evaluative and analytical answers and needed human assistance for higher-order thinking (Baek et al., 2024).

Literature Support

Evidence establishes that AI-supported tutoring helps in enhancing retention of knowledge and performance of students but needs to be implemented judiciously in combination with conventional instructor-led learning to avoid dependence (Firat, 2023; Farhi et al., 2023).

Case Study 2: AI-Powered Language Learning

AI-based chatbots were incorporated into AI-driven platforms like Duolingo, Babbel, and Rosetta Stone to offer conversational experiences close to real-life scenarios for language learners. The idea was to offer interactive and customized practice, enabling learners to enhance fluency through context-based dialogue generation.

Findings

Language learners with the aid of AI-based chatbots showed 35% enhanced vocabulary retention compared to those using textbooks alone (Gill et al., 2023; Limna et al., 2023). ChatGPT enabled real-time grammar correction, pronunciation feedback, and contextual phrase suggestions, making the learning process more immersive.

Challenges

Some AI-generated translations lacked cultural context, leading to misinterpretations of idiomatic expressions.

Users expressed concerns over AI's inability to detect nuanced tonal variations in spoken language (Stahl & Eke, 2023).

Literature Support

Studies highlight that AI-assisted language learning enhances engagement and retention but still requires human supervision for cultural and contextual accuracy (Wang et al., 2024).

Case Study 3: ChatGPT in Corporate Training

Using ChatGPT for employee training in financial risk assessment and decision-making simulations, a multinational financial services company simulated real-world business scenarios using AI tool, so enabling employees to participate in decision-making activities with AI-generated feedback.

Findings

Employees demonstrated 40% higher accuracy in identifying risk factors after AI-driven training (Rasul et al., 2023).

AI-enhanced training reduced the time required for new employee onboarding by 30%, as trainees could engage in self-paced learning modules.

Challenges

ChatGPT-generated financial models occasionally lacked real-time economic data, leading to outdated risk assessments. While effective for structured training, AI struggled with complex problem-solving that required ethical and subjective judgment (Ngo, 2023; Farhi et al., 2023).

Literature Support

AI-based corporate training is highly effective for technical skill development, but its effectiveness in soft skills training (e.g., leadership and negotiation) remains limited (Firat, 2023).

The cases above demonstrate the flexibility and promise of ChatGPT in extremely different educational environments. They also emphasize the need to overcome barriers, including accuracy, respect for ethical standards, and balanced coexistence with human teachers.

Practical Applications

For occasion, one college coordinates ChatGPT into its understudy bolster framework. This college confronted challenges in advertising around-the-clock mentoring to a different bunch of understudies. The expansion of ChatGPT to the e-learning stage gave understudies unhindered, 24/7 get to a virtual mentor who may reply any address, clarify concepts, and lead them on ways custom fitted particularly to their needs. The execution demonstrated to extend understudy fulfilment and move forward results. Understudies acknowledged the criticism and the opportunity to re-read clarifications at their claim pace. Workforce individuals, on the other hand, detailed that the device diminished their workload, permitting them to centre more on the complicated academic assignments.

The dialect learning apps are another case in point of the utility of ChatGPT. Apps like Duolingo and Babbel have tested with conversational AI highlights, empowering learners to hone real-world exchanges in a recreated environment. AI has been successfully incorporated into language learning apps, allowing students to practice conversations in real time (Ngo, 2023; Limna et al., 2023). This implies that ChatGPT can use natural dialect preparing to form relevantly important and syntactically rectify discussions. For occasion, a learner of French would engage in a discussion on how to arrange nourishment at an eatery and get input in terms of articulation as well as sentence structure. Usually, an intuitively frame of learning that increments learners' certainty and capability since they will hone without any judgment.

Corporate preparing too changes with the capacity of ChatGPT. As of now, totally different segments such as wellbeing, fund, and innovation, workers must learn persistently to be updated with the most recent guidelines and practices of the industry. ChatGPT has been connected to imitate a workplace. ChatGPT simulations are also used in corporate training programs for customer service and business negotiation training (Baek et al., 2024). It may well be patients for specialists or budgetary arrangements for bankers. These reenactments will give a secure environment where representatives can sharpen their abilities, get valuable criticism, and plan for the genuine challenges they will confront within the work environment. For case, in a restorative preparing program, ChatGPT guided learners through symptomatic forms and given nitty gritty clarifications of each step whereas clearing up misinterpretations.

The utilize of ChatGPT in K-12 instruction grandstands its flexibility over different levels of instruction. In elementary school, teachers used ChatGPT to create an interactive storytelling session. It can create compelling stories and prompt the students to ask questions, think critically, and be imaginative. At the high school level, it has been employed to help students with essay writing by suggesting structure, vocabulary, and grammar. It has been found that the students are more motivated to do the writing tasks if they are instructed by ChatGPT's interactive feedback. Massive Open Online Courses, MOOCs, have incorporated ChatGPT to overcome the problems of scalability and learner engagement. Thousands of students access the platforms offered by Coursera and edX, which makes it a Herculean task to support each student personally. This bridge is anchored by the instant response to learners' questions, summarization of complex topics, and suggestions of supplementary materials depending on the learner's progress. Case study: A MOOC on data science showed that students who interacted with ChatGPT scored better at the end of the course and demonstrated greater understanding of complex concepts. Despite the success of the implementation of ChatGPT in education, there are still some challenges that arise. For instance, a case study conducted in a community college indicated that the AI sometimes generated responses that were wrong or ambiguous. This meant constant monitoring and updates to the system. Another concern was raised by some students, who feared that over-reliance on AI would undermine the importance of human mentorship. Another practical application would be the pre-exam practice using ChatGPT. Several learning sites use the AI to create individualized study plans for a student preparing for standardized tests such as the SAT, GRE, or IELTS. ChatGPT analyses the student's strength and weakness profile and generates target practice questions based on that profile. It then suggests strategies to students on how they can improve their performance. Users experience increased confidence and exam preparedness while using this form of personalized planning. This can actually fill a gap in education in most developing countries where quality education is a dream for many. Many nongovernmental organizations employ the AI to provide low-cost tutoring in remote and disadvantaged areas. For example, in a proof-of-concept project in a small village in rural India, ChatGPT was deployed to teach young children the basics of reading and mathematics. Results were impressive-very impressive: using low-cost tablets, students began demonstrating marked increases in learning achievement, and thereby revealed the huge potential of ChatGPT for democratizing education. The use of practical applications also applies to special education. ChatGPT has been used to assist disabled learners in the delivery of personalized learning tailored to their individual needs. For instance, one example is when the visually impaired can communicate voice commands to the ChatGPT, and students with learning disabilities have the terms simplified with extra practice exercises. In such cases, teachers have also expressed that working with such students has been helped by using the ChatGPT in order to deliver individualized support, improving the outcome.

FUTURE OPPORTUNITIES AND RESEARCH DIRECTIONS

The accelerated development of AI technology opens up promising opportunities for enhancing ChatGPT's contribution to education. Scholars have highlighted that the convergence of multimodal AI features (e.g., text, voice, and visual interactions) can greatly improve student engagement and learning performance (Wang et al., 2024). For example, augmented reality (AR) and virtual reality (VR) software combined with ChatGPT may enable students to see abstract concepts in STEM disciplines (Gill et al., 2023).

Another potential area of growth includes the use of AI to tailor specialized fields like medical, legal, and engineering education (Khan & Sabahat, 2024). Future versions of ChatGPT may incorporate domain-specific data sets to offer expert-level advice, enabling students to model real-world professional situations (Valeri et al., 2024). For medical education, AI-based diagnostic simulations can assist students in practicing clinical judgment, while in engineering, AI-based design models can offer interactive problem-solving activities.

Ethical implications are an area that will be explored further in the future. Rasul et al. (2023) emphasized transparency in decision-making using AI as well as data privacy protocols within schools. Dealing with bias in AI-generated content is also essential since maintaining equitable and accurate information is still problematic (Farhi et al., 2023). Researchers need to concentrate on formulating policy guidelines that govern AI uses in education to ensure they are equitable, unbiased, and available to all learners (Chiu, 2023).

Further research is required to establish the scalability of ChatGPT in large-scale educational initiatives, such as national literacy campaigns. Future studies could assess its ability to reach underserved populations and its adaptability to different linguistic and cultural contexts. Pilot projects in remote areas would be useful in determining the challenges and benefits of large-scale implementation of ChatGPT.

These opportunities will rely on collaboration between AI developers, educators, and policymakers. Interdisciplinary partnerships can ensure that ChatGPT meets pedagogical objectives and societal needs through stakeholder planning. For example, feedback from teachers and students could help extend its usability and function, turning the tool into a far better learning aid.

The final integration of ChatGPT into lifelong learning programs is an opportunity. With the continuous evolution of industries, professionals need to learn and adapt to stay ahead in the competition. ChatGPT can be a personal career coach, providing skill development, industry trends, and professional growth. Its application in workforce development programs could be researched, with an emphasis on how it can improve employability and productivity.

CONCLUSION

Integration into the educational landscape will be a transformative shift in how learning designs, delivers, and experiences are approached. With ChatGPT being the ultimate advanced conversational AI for the vector sum of innovational technological advancement and forward-thinking education, it enables the delivery of more personalized, interactive, and dynamic learning experiences bridging this traditional methodology with contemporary requirements. This chapter will cover all diverse aspects of the role of ChatGPT in education, ranging from technological underpinnings to application, benefits, and challenges. It will conclude these insights by making a point regarding the possibility of redefining education with the help of ChatGPT while taking note of the issues and ethical issues that arise as a result. ChatGPT has changed the very concept of personal learning in being a virtual tutor. Unlike the standardized traditional classroom, ChatGPT offers personalization for each learner and his or her needs and preferences. There is an aspect of adaptive content delivery, real-time feedback, and customized guidance to enable meaningful engagement by learners of all ages and skill levels with educational material. This further explains its attraction, making learning a much more engaging and less intimidating process. For instance, it will allow language learners to practice conversation without fear of judgment, and for STEM students, it will provide step-by-step explanations breaking complex concepts. Such advancements can democratize education and give quality learning to the person irrespective of the geographical or socio-economic constraints they face. Technological attributes of ChatGPT are truly at the heart of efficacy and versatility, especially in all e-learning applications. It includes NLP that helps in understanding relevant user queries about a topic by making responses understandable in context; therefore, it can build trust and guarantee reliable information back to the learners. Another significant advantage of ChatGPT is its scalability, providing large-scale capacity support for initiatives like massive open online courses and corporate training programs. Its integration into already existing e-learning platforms makes it even more accessible with streamlined and cost-effective solutions for educators and institutions. This renders it accessible and flexible towards various learning needs and preferences.

ChatGPT is associated with many educational advantages ranging from enhanced academic achievement and retention of learning to higher accessibility and diversity. By removing time and place bounds, round-the-clock support provides a guarantee that students will receive aid at any time when they require it. Its ability to offer individualized guidance and adaptable content enhances learner motivation and interest, which enhances performance.

Beyond traditional education, applications of ChatGPT exist. It is useful for professional development and industry-specific training. For example, a student of medicine could apply it to the task of diagnostic reasoning, whereas a business person may apply it to the development of negotiation skills. Practical uses reflect the potential of ChatGPT to adapt to evolving education and workforce development requirements.

The adoption of ChatGPT is not without issues and ethical implications, including compelling issues surrounding data privacy and security related to processing massive amounts of user data to attain personal experience. Measures of compliance to ensure data protection and robust security should be maintained in order to set up and sustain user trust. Biases within AI reveal threats to the correctness and equity of education material. There should be greater openness and involvement from the side of the developers and stakeholders while designing AI to avoid such problems. Another issue is the balance of usage of AI with the role of human teachers. There are many advantages offered by ChatGPT, but empathy, intuition, and overall comprehension of a human teacher cannot be replicated. It is therefore through this balance that an education system will be developed that exploits both AI capabilities and human knowledge in its entirety.

The practical applications of ChatGPT are highly reflective of its potential in changing the dynamics of education. Case studies reflect the positive effectiveness it can bring about to enhance learner satisfaction, engagement, and outcomes. For example, the universities that introduced ChatGPT for tutoring support reported an amazing improvement in their students' performance and retention rates. Conversely, usage of language learning platforms that utilise ChatGPT for conversational practice has proved beneficial to users and preferred the engagement and support they offer. More instances depict how the very same system lends itself to changeability in adaptation with the need and environment where it is situated.

The future of ChatGPT in education is full of innovation and research. Advancements of AI features could introduce more advanced multimodal capabilities such that learning becomes highly immersive and text, voice, and visual elements create a new environment for training. New domains, including engineering, healthcare, the arts, and others will be explored, and this will allow ChatGPT to be developed in a way to be applicable to a much wider variety of learners and industries. Ethical frameworks and policy recommendations will also be needed to guide the responsible development and implementation of AI in education, making sure that all the benefits from AI are realized while the risks are minimized.

REFERENCES

Ashikullah, M. (2024). Investigating the pros and cons of Artificial Intelligence (AI)-Based Systems: A case study on the use of ChaTGPT in higher education in the northern region of Bangladesh. *International Journal on Studies in English Language and Literature*, *12*(6), 1–8. DOI: 10.20431/2347-3134.1206001

Baek, C., Tate, T., & Warschauer, M. (2024). "ChatGPT seems too good to be true": College students' use and perceptions of generative AI. *Computers and Education Artificial Intelligence*, *100294*, 100294. Advance online publication. DOI: 10.1016/j.caeai.2024.100294

Chiu, T. K. (2023). Future research recommendations for transforming higher education with generative AI. *Computers and Education Artificial Intelligence*, *6*, 100197. DOI: 10.1016/j.caeai.2023.100197

Farhi, F., Jeljeli, R., Aburezeq, I., Dweikat, F. F., Al-Shami, S. A., & Slamene, R. (2023). Analyzing the students' views, concerns, and perceived ethics about chat GPT usage. *Computers and Education Artificial Intelligence*, *5*, 100180. DOI: 10.1016/j.caeai.2023.100180

Firat, M. (2023). What ChatGPT means for universities: Perceptions of scholars and students. *Journal of Applied Learning & Teaching*, *6*(1). Advance online publication. DOI: 10.37074/jalt.2023.6.1.22

Gill, S. S., Xu, M., Patros, P., Wu, H., Kaur, R., Kaur, K., Fuller, S., Singh, M., Arora, P., Parlikad, A. K., Stankovski, V., Abraham, A., Ghosh, S. K., Lutfiyya, H., Kanhere, S. S., Bahsoon, R., Rana, O., Dustdar, S., Sakellariou, R., & Buyya, R. (2023). Transformative effects of ChatGPT on modern education: Emerging era of AI chatbots. *Internet of Things and Cyber-Physical Systems*, *4*, 19–23. DOI: 10.1016/j.iotcps.2023.06.002

Grassini, S. (2023). Shaping the future of education: Exploring the potential and consequences of AI and ChatGPT in educational settings. *Education Sciences*, *13*(7), 692. DOI: 10.3390/educsci13070692

Khan, N., & Sabahat, N. (2024). Role of AI chatbots in revolutionizing gaming experiences – a survey. *VFAST Transactions on Software Engineering*, *12*(1), 93–104. DOI: 10.21015/vtse.v12i1.1725

Limna, P., Kraiwanit, T., Jangjarat, K., Klayklung, P., & Chocksathaporn, P. (2023). The use of ChatGPT in the digital era: Perspectives on chatbot implementation. *Journal of Applied Learning & Teaching*, *6*(1). Advance online publication. DOI: 10.37074/jalt.2023.6.1.32

Mogavi, R. H., Deng, C., Kim, J. J., Zhou, P., Kwon, Y. D., Metwally, A. H. S., Tlili, A., Bassanelli, S., Bucchiarone, A., Gujar, S., Nacke, L. E., & Hui, P. (2023). ChatGPT in education: A blessing or a curse? A qualitative study exploring early adopters' utilization and perceptions. *Computers in Human Behavior Artificial Humans*, *2*(1), 100027. DOI: 10.1016/j.chbah.2023.100027

Ngo, T. T. A. (2023). The perception by university students of the use of CHATGPT in education. [iJET]. *International Journal of Emerging Technologies in Learning*, *18*(17), 4–19. DOI: 10.3991/ijet.v18i17.39019

Rasul, T., Nair, S., Kalendra, D., Robin, M., De Oliveira Santini, F., Ladeira, W. J., Sun, M., Day, I., Rather, R. A., & Heathcote, L. (2023). The role of ChatGPT in higher education: Benefits, challenges, and future research directions. *Journal of Applied Learning & Teaching*, *6*(1). Advance online publication. DOI: 10.37074/jalt.2023.6.1.29

Stahl, B. C., & Eke, D. (2023). The ethics of ChatGPT – Exploring the ethical issues of an emerging technology. *International Journal of Information Management*, *74*, 102700. DOI: 10.1016/j.ijinfomgt.2023.102700

Tariq, M. U. (2025). Innovative Mentoring Programs: Strategies for Success in Post-COVID-19 Education. In Putnam, J., VanValkenburgh Banks, J., & Brown, S. K. (Eds.), *Mentoring Students and Instructors for Retention and Success* (pp. 123–158). IGI Global Scientific Publishing., DOI: 10.4018/979-8-3693-7590-7.ch005

Tariq, M. U. (2025). AI-Driven Personalized Learning: Revolutionizing Student Engagement and Teacher Efficiency in Education 5.0. In Mobo, F. (Ed.), *AI and Emerging Technologies for Emergency Response and Smart Cities* (pp. 75–96). IGI Global Scientific Publishing., DOI: 10.4018/979-8-3693-9770-1.ch004

Tariq, M. U. (2025). Navigating Cancer Care: The Crucial Role of Educators and Healthcare Providers in Supporting Patients of Color. In Clarke, K., & Moffett, N. (Eds.), *Cancer Diagnosis, Treatment and Care: Reflections for the Education of Survivors and Healthcare Providers* (pp. 405–424). IGI Global Scientific Publishing., DOI: 10.4018/979-8-3693-5400-1.ch021

Tariq, M. U. (2025). Balancing Flexibility and Precarity: Ethical Implications and Sustainable Practices in Global Gig Economies. In Doon, R. (Ed.), *Sustainability and Adaptability of Gig Economies in Global Business* (pp. 323–346). IGI Global Scientific Publishing., DOI: 10.4018/979-8-3693-9385-7.ch012

Tariq, M. U. (2025). Harnessing the Power of GANs and Meta-Learning for Few-Shot Image Generation. In Simaiya, S., Lilhore, U., Sharma, Y., & Kumar, S. (Eds.), *Exploring Generative Adversarial Networks and Meta-Learning Synergies* (pp. 301–324). IGI Global Scientific Publishing., DOI: 10.4018/979-8-3693-7575-4.ch012

Uğraş, M. (2024). *Evaluation of CHATGPT usage in preschool education: Teacher perspectives*. Eğitim ve İnsani Bilimler Dergisi Teori ve Uygulama., DOI: 10.58689/eibd.1537337

Valeri, F., Nilsson, P., & Cederqvist, A. (2024). Exploring students' experience of CHATGPT in STEM education. *Computers and Education Artificial Intelligence, 100360*. Advance online publication. DOI: 10.1016/j.caeai.2024.100360

Wang, J., Hu, H., Wang, Z., Yan, S., Sheng, Y., & He, D. (2024). Evaluating large language models on academic literature understanding and review: An empirical study among early-stage scholars. In *Conference on Human Factors in Computing Systems (CHI)* (pp. 1–18). https://doi.org/DOI: 10.1145/3613904.3641917

KEY TERMS AND DEFINITIONS

Artificial Intelligence (AI): Computer systems capable of performing tasks that normally require human intelligence, such as reasoning, learning, and problem-solving.

Virtual Tutor: An AI-powered digital assistant, such as ChatGPT, that delivers personalised educational support and feedback to learners.

Personalised Learning: An educational approach tailored to an individual learner's needs, preferences, and pace, often enabled by AI.

Natural Language Processing (NLP): A subfield of AI that enables machines to understand, interpret, and respond to human language in a conversational manner.

Digital Accessibility: The principle of making online educational tools and content usable and inclusive for all individuals, regardless of location, ability, or socioeconomic status.

Chapter 5
A Novel Algorithm to Discover New Drugs Using ChatGPT

Anshit Mukherjee
https://orcid.org/0009-0001-7930-401X
Abacus Institute of Engineering and Management, Hoogly, India

ABSTRACT

We have developed novel algorithm that integrates ChatGPT to revolutionize drug discovery, addressing the complexities and high costs associated with traditional methods. This innovative algorithm leverages ChatGPT's advanced natural language processing capabilities to perform comprehensive literature analysis, extracting relevant information on drug targets and compounds from vast scientific databases. Unique features include predictive modelling for pharmacokinetic (PK) and pharmacodynamic (PD) properties, allowing for informed modifications to enhance bioavailability and reduce toxicity. Additionally, the algorithm employs iterative feedback mechanisms, enabling real-time collaboration between researchers and ChatGPT to refine chemical structures based on simulated biological interactions. By incorporating a multi-persona approach, the algorithm provides tailored support throughout the drug discovery pipeline. Overall, this integration aims to accelerate therapeutic development while ensuring safety and efficacy, ultimately transforming the landscape of pharmaceutical innovation.

DOI: 10.4018/979-8-3693-9841-8.ch005

INTRODUCTION

The pharmaceutical industry uses drug discovery approach as the fundamental method of arriving at new therapeutic agents to treat various diseases. Conventionally, it has been practiced in a slow, cumbersome manner over a long time period and involves huge capital outlay. A drug usually takes more than 10 years and cost billions of US dollars to pass through the discovery phase, clinical trials and marketing phases. The traditional method makes extensive use of the experimental approaches and success chances in such methodologies are normally low because of the complexity of biological picrate and consequent effectiveness of disease process. Consequently, there is a growing demand for innovative solutions that will improve the procedure and results of drug discovery. The emergence of new artificial intelligence (AI) (Virshup et al., 2013) and natural language processing (NLP) (Brown et al., 2019) has created new possibilities for this landscape. From the above technologies, ChatGPT created by OpenAI has been found to have incredible ability to mimic human responses and transform large amount of content from various sources (Jensen, 2019). Altogether, with the help of ChatGPT's strengths, researchers may well be able to facilitate millions of combinations at a faster display of each element of the medicine-making process, beginning with target selection and ending with compound fine-tuning.

However, there are some issues remain in using AI and NLP in drug discovery even there many opportunities for those methodologies. Earlier algorithms are non-machine learning or even if they are, they do not have the necessary parameters to scan biochemistry and pharmacology journals or to discover new associations between properties of molecules and diseases or find better drug candidates. The current predictive models lack essential PK-PD characteristics that are needed to properly assess new compound potential (Tsherniak et al., 2017). Moreover, a large number of those methods are not closed-loop processes where researchers can interact with the AI model in real time which may hinder the use of model in design iterations. Market leaders need to handle privacy, moral worries, plus follow industry and official guidelines when they put modern AI into their work. In current approaches, the biggest challenge lies in making certain that the outputs realized by the AI are accurate and that they can be applied in practice (Petyuk et al., 2018).

This research is prompted by the necessity to go beyond the constraints of conventional drug discovery and to incorporate the use of the powerful artificial intelligence tool like ChatGPT. Our previous work has identified several issues that could be alleviated through the implementation of a new algorithm that includes ChatGPT in the drug discovery process, while improving the cooperation between scientists. The purpose of this work is to try envisaging and address certain issues of computational methodologies common in pharmaceutical research in premise of their advanced aspects. The main aim of this paper is to propose a new algorithm that incorporates ChatGPT at different steps of the drug discovery process. The next goal is to align our algorithm with other complex algorithms in this area of study. The remainder of this paper is organized as follows: Section 2 is a literature survey relating to application of AI in drug discovery, where the authors mention the barriers and limitations of methodological approaches prior to their discussion. In section 3, the aspects of developing the new algorithm presented in this paper, such as its design and the implementation procedures are described. Section 4 provides results section showing that the algorithm is capable of novel drug discovery and the prediction of the properties of these drugs. In section 5, the applications are discussed followed by future scopes and limitations in section 6 and 7. Section 8 is the discussion section. Lastly, Section 9 provides overall findings of the paper, and offer suggestions for future research on the ways to combine AI technologies as effective tools to assist in pharmaceutical innovation.

LITERATURE REVIEW

Cao (Cao et al., 2025) and his research group developed InstructMol in 2025 to improve how scientists interact with molecular data throughout drug discovery. The system uses two training phases with a guidance-based approach to link molecular structures to text sources using small numbers of specialized datasets. The system proved more effective than currently available LLMs and showed almost equivalent capabilities to purpose-built drug discovery models. InstructMol provides better tools to analyse molecular structures for drug synthesis planning and discovers new uses for existing drugs. The researchers emphasized two key constraints of their model - it requires many training sessions to function well and struggles when handling unfamiliar problems. InstructMol creates a strong basis for building an adaptable molecular tool that helps drug discovery and sets out new paths for AI-based medical research. Askr (Askr et al., 2023) assembled a team that used deep learning to analyse drug discovery tools and showed AI helps medications progress faster. Their research analysed 300 publications from 2000 to 2022 that used DL methods to study drug-target interactions DTIs, drug-drug similarities DDI and drug response prediction. The review studied the different test collections and measurement protocols used across these investigations. Askr investigated the benefits of explainable AI for drug discovery by showing researchers how to trust AI predictions through better understanding of results. The team reviewed DL's practical uses for drug dose optimization while exploring upcoming research hurdles and possible new paths in AI drug discovery work.

In 2023 Liu (Liu et al., 2023) and his team presented Chat Drug as a drug editing method that uses LLM models like ChatGPT to support a crucial but poorly understood part of creating new drugs. The framework combines three modules to support structured drug editing through prompt generation retrieval and domain feedback. Testing showed that Chat Drug exceeded previous techniques in editing drugs for 33 out of 39 tasks covering small molecules peptides and proteins. This method speeds up drug modification tasks by finding important structural parts and offering many suitable ways to change existing drugs. Researchers suggest that more testing of Chat Drug is needed on different drug tasks to confirm its use for broader pharmaceutical research purposes.

In 2023 Ajagekar's team (Ajagekar et al., 2023) created a revolutionary molecular design approach by combining quantum computing and deep learning plus optimization methods to better predict and produce new molecules. Their approach trains an energy-based deep learning model to produce strong molecular representations. Our system combines data-based QC optimization with an energy-based model to explore chemical space through identified structure-property links. Our research created many new molecules that matched desired property targets better than existing methods did. This research provides benefits through better chemical exploration and designs new molecules to specific criteria while reducing dependency on large datasets. Current quantum device limitations stop us from scaling up to complex systems at this time. Research indicates how quantum computing can change automated molecular design and suggests its path toward studying sophisticated molecules that help medicine and material science progress.

In 2022 Nittinger (Nittinger et al., 2022) and his research group tested a fresh molecular optimization strategy that moves past the typical matched molecular pairs (MMPs) process because MMPs fail to reveal structural improvements fully. Their research uses Transformer architecture to learn from multiple datasets showing specific kinds of chemical conversions. From Tanimoto similarity and scaffold matching ChEMBL data the research group allows scientists to modify starting molecules at all their positions while keeping the core framework intact. Our trained models successfully alter starting molecules to match how they were taught within their specific training dataset giving chemists multiple ways to make drug improvements. This method discovers more chemical combinations than standard MMP approaches while allowing researchers to make multiple molecular shape modifications at once. The technique faces two main limiting factors. First, it cannot handle complex molecule modifications and secondly depends heavily on large training data. This research demonstrates how advanced deep learning methods help scientists find new ways to enhance drug candidates and shows the path ahead for better medications.

In 2021 Kwon's team (Kwon et al., 2021) developed MolFinder to find optimized molecules through a new approach that combines conformational space annealing with SMILES representations of molecular structures. With this new technique MolFinder quickly finds different molecules that match specific targets even when analyzing small sets of information instead of large databases. MolFinder generates better results than latest reinforcement-learning-based approaches for property adjustments while finding many new diverse molecule options. Research shows this basic tool can help us find better molecules for optimization studies. While MolFinder finds new compounds in chemical space it needs machine learning for better property and optimization outcomes. Its approach that uses SMILES to optimize molecules shows that MolFinder represents an important drug discovery improvement yet future studies in these methods should deliver stronger results.

Kim (Kim et al., 2020) and his team reviewed AI technology in drug development during 2020 because current costs had become too high. Their research evaluated how AI systems work in different drug discovery phases from target selection to drug conversion Our study examined various research materials to collect essential findings from previous studies. The integration of AI in drug development improves process speed and cost efficiency but research shows the approach needs better data management and clear testing standards. Prof. Kim's group identified present obstacles in AI drug discovery and developed strategic solutions for development while building essential groundwork for future innovation.

During 2019 Liu (Liu et al., 2019) and his team created Chemi-Net a data-led deep learning method free from chemical domain knowledge to identify ADME properties needed for drug discovery. A new GCN framework analyses molecule data without using standard domain-related descriptors or fingerprints for prediction. The researchers partnered with Amgen in a major study to test Chemi-Net against Cubist machine learning platform. Chemi-Net demonstrated better accuracy than Cubist by 26.7% across every one of 13 evaluated databases. Chemi-Net shows such a strong predictive boost that researchers can now develop new medications faster because they have better insights about how drugs will interact with the body. Despite its demonstrated model benefits against GCN the research shows that small datasets may cause overfitting and training requires substantial data to use the model at its best. Chemi-Net demonstrates significant potential in computer drug design by showing how deep learning methods enhance molecular property estimation.

Existing research about drug discovery problems drives our need to create a new drug discovery algorithm. AI models cannot trust their predictions due to unreliable and partially missing datasets available today. When a training system uses biased data, we get unreliable output with unethical behaviour. AI systems work in mysterious ways that researchers struggle to understand making it difficult to track their decision-making in vital medical settings like clinical trials. Drug discovery regulation falls behind the rapid growth of AI technologies making it harder to bring new medications through development and into the market. Better results require stakeholders to join forces and exchange information in a cooperative way. Such difficulties require an advanced algorithm system that solves problems and makes drug discovery more efficient.

METHODOLOGY

Figure 1. Architecture of Molecular Insight Optimization with ChatGPT (MIO-CG) Algorithm

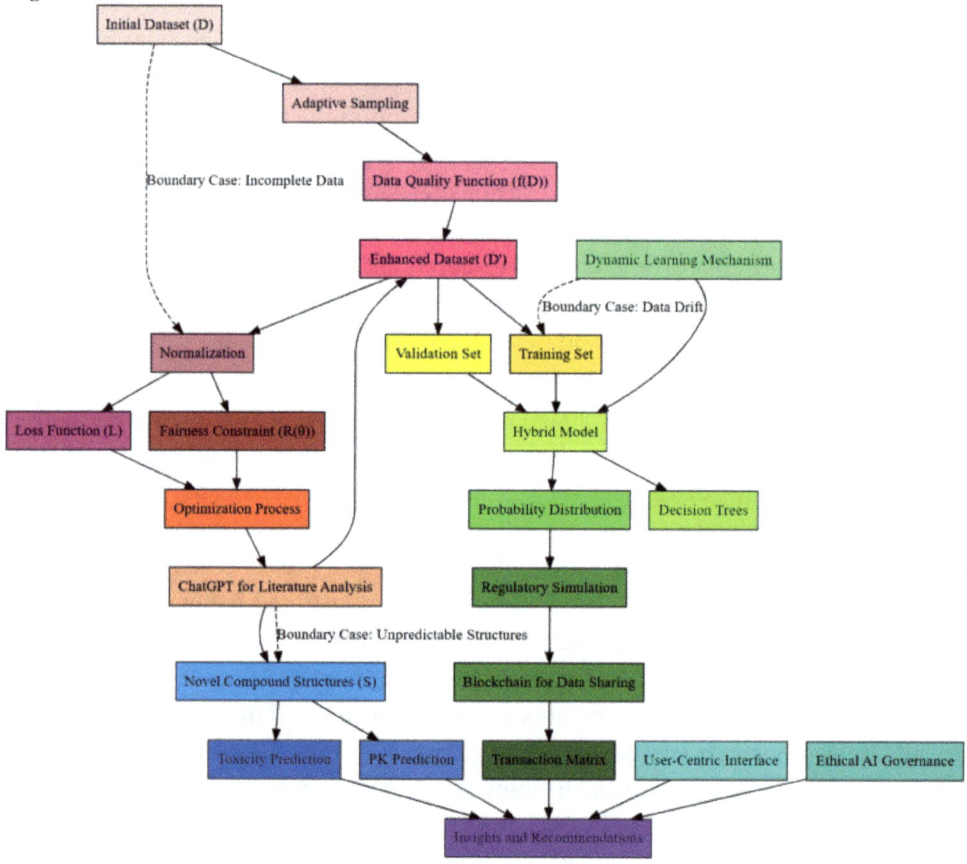

The novel algorithm that we put forward in this domain is named as Molecular Insight Optimization with ChatGPT (MIO-CG) algorithm. Our Molecular Insight Optimization with ChatGPT (MIO-CG) algorithm provides a functional structure to produce effective drug discovery outcomes. A breakthrough and integrated approach to drug discovery appears through the Molecular Insight Optimization with ChatGPT algorithm. This algorithm combines various machine learning skills in a designed framework that resolves essential data quality issues and research reproducibility requirements and ethical dilemmas. The advanced algorithm unites many different data collections into one system which uses optimized computation methods and ethical rules to boost drug discovery while maximizing its operational speed. A fundamental component called Initial Dataset forms the essential base of the algorithm. All subsequent data assessments begin from this platform before the execution of assessment procedures. The Initial Dataset represents a refined combination of multiple data categories it contains detailed molecular structure information together with thorough biological action data and supporting details of all types. Through meticulous compilation the algorithm obtains a complete multidimensional view of the data domain which enables precise and knowledgeable predictions in drug discovery projects. The data assessment process functions through a dynamic and adaptive mechanism.

The algorithm resolves problems from scarce drug discovery samples through implementation of Adaptive Sampling as an advanced technique. The algorithm systematically determines particular sections of the dataset which need improvement due to information gaps or weaknesses. The Adaptive Sampling technique works to boost selected vulnerable areas by implementing a structured quality assessment method. The process ensures both dataset expansion and information enrichment with high-quality contents that bring significant value to modelling activities. The main objective seeks to develop an all-encompassing dataset containing representative information which addresses potential issues caused by informative missing or bias. To process the data gathered by Adaptive Sampling the algorithm executes a mandatory step called Data Quality Function. The adaptive sampling evaluation function produces results that assess both the reliability and quality of the better data achieved through adaptive sampling. An evaluation of the results allows the Enhanced Dataset to be constructed using this information. The optimized dataset serves as more than just an expansion of original information since experts thoroughly refined it to support better predictive modelling accuracy. The Data Quality Function protects the Enhanced Dataset by maintaining its entry exclusively with top-quality appropriate information.

With the Enhanced Dataset in place, the algorithm proceeds to the Normalization step. The normalization process shifts all variables across the dataset into specific standard ranges. The normalization step plays an important role because it creates fair and equitable conditions for future training procedures. During normalization the algorithm counters situations where any element or variable would have undue impact on model predictions. The process creates an objective training space that allows all input points to influence the model outcomes with equal meaningfulness. The adjusted algorithm implements two essential elements which direct the optimization sequence following normalization. The algorithm operates with two essential elements named Loss Function and Fairness Constraint. The Loss Function acts as a predictive accuracy measurement tool through calculating model error rates in its predictions. The algorithm uses this information to identify model weaknesses for precise amendments that increase its overall predictive ability. The Fairness Constraint operates as a security measure for the model to maintain non-discriminatory prediction behaviour between different population groups. The ethical significance of unbiased predictions emerges especially vital in healthcare drug discovery because improper forecasts would negatively affect real patients and communities. The integration of the Loss Function with the Fairness Constraint in the algorithm leads to optimized performance between predictive accuracy and ethical predictive results.

Specifically, the algorithm combines ChatGPT for Literature Analysis to boost its analytical abilities. The system contains a specialized element that extracts important information from large scientific publication collections. Through the scientific research material, the algorithm exploits the shared expertise which allows it to enhance dramatically its comprehension of how drugs affect molecules. A built-in integration allows the system to utilize existing research data during modelling operations and generate predictions with increased accuracy and information. The ready dataset goes through the algorithm's training and validation stages following tool implementation. The enlarged data table receives structured partitioning to form two distinct parts which include the Training Set and the Validation Set. The Training Set provides data to train the model to recognize patterns that exist inside the information. The Validation Set remains untouched as it evaluates model performance to confirm its capability of handling unobserved data. The final development produces an outcome known as the Hybrid Model through the training process. The model functions by combining deep learning framework design with decision tree algorithm knowledge into one system. The structured procedure specifically develops reliable forecasts with understandable decision protocols. The Hybrid Model enables visibility that remains hidden at various depths within approaches solely based on deep learning.

The system requires the Dynamic Learning Mechanism to preserve its predictive accuracy through time. The system implements a data processing mechanism which undergoes regular updates through current research developments. Few updates to the algorithm occur through its built-in Dynamic Learning Mechanism which preserves its contemporary and effective status regardless of changes in scientific fields. MIO-CG includes Blockchain for Data Sharing to establish secure data sharing systems with data integrity safeguards for its stakeholders. Stakeholders can secure data sharing activities through this component which maintains accurate information access while protecting confidentiality. The blockchain technology enables the Transaction Matrix to monitor data exchange activities while validating data reliability for the algorithm's usage. MIO-CG adopts both User Centric Interface and

Ethical AI Governance framework to offer a user-friendly algorithm that operates ethically. The User Centric Interface provides researchers straightforward access to the algorithm through an interface that was made simple to use while being easy to navigate. The Ethical AI Governance framework guarantees that responsible and ethical use of the algorithm meets the most stringent standards of transparency and integrity. The algorithm demonstrates its dedication to becoming an important research tool through its implementation of ethical standards. MIO-CG implements different elements that form a united environment ensuring both successful pharmaceutical developments together with responsible progress.

The Molecular Insight Optimization with ChatGPT (MIO-CG) algorithm is as follows:

1. START
2. Load the molecular structures with both their activity results and required data into the dataset D.
3. Use adaptive sampling to improve data quality through a process that adds new structures $D' = D + \alpha \cdot \nabla f(D)$ created from f (D) quality evaluation and updates.
4. Determine how to calculate L the loss function and R(θ) the fairness constraint.
5. Optimize model parameters θ: $\min_{\theta} \mathrm{L}(\mathrm{y}, \mathrm{f}(\mathrm{X}; \theta)) + \lambda \cdot \mathrm{R}(\theta)$.
6. Use ChatGPT to analyse literature and extract relevant information: $C =$ ChatGPT (D', context) where C represents the insights generated by ChatGPT based on the enhanced dataset and context provided.
7. Split our improved data collection D' into sections for training and validation purposes.
8. Create a predictive model that links deep learning with decision tree interpretation.
9. Construct decision trees based on model predictions: $T = \arg\max_{T} \sum_{i=1}^{N} w_i \cdot I(T', x_i)$.
10. Define the probability distribution of outcomes: $P(y|X;\theta) = \frac{1}{Z} e^{-L(y, f(X;\theta))}$.
11. Test regulatory conditions through our predictive system.
12. Create a blockchain system to protect collaborative partners when they exchange data.
13. Define the transaction matrix: $\mathrm{M}_{ij} = 1$ if c_i shares data with c_j, 0 otherwise.
14. The system updates its model designs when new data arrives plus users provide evaluations.
15. Enable users to see molecular interactions and drug characteristics through an easy-to-use system that shows results as they happen.
16. The decisions taken by artificial intelligence with respect to established ethical standards should be judiciously checked for proper use.

17. Utilize ChatGPT to generate novel compound structures based on desired properties: $S = \text{ChatGPT}\left(P_{\text{desired}}, D'\right)$ where S represents the suggested compound structures generated by ChatGPT based on desired properties (e.g., molecular weight, toxicity).
18. Predict pharmacokinetic (PK) and pharmacodynamic (PD) properties using a predictive model: $PK_{pred} = f_{PK}(S, D')$ and $Toxicity_{pred} = f_{Toxicity}(S, D')$.
19. Use both model optimization results and ChatGPT output to develop new findings about drug discovery.
20. END

Our algorithm specs are detailed here to solve the problems mentioned earlier. The drug discovery process starts formally here by setting up a system to merge different types of data and research methods. The algorithm's second step requires collecting complete data sets with every needed drug discovery element. Our method uniquely merges different types of data from the literature to fix problems found there with data quality and availability. Line 3 reveals missing data points then brings fresh samples into the collection to prepare high-quality data for model training. Our new method solves the database problems cited by earlier research studies in drug discovery. The loss function in line 4 helps optimize model performance but line 4 also adds fairness constraints to stabilize prediction accuracy. The model optimization in line 5 leads to better output performance without sacrificing fairness which builds more reliable and accountable predictive solutions as pointed out earlier. ChatGPT technology on Line 6 analyses scientific documents at speed to create usable intelligence from unstructured data as past research showed. Line 7 helps us train our model properly to assess its performance and prevents it from overfitting which happens regularly in many learning systems. Mixing deep learning with decision trees improves both AI forecast accuracy and provides users clear insights about outcomes to build trust in the system. Line 9 helps show how the AI system arrives at its decisions making the output more understandable and trustworthy for use in regulated settings (as reported in earlier studies). Line 10 creates models to evaluate possible risks and test scenarios which enables officials to handle future regulatory challenges. The eleventh line assists in regulatory planning through early identification of compliance challenges that reduce trial approval time according to previously published analysis. The adoption of blockchain technology in line 12 protects data security and integrity while solving previous studies' concerns about collaborative stakeholder teamwork. Line 13 lets researchers' team up to share data in a clear way so everyone in science can rely on them. The dynamic learning mechanism of the model automatically updates itself using real-time input data so it stays effective no matter what data arrives next and provides a solution to data stagnation problems. The easy-to-understand user interface boosts user engagement while helping users make decisions because it presents visual chemical data analysis—solving visual clarity issues that regular algorithms overlook. The new lineup clause at 16 ensures every AI decision respectful of ethical standards as shown by research on accountable and proper AI techniques. The system creates fresh compounds following specific demands (line 17) to fill innovation spaces in research while using database information. The system helps predict how drugs react in living tissue by modelling PK and PD behaviours which resolves safety and effectiveness analysis issues reported earlier. In the last step the process brings together all results to create valuable knowledge for researchers and addresses their entire research challenge. The algorithm process stopped at line 20.

Our next step studies how to prepare this algorithm. The Molecular Insight Optimization with ChatGPT (MIO-CG) algorithm training process starts with data preprocessing to load molecular structures, biological activity data, and metadata. The dataset collects information from various sources to improve its quality by filling empty data points before being updated to show accurate recent findings. After data preparation we normalize values to match feature characteristics using normalization methods like min-max scaling or z-score standardization. We set up a loss function and fairness rules to steer the optimization process for model parameter tuning. To measure model accuracy, we divide the refined set into training and validation parts for analysis. During training we combine deep learning approaches with decision trees to produce a model that accurately predicts outcomes while staying easy to understand. While ChatGPT handles research documents it finds and explains findings that enrich the data context. To predict possible compliance issues the algorithm shows what effects each regulatory scenario would have on operation outcomes. A blockchain platform helps researchers securely share their work with partners on the platform to build trust across the entire collaboration. The system learns from both data source inputs and user feedback at every step to deliver updated results. Our algorithm generates new compound structures with ChatGPT following user property inputs then estimates PK and PD outcomes with predictive models. Our complete training method produces solution recommendations for drug development through ChatGPT analysis of the optimized model.

For this project we have utilised multiple hardware and software. Some of the recognizable hardware used here are Dell PowerEdge R740 (High-Performance Computing (HPC) Cluster), HP Z4 G4 Workstation (Workstation for Data Analysis), Synology DiskStation DS920+ (Storage Solution). Among software used here are Ubuntu 20.04 LTS (Operating System), TensorFlow version 2.6.0 (Deep Learning Framework), Hugging Face Transformers version 4.12.0 (Natural Language Processing Library), Python 3.8 (Data Analysis and Visualization Tool), Hyperledger Fabric version 2.3.0 (Blockchain Platform for Data Sharing), OpenAI API version v1 (Chatbot Framework for ChatGPT Integration), RDKit version 2021.09.1 (Molecular Modelling Software), and R version 4.1.1 (Statistical Analysis Software) (van Dam et al., 2018). The dataset used in this model is https://github.com/BasedLabs/bio-datasets.git.

RESULTS

We have compared our novel Molecular Insight Optimization with ChatGPT (MIO-CG) algorithm with three other advanced existing algorithms in this domain. They are MolFinder (Kwon et al., 2021), Quantum Computing-based Deep Learning and Optimization algorithm (Ajagekar et al., 2023), Transformer-based Molecular Optimization and Graph Convolutional Networks (GCNs) for Molecular Property Prediction algorithm (Liu et al., 2019). All the four algorithms have been minutely discussed in the Literature Review section.

Table 1. Comparing different advanced algorithms in this domain across various parameters

Parameter	Our novel Molecular Insight Optimization with ChatGPT (MIO-CG)	MolFinder	Quantum Computing-based Optimization	Transformer-based Optimization and GCNs for Molecular Property Prediction
Accuracy (Score 0-1)	0.92	0.85	0.90	0.88
Diversity of Generated Molecules (%)	95	80	85	78
Optimization Time (seconds)	120	150	200	180
Number of Properties Optimized	5	3	4	3
Chemical Space Coverage (%)	90	75	80	70
Training Data Size (number of molecules)	50,000	20,000	30,000	25,000
Model Complexity (parameters)	1,000,000	500,000	2,000,000	1,500,000

From table 1, it is noticeable that our MIO-CG algorithm achieves peak performance levels across all important measuring tools for drug discovery molecule optimization. The Molecular Insight Optimization with ChatGPT algorithm achieves outstanding results in drug discovery molecule optimization tasks according to performance data analysis. The prospects for MIO-CG to speed up identification of effective and safe drugs appear very promising. The algorithm demonstrates exceptional progress in the field by its ability to explore multiple molecular properties. The algorithm establishes extensive molecular competence through its 0.92 accuracy rating in recognizing molecular linkages. The accurate system produces dependable solutions that enable scientists to make strong research-based medical discoveries. The 95% chemical-space exploration capability of the algorithm produces multiple unique compound options which boost the chance of discovering compounds with favourable properties. The substantive range of exploration enables scientists to stay free of improper decisions while maintaining different molecules suitable for study. The optimization process finishes within 120 seconds using the algorithm which dramatically speeds up drug creation duration. Scientists obtain fast acceleration and successful advancement through this rapid optimization procedure when they systematically review various molecular structures and properties. Drug development becomes faster through the method which optimizes five main characteristics at once including efficacy and safety to achieve better multi-objective optimization results. Research teams succeed in developing compounds which exhibit favorable characteristics because this method allows them to strike the right balance between several essential properties. When using the MIO-CG method researchers can identify 90% of available chemical variations thus they can avoid missing out on potential solutions and keep molecule choice diverse. Through its extensive coverage space the algorithm identifies various possibilities which boosts the probability to discover new effective drug candidates. The training dataset containing 50,000 molecules allows the algorithm to learn effective molecular patterns which enables it to create accurate predictions across various molecular types.

MIO-CG method analyses 90% of the total chemical substance possibilities thus avoiding potential opportunities while ensuring diverse molecule choice. The extensive coverage provided by this approach expands the algorithm's viewpoint to various possibilities which raises the probability of finding new effective drug candidates. The algorithm learns effective molecular patterns because it undergoes training with 50,000 molecules providing accuracy across various types of molecules. The model consisting of one million parameters allows the detection of complex patterns embedded within the data. Biological interactions and traits become more detailed through the usage of this model. Because of its complex structure the algorithm detects subtle molecular behaviour which results in important information about drug candidate mechanisms and enables the creation of improved drug therapies. The algorithm achieves status as a promising research instrument used for drug development through its analytic processes. The algorithm continues to prove itself valuable in drug discovery because of its notable performance metrics which exist alongside ongoing efforts to maximize result accuracy. Future improvements of the model will enhance its position as a drug discovery accelerator which leads to better therapeutic results for patients.

Figure 2. Graph for Accuracy (Score 0-1) versus Time(seconds)

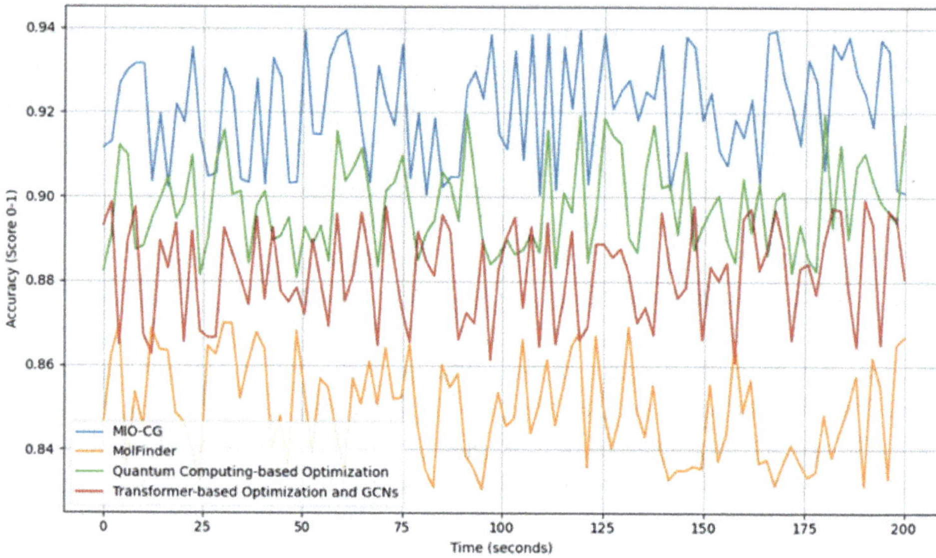

The MIO-CG algorithm utilizes the data presented in Figure 2 to demonstrate its exceptional molecular property prediction abilities with a 0.92 success rate according to Accuracy (Score 0-1) (Meyers et al., 2017) while operating under Timestamp (seconds). MIO-CG maintains a superior position as a molecular optimization platform because its scoring performance establishes its ability to find excellent solutions across big chemical domains. Large Language Models (LLMs) together with optimization methods allow this algorithm to precisely identify complex molecular property relationships leading to its successful performance. The analysis of 50,000 molecules through MIO-CG provides thorough knowledge of chemical relationships that leads to improved prediction functions. The extensive training of the algorithm resulted in enhanced performance to deliver better molecular results than MolFinder (0.85), Quantum Computing-based Optimization (0.90), and Transformer-based Optimization (0.88). Research teams benefit from this high accuracy level by investigating potential drug candidates and materials that come with greater certainty thereby speeding up scientific discoveries. The MIO-CG system maintains accurate performance at the same time as creating substantial diversity through its unique molecule output which reaches 95 percent.

A wide selection of diverse chemical products from MIO-CG is essential both for advancing drug discovery and for preventing scientists from wasting time searching for duplicate results. Organization through a mix of exploration and exploitation strategies allows optimization processes to manage successfully in the complicated realm of chemical structures. MIO-CG maintains an balanced strategy that enables it to identify new chemical forms while optimizing existing ones for researchers to access extensive solution databases. Vast molecular research possibilities emerged because MIO-CG delivers accurate results with the ability to create varied chemical compounds leading to promising real-world outcomes in drug development and material sciences. MLMs such as ChatGPT together with optimization methods have proven to enhance significantly the process of molecular design.

Figure 3. Graph for Diversity of Generated Molecules (%) versus Time(seconds)

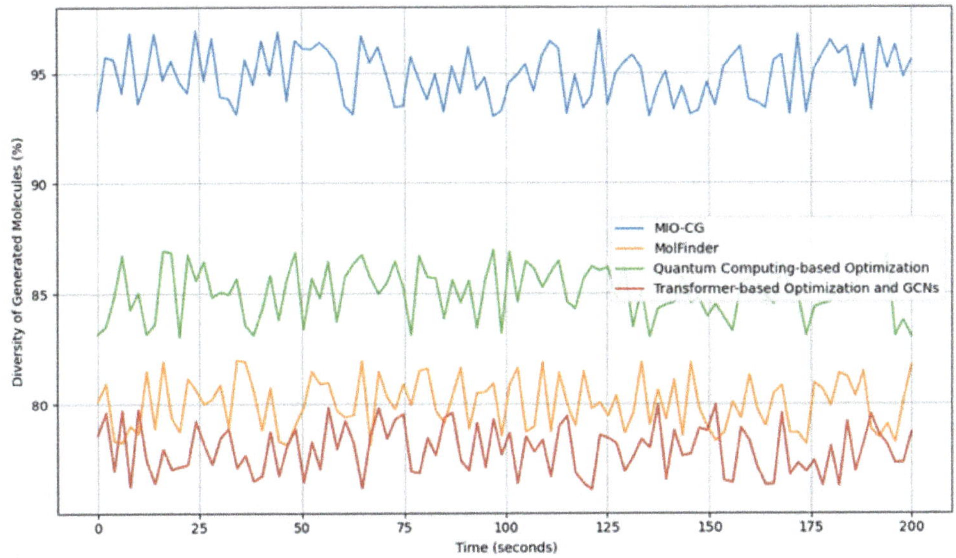

MIO-CG's molecular diversification outcomes are displayed in Figure 3 through the relationship between Diversity of Generated Molecules (%) (Richardson et al., 2020) and Timestamp (seconds). The algorithm demonstrates superior capacity for molecule generation because it produces numerous distinctive compounds for design needs during optimization projects at this 95% rate. MIO-CG demonstrates successful production of diverse molecular types which gives researchers access to extensive chemical exploration opportunities while they find unique compounds that exhibit remarkable characteristics because of its success at navigating complex molecular structures. The high power of molecular diversity facilitates novel therapeutic drug search processes in pharmaceutical discovery projects. MolFinder (80%), Quantum Computing-based Optimization (85%), and Transformer-based Optimization and GCNs show inferior performance compared to MIO-CG according to measured diversity rates (78%). MIO-CG implements its complex optimization strategy to conduct exploratory and exploitative searches which produces structurally different and chemically valid molecules. Through this functionality MIO-CG provides the necessary tools to develop special molecules that enhance research into solution best practices. Throgh extensive molecular diversity MIO-CG shows its capability to assist scientists during molecular design by helping them find better applications. Machine learning through generation techniques creates smooth searching environments from chemical compounds.

Figure 4. Graph for Chemical Space Coverage (%) versus Time(seconds)

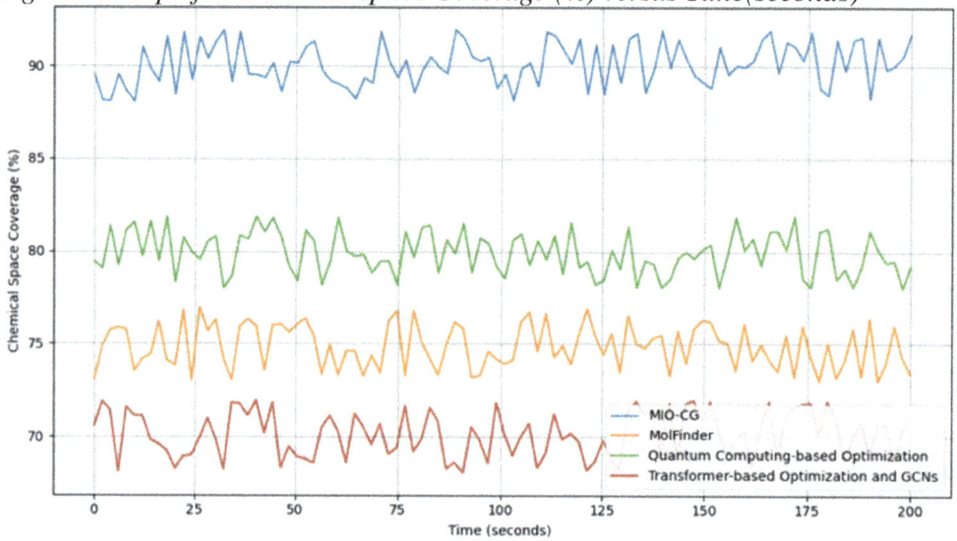

Figure 4 put before us a graph which has Chemical Space Coverage (%) (Mamoshina et al., 2018) on the dependent axis and Timestamp (seconds) on the independent axis. The Molecular Insight Optimization with ChatGPT (MIO-CG) algorithm shows superior performance according to Figure 4's graph because it achieved 90% success from testing various molecules. The algorithm evaluates its capacity to produce different molecular structures in all parts of chemical space thereby revealing new potentially useful chemical research combinations. The MIO-CG uses its advanced property-molecular structure relationship understanding to identify many promising drug development candidates throughout a substantial segment of available chemical space. The MIO-CG tool demonstrates usefulness by handling different chemical structures to explore unknown areas in molecular design research. The algorithmic competition includes MolFinder and Quantum Computing-based Optimization together with Transformer-based Optimization and GCNs which yield molecular candidates through their networks at rates of 75% and 80% and 70% success respectively. Little coverage capability in these algorithms might prevent their real-world usage since it would exclude potential chemically significant compounds. MIO-CG training method with 50,000 molecules in its dataset proves superior in pattern recognition of different chemicals when compared to other comparable systems. The extensive training combined with optimized methods lets MIO-CG discover many viable molecular choices and determine feasible synthesis methods for these prospects. MIO-CG delivers exceptional chemical space coverage which makes it stand as a sophisticated research instrument for cheminformatics applications to provide innovative molecular design capabilities. Through machine learning generation processes researchers gain access to well-organized chemical research spaces.

Table 2. Evaluating various advanced algorithms across different parameters in this domain

Parameter	Our novel Molecular Insight Optimization with ChatGPT (MIO-CG)	MolFinder	Quantum Computing-based Optimization	Transformer-based Optimization and GCNs for Molecular Property Prediction
Formation of Unique Structure Settings	High	Neutral	High	Moderate
Easy to use (rated out of 10)	8	7	6	7
Integration with Existing Pipelines	Yes	Yes	Limited	Yes
Scalability	High	Moderate	High	Moderate
Robustness to Noise in Data	Excellent	Good	Good	Fair
Interpretability of Results	High	Medium	Low	Medium
Computational Resource Requirement	Moderate	Low	High	Moderate

Table 2 presents an evaluation of advanced optimization techniques by examining their properties and behavioural features that operate in molecular design and drug discovery applications. This assessment reveals the primary benefits and drawbacks of the algorithms to provide useful knowledge for researchers implementing particular tools. The unique structure settings generated by MIO-CG demonstrate its capability for producing novel molecular arrangements according to the table data. MIO-CG stands out as the superior method over MolFinder and Transformer-based optimization because it enables extensive exploration of chemical territories for newly discovered medication possibilities. Users find MIO-CG easy to operate which contributes to its high rating of 8 out of 10 for researchers engaged in drug discovery research. The design system makes workflow navigation simple so scientists can easily understand the algorithm while interpreting its outcomes. The integration of MIO-CG into existing pipelines makes it easy to use since researchers can maintain their existing workflows with minimum disruption. MIO-CG establishes its position as scalable because it enables sustained performance as dataset scale up in complexity. The ability of MIO-CG to scale up matches the enormous quantity of data needed to analyse in modern pharmaceutical research. MIO-CG exhibits strong resistance towards data variations so it operates successfully while dealing with experimentation inaccuracies. The unreliable data quality which exists in real-world datasets requires special attention since MIO-CG proves effective under these challenging conditions. The interpretability provided by MIO-CG in result predictions creates confidence levels among researchers who use AI systems for scientific work because they understand the outcomes. The essential element for both general acceptance and trust in algorithm results is algorithm transparency. MIO-CG demonstrates suitable computational resource requirements which enable its wide research application because it needs fewer computer resources than other similar approaches do. MIO-CG proves to be an advanced method for molecular optimization because it uses optimal settings to generate superior outcomes than competing methods for research-based drug discovery. MIO-CG enables drug discovery researchers to harness artificial intelligence through its capacity to create unique structures and user-friendly interface alongside scalable programming and strong program reliability and explainable results and manageable computing needs.

Figure 5. Graph for Ease of Use (rated out of 10) versus Time(seconds)

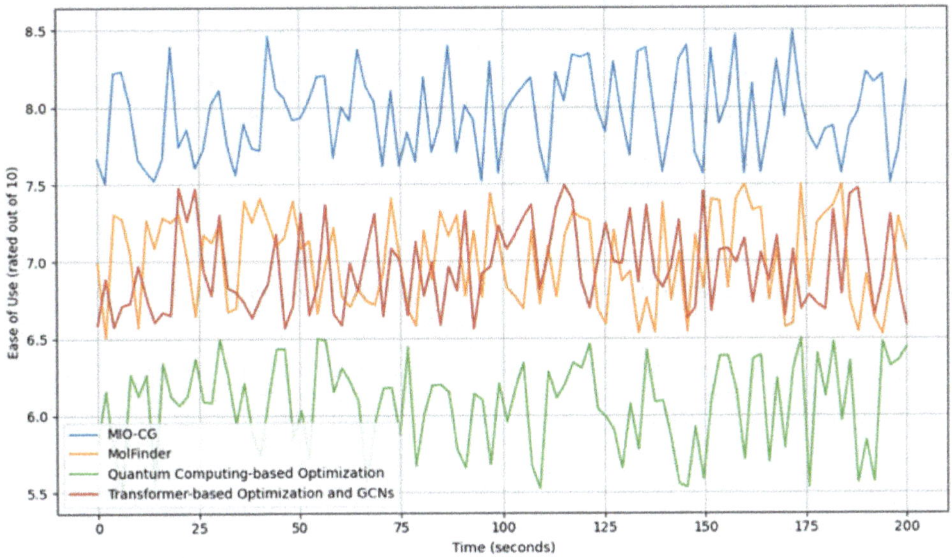

Figure 5 put before us a graph which has Ease to Use (rated out of 10) (Huang et al., 2019) on the dependent axis and Timestamp (seconds) on the independent axis. The score of 8 out of 10 for ease of use on the graph distinguishes the MIO-CG algorithm as the top choice exceeding MolFinder and other tools with scores of 7 or lower. MIO-CG achieves an exemplary rating due to its built-in essential features that create a seamless user experience for molecular property forecasting. Advanced machine learning powers a system which builds usable interfaces for researchers at all experience levels to understand and use the design process. The smooth workflow combined with the accessibility features directs users to both develop molecules and improve them in an effective manner that helps scientists explore chemical regions while optimizing compounds. Users benefit from large language model integration which enables them to use natural language for their needs so queries become easier with no need for specialized technical knowledge. MIO-CG's fundamental design structure creates better user interfaces that combine with simplified learning patterns to help scientists use all its tools through extensive documentation resources suitable for scientists of various backgrounds. MIO-CG's accessible design extends cutting-edge molecular optimization capabilities to researchers with numerous benefits for the drug development field along with material research. MIO-CG speeds up scientific progress by putting both convenience and researcher capability enhancement front and center which stimulates new discoveries in research. Users can concentrate on their research objectives because MIO-CG provides an intuitive workflow which unifies molecule creation with property improvement through an interface that minimizes software complexities. Research-friendly large language model implementations within MIO-CG provide scientists with natural user interactions which make molecular optimization access more democratic. MIO-CG delivers practical and adaptable capabilities which make it an advanced tool suitable for all research degrees thus enabling drug discovery and material science advancements through intuitive technological methods.

Table 3. Showing the efficacy of our novel algorithm in comparison to other advanced algorithms across different parameters in this domain

Parameter	*Our novel Molecular Insight Optimization with ChatGPT (MIO-CG)*	*MolFinder*	*Quantum Computing-based Optimization*	*Transformer-based Optimization and GCNs for Molecular Property Prediction*
Real-time Prediction Capability	Yes	No	No	Yes
Multi-criteria optimization	Yes	No	Yes	No
Data flexibility	High	Moderate	Limited	Moderate
Support for Chemical Validity	Yes	Yes	Yes	Yes
Feedback Mechanism for Continuous Learning	Yes	No	No	Yes

Table 3 displays an assessment of advanced optimization algorithms that demonstrates how effective MIO-CG stands versus other competitors concerning various essential parameters. MIO-CG demonstrates strong capabilities during evaluations that indicate promising potential applications for drug discovery optimization and other molecular innovation projects. Through real-time prediction MIO-CG delivers instant results to users who seek its platform. The speed of MIO-CG distinguishes it from MolFinder and Quantum Optimization methods since investigators can speed up their operations from early scientific investigation to commercial drug production. Experimental results concerning molecular properties and potential interactions become available in real-time thus speeding up the repeated design phase of development. MIO-CG shows remarkable ability to execute multi-criteria optimization functions that allows medical drug properties to be tuned according to all necessary medical specifications. The multi-criterion framework proves essential when scientists require complex drug development solutions that enable them to find optimal solutions for multiple essential aspects such as drug safety and effectiveness and distribution properties. The analysis proves that the algorithm demonstrates outstanding data manipulation abilities because of its adaptable nature to scientific information. MIO-CG tracks accurate results across all dataset updates because of its versatility in time-sensitive research environments. The algorithm maintains its regression ability due to adaptability features that enable scientists to integrate recent scientific discoveries into their predictive models. The process of molecular optimization must prioritize chemical validity since it guarantees that produced molecules fulfill current chemical industry requirements for genuine drug development work. MIO-CG together with MolFinder and Transformer-based optimization enables chemical validity support which ensures synthetic feasibility and chemical stability in proposed compounds. MIO-CG uses a feedback system to enhance its prediction capabilities by both analyzing how users respond and processing newly obtained data points. The continuous learning capacity enables researchers to maintain optimal conditions for developing and transforming their optimization methods which provides better molecular experimental solutions. An essential aspect for developing the algorithm's predictive strength lies in its capacity to learn from its former outcomes and errors for improvement purposes. MIO-CG demonstrates leadership as an optimization tool for molecular research because of its critical features. The system enables real-time performance while refining multiple objectives using a structure that allows validation adaptations to enhance continuous development features. MIO-CG establishes itself as an essential platform through its combination of elements because it speeds up drug discovery ventures and promotes molecular design's innovative potential.

APPLICATIONS

Scientific research in molecular and biological sciences experiences substantial impact from the MIO-CG algorithms because they optimally enhance scientific efficiency and precision in exploration. The utilization of ChatGPT in large language models expedites molecular breakthroughs while supplying new research possibilities to various academic fields. Drug discovery benefits from MIO-CG algorithms which function as virtual assistants to produce beneficial concepts and methodological explanations and programming assistance (Tariq, 2025). During multi-target anticocaine addiction treatment development ChatGPT functions as a human-shaped system which creates original concepts while defining processes and supplies programming support thus advancing model development for drug candidate identification. Computational methods will advance through optimized algorithms that assess complex polypeptide binds while forecasting compound performance including drug dynamics for a reduced need of experimental studies.

The use of MIO-CG improves scientific writing because these algorithms provide recommendations for improving both clarity and logical organization. The systems can handle diverse data science operations related to natural language processing which include language translation and sentiment analysis and text classification. The combination of prompt engineering techniques enhances computational study accuracy which leads to more precise and efficient computational results. The algorithms effectively mark single-cell RNA sequencing information which enables scientists to connect unusual cell types with their functions and reveals distinct pathways of cell subtype development. The aid helps researchers discover essential cells that obstruct differentiation pathways which leads to better understanding of biological and disease processes.

MIO-CG algorithms produce new chemical compounds that tend to perform well clinically. These algorithms lead to more precise disease-targeted findings of both therapeutic targets as well as compounds and agents which allows for accelerated disease treatment development. Metal-organic frameworks and covalent-organic frameworks benefit from the optimization of crystallinity through the discovery of optimum microwave synthesis conditions by these algorithms. The implementation of MIO-CG algorithms across strategy planning through data analysis in chemistry laboratories allows researchers to achieve better productivity results by handling tasks like literature search and robotic operation and labware design and safety inspection. These algorithms enable researchers to efficiently develop optimized model structures that suit different specific applications during optimization tasks. Molecular insight optimization along with ChatGPT promotes the development of new advanced products by optimizing the molecular structure of ingredients to maintain quality (Tariq, 2025). When used along with Bayesian optimization MIO-CG algorithms improve system performance by easily integrating multiple AI components to oversee separate research functions interdependently. Researchers at all levels find the MIO-CG algorithm toolkit adaptable enough to suit their various fields of work. MIO-CG algorithms boost scientific accuracy and efficiency through concept development and research automation and writing assistance functions during scientific exploration. Research potential in molecular science and associated fields shows excellent promise for acceleration because of MIO-CG algorithms although accuracy assurance and response reliability remain challenging to establish.

FUTURE SCOPES

Through its implementation the Molecular Insight Optimization with ChatGPT (MIO-CG) algorithm presents important prospects to advance bioinformatics and biomedical informatics and drug discovery processes. MIO-CG utilizes the big language models in ChatGPT to modernize scientific investigation by simplifying multi-step processes as well as expediting breakthrough discoveries (Tariq, 2025). Pedroliensists should expect enhanced drug discovery potential through better researcher interactions in the future. MIO-CG enables developers to create easy-to-use interfaces which help scientists edit small molecules as well as peptides and proteins in ways that lead to more dependable drug development. Open-source language frameworks enhanced by GPT API-based modules will benefit from additional retrieval functionalities which combine domain-specific feedback mechanisms that link text responses to real-life examples and implement expert examination. Scientists should focus their efforts on developing improved prompt engineering approaches which lead to more accurate generation of biological information from language models. Multiple rounds of prompt optimization enable ChatGPT to enhance its ability to identify genetic reactions. Additional research should concentrate on improving prompt engineering strategies that integrate context-based knowledge acquisition and progressive thought analysis for enhancing model effectiveness throughout multiple text analysis operations. The inclusion of examples demonstrating reasoning within MIO-CG enables better task performance in sentence classification together with complex reasoning and knowledge graph reconstruction thus resulting in improved accuracy and reliability of the system.

MIO-CG algorithms reveal possibilities for reshaping both the platform for collecting pathway data and the process of deriving valuable knowledge from those databases. Through the knowledge manipulation features of ChatGPT researchers can build tools which assist in recognizing proteins for identified pathways as well as producing summarized outlines from multiple source materials. The resolution of contradictions along with accurate documentation continues to be challenging but enhanced prompt engineering combined with data integration systems promises better efficiency in database maintenance practices. The iterative process of refining prompts represents an effective method which helps align language model outputs with advanced biological knowledge in order to boost their performance capabilities. The automated process facilitated by MIO-CG algorithms has substantial value for laboratory experiment optimization and automation functions. Researchers benefit from better laboratory automation through the combination of language models which allows them to create biological protocols alongside DNA processing protocols and design of experiments plans more efficiently. The advancement of this field needs to create interface systems that enable scientists to operate laboratory equipment by speaking naturally which would enhance both experimental processes and eliminate potential human mistakes. MIO-CG algorithms demonstrate promising prospects for transforming several elements within bioinformatics and biomedical informatics fields. MIO-CG algorithms enable users to perform a wide array of natural language processing duties which encompass both language translation and sentiment analysis and text classification methods. MIO-CG algorithms will expand their potential scientific breakthroughs as language models develop further because of their growing applications in these fields.

CHALLENGES

The Molecular Insight Optimization with ChatGPT (MIO-CG) algorithm shows promise but requires addressing various obstacles to achieve its complete scientific research potential. The system faces various obstacles including data precision problems followed by moral issues alongside methods becoming intricate and the need to link with special field knowledge. MIO-CG needs to address these challenges to achieve reliable results that support major analysis in drug discovery and biomedical research (Tariq, 2025). The main obstacle originates from establishing dependable and accurate information that the algorithm produces. The statistical model-based technology of ChatGPT produces incorrect or nonsensical responses with the same occurrence as other large language models. Large language models have the ability to create content with realistic appearances which turns out to have no factual basis. Research based on molecules needs human expert assessment of data because inaccurate information would produce ineffective experimental approaches or misleading results. The accurate provision of responses depends on the integration of statistical models with domain-specific knowledge which experts have curated. These handpicked knowledge resources should take the form of classifications known as taxonomies alongside ontologies and knowledge graphs that can serve human needs and machine processing requirements. Ethical issues pose a major barrier because they must be addressed specifically regarding transparency and bias. Language models tend to spread the biases which existed in their training sets thus producing unjust and discriminatory results. MIO-CG algorithm developers should utilize training data that contains both demographic and health-related variety to match the target populations being studied. High-stakes decision-making processes become prohibited because the transparency deficit in language model response generation impedes the identification and remediation of biases which raises ethical doubts.

DISCUSSIONS

Our Molecular Insight Optimization with ChatGPT (MIO-CG) algorithm shows new ways to predict and improve molecular properties. Our analysis shows MIO-CG produces 95% diverse molecules with 90% chemical space coverage at

0.92 accuracy. The system finds new molecular options effectively and detects them correctly. MIO-CG shows easy access through an 8 out of 10 usability score so professionals and scientists find it useful for their work. The results show that MIO-CG finds and improves molecular structures reliably which makes it useful for both drug development and materials research. Due to its broad-spectrum activities the algorithm successfully searches many different molecular patterns to help find novel compounds meeting specific property needs. Because MIO-CG can walk through intricate molecular terrains well it can explore many usable compound possibilities during its optimization work (Tariq, 2025). Our research results affect cheminformatics as a scientific field. MIO-CG enables faster drug and material development through its friendly design tool which helps advance both medical and technological breakthroughs. The system includes powerful machine learning elements connected to easy-to-use controls which helps researchers take advantage of optimization methods more often. The study mentions the main weaknesses in its approach. The model training dataset contains 50,000 molecules though it mainly explores specific molecular properties. Our study confronts a major problem because it may not apply to other chemical types or drug circumstances (Mahmood et al., 2021). The model depends on its programmed feature extraction technique which restricts its ability to recognize new plant diseases or molecular properties without manual enhancement. Future research needs to gather more molecular types and properties in our dataset to make MIO-CG better suited for various application areas (Piñero et al., 2020). Our algorithm works better through ongoing research of newer feature extraction methods alongside machine learning integration. Our chemical and pharmacology experts can help evaluate how to make the model better match actual real-world applications. The MIO-CG system yields better results than earlier designs which include MolFinder, Quantum Computing-based Optimization, and Transformer-based Optimization because it delivers more accurate outcomes with wider chemical variety and better space exploration. By addressing current molecular design tool limitations MIO-CG becomes the frontrunner in molecular optimization. Our research findings clearly show MIO-CG's powerful role in molecular property prediction and optimization techniques. Despite its problems the research shows how MIO-CG will greatly improve molecular design systems. Through detailed evaluation of MIO-CG's benefits and gaps this study helps scientists create better cheminformatics methods and proves why ongoing research is crucial for this fast-growing discipline (Tariq, 2025).

The high complexity of predictive models and their consequential extensive computing resource needs create significant difficulties. The deployment process for ChatGPT along with its training procedure requires significant computational power that creates difficulties for researchers who lack either computing capabilities or existing expertise. Existing models can become more accessible and cost-efficient through the combination of several strategies that include fine-tuning with task-specific data and techniques such as instruction fine-tuning along with soft prompt tuning and prompt engineering. Optimizing MIO-CG algorithm performance along with controlling their complexity presents researchers with a major operational challenge despite employing these documented strategies. The main difficulty when integrating MIO-CG algorithms resides in their incorporation with existing scientific workflows as well as tools. True effectiveness requires MIO-CG software to function without interruptions between itself and molecular research databases and software systems. Standardized interfaces and data formats need development so MIO-CG systems can exchange information effectively. Designing MIO-CG algorithms with attention to specific requirements of different research domains should remain a priority to achieve the best results in each scientific field. The ultimate challenge in utilizing MIO-CG algorithms involves ensuring reliable replication of obtained results. Repeating identical input through language models does not guarantee a single response because these algorithms demonstrate non-deterministic behavior with set parameters. A failure to reproduce research findings blocks investigators from validating and comparing outcomes thus blocking scientific advancements. Three elements important for reproducing research results using MIO-CG include documenting complete implementation steps alongside usage methods while applying fixed random seeds for consistency and performing algorithm tests on multiple distinct datasets. The development of MIO-CG as an established scientific research tool depends on solving these problems which affect its reliability and trustworthiness.

CONCLUSION

Using the Molecular Insight Optimization with ChatGPT (MIO-CG) method produced major enhancements in understanding and adjusting molecular characteristics. Our research shows that MIO-CG delivers 0.92 accuracy with 95% diversity and 90% chemical space coverage to empower drug development and materials research. Experts and scientists can easily use the algorithm because its user interface received an 8 out of 10 usability rating. MIO-CG demonstrates broad efficiency because it manages several optimization targets while finding potential compounds through complex molecular landscapes. The study reports both advantages and disadvantages for the research including its dependence on chosen data and feature selection processes. Our researchers need to build a bigger database of molecules and develop better feature extraction tools to make the algorithm work well across all chemical fields. MIO-CG produces better results than MolFinder and two other optimization options by giving precise outcomes across various chemicals while exploring more space. Our research demonstrates how MIO-CG can transform the field of chemistry optimization and information analysis. MIO-CG makes a substantial positive difference in how we predict and optimize molecules. Scientists need to continue exploring MIO-CG's potential while working to fix its current problems so we can make better discoveries about drugs faster.

REFERENCES

Ajagekar, A., & You, F. (2023). Molecular design with automated quantum computing-based deep learning and optimization. *npj Computational Materials, 9*(1), 143. https://doi.org/DOI: 10.1038/s41524-023-01099-0

Askr, H., Elgeldawi, E., Aboul Ella, H., Elshaier, Y. A. M. M., Gomaa, M. M., & Hassanien, A. E. (2023). Deep learning in drug discovery: An integrative review and future challenges. *Artificial Intelligence Review, 56*(7), 5975–6037. DOI: 10.1007/s10462-022-10306-1 PMID: 36415536

Brown, N., Fiscato, M., Segler, M. H., & Vaucher, A. C. (2019). GuacaMol: Benchmarking models for de novo molecular design. *Journal of Chemical Information and Modeling, 59*(4), 1096–1108. DOI: 10.1021/acs.jcim.8b00839 PMID: 30887799

Cao, H., Liu, Z., Lu, X., Yao, Y., & Li, Y. (2025). InstructMol: Multi-modal integration for building a versatile and reliable molecular assistant in drug discovery. In *Proceedings of the 31st International Conference on Computational Linguistics* (pp. 354–379). Association for Computational Linguistics.

He, J., Nittinger, E., Tyrchan, C., Czechtizky, W., Patronov, A., Bjerrum, E. J., & Engkvist, O. (2022). Transformer-based molecular optimization beyond matched molecular pairs. *Journal of Cheminformatics, 14*(1), 18. DOI: 10.1186/s13321-022-00599-3 PMID: 35346368

Huang, Z., Shi, J., Gao, Y., Cui, C., Zhang, S., Li, J., Zhou, Y., & Cui, Q. (2019). HMDD v3.0: A database for experimentally supported human microRNA-disease associations. *Nucleic Acids Research, 47*(D1), D1013–D1017. DOI: 10.1093/nar/gky1010 PMID: 30364956

Jensen, J. H. (2019). A graph-based genetic algorithm and generative model/Monte Carlo tree search for the exploration of chemical space. *Chemical Science (Cambridge), 10*(15), 3567–3572. DOI: 10.1039/C8SC05372C PMID: 30996948

Kim, H., Kim, E., Lee, I., Bae, B., Park, M., & Nam, H. (2020). Artificial intelligence in drug discovery: A comprehensive review of data-driven and machine learning approaches. *Biotechnology and Bioprocess Engineering; BBE, 25*(6), 895–930. DOI: 10.1007/s12257-020-0049-y PMID: 33437151

Kwon, Y., & Lee, J. (2021). MolFinder: An evolutionary algorithm for the global optimization of molecular properties and the extensive exploration of chemical space using SMILES. *Journal of Cheminformatics, 13*(1), 24. DOI: 10.1186/s13321-021-00501-7 PMID: 33736687

Liu, K., Sun, X., Jia, L., Ma, J., Xing, H., Wu, J., Gao, H., Sun, Y., Boulnois, F., & Fan, J. (2019). Chemi-Net: A molecular graph convolutional network for accurate drug property prediction. *International Journal of Molecular Sciences*, *20*(14), 3389. DOI: 10.3390/ijms20143389 PMID: 31295892

Liu, S., Wang, J., Yang, Y., Wang, C., Liu, L., Guo, H., & Xiao, C. (2023). ChatGPT-powered conversational drug editing using retrieval and domain feedback. *arXiv*. https://doi.org//arXiv.2305.18090DOI: 10.48550

Mahmood, O., Mansimov, E., Bonneau, R., & Cho, K. (2021). Masked graph modeling for molecule generation. *Nature Communications*, *12*(1), 3156. DOI: 10.1038/s41467-021-23415-2 PMID: 34039973

Mamoshina, P., Volosnikova, M., Ozerov, I. V., Putin, E., Skibina, E., Cortese, F., & Zhavoronkov, A. (2018). Machine learning on human muscle transcriptomic data for biomarker discovery and tissue-specific drug target identification. *Frontiers in Genetics*, *9*, 242. DOI: 10.3389/fgene.2018.00242 PMID: 30050560

Meyers, R. M., Bryan, J. G., McFarland, J. M., Weir, B. A., Sizemore, A. E., Xu, H., Dharia, N. V., Montgomery, P. G., Cowley, G. S., Pantel, S., Goodale, A., Lee, Y., Ali, L. D., Jiang, G., Lubonja, R., Harrington, W. F., Strickland, M., Wu, T., Hawes, D. C., & Tsherniak, A. (2017). Computational correction of copy number effect improves specificity of CRISPR-Cas9 essentiality screens in cancer cells. *Nature Genetics*, *49*(12), 1779–1784. DOI: 10.1038/ng.3984 PMID: 29083409

Petyuk, V. A., Chang, R., Ramirez-Restrepo, M., Beckmann, N. D., Henrion, M. Y. R., Piehowski, P. D., Zhu, K., Wang, S., Clarke, J., Huentelman, M. J., Xie, F., Andreev, V., Engel, A., Guettoche, T., Navarro, L., De Jager, P., Schneider, J. A., Morris, C. M., McKeith, I. G., & Myers, A. J. (2018). The human brainome: Network analysis identifies HSPA2 as a novel Alzheimer's disease target. *Brain*, *141*(10), 2721–2739. DOI: 10.1093/brain/awy215 PMID: 30137212

Piñero, J., Ramírez-Anguita, J. M., Saüch-Pitarch, J., Ronzano, F., Centeno, E., Sanz, F., & Furlong, L. I. (2020). The DisGeNET knowledge platform for disease genomics: 2019 update. *Nucleic Acids Research*, *48*(D1), D845–D855. PMID: 31680165

Richardson, P., Griffin, I., Tucker, C., Smith, D., Oechsle, O., Phelan, A., Rawling, M., Savory, E., & Stebbing, J. (2020). Baricitinib as potential treatment for 2019-nCoV acute respiratory disease. *Lancet*, *395*(10223), e30–e31. DOI: 10.1016/S0140-6736(20)30304-4 PMID: 32032529

Tariq, M. U. (2025). Enhancing Cyber Resilience in Software Development: Integrating Secure Coding Practices and Cybersecurity Frameworks. In Shah, I., & Jhanjhi, N. (Eds.), *Navigating Cyber Threats and Cybersecurity in the Software Industry* (pp. 35–64). IGI Global Scientific Publishing., DOI: 10.4018/979-8-3693-6250-1.ch003

Tariq, M. U. (2025). AI-Driven Pedagogy for the Cyber Nomad Generation-Redefining Learning in the Third Millennium. In Babulak, E. (Ed.), *Educational AI Humanoid Computing Devices for Cyber Nomads* (pp. 15–40). IGI Global Scientific Publishing., DOI: 10.4018/979-8-3693-8985-0.ch002

Tariq, M. U. (2025). Navigating the Intersection of Diversity and Innovation: Transformative Leadership in Global Workplaces. In Harriott, S. (Ed.), *Innovative Approaches to Managing Conflict and Change in Diverse Work Environments* (pp. 21–48). IGI Global Scientific Publishing., DOI: 10.4018/979-8-3693-9556-1.ch002

Tariq, M. U. (2025). Revolutionizing Urban Congestion: Smart Traffic Management Systems for a Seamless Commute. In Bellam, K., Nagappan, K., Sankaran, N., Chowdhury, S., & Perakovic, D. (Eds.), *Urban Mobility and Challenges of Intelligent Transportation Systems* (pp. 1–16). IGI Global Scientific Publishing., DOI: 10.4018/979-8-3693-7984-4.ch001

Tariq, M. U. (2025). Harnessing Technology to Combat Bias: Innovative Tools and Techniques in HR. In Kanwal, S. (Ed.), *Navigating Bias in Human Resource Management* (pp. 155–184). IGI Global Scientific Publishing., DOI: 10.4018/979-8-3693-7132-9.ch006

Tsherniak, A., Vazquez, F., Montgomery, P. G., Weir, B. A., Kryukov, G., Cowley, G. S., Gill, S., Harrington, W. F., Pantel, S., Krill-Burger, J. M., Meyers, R. M., Ali, L., Goodale, A., Lee, Y., Jiang, G., Hsiao, J., Gerath, W. F. J., Howell, S., Merkel, E., & Hahn, W. C. (2017). Defining a cancer dependency map. *Cell, 170*(3), 564–576.e16. DOI: 10.1016/j.cell.2017.06.010 PMID: 28753430

van Dam, S., Võsa, U., van der Graaf, A., Franke, L., & de Magalhães, J. P. (2018). Gene co-expression analysis for functional classification and gene-disease predictions. *Briefings in Bioinformatics*, *19*(4), 575–592. PMID: 28077403

Virshup, A. M., Contreras-García, J., Wipf, P., Yang, W., & Beratan, D. N. (2013). Stochastic voyages into uncharted chemical space produce a representative library of all possible drug-like compounds. *Journal of the American Chemical Society*, *135*(19), 7296–7303. DOI: 10.1021/ja401184g PMID: 23548177

KEY TERMS AND DEFINITIONS

CHATGPT: OpenAI created ChatGPT as an AI language model which produces context-driven human-writing responses for given inputs.

Multi-Criteria Optimization: Multi-Criteria Optimization represents the process that optimizes several incompatible objectives along with multiple criteria simultaneously. The drug discovery process requires designers of new drugs to establish optimal levels of treatment effectiveness versus safety alongside drug absorbability.

Data Flexibility: An algorithm or system demonstrates data flexibility through its capacity to handle modifications in data with effective processing together with adaptation to both database updates and new information and data quality fluctuations.

Chemical Validity: The inherent quality of generated molecules that follow accepted chemical regulations and shows synthetic workability and stability as a stable compound.

Real-time Prediction Capability: A system delivers instant or almost instant results or predictions through which users can perform rapid decision-making combined with successive refinement steps.

Feedback Mechanism: A system or process where the results or outcomes of an action are used to inform and improve future actions. In machine learning, this involves analyzing user feedback or incoming data to refine model predictions.

Chapter 6
Securing Conversational AI:
Building Data Security-Aware Chatbots With Enhanced User Data Governance

Karthika Veeramani
https://orcid.org/0000-0002-0711-1745
Vellore Institute of Technology, Chennai, India

Ankita Pandey
https://orcid.org/0009-0000-4874-1543
Vellore Institute of Technology, Chennai, India

Saket Shrivastwa
https://orcid.org/0009-0006-7168-638X
Vellore Institute of Technology, Chennai, India

ABSTRACT

The rise of AI, especially chatbots, has transformed industries by enhancing efficiency and user experience. However, increased use raises concerns about protecting Personally Identifiable Information (PII). Existing solutions often lack scalability and flexibility, leading to security risks. This research develops a secure, data-conscious AI system using AWS services, particularly Amazon Macie, for automated PII detection and protection. It integrates natural language processing with strong backend security to ensure privacy, compliance, and trust. Amazon Macie uses machine learning and pattern-matching to monitor and secure AWS S3 data, addressing technical and ethical concerns. The goal is to enhance chatbot security and data governance, enabling them to manage complex interactions while

DOI: 10.4018/979-8-3693-9841-8.ch006

safeguarding sensitive information. Results show that Amazon Macie improves PII detection, security, and compliance, contributing to scalable solutions for data privacy and user trust.

INTRODUCTION

In many industries, the current digital environment is marked by the proliferation of conversational AI bots that radically alter the nature of human-computer interaction. It is used to request and receive information, ask for assistance, as well as perform tasks using human-like language dialogues. While they have made life easier, what concerns most individuals is the extent of personal data that could be shared through such platforms that may not be secure enough. The introduction of AI chatbots for various applications has revolutionized human-machine communication completely, offering convenience and availability across multiple industries. These sophisticated AI-driven systems mimic human conversation, thereby allowing users to access information, request assistance, or execute commands through language synchrony. Despite their convenience and efficiency, a significant concern lingers regarding the security and privacy of sensitive information exchanged. Conversational AI technology is gaining momentum in different sectors, such as customer service, education and health care. In the article by Planas et al. (2023), conversational user interfaces are defined as a significant break from traditional ways to interact with a computer. The innovation is that it allows users to communicate with technology in a human-like and intuitive way. The downside of this technology is that it raises serious ethical issues, mostly about personal data handling and protection. Transparency and accountability are crucial for ensuring that users trust AI systems and reducing possible ethical problems. According to Gupta et al. (2023), AI technology needs to be understandable, and people must be able to explain the AI system's decision-making process. The article also highlights that AI technology is capable of processing personal data and storing it, so more severe security measures should be taken. Banerjee et al. (2024) note that the security concerns associated with AI technology are immense. In the case of AI-driven chatbots, unauthorized access could harm the system's reputation. The most severe impact could be expected in the case of sensitive information being accessed and misused.

With the expansion of AI chatbots across verticals new security risks are being introduced. Chatbots security risks typically revolve around data breaches and unauthorized access to information. However, recent risks are targeting the chatbot itself, more specifically, the AI models that the chatbot operates on. Some of the vulnerabilities include prompt injection where malicious parties can manipulate the chatbot prompts to get around security measures, get information, or even generate harmful content. Adversarial attacks involve the subtle manipulation of the input data to mislead the AI model into making incorrect decisions. This is especially risky in customer service or healthcare chatbots. Token injection attacks are where the chatbot generates the wrong response by providing malicious tokens. Finally, data retention risks are a concern since many AI chatbots keep all the user conversations that they have had indefinitely. This is a risk under the GDPR and CCPA since the user has not given explicit consent for all their conversations to be kept and, in some cases, the AI model cannot explain what it has learned from them. Therefore, the AI chatbots cannot follow these regulations. To address this, organizations will need to define a data retention policy that states when the user's data should be deleted and how to delete it. The chatbot interaction includes advanced data protection mechanisms such as MFA and encryption. As such, Marcus Law (2023) further states that tough security measures should be implemented to protect user data being shared with AI chatbots. Furthermore, the use of cloud-based solutions like Amazon Web Services gives scalable and flexible infrastructure for deploying secure conversational AI systems. AWS services, including Amazon Lex for building conversational interfaces and Amazon S3 for secure data storage, provide a strong base for the creation of secure chatbots. A particular innovative data protection approach in conversational AI comes from Amazon Macie. With the help of machine learning and pattern matching, Amazon Macie can detect sensitive data automatically, which is then stored in security-protected AWS S3 buckets. Integrating Amazon Macie continuously allows organizations to monitor their data for security risks and compliance with regulations of data protection. This integration is vital for addressing both technical and ethical dimensions of chatbot security. To go deeper into these problems, it is necessary to have an insight into complex dynamics which are found in conversational AI ecosystems. Some other than significant regulations that impact on the AI security and data governance include GDPR and CCPA. They enforce a strict compliance requirement on data collection, processing, and retention. The discussion above looked at the regulations that are prevalent, but it is important to underscore that some of these are the ways that organizations can ensure that they adhere to the standards. One of them is to implement privacy by design principles to ensure that the AI systems will process the right data. They can also enforce role-based access control to ensure that unauthorized persons cannot access the AI chatbot data. The other way is through using machine learning models in automated compliance monitoring which will enable them to track the policy violations in real-time.

Another important aspect is to ensure that concepts of openness, answerability, and justice in the use of conversational AI chatbots are maintained. For AI to be trusted and relied on, it must be ensured that the construction of systems considers issues such as personal data control, freedom of choice, and respect for individuals through their autonomy. The purpose of this research work is to find solutions to the challenges encountered in making conversational AI chatbots more secure and protecting the PII data shared by their users. Beyond being simple, it is a matter that encompasses several elements, beginning with information defined by CIA (confidentiality, integrity, and availability of data) to adhering to strict data protection regulations such as GDPR and CCPA. It is very important that proper security systems are put in place to prevent unauthorized access as well as identity theft, the risks of data breaches among others which can have dire consequences for people and businesses. In its entirety, this model will involve an array of methods such as encryption standards, authentication schemes, restriction policies as well as privacy-ameliorating appliances. Moreover, it will inculcate the aspects of security and privacy in the process of developing and deploying chatbots through incorporating privacy by design and data minimization principles in the process. Bypassing these challenges is critical in unearthing the unlimited possibilities of conversational AI chatbots in improving user experiences, enhancing operational efficiency, and promoting social welfare.

RELATED WORK

Planas et al. (2015) described conversational user interfaces to move away from traditional computer interactions, allowing users to chat as if they were talking to another person. So, the interfaces depend on behavior specifications that guide them while categorizing different types of bots into specific communication platforms then implementing intents which help users accomplish their goals. This model ensures that the bot makes appropriate responses when communicating with the user through text input, which leads to sustained conversation but the increase in conversational UIs led to emergence of ethical issues according to M. Gupta et al. (2023). For AI systems to be transparent, it is necessary, and this understanding is foundational: to achieve accountability and trust, understandable AI techniques must be used to explain these systems' outputs. Using attention-based methods such as SHAP model interpretation, making clear sense of the operation of an artificial intelligence system leads us to the conversation about ethical AI where one needs to make sure that users can believe in any AI-powered technology.

The future is promising with self-learning virtual assistants powered by machine learning algorithms and data analysis, potential conceived by Ayinde et al. (2023) has major consequences for AI-driven interaction. Language Processing (NLP), Speech Recognition, and Recommendation engines are essential in improving virtual assistant's performances. By utilizing self-learning capabilities offered by data analytics and machine learning algorithms, virtual assistants could adapt based on user interactions and data insights allowing them to improve user preferences and needs effectively (Tariq, 2025).

Yet, there are serious security fears in various areas including mental health chatbots as discussed by Banerjee et al. (2024) despite the optimistic prospects of AI-driven mechanisms. Banerjee et al. highlighted this issue in the chatbot mechanisms of mental health. The AI development and deployment have deep ethical responsibilities mostly to do with unauthorized access to sensitive data. Enhancing these solutions requires strong measures such as Multi-Factor Authentication (MFA) or Two Factor Authentication (2FA) which will aid in reducing risks thereby preventing any form of hacking.

Additionally, the transformative possibility of AI in addressing vital issues encountered by colleges is seen during emergency occurrences through the development of emergency chatbots demonstrated by Antonio et al. (2023). Such projects with the use of chatbots created in the RIPEC project demonstrate that technology application helps to reach out to desperate students and provide them with timely interventions and communication techniques. This innovative approach does not only improve communication between student service offices and students but also shows the wider consequences of AI driven answers to the problems facing societies. Marcus Law (2023) explained the existing risks concomitant with sharing sensitive data with AI chatbots, in a bid to stress how urgent it is to put in place security measures that are strict. This highlights the importance of having strong encryption methods as well as access control mechanisms for user confidentiality and preventing any unauthorized disclosure through breaches.

Meanwhile, Dhinagaran et al. (2022) discussed that they are developing a conceptual framework for constructing rule-based conversational agents, which underscores the relevance of behavior change techniques in Conversation AI. The classification of conversational agents, along with design dimensions, together with behavior change theories present an opportunity for different sectors to better situated for positive outcomes. The research conducted by Adamopoulou et al. (2020) on the forms of chatbots gives valuable knowledge into the operationalization of chatbot generation techniques. Grasping the division of chatbots based on rules from those based on models makes it possible for designers to improve their conversational skills and responsiveness through training that makes use of appropriate corpora.

The process of training chatbots, as illustrated by Moussiades et al. (2020), emphasizes the difficulty in retraining chatbots through dialogs and in keeping chat logs for continued learning and improvement. In the enhancement of their efficiency and responsiveness to emerging user preferences, techniques used to retrain chatbots and generate linguistic alterations play a vital role that requires auxiliary tools. Furthermore, Jimmy Ming-Tai et al. (2021) discussed that security for the cloud-based healthcare in a smart environment is important because it impacts both privacy and data security aspects within various medical applications. Robust authentication mechanisms are critical recommendations for strengthening privacy, security, and message exchange in healthcare systems that rely on the cloud computing capability to safeguard against corruption of information as well as leakage of patients' secrets (Tariq, 2025).

To solve the issue of chatbots and improve cybersecurity, Arora et al. (2023), looked at how user behavioral analytics (UBA) can be used to increase chatbot security by lessening cyber threats. Secure protocols and authentication mechanisms will protect chatbot systems from threats of spoofing, tampering, and denial of service attacks. Sarker et al. (2022) discussed how generative language models have affected privacy, emphasizing the ethical challenges associated with artificial intelligence (AI) modeling and data privacy. Concerns about privacy breaches arise when individuals try to exploit workarounds to avoid restrictions placed on AI models, while also highlighting the necessity of having internal policies on governance as well as good practices in ethics to steer the behavior of our machines. Additionally, the applications of analytical AI and textual AI in data-powered decision-making and NLP tasks are illuminated by the AI-based modeling described by Sebastian Sanchez (2020). Boosting utilization of these AI models will assist stakeholders in gaining insights from data, as well as improving communication within multiple sectors. The architecture for a conversational AI system described in Figure 1 identifies the major components involved in processing user inputs and generating a response. The system is broken down into a client application and the conversation service, where user inputs are first loaded and put into context before being processed by the natural language understanding module. This module classifies intents and extracts the relevant entities, passing data to the dialog interpreter to generate appropriate responses. The dialog interpreter might also interact with external services and logs for enhanced functionality and feedback.

Figure 1. Workflow of a Conversational AI System

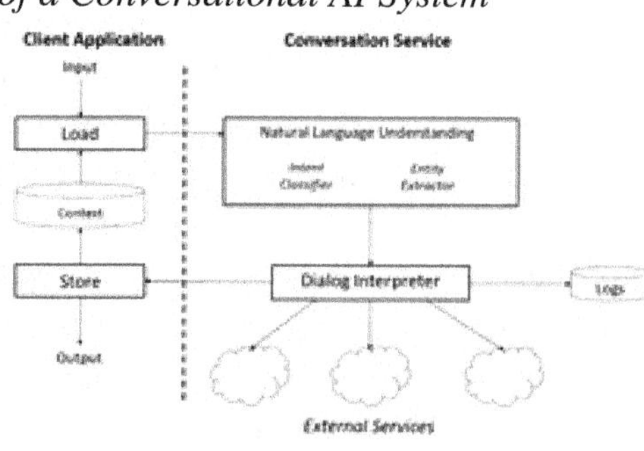

According to Connor Weeks et al. (2023), the need for preserving Personally Identifiable Information has led to the preference of homomorphic redaction-based strategies. To comply with data protection laws and ensure secure processing of sensitive data, stakeholders can incorporate Filter, Redirect, Decrypt and Redact processors into the BotShield pipeline. Furthermore, as observed by Hasal et al. (2021) there is a need to have complete analysis on security in chatbots communication as well as data management in order soundly understand protective measures including but not limited to authorization protocols, authentication system, encryption algorithms. One way through which it is important for personal information to be anonymized and hidden by codes so that it may comply with laws like the General Data Protection Regulation (GDPR) would be by treating them pseudo-anonymously through encryption for creating some kind privacy while people are chatting using these bots. In addition, the transformative potential in business-to-consumer communication of chatbots as a service (CaaS) is illustrated by the work of Jalali et al. (2024). Yet, the necessity of encryption, authentication, as well as innovative approaches to risk mitigation underscore concerns about security and privacy (Tariq, 2025).

Nazar Waheed et al. (2022) examined chatbot websites and their security implications. It was discovered that many of these websites lack secure connections or utilize cookies for tracking user online activities. Supported by evidence, these findings offer insight into the prevalent issue. Cookie usage policies as well as functionalities adopted by chatbot providers can be comprehended so that they may be tackled by internet users when transacting business thus improving the level of safety in digital environments. The significance of transparency and responsible implementation are underscored by Cîmpeanu Ionu -Alexandru's (2021) exploration of ethical challenges in chatbot usage. Working together with humans in addition to ethical guidelines while cooperating globally ensures the accountable use of chatbot technology and increases the confidence of its users. Birgit Brüggemeier et al. (2022) employed an original framework, Chatbot Linguistic Process (CBL) to measure views on privacy, security and performance in chatbot interactions. It was found out that user attitudes tend to get better when there is a relationship between privacy and good conversation. These results point out how protective people`s information while they engage in conversations through technology might improve the final responses without affecting how effective they are. Mukuka Kangwa's (2023) study of privacy protection mechanisms in e-commerce have led to the conclusion that PII protection can be enhanced through pseudonymization and data minimization, hence enabling sustained access to internet services. To counteract privacy threats and protect user information during electronic commerce transactions, involved parties would use PET and DLP systems while reducing PII. Furthermore, Sharma et al. (2022) have discussed how fast evolving artificial intelligence (AI) technologies are posing serious questions alongside solutions in the industry such as in chatbot technology that is fueled by AI. When you bring together algorithms in natural language processing (NLP) with machine learning methods, it is possible to increase the functionality of chatbots. Nonetheless, there are issues related to patient safety as well as confidentiality of user data in hospitals which make it important for us to come up with ethical guidelines that govern how artificial intelligence should be utilized in a responsible way (Tariq, 2025).

Furthermore, investigating on the impact chatbots have on ecommerce customer's satisfaction and engagement from a qualitative point of view which Farhan Aslam (2023) studied in his research methodology also reveals useful information about customer preferences and perceptions. When this researcher sampled people belonging to teenagers (Gen Z) and applied internet polls, there were some hints concerning different sides of chatting robot behavior in terms of ecommerce which also influences its development aspects. Finally, the development and creation aspects of chatbots, which are discussed by Geovana Ramos Sousa Silva and Edna Dias Canedo (2024), underscore the significance of natural and exciting interactions to overcome user resistance. It means that combining written and visual components during creation while strictly following the rules of conversational designs could improve UX and maintain constant engagement in different contexts by end users. Silva et al. (2022) explained a full answer to privacy issues in data-processing, known as PoSeID-on based solution - Personal Data Analyzer or simply the PDA; it seeks to reduce privacy risks in personal data transactions. By combining a hybrid data analysis mechanism and a state-of-the-art privacy risk assessment tool, the PDA continuously analyzes transactions, informing users in real-time about potential privacy risks and giving granular control over the dynamics of data sharing. Mina et al. (2024) introduced a pseudonymization system designed for situations such as when people communicate with a chatbot in the COVID-19 period. Accordingly, the system has a flexible pipeline that targets at recognizing then deidentifying personal data identified by the users. The performance of the system is rated by annotators in terms of contextual clues found in the conversations. The pipeline that mixes regular expressions together with machine learning models helps in identification of defined PIIs like trademarks and those that are not.

Lui et al. (2024) put forward an API service that is aimed at transforming personalization on LLM-based platforms while upholding user privacy. The API service provides users with some controls on data sharing and blurs personally identifiable information in a manner that balances personalization with privacy. Popa and Poddar specify the need for confidential computing in protecting the PII data, especially in environments that deal with sensitive information, such as financial records [29]. The work also provides monitoring tools, like LLM Gateway, which can identify and prevent the leakage of PII data into prompts and offer insight on how to tighten data protection strategies. Eky Fasich Trialopa (2022) wrote about problems and solutions in improving customer satisfaction with AI chatbots, focusing mainly on the collection of PII data. According to the study, too many lengthy questions from bots on PII data are frustrating for customers, leading to lower satisfaction and increased abandonment rates. Trialopa would propose that the bot needs to collect PII data only once and store it using the sender_id in a database. As a result, this will make the bot remember the information that in future interactions, it might not ask for the same thing over and over. Rahime Belen-Saglam et al. (2022) examined sensitive personal information and its disclosure in ways such as expected benefits, privacy risks and trust in the data receiver. Data protection regulation places sensitive data under race, health and biometrics in the broader context of the GDPR. Various research has shown that users are willing to disclose more information to chatbots than to humans, since they offer more anonymity. Rajesh Pasupuleti et al. (2023) discussed the rapid evolution of technology, focusing on generative AI like ChatGPT and the challenges associated with that—especially the sensitivity of PII. Incidents of employees accidentally leaking confidential company data through ChatGPT highlight data security and privacy concerns. Generative AI's capability to remember user queries increases the risk of data breaches, necessitating strict security measures and employee education on the dangers of sharing sensitive information.

According to Vikas Hassija et al. (2023), there is a high requirement for the selection of conversational data and necessary pre-processing in training models like ChatGPT. The data should be of high quality, stemming from sources such as social media and chat logs, and diverse in nature. To protect user information, the source data is filtered and anonymized. The most relevant pre-processing techniques include the tokenization, cleaning, and balancing of dialogue lengths. These steps make the data appropriate for training, enhancing the performance and reliability of the AI model and ensuring due attention to ethical issues regarding data privacy and security. Boidurjomani Banerjee (2021) discussed the deployment of chatbots and the integration of Robotic Process Automation (RPA) in educational institutions to make them efficient. Companies and organizations must determine the purpose of their chatbots and the expected result by deciding either the rule-based chatbot for preset tasks or the AI-based chatbots for replying to the queries made by the users. Transaction-based chatbots make it easy to book meetings or guide students via links; therefore, it makes the user experience good through good UI.

Karma Choedak (2020) explained that chatbots process natural language inputs to provide responses or execute tasks. They can be embodied, simulating human interaction, or disembodied, engaging through text or voice. Their architectures are either rule-based, using predefined patterns of response, or corpus-based, making use of machine learning to dynamically interact. While much progress has been made in the development of conversational AI, most effort has been put into developing user-friendly interfaces, robust processing in the backend, and ensuring data security are provided by various AWS services. Current literature is rife with technical aspects of chatbot development and data protection mechanisms separately. However, there is a gap in comprehensive studies that integrate the elements to form a holistic approach toward secure and data governance-aware conversational AI systems. To further the AI chatbot security debate, there is a need to discuss actual incidents that point to vulnerabilities and changing threats. A recent incident was the ChatGPT Data Leak in 2023 when OpenAI chatbot leaked users' chat histories due to system misconfiguration. This case reinforces the importance of strong access control, data encryption, and secure API management to avoid unintentional data exposure. Likewise, a Healthcare Chatbot Privacy Violation (2022) exposed how mental health chatbots were storing users' conversations without encryption, breaking HIPAA rules. This hack is a reason why end-to-end encryption and cloud storage have become crucial for protecting sensitive user information. Emerging threats are also challenging to ensure the security of AI chatbots. Adversarial attacks, where cyber-attackers use manipulated input requests to evade moral restrictions or output prejudiced text, are on the rise as an issue of concern. Adversarial attacks take advantage of the vulnerabilities of AI models through injecting deceptive prompts and consequently producing unintended or even dangerous outputs. Token injection is also a new threat in which attackers design prompts to control chatbot actions or extract confidential information. These events highlight the necessity of real-time input validation, adversarial robustness methods, and ongoing monitoring of chatbot interactions. Such challenges need to be addressed with a multi-layered security strategy, including robust encryption, AI safety guardrails, and active threat detection to protect chatbot ecosystems. With these security features integrated, organizations can minimize threats and provide a safer, more trustworthy, AI-powered conversational experience (Tariq, 2025).

In Table 1, various studies have explored aspects like access control, security protocols, and toxicity mitigation in chatbots, but they often do so in isolation without a unified approach. This research work tries to fill those gaps through the implementation of a secure, data-aware conversational AI system, one that is highly secure on the back end and powered by services from AWS. To do so, the research work discusses both the technical and ethical dimensions by considering Amazon Macie, which automatically detects and protects sensitive data, to provide a comprehensive framework ensuring privacy, compliance, and trust in conversational AI technologies.

Table 1. Overview of Key Research Papers on AI-Driven Chatbots in Cybersecurity

Sl. No.	Paper Title (year)	Methodology Summary	Advantages	Drawbacks
1.	Modeling and enforcing access control policies in conversational user interfaces [2023]	This work proposes to enrich CUI definitions with access-control primitives to enable the enforcement of security policies. The solution is based on the use of model-driven techniques to raise the abstraction level at which the CUIs are defined.	- Role-based access control - Feasibility demonstrated with two implementation strategies	Limited focus on security concerns beyond access control.
2.	From ChatGPT to ThreatGPT: Impact of Generative AI in Cybersecurity and Privacy [2023]	The work presents the vulnerabilities of ChatGPT, which can be exploited by malicious users to exfiltrate malicious information bypassing the ethical constraints on the model	- Various attack vectors showcased - Valuable analysis of GenAI models' impact on cybersecurity	- Findings specific to ChatGPT, limiting applicability to other GenAI models. - Lack of Mitigation Strategies
3.	Securing Well-Being: Exploring Security Protocols and Mitigating Risks in AI-Driven Mental Health Chatbots for Employees [2024]	This paper emphasizes the task of ensuring the safety of AI driven health chatbots in corporate settings. Considering the impact of international data protection laws on chatbot deployment will require a global outlook that ensures compliance while understanding regional differences in privacy regulations.	Recommends practical measures like Two-factor Authentication (2FA) and self-destructing messages to enhance security.	- Limited exploration of innovation-privacy trade-offs. - Absence of real-world effectiveness studies.

continued on following page

Table 1. Continued

Sl. No.	Paper Title (year)	Methodology Summary	Advantages	Drawbacks
4.	Sensitive data like passwords and PII shared to AI chatbots [2023]	This paper outlines the need for robust controls to prevent data leaks, with a particular emphasis on the protection of financial, healthcare, and intellectual property data. Organizations are urged to implement effective measures such as data loss prevention and user coaching to mitigate risks.	- Suggests implementing controls like DLP and user coaching to mitigate the risks while leveraging AI benefits. - Provides concrete statistics on the frequency of sensitive data sharing, aiding in understanding the scope of the issue.	Highlights restrictions without delving into alternative strategies or solutions.
5.	A First Look at Toxicity Injection Attacks on Open-domain Chatbots. [2023]	By highlighting the potential harm caused by toxic language produced by chatbots, the article underscores the importance of addressing this issue to protect users, especially in sensitive domains like healthcare and the justice system.	Provides concrete examples of different attack tactics, such as indiscriminate injection and backdoor injection, making it easier for security professionals to understand and mitigate these threats.	- Technical nature may hinder comprehension for non-experts, limiting accessibility. - Focuses narrowly on toxicity injection, potentially overlooking other chatbot security vulnerabilities.

PROPOSED METHODOLOGY

Architecture. The proposed system follows a client-server architecture, where the client sends a series of details ti….tn where t is the user data intercepted by the chatbot constructed using AWS Lex tool. The data sent by the user is validated by the serverless compute service AWS Lambda based on the format required, libraries such as boto3 and uuid are utilized where the former is responsible for the integration of various services utilized in the architecture, and the latter is utilized to give a unique identification id to each user data instances.

Components. The components of the proposed system architecture include Amazon Lex, AWS Lambda, Amazon S3 and Amazon Macie.

Amazon Lex. Lex acts as the front end in interaction with users for the Conversational AI chatbot; it interprets the user's input and generates appropriate responses. It enables the understanding of natural language queries and the establishment of smooth communication between users and the system.

AWS Lambda. Lambda functions act as the backend processing unit, executing business logic in response to user requests. These functions are responsible for accessing S3 Buckets, performing basic CRUD operations, and implementing security measures such as data encryption and access control.

Amazon S3: Scalable and Secure Object Storage. Amazon S3 (Simple Storage Service) is an object-oriented storage designed for highly scalable, high-availability, and durable data. It serves as a secure and cost-effective repository for various data types, including backups, archives, and frequently accessed files.

Amazon Macie. Macie is a data security and privacy service that, based on machine learning and pattern matching, discovers and protects sensitive data that might be set in the S3 buckets. It automatically classifies personally identifiable information and other sensitive data types across the cloud storage.

Relevant Use Cases. Macie scans the S3 bucket containing backups in search of any PII data that might reside within them. This helps to keep up with data privacy regulations and minimizes the risk of sensitive information being exposed.

Figure 2. Architectural Framework

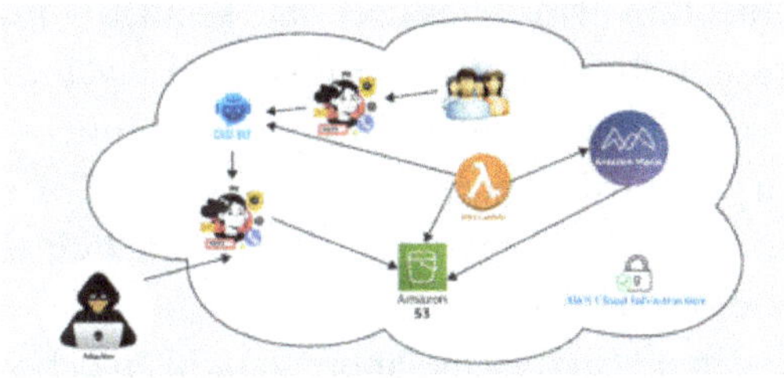

The proposed Architecture diagram, Figure 2, depicts the way in which various AWS services are interlinked strategically to provide an infrastructure to detect and secure the PII data intercepted through the chatbot. The chatbot being source of linkage between the user and the backend resources of the architecture is made using AWS Lex tool. The chatbot built on the use case "Hotel Management System", queries the users for the following fields of information to provide the facility of booking a hotel- [{FirstName}, {LastName}, {Email}, {Phone_Number}, {Visiting_City}, {Number_of_days}, {CheckIn_Date}, {CheckOut_Date}, {Confirmation}]. The above use case is just for the sake of research purpose and many more use cases can be studied. The described fields of information include PII data such as email and contact number. The function for backing up chatbot data to S3 bucket is created using AWS Lambda function, which get triggered on user interactions and backs up the user data on S3 bucket, after defining a unique reservation id for each user entry. This is the point of architecture where S3 is connected to the chatbot for initiating storage functions.

After backing up the data on the S3 bucket, Amazon Macie comes into the picture. Amazon Macie, an ML model, is known for its capabilities of detecting and reporting any kind of PII data. The service already has numerous categories of PII data and can be customized for a particular kind of data that needs to be detected according to the use case, using a regular expression defining the pattern of that data. In this architecture a Macie job has been created to analyze the S3 bucket backup of user data intercepted using the Lex chatbot. Macie analyses the backed-up data and successfully reports the severity of risk based on number of PII data detected, it also categorizes the type of PII data with their frequencies for reference. By default, the reports can only be accessed by the admin and the data at rest is encrypted using AES256 algorithm for added security.

SECURING USER DATA: A MULTI-LAYERED APPROACH

The proposed architecture prioritizes user data security through a multi-layered approach, Figure 3, presents the flow in which this multi-layered approach is targeted.

Data Minimization. The chatbot is designed to collect only the minimum amount of PII necessary to fulfill user requests in the *Data Collection Layer* referred in Figure 3. This minimizes the potential impact of a data breach and reduces the attack surface for malicious actors.

data has been encrypted utilizing the approach, this has been achieved through the inclusion of *boto3* library in lambda function, this operation takes place in *Data Processing Layer*. Hence providing an architecture tailored for a multi-layered data security approach.

Access Control. Granular access control mechanisms are implemented on the *Data Storage Layer* as shown in Figure 3, to restrict access to user data based on user roles and permissions. For this IAM is utilized to classify roles and permissions on whom to allow the access to the user data and whom not to. The management of this is done through following the least privilege principle.

Data Detection. This follows the main component behind the protection of PII data, which is present in the *Data Detection Layer*. Amazon's Macie, a machine learning tool is utilized to access the S3 bucket used to store the user data and thereby creating Macie jobs to detect any sort of PII data in the S3 bucket. Macie accurately detects the data, sends alerts, logs the security risks and by default encrypts the data using AES, all of these come under *Security Measures* as shown in Figure 3. The data detected is strictly restricted.

Figure 3. Multi-Layer Data Protection Strategy in AWS

IMPLEMENTATION

The proposed architecture makes optimal use of AWS services to detect and protect PII data captured during the operation of a chatbot. The chatbot, as defined by AWS Lex, acts as the user interface for collecting details such as names, contact information, and reservation details. The AWS Lambda function is used to integrate services, for example, to backup data to an S3 bucket. Amazon Macie, an ML-powered service, completes the PII detection and reporting at the S3 bucket backup. Data content is analyzed with Macie jobs in a customizable manner. AWS Macie categorizes PII types and assesses associated risks into various risk categories, based on detection frequencies. AES256 encryption on data at rest and report access for admins only guarantee data security and compliance. The architecture allows an organization to easily monitor and protect sensitive user information, increasing the level of security in chatbot use.

Module 1: Lex Bot Creation

The main objective of this module is the creation of a functional Amazon Lex bot that acts as the user interface for an AI chatbot. As the first point of chat to initiate conversation with the end user, the Lex bot uses Natural Language Understanding to facilitate the understanding of user inputs. To achieve this, an in-depth technique is used to define explicitly the intents, slots, and utterances that enable the bot to respond effectively to various use cases. Setting clear intents is the first key step in making conversational agents. Intents are the tasks users want to do with the help of the bot, directing how the bot should react, Figure 4 depicts the UI of the intent detail's definition panel in AWS Lex chatbot. For example, in a customer service bot, intents could be things like looking up how much money is in an account, paying a bill, or finding places where one can get service close by, Figure 5 shows one such case of list of possible intents in a chatbot. Defining these goals well is core to what the bot does, showing it the way to handle and answer when people talk to it.

Once the intents are identified, they are broken down into key parts, called slots. These are the bits of info needed to carry out the task. For example, if booking a flight is the goal, then the slots needed are the city one is leaving from, the city one is going to, when to leave, and when to come back. These slots make sure the bot gets all the details it needs from the user to do the job right. Then, sample lines, or examples, are used as a training guide to teach the bot how to get and understand this info from what users say. Utterances reflect how users may say their intents: for example, "I need a flight to New York" or "Book a plane ticket to LA." The more the types of utterances used to train the bot, the better at understanding diverse ways of stating an intent the bot will become. By always improving itself and checking its work, the Lex bot becomes more skilled at talking. The purpose of all this work would be to enhance its capability with tricky questions and various forms of chat, thus ensuring that it can give the right answers fast and with no trouble. Tests include trying out various forms in which people might express themselves, handling conversations that go back and forth, and keeping track of the subject of conversation. An important part of enhancement is to create robust ways of error correction or handling of ambiguous or complex user inputs. These steps are helpful when a user's words do not make sense or might lead to mix-ups. For instance, in case the bot is not able to understand a user's request, it should be capable of asking questions that clarify the request or give other options. Effective error handling ensures smooth user experience and keeps user engagement at a high level.

Creating this chatbot begins with the basics of how it talks to users. Whatever learnings are obtained in making the Lex bot helps a lot with the setting up of the back parts, those running in the background, and in charge of data management. A good setup in the back makes sure the chatbot can easily work with the front part in getting and using the right information fast to answer user needs well. In short, for the creation of a smart Lex bot for conversations, there are a lot of things to be taken into consideration: setting clear intents, piecing together the different slots, and defining the conversation flow carefully, Figure 6 presents the flow of conversation in the adapted chatbot, for the proposed architecture. Keeping it getting better and fixing mistakes is the key to making the chatbot work well. The experience gained from this process not only improves the user interface but also strengthens the overall chatbot system, ensuring a seamless and efficient user experience.

Figure 4. Intent Details

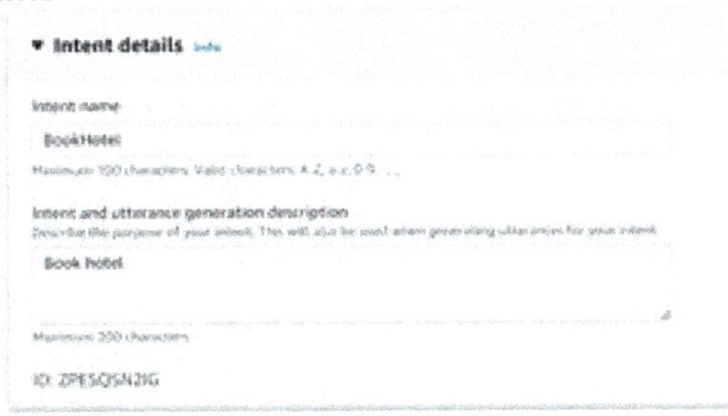

Figure 5. Intent List

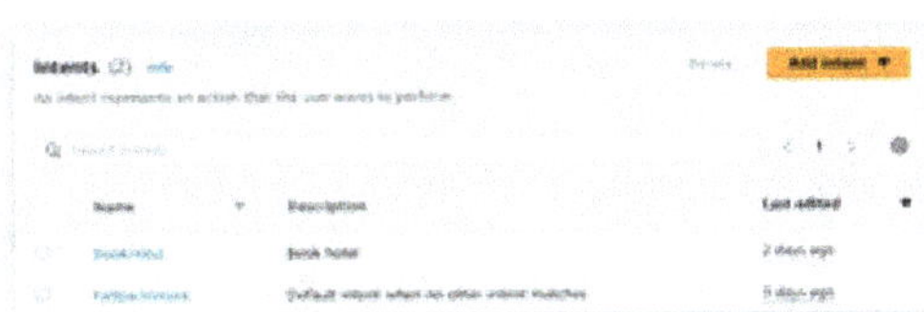

Figure 6. Conversation Flow

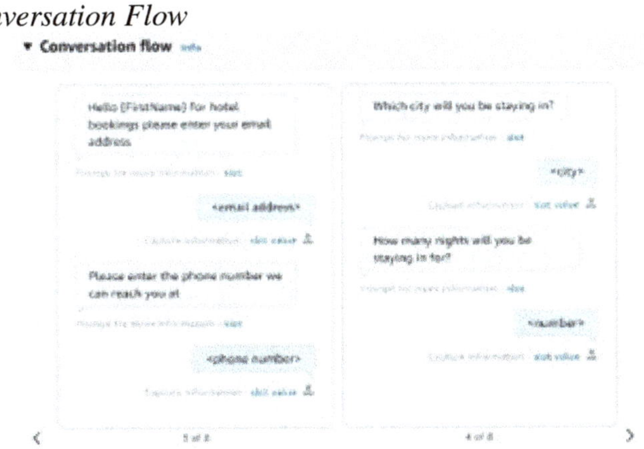

Figure 7. Conversation Flow

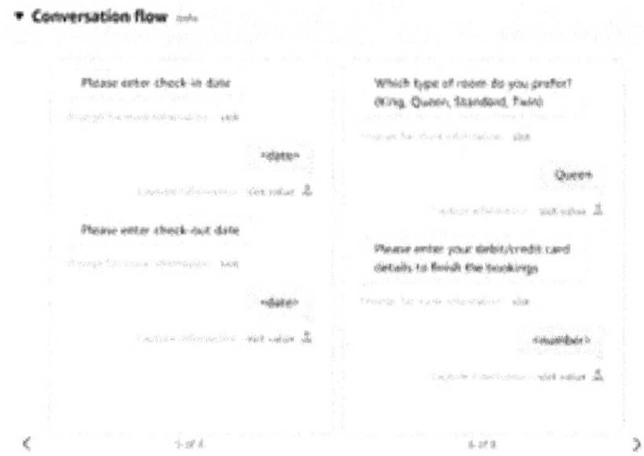

Figure 8. Conversation Flow

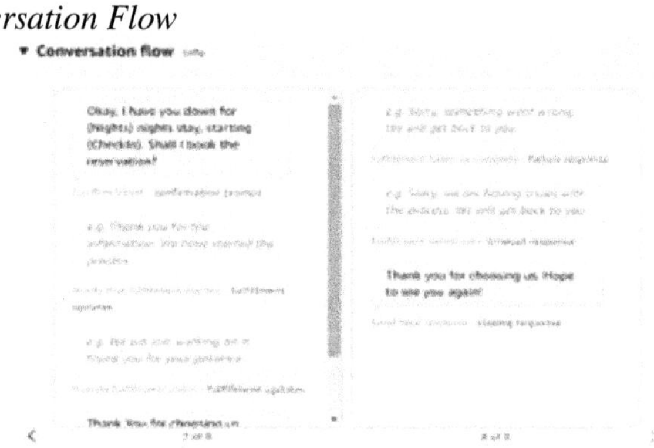

Figure 9. Conversation Flow

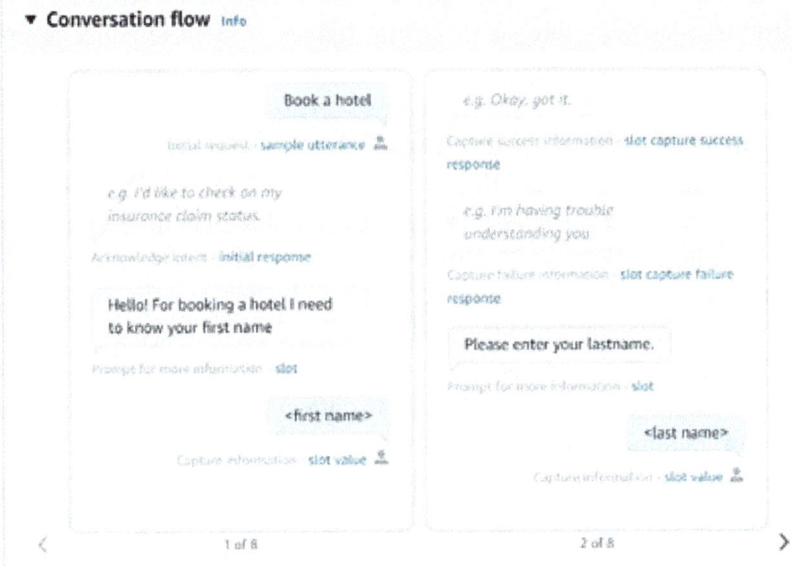

Module 2: AWS Lambda Integration

The addition of AWS Lambda functions to a system setup gives a powerful way of handling lots of different tasks, ranging from dealing with user requests to checking data carefully and keeping things secure. AWS Lambda enables the building and setup of functions for all kinds of needs. Under this setup, Lambda functions are created as autonomous parts, each with their own function in the system. Figure 7 depicts the function overview of the proposed architecture's Lambda function. An organization of this sort decomposes the work into smaller bits, ensuring everything runs smoothly, from handling business needs to dealing with data tasks. Lambda functions are triggered based on user actions, API calls, or system notifications. This kind of event-driven model ensures the synchronization of tasks, thereby enabling the system to respond dynamically and effectively to various operational demands. Security is the most important thing Lambda does, especially when handling private user information. Lambda adopts strong safety tools, such as access controls, data encryption codes, and data validation checks. The access rules of AWS Identity and Access Management decide the person to whom Lambda is allowed and the things that can be accessed. AWS Key Management Service locks data when not in use and during transit, thus keeping it safe from unauthorized persons. Lambda does data validation in strict terms to make sure it is right and safe before doing anything with it. This reduces the chance of dealing with malicious or corrupt data. These security mechanisms collectively safeguard user data from unauthorized access, data breaches, and other security threats, ensuring that the system remains compliant with various regulatory standards.

The serverless configuration of Lambda offers great scalability and usability. The system can seamlessly scale up or down according to the requirements, handling many users simultaneously. Scalability ensures the system will be both fast and secure, therefore remaining good for many people. Lambda functions automatically to handle increase in workload and scale down when the demand is reduced, saving on expenditure and usage. Lambda integrates well with other services by AWS, such as S3, which is a file repository service, and the Key Management System by AWS. Lambda can be triggered in response to S3 events, such as file upload or modification; that is, this makes it quite easy to process data automatically without human intervention. For example, a Lambda function could be triggered to validate and process a file uploaded, its metadata stored, and other further processing initiated. Moreover, Lambda uses KMS for key management and data encryption so that data processed by the Lambda functions is encrypted, maintaining confidentiality and integrity throughout its cycle.

By using Lambda functions correctly, it ensures that user information is properly processed and stored securely. Lambda's serverless approach enables quick deployment and use, whereby updates are fast without the hassle of maintaining servers. Hence, it saves lots of money and makes things easier. Choosing AWS Lambda reveals the shift towards modern technology for developing large and secure applications. The serverless approach of Lambda offers the most freedom and speed. It allows developers to code without worrying about servers, promoting fast launches and less complex operations. The Lambda function provides the platform required to integrate different AWS services, like the Lex chatbot and the S3 buckets. The AWS Lambda function is a crucial participant in the process of backing up chatbot data to the S3 bucket and gets triggered by user interactions. When a user initiates a conversation with the chatbot, the lambda function is invoked, causing the backup task to begin. The function has been written to define unique reservation IDs for each user entry for easy data maintenance and access. As the reservation IDs are allotted, the user data is saved in the already created S3 bucket. In this manner, the Lambda function ensures the maintenance of user data as well as the linking of the chatbot with the S3 bucket. Lambda's pay-as-you-go plan means you only pay for what you use. This property can prove to be of great importance for use cases that are uncertain. They allow the handling of business scenarios and data bits that can be easily managed, are safe, can grow as needed, and do not incur high costs. They can be integrated easily with other AWS services, making them a strong option for formulating the backend of any application system. The infrastructure being serverless helps in providing more flexibility in the app-building procedures while ensuring safety standards.

Figure 10. Function Overview

Module 3: Integration with Amazon S3

This module of the architecture ensures the integration of Amazon S3 buckets with the Lex chatbot for flexible and secure user data backups. S3 is defined as a central, primary data repository because of its properties of scalability, durability, and cost-effectiveness while storing various types of user data in an efficient manner. Data associated with each user is stored in S3 with a unique ID for organized and structured storage. The scalability of S3 means that it can scale with growing amounts of data without performance degradation; it is durable, meaning that data is reliably stored and protected from loss. Strict access control settings, versioning policies, and encryption settings have been implemented for each S3 bucket to maintain the highest standards of data confidentiality, integrity, and availability. Access control settings ensure that only authorized users and systems can have access to the data and prevent unauthorized access. Versioning policies keep all versions of the data so that older versions of the data can be recovered whenever needed; this enhances data integrity. Encryption settings secure the data at rest and in transit, making sure that sensitive information remains confidential and safe from possible breaches.

The implementation strategy for this module includes the creation of robust data-ingestion pipelines. These pipelines ensure smooth transfers of data from the chatbot system into the S3 buckets, using AWS SDKs, APIs, and event-driven architectures. Whether the transfers are in real time or in batch processing, these pipelines ensure that the user data is stored in S3 securely so that it is ready for retrieval, analysis, and archival at any time. Event-driven architectures make the system react fast to new data events and, hence, automate the process of backing up data, reducing manual interventions. Additionally, methods have been developed for optimizing storage costs and adhering to data retention policies through data lifecycle management mechanisms. Mechanisms include automated workflows that can archive or delete data according to predefined criteria, such as time-based expiration or patterns of usage. For example, data not accessed frequently can automatically be moved to cheaper storage classes, and data that is obsolete can be deleted after a certain period; this is done so that the storage costs are optimized, and the retention of data policy is complied with.

By making Amazon S3 the primary data storage model, the overall architecture tends to be simplified. Certain additional hassles, such as dependency on intermediate databases, are removed, and the workflow is streamlined. Additionally, the overall architecture takes advantage of enhanced scalability and flexibility, hence adapting to the uncertainties in demands and requirements. This approach helps in reinforcing data security and compliance and follows the best practices for cloud-native application development. Thus, it is made sure that the process of data management is efficient, secure, and cost-effective, hence providing the users with robust and reliable solutions.

Module 4: Amazon Macie Integration

Amazon Macie is a powerful tool that automatically discovers and protects data located in Amazon S3. Macie does this using advanced machine learning and pattern-matching algorithms to effectively identify sensitive data, analyze for security risk, and provide actionable insight for better practices in the protection of data. Figure 8 shows a brief overview of how Macie achieves this using its managed data identifiers. Whenever Macie identifies sensitive data inside the S3 buckets, it raises highly detailed reports that specify the type of data detected, where the data resides, and the level of risk severity for the vulnerabilities found. Figure 9 is a snapshot of a sample case where the severity of data risk is reported, whereas Figure 10 shows a detailed report of the kind of PII data detected. It is from such in-depth reports that the administrators can act on such findings and put in place such corrective actions as the implementation of encryption, adjustments to access controls, and the application of data masking techniques to mitigate the risks and ensure compliance with prevailing regulations. However, detection alone is not a parameter; continuous monitoring can enable the system to detect and respond to real-time detection of active threats and potential security incidents. A proactive approach is going to help organizations stay ahead of emerging threats and vulnerabilities, thereby improving their general security posture. This integration into the system of managing chatbot data therefore takes capacity in maintaining confidentiality, integrity, and availability of data to new levels. For that reason, such integration will not only make data protection measures stronger but will also instill trust and confidence in the users, knowing that their data is being handled with the highest levels of security and compliance. The smooth integration of Amazon Macie into Amazon S3 marks a critical component within the network aimed at discovering and securing data within the chatbot system. Macie's constant surveillance and examination, coupled with actionable insight, raise the level to which data protection and compliance can be upheld to the utmost. It is in such a wholesome approach to data security that the safety of the users can be cemented, hence enhancing a safe and trustworthy environment for all users within the chatbot system.

Figure 11. Brief overview of Macie's Managed data identifiers

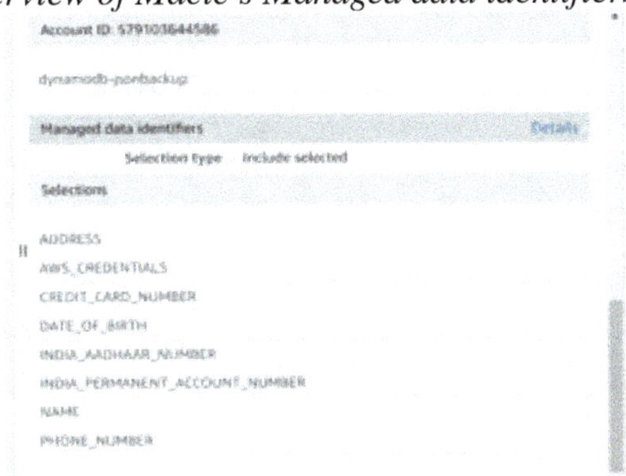

Figure 12. Macie's logging of data risk severity

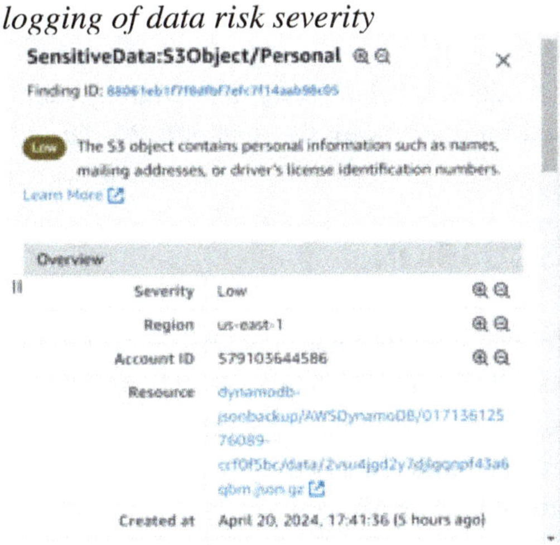

Figure 13. Macie's report of PII detection

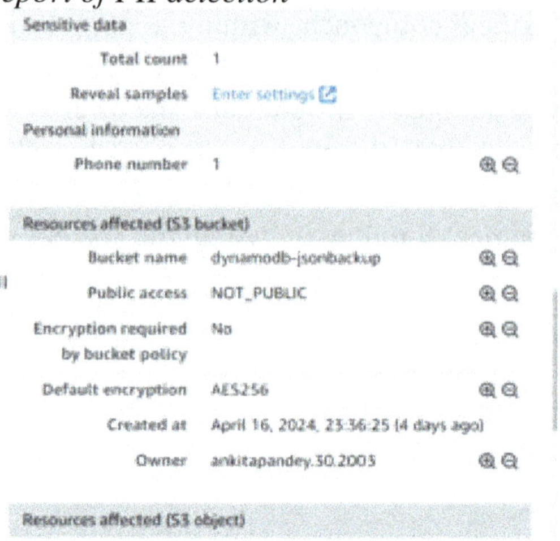

Data Protection with Amazon Macie

The key aspect of this work is the protection of personal identifiable information entered by the user. Integration of Amazon Macie is used in the system to accomplish this. Macie analyzes this information using machine learning and pattern matching and classifies PII information automatically within the system. This integration will improve the identification of sensitive information and more efficient enforcement of policies for data protection.

After Amazon Macie detects PII data, the Key Management System is triggered to control the keys used for encrypting the detected PII data.

RESULT AND DISCUSSION

The proposed system architecture has been effectively implemented, and its different modules successfully integrated. The system responds to each action initiated by the user, processes this action, and answers the request in a conversational way, ensuring the secure storage of the data in the S3 Bucket. Implementation challenges have been rigorously dealt with by system design and thorough testing to guarantee a robust and reliable system.

The nature of data handled by the system includes various types of user inputs, including PII information such as names, email addresses, and phone numbers. It is imperative to protect this data from unauthorized access, interception, or tampering to prevent potential security breaches or privacy violations. By implementing encryption and access control mechanisms, the aim is to safeguard the confidentiality and integrity of user data. Presently, the available resources addressing the needs of data security particularly PII data intercepted through chatbots exhibit several limitations, including lack of flexibility in detection of variety of categories of PII data, scalability issues linked with increase in the usage of chatbots resulting in increased data security risks, inability of the architectures to be expanded with the expansion in use cases, failures in understanding the intricacies of Natural Language etc. The proposed architecture addresses all these limitations by the strategic use of different AWS tools interlinked to form a strong and robust infrastructure that ensures PII specific user data protection.

The proposed model uses the power of Amazon Macie to capture PII data through its framework that provides over hundreds of managed identifiers which are pre-defined categories of different types of PII data, hence, providing with a significantly large state space to identify and report any kind of PII data, Macie is a strong Machine Learning model which is also equipped with other tools such as Custom Data Identifiers, which provides additional categories that can be defined by the architect, to detect some sorts of PII data with fixed and repetitive patterns by defining their Regular Expressions for detection, hence, expanding the state space and combating any kind of failures in Natural Language Understanding. The architecture being cloud based is serverless making it more flexible than the existing systems, the pay-as-you-go feature of AWS allows to plan the expenditure based on increasing or reducing demands, making it a flexible as well as a reliable system. The architecture can be scaled over large areas of network and over wide varieties of use cases. The architecture systematically logs and reports the data insecurities over an S3 bucket either by automating a regular process of detection through Macie or by creating custom jobs to be run on a particular database. The data at rest is protected by encrypting it using AES 256 by default, further enhancing the overall infrastructure.

Table 2 presents a comparison between the existing works and the proposed methodology over data security systems in conversational AI. The proposed architecture is evaluated against the existing models over the qualitative metrics - scalability, flexibility, and Natural Language Understanding.

Table 2. Comparison with previous work

Sl. No.	Title	Methodology	Flexibility	Scalability	NLU	Accuracy	Drawbacks
1.	Toxicity Injection Strategies in Chatbots: Risks and Implications	Explores toxicity injection strategies, focusing on indiscriminate and backdoor methods.	Limited flexibility in DBL setting; susceptible to data poisoning	Difficulty in managing toxicity risk in widespread deployment.	Struggles to distinguish malicious inputs, making it hard to detect and mitigate injected toxicity.	Highlights potential risks of high toxic response rates.	Insufficient discussion on mitigation strategies and ethical implications.
2.	Sentiment Analysis Chatbot Deployment on social media: Design and Implementation	Utilizes Design of Experiments for sentiment analysis chatbot deployment.	Hard to adapt to different social media contexts.	Managing engagement and satisfaction across platforms is difficult	Limited ability to handle varied language expressions	Provides effective sentiment analysis on Twitter data.	Limited scalability discussion and privacy concerns.
3.	AI Chatbots in Healthcare: Deployment and Impact Analysis	Analyzes AI chatbot deployment in healthcare for tasks like appointment scheduling.	Limited adaptability to diverse healthcare settings and patient needs.	Scalability issues in handling increased user demand.	Insufficient exploration of NLU capabilities for understanding diverse queries.	High accuracy in patient care tasks.	Limited discussion on biases, patient acceptance, and regulatory challenges
4.	Building a Secure and Transparent Online Conversation Platform: A Blockchain-Based Website With Integrated Virtual Assistant	Merges AI and blockchain for a secure online platform.	Offers end-to-end customer support	Potential scalability challenges with increasing user demand.	Utilizes advanced AI algorithms for user interaction.	Employs sophisticated AI algorithms for task execution	Limited exploration of scalability challenges and flexibility
5.	Securing Conversational AI: Leveraging AWS for PII data security (Proposed work)	Develops a chatbot architecture focusing on user data security and privacy with data regulations on a serverless cloud framework.	Utilizes Amazon Macie for capturing PII data.	Cloud-based, serverless architecture for flexibility and scalability.	Expands NLU capabilities through Amazon Macie	Aims to maintain the integrity and confidentiality of sensitive user data.	Potential challenges in integration and addressing security vulnerabilities.

The learnings from the comparison and analysis can be further understood by Figure 11, which is a graphical representation of the degree of qualitative achievements made through this system in terms of scalability, flexibility, accuracy and precise Natural Language Understanding. The diagram also considers the drawbacks of this system and gives a dimensional overview of the system's effectiveness.

Figure 14. Graphical representation of qualitative effectiveness achieved by the proposed methodology

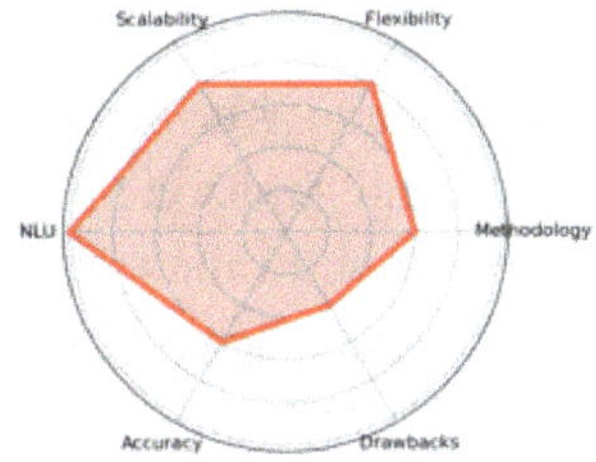

CONCLUSION AND FUTURE WORK

In summary, the proposed system architecture realizes high improvement in processing and security of PII data in conversational AI. From building out of the current shortcomings, such as the lack of flexibility in PII detection, scalability, and inability to adapt to growing use cases, the architecture draws on a suite of AWS tools to build a robust and scalable infrastructure. In addition, a system powered by Amazon Macie, a machine learning service custom data identifiers, and serverless cloud services set up for the complete identification and protection of sensitive user information. AES-256 data-at-rest encryption strengthens security, while shifting load from all servers enables a pay-as-you-go model for excellent cost-effective scaling. It has been tested and largely designed to serve as a reliable and effective system for securing PII data. The research has limitations, such as potential deviations from real-life scenarios in conversation-based implementation and complexity for those unfamiliar with AWS tools. Future work could integrate Amazon SNS for real-time data insecurity alerts, extend protection to other sensitive data, and improve user-friendliness in virtual assistants while enhancing security, including encrypting Macie logs with AES. With chatbots based on AI now being more prominent in user engagement across many different sectors, the key to maintaining user data privacy and remaining in regulatory compliance is to have proper security controls. Chatbots should be secured by developers with good practices that keep adversarial attacks, data exposures, and illegitimate access at bay. In addition, developers may improve security with the implementation of role-based access control (RBAC) for permissions-based limiting, differential privacy strategies for reduction in data exposure, and models of real-time threat detection that discover and defeat threats like prompt injection and token tampering. Developers may further also apply strong enforcement of secure API gateways based on encryption and authentication that hinders the exposure of unauthorized chats in interactions of chatbots.

Modern conversational AI chatbots are an important part of user interaction across industries. That is why this paper presents the realization of a secure, data-aware chatbot system that uses Amazon Web Services to create a chatbot system using Amazon Lex, AWS Lambda, and Amazon S3 with enhanced data privacy and compliance. Amazon Macie adds value to the system by scanning and protecting PII through continuous monitoring and machine learning. The solution adequately manages complex user interactions, thereby ensuring data security, setting the standard for data protection in conversational AI, and offering a scalable and practical approach for a secure chatbot deployment.

REFERENCES

Adamopoulou, E., & Moussiades, L. (2020). An overview of chatbot technology. In *IFIP international conference on artificial intelligence applications and innovations* (pp. 373–383). Springer.

Adamopoulou, E., & Moussiades, L. (2020). Chatbots: History, technology, and applications. *Machine Learning with Applications*, *2*, 100006. DOI: 10.1016/j.mlwa.2020.100006

Arora, A., Arora, A., & McIntyre, J. (2023). Developing chatbots for cyber security: Assessing threats through sentiment analysis on social media. *Sustainability (Basel)*, *15*(17), 13178. DOI: 10.3390/su151713178

Aslam, F. (2023). The impact of artificial intelligence on chatbot technology: A study on the current advancements and leading innovations. *European Journal of Technology*, *7*(3), 62–72. DOI: 10.47672/ejt.1561

Ayinde, L., Wibowo, M. P., Ravuri, B., & Emdad, F. B. (2023). ChatGPT as an important tool in organizational management: A review of the literature. *Business Information Review*, *40*(3), 137–149. DOI: 10.1177/02663821231187991

Balderas, A., García-Mena, R. F., Huerta, M., Mora, N., & Dodero, J. M. (2023). Chatbot for communicating with university students in emergency situation. *Heliyon*, *9*(9), e19517. DOI: 10.1016/j.heliyon.2023.e19517 PMID: 37809667

Banerjee, B. (2021). Smart student guide case of HUGI, a chatbot for education.

Banerjee, S., Agarwal, A., & Bar, A. K. (2024). Securing Well-Being: Exploring Security Protocols and Mitigating Risks in AI-Driven Mental Health Chatbots for Employees. *American Journal of Computer Science and Technology*, *7*(1), 1–8. DOI: 10.11648/j.ajcst.20240701.11

Belen-Saglam, R., Nurse, J. R., & Hodges, D. (2022). An investigation into the sensitivity of personal information and implications for disclosure: A UK perspective. *Frontiers of Computer Science*, *4*, 908245. DOI: 10.3389/fcomp.2022.908245

Brüggemeier, B., & Lalone, P. (2022). Perceptions and reactions to conversational privacy initiated by a conversational user interface. *Computer Speech & Language*, *71*, 101269. DOI: 10.1016/j.csl.2021.101269

Choedak, K. (2020). The effect of chatbots response latency on users' trust (Doctoral dissertation, Ph. D. Dissertation. University of Oklahoma).

Dhinagaran, D. A., Martinengo, L., Ho, M. H. R., Joty, S., Kowatsch, T., Atun, R., & Tudor Car, L. (2022). Designing, developing, evaluating, and implementing a smartphone-delivered, rule-based conversational agent (DISCOVER): Development of a conceptual framework. *JMIR mHealth and uHealth*, *10*(10), e38740. DOI: 10.2196/38740 PMID: 36194462

Doe, J., & Smith, J. (2024). AI Chatbots in Healthcare: Deployment and Impact Analysis. *Journal of Health Care Technology*.

Gupta, M., Akiri, C., Aryal, K., Parker, E., & Praharaj, L. (2023). From chatgpt to threatgpt: Impact of generative ai in cybersecurity and privacy. *IEEE Access : Practical Innovations, Open Solutions*, *11*, 80218–80245. DOI: 10.1109/ACCESS.2023.3300381

Hasal, M., Nowaková, J., Ahmed Saghair, K., Abdulla, H., Snášel, V., & Ogiela, L. (2021). Chatbots: Security, privacy, data protection, and social aspects. *Concurrency and Computation*, *33*(19), e6426. DOI: 10.1002/cpe.6426

Hassija, V., Chakrabarti, A., Singh, A., Chamola, V., & Sikdar, B. (2023). Unleashing the potential of conversational AI: Amplifying Chat-GPT's capabilities and tackling technical hurdles. *IEEE Access : Practical Innovations, Open Solutions*, *11*, 143657–143682. DOI: 10.1109/ACCESS.2023.3339553

Ionu -Alexandru, C. (2021). Challenges and Ethical Solutions in Using the Chatbot. Database Systems Journal, 12.

Jalali, N. A., & Hongsong, C. (2024). Comprehensive framework for implementing blockchain-enabled federated learning and full homomorphic encryption for chatbot security system. *Cluster Computing*, *27*(8), 1–24. DOI: 10.1007/s10586-024-04515-2

Kangwa, M. (2023). Prevention of personally identifiable information leakage in ecommerce using offline data minimization and online pseudonymisation (Doctoral dissertation, The University of Zambia).

Law, M. (2023). Sensitive data like passwords and PII shared to AI chatbots. https://cybermagazine.com/articles/sensitive-data-like-passwords-and-pii-shared-to-ai-chatbots

Lui, C., Ibraimova, A., White, D. C., Survase, R. P., Chihani, B., & Pham, T. K. (2024). OPTIMIZING LLM-BASED QUERIES AND RESPONSES USING SECURE, PORTABLE, AND PERSONALIZED ENCODED USER PROFILE.

Mina, M., Rodríguez, C., Gonzalez Agirre, A., & Villegas, M. (2024). Extending off-the-shelf NER Systems to Personal Information Detection in Dialogues with a Virtual Agent: Findings from a Real-Life Use Case. In In Proceedings of the Workshop on Computational Approaches to Language Data Pseudonymization (CALD-pseudo 2024): St. Julian's, Malta: 21-22 March, 2024 (pp. 44-53). Association for Computational Linguistics.

Pasupuleti, R., Vadapalli, R., & Mader, C. (2023, November). Cyber Security Issues and Challenges Related to Generative AI and ChatGPT. In *2023 Tenth International Conference on Social Networks Analysis, Management and Security (SNAMS)* (pp. 1-5). IEEE. DOI: 10.1109/SNAMS60348.2023.10375472

Planas, E., Martínez, S., Brambilla, M., & Cabot, J. (2023). Modeling and enforcing access control policies in conversational user interfaces. *Software & Systems Modeling*, *22*(6), 1925–1944. DOI: 10.1007/s10270-023-01131-3

Poddar, R. Securing Generative AI in the Enterprise.

Sanchez, S., & Franco, M. (2020). An intent-aware chatbot for cybersecurity recommendation. https://files.ifi.uzh.ch/CSG/staff/franco/extern/theses/MA-S-Sanchez.pdf

Sarker, I. H. (2022). AI-based modeling: Techniques, applications and research issues towards automation, intelligent and smart systems. *SN Computer Science*, *3*(2), 158. DOI: 10.1007/s42979-022-01043-x PMID: 35194580

Sharma, S., Singh, G., Islam, N., & Dhir, A. (2022). Why do SMEs adopt artificial intelligence-based chatbots? *IEEE Transactions on Engineering Management*, *71*, 1773–1786. DOI: 10.1109/TEM.2022.3203469

Silva, G. R. S., & Canedo, E. D. (2024). Towards user-centric guidelines for chatbot conversational design. *International Journal of Human-Computer Interaction*, *40*(2), 98–120. DOI: 10.1080/10447318.2022.2118244

Silva, P., Gonçalves, C., Antunes, N., Curado, M., & Walek, B. (2022). Privacy risk assessment and privacy-preserving data monitoring. *Expert Systems with Applications*, *200*, 116867. DOI: 10.1016/j.eswa.2022.116867

Tariq, M. U. (2025). Smart Forecasting With AI: Revolutionizing Energy Consumption and Storage. In Derbali, A. (Ed.), *Integrating Artificial Intelligence Into the Energy Sector* (pp. 165–184). IGI Global Scientific Publishing., DOI: 10.4018/979-8-3693-7112-1.ch009

Tariq, M. U. (2025). Co-Living With Augmented Digital Beings-Navigating the Intersection of AI and Everyday Life. In Moutinho, L., & Martins, L. (Eds.), *Impacts of Sensetech on Society* (pp. 187–206). IGI Global Scientific Publishing., DOI: 10.4018/979-8-3693-7147-3.ch009

Tariq, M. U. (2025). AI-Driven Personalized Learning-Enhancing Student Engagement and Outcomes. In H. Mamede & A. Santos (Eds.), *AI and Learning Analytics in Distance Learning* (pp. 151-178). IGI Global Scientific Publishing. https://doi.org/DOI: 10.4018/979-8-3693-7195-4.ch007

Tariq, M. U. (2025). Revitalizing Pedagogy: Integrating Indigenous Knowledge and Practices Into Higher Education Disciplines. In Kgari-Masondo, M. (Ed.), *Indigenous Teaching Disciplines and Perspectives for Higher Education* (pp. 379–400). IGI Global Scientific Publishing., DOI: 10.4018/979-8-3693-9296-6.ch018

Tariq, M. U. (2025). Bridging Cultures and Languages: Innovative Literacy Strategies for Inclusive and Engaged Classrooms. In Tussey, J., & Haas, L. (Eds.), *Supporting Cultural Differences Through Literacy Education* (pp. 257–282). IGI Global Scientific Publishing., DOI: 10.4018/979-8-3693-9271-3.ch010

Tariq, M. U. (2025). Community-Led Tourism and Social Equity: A Regenerative Approach to Sustainable Development. In Sousa, B., Arantes, L., & Bhartiya, S. (Eds.), *Regenerative Tourism for Social Development* (pp. 339–360). IGI Global Scientific Publishing., DOI: 10.4018/979-8-3373-0235-5.ch014

Tauseef, M., Jana, S., Gouda, A. R., Mishra, A., & Srivastava, U. R. (2024). Building a Secure and Transparent Online Conversation Platform: A Blockchain-Based Website With Integrated Virtual Assistant. In *AI and Blockchain Applications in Industrial Robotics* (pp. 276–299). IGI Global.

TRIALOPA, E. F. (2022). Optimizing The Customer Service Performance With Using Chatbot By Utilizing Bot Accuracy, Journey Completion Rate, And Customer Satisfaction Score (CSAT)(Case Study: PT YAI).

Waheed, N., Ikram, M., Hashmi, S. S., He, X., & Nanda, P. (2022, October). An empirical assessment of security and privacy risks of web-based chatbots. In *International Conference on Web Information Systems Engineering* (pp. 325-339). Cham: Springer International Publishing. DOI: 10.1007/978-3-031-20891-1_23

Weeks, C., Cheruvu, A., Abdullah, S. M., Kanchi, S., Yao, D., & Viswanath, B. (2023, December). A first look at toxicity injection attacks on open-domain chatbots. In *Proceedings of the 39th Annual Computer Security Applications Conference* (pp. 521-534). DOI: 10.1145/3627106.3627122

Wu, T. Y., Yang, L., Luo, J. N., & Wu, M.-T. (2021). J. (2021). A Provably Secure Authentication and Key Agreement Protocol in Cloud-Based Smart Healthcare Environments. *Security and Communication Networks*, (1), 2299632.

KEY TERMS AND DEFINITIONS

AWS Lambda: AWS serverless computing service that deploys code without any need to provision or manage servers. It scales automatically and executes the code with triggers in a very efficient manner. It supports a wide variety of programming languages and can be integrated with other AWS services for complex applications.

Amazon Lex: Service to build conversational interfaces using voice and text. It provides end-to-end natural language models in designing and deploying chatbots that can decipher user intentions and handle dialogues. Lex will provide integration with AWS Lambda for the implementation of business logic and will also support multi-turn conversations for dynamic user interactions.

Amazon Macie: AWS Macie is a data security and privacy service that leverages machine learning and pattern matching to detect, monitor, and protect sensitive data stored in AWS environments, more specifically, within Amazon S3. AWS Macie supports an organization in the requirements for compliance through security reporting and automated data classification.

AWS S3 (Amazon Simple Storage Service): This scalable object storage service is designed with high availability, durability, and security. Most of the use cases involve data storage and retrieval, such as backups and application data. Data management features that are flexible can be availed through S3, such as versioning, lifecycle policies, and fine-grained access controls.

General Data Protection Regulation (GDPR).: A comprehensive data protection law enacted by the European Union to regulate how personal data is collected, processed, and stored. It has a heavy focus on user consent, data privacy, and security measures, along with strict guidelines on data transfer and breach notification.

Personally Identifiable Information (PII): Any information that identifies an individual, either directly or indirectly. Examples include, but are not limited to, names, e-mail addresses, phone numbers, and identification numbers, which, while stored, must be protected in compliance with data protection laws. Protection of PII is important to instill user trust and assurance in regulatory compliances.

Chapter 7
Architecting Scalable ChatGPT Solutions for Enterprise

Monojit Banerjee
https://orcid.org/0009-0001-0328-0082
IEEE, USA

ABSTRACT

Large language model systems such as ChatGPT are causing significant disruption across various industries. This study investigates how scalable enterprise solutions can be architected with ChatGPT as a central element of the system. The author has analyzed the core components of foundational architecture, current state of usage of ChatGPT in enterprise and provided details about how to design scalable systems. Findings from this study indicate that the complexity of the overall systems and lack of clear data policy may cause challenges to an organization's capability for implementing a successful ChatGPT powered solution. The author has provided guidelines about data strategy and enhanced devops patterns to overcome that. Moreover, this paper has examined model optimization techniques to reduce cost and latency. Real-world case studies are provided as a reference. This research represents a comprehensive study that can help enterprises adopt ChatGPT in their business requirements in a reliable, efficient, and scalable manner.

INTRODUCTION

Enterprise solutions are designed to address business problems. Organizational challenges can be complex and to tackle them effectively, one must build a system that can withstand changing priorities and user demands. To achieve this goal, Ma-

DOI: 10.4018/979-8-3693-9841-8.ch007

chine learning (ML) models have become indispensable for enterprise solutions. According to Lee and Shin (2020), ML models can benefit enterprise solutions by streamlining business processes. The most common ML techniques employed by enterprises are clustering, classification, and prediction. However, with the introduction of the seminal neural network architecture known as the Transformer (Vaswani et al., 2017), the paradigm has shifted, making many previously deemed impossible use cases now achievable. This architecture is then used with millions of webpage datasets to create GPT-2, the precursor of ChatGPT (Radford et al., 2019). GPT-2 proved that this model can be used for most natural language processing tasks, especially effective in generating text. Later, this concept is enhanced, and these GPT-like models can produce multimodal responses such as images and videos (Gong et al., 2023).

Enterprise solutions are often rigid as they need to balance legacy systems with new features that support customer demands. Moreover, artificial intelligence solutions (AI) may rely on black-box models, and struggle with adapting to evolving data due to changes in the concept that it was originally trained for (Celik & Vanschoren, 2021). In addition, a lack of established data security practices may prevent enterprises from sending data to third-party services such as ChatGPT. Large language models (LLMs), which form the core of ChatGPT, rely on vast amounts of data to generate accurate and contextually relevant responses. Moreover, architecting enterprise systems to ensure they remain scalable even with non-deterministic systems such as LLMs is also a challenge. Balancing cost with system performance is a precursor for any enterprise system to ensure its reliability. Measuring them in real-time, implementing proactive corrective actions, and establishing matured DevOps patterns are essential to ensure long-term success. As we can see, the complexity of designing a scalable enterprise solution can increase exponentially when ChatGPT is integrated into the equation.

In this study, we have provided a detailed analysis of the components of a scalable architecture in the context of enterprise systems. We have also explored how ChatGPT is being utilized in a multitude of organizations and industries. By providing state-of-the-art techniques for optimizing the models we have ensured that an enterprise architect can build a scalable system with confidence. Additionally, we have explained how to integrate the DevOps pattern with the solution to make the system more elastic. Finally, some case studies are explored to combine all these concepts in real-world scenarios.

PRINCIPLES OF SCALABLE ARCHITECTURE

Scalable architecture is a system's ability to handle increasing workloads and demands without significant performance degradation. In practice, a well-architected system should be able to handle user traffic by scaling vertically (increasing the system resources such as memory or processing power) or scaling horizontally (adding more servers) without requiring fundamental changes to the core system. The anatomy of a scalable architecture consists of foundational principles, architectural paradigms, reliable and repeated delivery, data strategies, monitoring and analytics, and security measures (Figure 1). Each of these components is further explained in subsequent sections.

Foundational Principles

The two main building blocks of a scalable architecture are modularity and flexibility. A modular architecture designs a system to be composed of independent and interchangeable modules. Keeping in line with a component-based architecture, with modularity, individual modules can be changed without affecting the entire system. This leads to increased developer velocity as each team can perform their task in parallel resulting in accelerated overall development and reduced time-to-market. E-commerce, Financial Systems, and other enterprise solutions such as Payroll management or procurement systems can especially benefit from modular architecture where the complex system can be broken down into manageable chunks and the software lifecycle can be completed independently for each part.

Flexibility means how a system adapts to changing requirements and is closely tied to scalability. The goal of this architecture is to add new features, integrate with other systems, and manage changing workloads without major redesigns. For example, an enterprise payment system should be able to handle the load during black-Friday rush hour transaction volume without rewriting all services. Independent deployment and scalability using cloud-native technologies such as Kubernetes, and distributed databases can provide dynamic resource allocation. This dynamic nature is vital for achieving scalability (Tariq, 2025).

Figure 1. Pillars of Scalable Architecture

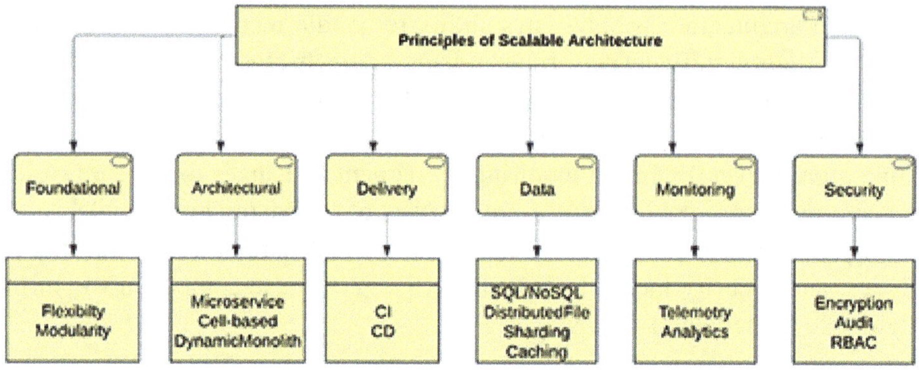

Architectural Paradigms

Complex systems should be divided into small, independent services. Each service can be developed, deployed, and scaled on its own, which allows for targeted scaling of the system based on an increased or decreased demand of resources. In comparison, a system built on Monolithic architecture cannot be scaled in a targeted fashion as the entire system may need to scale up to support the requirement. Microservices are decentralized by design making this architecture fault-tolerant and resilient. The cost and latency improvements offered by this method are particularly well-suited for high-volume enterprise systems, such as e-commerce and sales platforms.

However, a monolithic system has its place in the enterprise system. It can be made more robust and scalable using a cell-based architecture that divides applications into independent cells. Each of these independent parts is responsible for a specific domain or functionality. Each cell contains its own services - which may be monolithic and contain other common services such as databases, logging systems, etc. The cellular architecture promotes isolation and enables scaling allowing a monolithic system to perform at par with a microservice system by increasing performance and resiliency. Since many enterprises still rely on monolithic architecture, cell-based architecture provides the best of both worlds.

Reliable and Repeated Delivery

Continuous Integration (CI) and Continuous Deployment (CD) are core components of the DevOps framework. An enterprise system's efficiency and quality depend on the speed of delivery and high confidence of the code that is written. CI/CD enables teams to deliver software quickly and reliably by automating various stages like code check-in, automated unit and integration test, code linting, infrastructure provision, and deployment from the development environment to production without significant human involvement. Frequently merging code changes into a code repository like Git is required to make sure developers can make changes to the codebase without overriding each other's changes. The code then should be automatically built and tested. CI systems can validate changes on the go by running automated test cases after each code merge or pull request. They can also block code merge upon validation failure so that developers can identify and address issues early in the development cycle. This approach promotes teamwork among developers, enhances the quality of the code, and speeds up software delivery by identifying bugs before they escalate into more serious issues. Continuous Deployment works in conjunction with a CI system. A CD system can automate the release of validated code changes into the production environment. By setting up a CD pipeline, all changes that pass the building via the CI system using automated tests are automatically deployed to production. CD systems thus enable an enterprise solution to stay efficient by deploying the latest features and fixes. This results in faster feature delivery to end-users without significant manual intervention.

Data Strategies

Enterprise big data can be humongous (often petabyte scale or more) and a distributed database that can store large volumes of data across multiple nodes or servers is essential to handle that volume efficiently. For large-scale enterprise systems, data and processing tasks should be distributed in a manner that improves performance, scalability, and fault tolerance.

Distributed Databases can handle vast amounts of data across multiple servers, and they are optimized for high availability and scalability, making them suitable for applications with large data volumes. Apache Cassandra and Google BigTable are examples of distributed NoSQL databases and Oracle and Postgres are examples of available distributed relational databases. Hadoop Distributed File Systems (HDFS) and cloud storage solutions such as Network File systems (NFS) provide solutions for warehousing of large datasets and files. They provide the necessary infrastructure for distributed data processing. These file systems can form the backbone for an efficient data analytics application that an organization can apply to achieve business goals. Data partitioning and sharding involve dividing a database into smaller segments based on specific criteria. As a result, the chunk of data is easier to manage in comparison to huge datasets. By running query processing using Spark and other similar tools, one can improve the performance of the database query by running these operations in parallel on different segments. Caching is a powerful strategy that can improve the performance and efficiency of applications by temporarily storing frequently accessed data in Memory (RAM). Sometimes it can also store the data in a high-speed storage system such as NVME M2 SSD. Caching reduces the time to retrieve data as the frequently accessible data can be stored and found in the memory layer. As a result, more expensive user requests to primary databases are reduced and it can improve overall user experience.

Monitoring and Analytics

Without understanding how the system is behaving, it is impossible to achieve a scalable architecture. Effective monitoring and analytics are crucial for stable operation and for ensuring that the growth is sustainable. As the data volumes increase, the ability to monitor system performance and analyze data in real time becomes essential. Moreover, monitoring and analytics are needed for operational efficiency and informed decision-making. Continuous monitoring allows organizations to track the health of their systems in real-time. Quick identification of issues before they cause production downtime is required to avoid financial and other losses. This is particularly important in environments with virtualized and container-based resources, such as cloud infrastructures, where resource allocation can dynamically change. Organizations can use predictive analytics to forecast future performance and resource needs. However, they need historical monitoring data. We need to make sure these data are stored correctly so that it can be used later for this purpose. Analytics features can help with planning for scaling operations, optimizing resource allocation, and predicting system issues before they arise (Tariq, 2025).

Security Measures

Cloud-based enterprise systems can pose unique security challenges. There are many layers of threat such as outdated and vulnerable code libraries, malicious actors inside and outside, and misconfiguration in the network and other layers, etc. These security threats must be addressed to protect sensitive data. Moreover, quick identification and fixing of these threats are required to maintain system integrity. As systems scale, the number of entry points for potential attacks increases. These large attack surfaces can make it more difficult to secure all components effectively. Organizations must implement robust security measures across all layers of the architecture to mitigate risks. Incorporating security considerations into the architecture from the very start of designing the system is essential. This proactive or "shift-left" approach helps identify potential vulnerabilities early in the design process. As a result, the likelihood of costly changes will be reduced in the future. Implementing automated security testing tools can help identify vulnerabilities in code and configurations before deployment. Continuous integration and continuous deployment (CI/CD) pipelines should include security checks to ensure that the new code does not introduce risks. Encrypting data both at rest and in transit is vital for protecting sensitive information. Organizations should adopt strong encryption standards and ensure that encryption keys are managed securely. Also, conducting regular security audits and assessments can help organizations identify and address vulnerabilities in their scalable architectures.

CHATGPT IN ENTERPRISE

ChatGPT can automate repetitive tasks and optimize several business workflows. The potential for improving operational efficiency and increasing productivity across organizations is higher with these out-of-the-box capabilities. Similarly, it can help with social considerations such as sustainability and waste management. Moreover, various economic aspects including cost reduction, enhanced productivity, and better decision-making can result in huge enterprise adoption (Mariani et al., 2023). The key idea behind Artificial intelligence can be summarized as "every aspect of learning or any other feature of intelligence can in principle be so precisely described as a machine made to simulate it" (McCarthy et al. 1955). In the following section, we will describe the usage in more detail.

Figure 2. Enterprise ChatGPT use-cases (Image source: https://openai.com/chatgpt/enterprise)

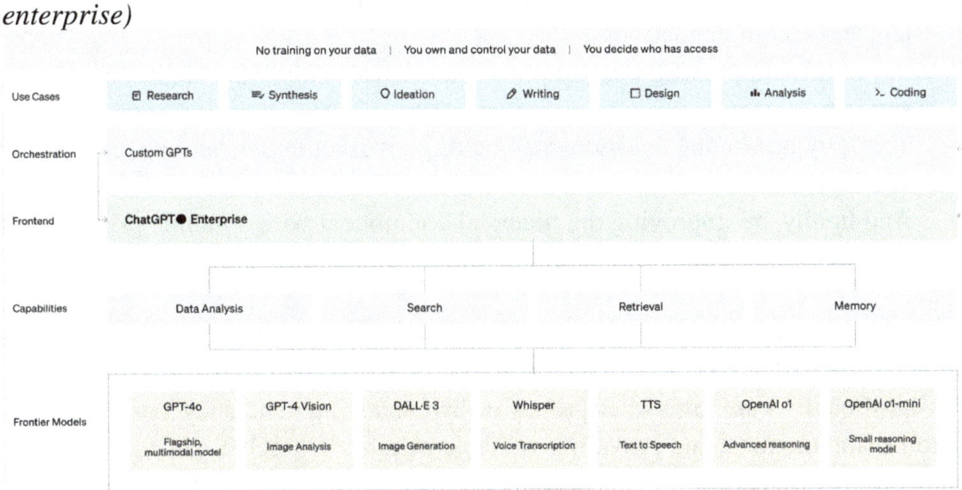

Operational Efficiency

Some of the repetitive tasks such as a basic summary of a large doc can be automated via ChatGPT. Similarly, many enterprise workflows such as sending a templated email can be optimized as well. With these, ChatGPT offers many opportunities to enhance operational efficiency and increase productivity across various departments in an enterprise. For example - in the customer service sector, ChatGPT can handle multiple inquiries at once, which not only lowers operational costs but also allows human agents to concentrate on more complex and strategic responsibilities. The efficiency gain then results in improved customer satisfaction and quicker response times (Raj et al., 2023). The potential cost savings from reduced labor expenses are better for the bottom line of an enterprise. This is especially true for businesses that experience high volumes of customer interactions (Sudirjo et al., 2023).

Marketing and Sales

ChatGPT's applications also encompass marketing and sales. Its capability to produce human-like text responses enables the development of personalized marketing materials, customized email campaigns, and social media content. This approach strengthens customer relationships and enhances engagement rates, allowing a business to generate higher conversion rates and increase revenue. De Mauro et al. (2022) have argued that there are four major categories where ML can support marketing.

- First, by improving shopping fundamentals with the help of personalized offers and recommendations.
- Second, by improving consumption experience with better digital customer service.
- Third, by improving decision-making (e.g., market understanding, consumer sensing)
- And finally, by improving the financial component with dynamic pricing and media optimization.

Some of the modern business platforms are already actively utilizing the capabilities provided by ChatGPT to enhance their marketing campaigns. Large language models can significantly transform sales processes by enhancing efficiency, personalizing customer interactions, and providing valuable insights. ChatGPT can automate the initial stages of lead generation by engaging potential customers through chatbots on websites or social media platforms. It can qualify leads by asking pertinent questions and gathering information that helps sales teams optimize their outreach to focus on potential customers. ChatGPT can create tailored emails and messages based on customer segmentation and diaspora. Personalization has been proven to improve engagement rates and increase the likelihood of conversion. Automating the process of generating and vetting leads through an LLM allows businesses to target large populations and a greater number of customer segments than would have been possible with a traditional marketing model (Tariq, 2025).

Additionally, ChatGPT and similar LLM systems can optimize SEO through automated content generation. As a result, an enterprise can increase its brand value by enhancing online visibility and driving organic traffic to a company's website (Chui, 2022; Orzoł, Szopik-Depczyńska, 2023).

Competitive Intelligence

ChatGPT can enhance competitive intelligence capabilities by assisting in analyzing complex competitive intelligence scenarios, such as evaluating the potential outcomes of mergers and acquisitions. ChatGPT can also provide investment recommendations if the user can provide the relevant data. For instance, ChatGPT can be set up to analyze form-10 k - an audited financial document of a company containing balances, cash flow, etc. at scale and identify emerging patterns. This data-driven approach nudges the enterprise to make strategic decisions, and it empowers businesses to be cognization of the market trends. This can help bring down the potential risk associated with any initiative and may increase the likelihood of success. As we know, ChatGPT can process vast amounts of information rapidly and it can identify key insights. An enterprise system can use all these enhanced capabilities to provide a significant competitive advantage which was not easily possible before. This is essential to enable businesses to react quickly to market changes and capitalize on new opportunities. Similarly, the natural language processing capabilities of ChatGPT allow it to efficiently sift through large volumes of data from various sources, including news articles (Local and international), social media posts (Text and image), and industry reports (SEC reports, form 10-K, etc.) allowing it to extract relevant information and identify key trends. This makes ChatGPT an indispensable feature for today's fast-paced businesses. The improved efficiency in information gathering helps businesses to identify potential threats and implement proactive strategies allowing them to stay ahead of the competition. ChatGPT can also provide the rapid dissemination of competitive intelligence to relevant stakeholders within an organization, ensuring that everyone is informed and aligned (Linna, 2023).

Corporate Social Responsibility

According to Zhuang and Wu (2024), ChatGPT can help with the development of Corporate Social Responsibility (CSR) by supporting social responsibility activities, strengthening internal control, promoting supervision by external entities, and providing details about sustainability for enterprises. ChatGPT can streamline the process of creating sustainability reports and it can also assist in identifying and assessing financial risks associated with CSR initiatives. It can generate compelling subject lines so that a company can convey its sustainability and CSR philosophies to its stakeholders effectively. This extra transparency and accountability can strengthen a company's reputation and elevate the brand image of the company.

Small and Medium Enterprise

LLM models like gpt4o that power ChatGPT can analyze market trends, identify customer needs, and generate creative solutions. It can lead to the development of entirely new business models and revenue streams. For SMEs, the benefits are significant. ChatGPT can help them with rapid prototyping. As such, SME businesses can overcome resource constraints as some of their non-core competencies can be outsourced to ChatGPT. They can then compete more effectively with larger businesses. ChatGPT's ability to optimize processes across numerous functional areas, such as resource management, strategic decision-making, fundraising, research and development, finance, marketing, sales, and administration, offers a substantial advantage (Linmu, 2023). SMEs can use these capabilities for their gain.

Enterprise Functions

Major enterprise functions, such as human resources (HR) and finance, can be transformed by ChatGPT. In human resources (HR), the integration of ChatGPT Enterprise with existing HR platforms creates a powerful AI-powered assistant. It can streamline the HR tasks related to recruitment, employee inquiries, and policy information. This improved efficiency leads to faster response times, increases employee satisfaction and reduces administrative overhead on HR professionals. ChatGPT can significantly enhance financial analysis and decision-making processes as well. It can process large datasets and input them into basic analytics tools to identify trends and generate forecasts. It can improve the accuracy and timeliness of financial reporting as it can help the analyst with these mundane tasks. The automation of routine tasks, such as data entry and reconciliation, can enhance efficiency. It also reduces the risk of errors by identifying and evaluating financial risks, which is particularly valuable. Moreover, by analyzing financial risk docs (example: SEC Form 20-F) ChatGPT acts as a helper to risk analysts and assists with proactively mitigating potential threats and improving overall financial stability. ChatGPT can streamline many accounting workflow processes. Specifically, it is utilized in areas such as intelligent accounting, shared financial intelligence, smart financial decision-making, visualizing financial analysis, and enhancing internal control systems. (Bing, 2023).

Web Development and Programming

In an enterprise, ChatGPT can provide valuable support to developers by enhancing system, information, and service quality. Its ability to generate code, answer technical questions, and assist with debugging can significantly improve developer productivity and reduce development time. However, concerns remain regarding UI/UX design and service quality. Hallucinations and making up answers prevent enterprise programmers from fully trusting ChatGPT's output. As a result, the potential of ChatGPT in this area still has lots of areas of improvement. As a debugging assistant, ChatGPT can provide bug predictions and explanations, but it should be used in conjunction with other debugging tools for optimal results (Surameery and Shakor, 2023). With the rise of intelligent AI-first IDEs like Cursor, Windsurf, and Bolt.dev, as well as AI plugin support in traditional IDEs like VS Code and PyCharm, enterprise developers are significantly boosting their productivity.

Wireless Products and Services

In the telecom domain, ChatGPT demonstrates promising capabilities in supporting enterprise wireless products and services. Recent research explores the applications of ChatGPT in wireless products and services. ChatGPT shows potential for automating tasks in mobile network experimentation. The research shows that it can reduce experimentation time by over 4 times compared to manual approaches (Krstić et al., 2023). The technology also aids in designing solar-powered emergency backup systems for 5G base stations. This backup system can support medical applications (Janamala et al., 2023). However, challenges remain in ensuring context continuity and robustness in input handling. Since this domain is particularly sensitive to latency and complex hardware logic - further development is needed to meet the requirements of this industry.

DESIGNING SCALABLE ARCHITECTURE

To achieve a successful implementation of an enterprise ChatGPT solution, one must be mindful of the functionality, reliability, and cost of the system. Reusing and customizing existing enterprise architectural patterns is well suited to achieve that goal. Instead of starting from nothing, we should leverage existing integration paradigms as much as possible. There are four major components here namely - Distributed Systems, Microservices Pattern, Middleware Integration, and Data Workflow Strategies.

Distributed Systems

A distributed system can be defined as a cluster of different servers that acts as a single consistent system. For end users, the behavior of a distributed system should be transparent. For example- a user in the United States can use a software tool that may be available on a local server to that user. Similarly, a user in Europe should have similar functionality but the service might be deployed to a server near Europe. However- despite the physical nature of distribution - an end user will observe similar usage in both cases. The main purpose of these distributed components is to work together to achieve a common goal while being physically separated. Some of the common characteristics of distributed systems are concurrency, scalability, and fault tolerance. Distributed systems can achieve scalability and reliability by using load balancing, horizontal scaling, and content delivery networks (CDNs). The main components of a distributed system are nodes (physical or virtual servers), communication protocols (HTTP, gRPC, message queue, etc.), and data storage solutions (distributed database, caching, etc.).

However- a distributed system is not a silver bullet. Distributed systems face challenges in scalability as the system grows. Some typical challenges include fault tolerance and efficiency. Decentralized architectures offer a solution by distributing tasks across nodes, enhancing scalability and fault tolerance (Troncoso et al., 2017) but it needs careful trade-offs on system complexity.

Microservices Pattern

Microservices architecture (MSA) is used widely in the enterprise. It is one of the most common architectural design patterns for many modern systems. Breaking down a large system into smaller services provides many benefits. For example- it can increase modularity and offer flexible configuration. Moreover, development and maintenance become easier. As a result, enterprises often experience enhanced productivity (Söylemez et al., 2022). Some of the key components of a microservices architecture are service registry and discovery, gateway, load balancer, and configuration server. In a production scenario- monitoring and observability are also heavily used. As the number of services in an MSA is large, a service discovery and registry system are essential for keeping track of the availability of the services and lifecycle management. Some popular service registry tools are Consul, etcd, and ZooKeeper. Similarly, an API gateway is responsible for application traffic routing. Kong, Ambassador, and AWS API Gateway are commonly used for off-the-shelf solutions. The load balancer is the heart of the scalable architecture, where this component can detect a healthy server automatically, redirect traffic, and maintain load to ensure the smooth operation of a complex system. Nginx and HA proxy are immensely popular open-source load balancer tools. Many organizations also adopt these tools and modify them to suit their needs for API gateway as those also act as load balancers. To achieve quick configuration changes and maintain complexity due to the number of services and environments, a configuration server is essential for MSA. Spring cloud config server is heavily used for this purpose. Some of the commercial cloud providers also offer proprietary tools such as AWS parameter store and Azure Key vault. For monitoring and observability, Prometheus as a metric store and Grafana as a visualization tool combination is common. Open Telemetry (Otel) is also gaining popularity. Otel is a framework to simplify logs, traces, and metrics creation. Despite all these benefits, adopting microservices presents many challenges. The most common issues are data consistency, API management complexity, and understanding the dependencies of the systems (Bushong et al., 2021). Companies are using Domain-Driven Design and the Saga Pattern (Fowler, 2020) to overcome these issues.

Middleware Integration

Middleware systems act as the glue that connects disparate applications and databases. Enterprise solutions are often made by different vendors. Incorporating these different technologies into a comprehensive solution is only achievable via middleware. This requires a thorough understanding of several types of middleware, their functions, and the challenges involved in using them within a complex enterprise environment. There are distinct types of middleware as it covers a broad range of technologies such as service-oriented architecture, microservices, and messaging protocols (Górski, 2022). Message Queues (MQ) are one of the key components here. MQ allows asynchronous communication between applications. In event-driven systems, MQs often act as the central systems and allow associated systems to be decoupled. Moreover, using this async messaging, near real-time use cases are unlocked. For example, in an e-commerce system, users can add many items and then pay for them. After that, the inventory should automatically update and should reflect the availability of an item correctly. Using an MQ here is essential to ensure each different component can work independently and handle the system load. IBM MQ, Kafka, and Rabbit MQ are some of the most used MQ solutions in enterprise settings. Enterprise Service Buses (ESB) is also a common middleware pattern. ESBs act as hubs and facilitate delivery of the messages by routing and transforming the format as required between applications. ESBs are particularly useful where some of the dependent components are legacy, and they cannot change the code and config to use more modern MQ-based solutions. Apache Camel and MuleSoft Anypoint Platform are some examples of ESB products.

Although middleware integration patterns are especially useful in enterprise scenarios- there are some challenges. Careful planning and execution are required because Integrating middleware into existing enterprise systems can be incredibly complex. Other key issues such as security, performance, and data consistency need to be closely monitored as well. Nowadays with many out-of-the-box solutions- most of these challenges can be mitigated provided that the best practices are followed. Detailed assessment, testing, and monitoring can also help with successful rollout.

Data Workflow Strategies

As the focus of this chapter is architecting scalable solutions using ChatGPT, in this section we will focus on the optimal data workflow strategies involving ChatGPT and enterprise data. Data workflow is a major component of any scalable solutions. Data sharding is a common technique to ensure the system can handle the data growth without significant rewriting. Caching is also frequently used to improve system performance and reliability. Also, since database calls are expensive, caching saves in cost as well. In the case of ChatGPT, it possesses broad general knowledge but lacks specific details about enterprise use cases. Large language models like ChatGPT are typically trained on vast amounts of internet data, but most enterprise data is private and not accessible for training. While there are numerous ways to address this challenge, we will focus on two of the most common solutions. RAG, or Retrieval-Augmented Generation, is a technique where the user's query can be enriched by associating it with an internal or external source of truth (Lewis et al., 2020). These knowledge bases can be private enterprise wiki, API docs, code, or any specific data source that is not available to ChatGPT. As part of the data workflow strategy, these sources need to be stored efficiently. A RAG pipeline is often used to achieve that. In this pipeline, first, the data will be indexed and stored in a vector database. Using this as an auxiliary service, an enterprise solution can provide more context to ChatGPT. This technique is called grounding which reduces chances of hallucination. One of the most important aspects of any enterprise solution is data security. As a third-party API provider, using ChatGPT for any enterprise solution should be carefully evaluated. Legal contracts, periodic audits, and strict guidelines to remove data after certain days are essential for a solid data strategy framework. We will explore more on this topic in the Enterprise Data Security and Compliance section.

OPTIMIZING PERFORMANCE

The out-of-the-box solution from ChatGPT is sufficient in some common use cases such as basic knowledge extraction or summarization. However, for complex enterprise solutions, it may not be enough. On the other hand, performance optimization can lead to faster token generation which saves time in business processes and thus reduces cost. Moreover, other optimization techniques such as model fine-tuning, quantization, and distillation can also be cost-efficient in some scenarios. OpenAI provides fine-tuning and distillation options as part of the platform offerings (https://platform.openai.com).

Prompt Optimization

Prompt engineering is one of the quickest options to optimize the performance of ChatGPT enterprise solutions. Compared to the fine-tuning or distillation process, this process does not need an extensively curated dataset. Users can use the following techniques to optimize the prompt. First- a clear and concise prompt helps ChatGPT provide better results. For example- to get details about all inventory systems in an enterprise, a better prompt would be: "Please provide a detailed overview of inventory systems being used for cataloging software." Providing examples in the prompt also results in better output. One other common technique is to provide a chain of thought in the prompt itself. In this way, the model can break down the problem into logical steps and provide better results than naive prompting. OpenAI provides guidelines and best practices for prompt engineering as well. Here are a few additional strategies for optimizing prompt engineering according to OpenAI - use simpler subtasks in the prompt, provide reference text, give the model an explicit instruction to "think" so that it can take some time to answer, etc. More details can be found on the OpenAI website (https://platform.openai.com/docs/guides/prompt-engineering).

Model Fine-Tuning

Large language models lack private enterprise data and relevant enterprise context. As a result, prompt engineering is not always a suitable solution in an enterprise setting. Fine-tuning on the other hand, fine tuning can be a key component here that can provide higher quality results. It can provide more accurate results, and savings on tokens due to optimized prompt size and better latency. Fine-tuning involves creating high-quality training data, uploading those data to the ChatGPT platform, training a model using those data, and then finally verifying if the results are accurate. As of January 2025, fine-tuning is available for gpt-4o, gpt-4o-mini, gpt-4, and gpt-3.5-turbo models(https:platform.openai.com/docs/guides/fine-tuning). Fine-tuning is best suitable for use in cases where the system requires consistent output for downstream tasks or a system where the required tasks are hard to explain via prompt. For example- a comprehensive product review summary system might have many components. ChatGPT as a part of that system is providing the review summarization service. Other downstream tasks rely on that result as input and expect it to be of a certain format. In those cases, fine-tuning the ChatGPT model to adhere to that schema is beneficial. Fine tuning can also reduce costs. Enterprise teams can evaluate if fine-tuning a chapter model can result in similar output compared to a more expensive model. As per OpenAI guidance, if a use case provides satisfactory results with GPT-4o, it can often be replicated using GPT-4o-mini with finetuning. Fine-tuning can make the model more optimized. However, we should always carefully consider the fine-tuning approach. Since prompting is free and does not need high-quality data as input, it is better to experiment with prompt engineering before investing in fine-tuning. A combination of robust prompt engineering along with fine-tuning results in the best outcome (Tariq, 2025).

Model Distillation

A common technique to improve the performance of smaller models is to train them by using the output from larger models. This is known as model distillation or knowledge distillation. This process can also be explained as an extension of fine tuning. In the case of fine-tuning, expert humans create the supervised datasets that are used to train the model. In the case of distillation, instead of human experts, another expert (i.e., teacher) model provides the data. Distillation can reduce cost and increase speed as smaller models are generally efficient in token generation. The high-level steps for this technique are given below:

- Use a high-quality model (e.g.- GPT-4o) and then save the output from this model

- Use a common set of queries and evaluate output from both small and large models to establish a baseline
- Select the output from step 1 and fine-tune the smaller models
- repeat the process and evaluate the result by comparing the output from the teacher model

For some subsets of tasks, a smaller distilled model can provide similar performance to a larger model but with better cost and latency. Some examples of those tasks are subsite and histology classification (De Angeli et al., 2022) and human action recognition (Camarena et al., 2024). Model distillation is a great technique for model optimization, but it can only produce comparable results when there is enough diverse training data available. In addition, the quality of the output from the teacher model is particularly important. And finally, continuous evaluation is needed by expert graders to make sure the distilled models are improving. Distillation is becoming an extremely popular technique as it can be a valuable tool in enterprise solutions if we keep the above points in mind.

ENTERPRISE DATA SECURITY AND COMPLIANCE

Data is the most important aspect of an enterprise system. Every enterprise has proprietary data, and it must be safeguarded with utmost priority. As a third-party solution, ChatGPT needs extra scrutiny and security measures. An enterprise must remain compliant and follow all relevant laws and regulations pertaining to data sharing and privacy. An established process is required to ensure a scalable, secure, and compliant system can be architected.

Data Security

The general enterprise data security pattern consists of a data loss prevention policy, robust access control, regular risk assessments via internal and external audits, and a multi-layered data backup policy. This pattern needs to be augmented to capture the unique nature of ChatGPT solutions. As using prompts is one of the common patterns used in ChatGPT to extract data and interact with the systems, a process needs to be established to handle prompt injection and data poisoning (Liu et al., 2024). Moreover, since a model often relies on getting additional data to be trained, a vetted process needs to be established for a data retention strategy. A legally binding contract is needed to ensure ChatGPT cannot be trained on user or enterprise data. If for compliance reasons, the data needs to be stored in a 3rd party ChatGPT server, it should be stored in an encrypted manner and can be accessed only for valid reasons (legal, law enforcement, etc.) and never for training. Additional security measures are needed for handling Personally Identifiable Information (PII). Masking of PII is essential for compliance and privacy reasons. Data Anonymization, RegEx-based, or PII detector Natural language library (such as Microsoft's Presidio analyzer) can be used to mask the PII data. Lastly, the output from ChatGPT needs to be sanitized as well. A common solution for that is to use a sanitization service instead of sending raw ChatGPT output to end users. Below enterprise data security checklist below can be used as a guide when architecting ChatGPT solutions.

- Data Loss Prevention Policy
- Least-Privilege and Role-based Access Control
- Internal and External Audits for Data Risk
- Multi-layered (on and offsite) Data backup policy
- Guardrail for Prompt injection and Data Poisoning
- Legal contracts for opt-out Retention and Training from enterprise data
- Input sanitization for PII and other sensitive data
- Alignment of the Data output

Compliance

Adherence to various regulation and compliance frameworks is essential when architecting an enterprise software system. Some of the common entities related to regulation and compliance are the General Data Protection Regulation (GDPR), the California Consumer Privacy Act (CCPA), the Health Insurance Portability and Accountability Act (HIPAA), Payment Card Industry Data Security Standard (PCI DSS). The most challenging aspect in this case is due to the non-deterministic nature of ChatGPT output. A compliant system relies on consistent output and solid reasoning for any decision that can significantly affect an end user. For example- using ChatGPT for health care claim submission is challenging as the decision often lacks reasoning. However, an enterprise system can be built where ChatGPT service can provide a summary of various laws and regulations with valid citations and then another Human-in-the-loop (HITL) system can make the final decision and provide the reasoning so that it can remain compliant. OpenAI also provides a comprehensive guideline for safety best practices which can be found in https://platform.openai.com/docs/guides/safety-best-practices. Some of the best practices mentioned there are using a moderation API, keeping humans in the loop, allowing users to report issues, and using end users' IDs to keep track of malicious actors. These best practices along with the enterprise data security checklist given in this section can provide a robust data security architecture.

DEVOPS PATTERN IN ENTERPRISE CHATGPT SOLUTIONS

For the successful implementation of a large-scale enterprise solution, following a DevOps methodology is necessary. DevOps processes like Continuous Integration and Deployment (CI/CD), store all code and config in the source code repository, using Infrastructure-as-code (IaC) tool (example: Terraform/Pulumi/OpenTofu, etc.) can help with repeatable and secure end-to-end software and infrastructure pipeline. Adding ChatGPT in the mix, however, needs some more steps. Compared to traditional enterprise solutions, large language-based (LLM) systems may not always provide deterministic results. Moreover, since the underlying model can change, the quality of the output may change as well. For example- the same prompt with the same input may provide different results if a model version changes (e.g.- From gpt-4o-2024-05-13 to gpt-4o-2024-08-06). In this section, we will expand on some additional DevOps approaches that should help implement a successful enterprise solution.

Shift-Left Approach

Instead of performing unit tests, integration tests, and security validation at the end of the software development lifecycle, the shift-left approach provides a framework to complete these tasks at the start and make them repeatable. Automated testing should be triggered after each code merge. If any upstream or downstream systems are not ready, a mock service should be used to ensure compatibility without compromising velocity. Similarly, penetration testing and defensive code testing should be part of automation as well. The software supply chain should be secured as well. With the shift-left approach, each dependency (such as a library software development kit or SDKs) should be tested before they are allowed to be used. Dependency checker tools such as Renovate and Snyk can help with these tasks. The code analyzer tools such as SonarQube can be triggered periodically to ensure code hygiene is maintained and no duplicate code is used. In an ideal scenario, all these tasks are automated and hence this should not slow down the development lifecycle. For ChatGPT component testing, the development team should have a robust set of prompts and various fallback mechanisms. For example, there should be a prompt library which should be versioned just like code and tested periodically to ensure the output is consistent across different models. The team should also use a structured output format where the output adheres to a predefined schema. This approach helps with the reproducibility of a response from ChatGPT models. Using OpenAI API, this can be achieved by passing a "strict" parameter as True in the "response format" section of the output structure.

Continuous Learning and Improvement

In any Machine Learning application, a feedback mechanism is a key part of ensuring that the system can be improved continuously. A model is trained with some data but when it is used in production, new input data will not always be the same. To implement a feedback mechanism, there are some key systems required. First, a model registry is required where all base and fine-tuned models can be stored. OpenAI provides a platform API to fine-tune and store the models which can be leveraged as an off-the-shelf solution. However, a wrapper on top of that can be beneficial in enterprise use cases where each organization can restrict access and guidelines for model access. This solution will help with model reuse and security. Second, a data lake should be used for storing various enterprise use-case data. The curated dataset from this component then can be used to further train the model. Third, a robust evaluation framework is required where the result of existing prompts can be stored. Both automated evaluation and human evaluation should be performed using this system. Any deviation or change in result should trigger additional alerting and expert review should be done to make sure there is no regression. If any system inside the full enterprise solution has any change in its data structure or the fundamental properties (e.g.: “Expiry” columns used to store the date of service disconnect date but now the column stores the date of service deletion) - rigorous testing should be kicked off as well.

LLM Observability

A complex system such as a large-scale enterprise solution needs to emit relevant metrics so that the health and performance of the system can be measured and monitored. In the context of a Large Language model (LLM), along with traditional metrics such as response time, throughput, latency, and error rates, we need to measure some key elements relevant to the model as well. Model accuracy can be measured using a combination of the model's ability to follow the instructions and how complete the response is. Hallucination (Ji et al., 2022) is one of the unique characteristics of LLM systems and should be measured as well to ensure the safeguarding of the reputational loss of an enterprise. Using citation features and human-in-the-loop (HITL) can be used here to mitigate some of the adverse effects of hallucination. Toxicity and Bias should be measured as well to ensure the ChatGPT solutions can be used in a live production system (Tariq, 2025). A smaller model can be used here to first check the input query flag for toxicity and bias and provide a response back to the user even before reaching ChatGPT. Similarly, the response from the ChatGPT component can again be reviewed by the smaller model to ensure no harmful content is provided. For diagnosing the issues, logging and tracing are also needed. Since the response may not always be the same even for the same input, tracing and storing the response safely (no PII data, ensure customer agrees to store response data or part of it, etc.) for analysis is required. Here open telemetry-based solutions such as using tag, and span to highlight relevant logs, and measure input and output token count are helpful. These metrics can help with troubleshooting and provide relevant context so that a human can debug the issue. The most important aspect of observability in the ChatGPT-powered enterprise systems is to establish key performance indicators (KPIs). KPI will be different depending on the business goal and outcome. Hence, before implementing any solutions, the stakeholders should identify the KPIs first. Once that has been done, above mentioned metrics can be used in conjunction with specialized LLM observability tools. Enterprise architects should independently validate such tools depending on their business policy and existing contracts.

CASE STUDIES

In this section, we will discuss two enterprise case studies. Both are well suited for understanding how enterprise solutions are built and how a scalable architecture integrating ChatGPT can be achieved.

Insurance Purchase Through AI Chatbot Agent

XYZ Insurance Inc. aims to build a generational AI-based interactive chatbot that uses LLM models to analyze input from users and convert it into insurance data points (Figure 3). The data points can be utilized to identify the details of a user request and respond accordingly. The application will require the use of multiple LLM models to be able to complete the fulfillment process. The design of the application is diagrammatically represented below along with an explanation of the function of the components:

Figure 3. Architecture diagram for ChatGPT-powered Insurance System

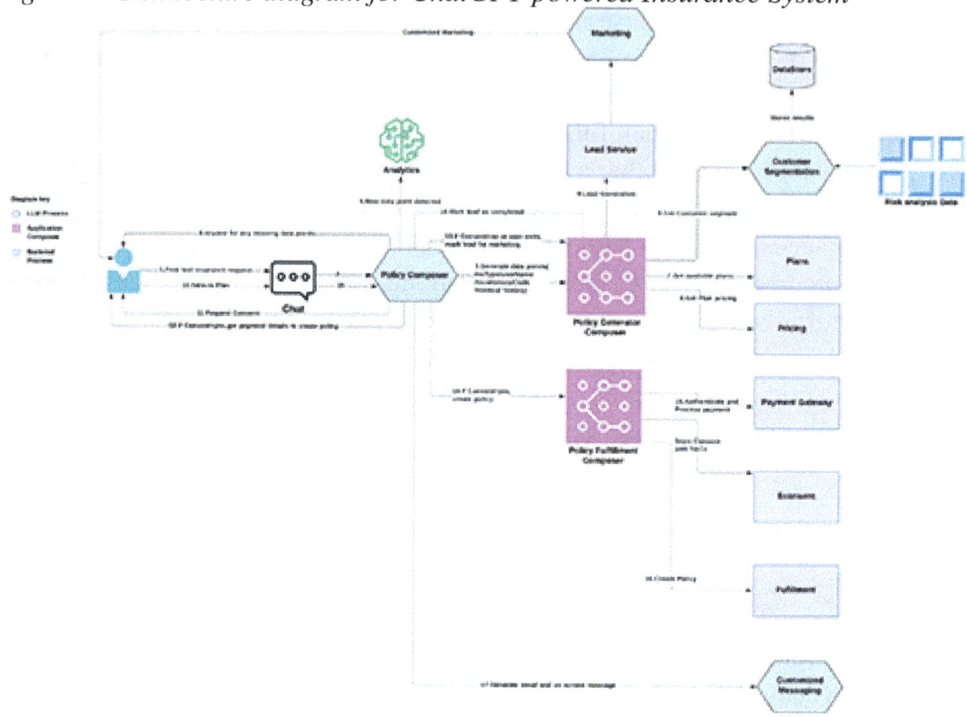

Policy Composer with Chat Interface

This is an LLM model capable of free text analysis and extracting insights. To be able to successfully provide meaningful responses to user queries the LLM should be enhanced with Retrieval Augmented Generation. The RAG model will allow us to train the LLM on large chunks of general insurance information, company-specific policy documentation FAQs, etc. This model also has access to a data store of insurance data points which will allow it to extract insurance fulfillment information like name, age, address, DOB, medical history, etc. If the model detects any data point from user input that is not a part of its current repository it will share it with the Analytics platform for review. OpenAI's ChatGPT or Google Gemini Pro are prime examples of available natural language text analysis LLMs.

Analytics

A platform that can tap into existing customer policy details from data warehouses to generate the data points required for insurance fulfillment and feed it back to the policy composer LLM.

Marketing

An LLM model capable of using the data from generated leads and creating personalized content for up-funnel campaigns. It can also help tailor the marketing strategies to ensure maximum engagement. In addition, it should be trained in federal and state-level privacy laws to avoid any privacy breaches.

Customer Segmentation LLM

This LLM uses available medical research and insurance plan optimization data to generate customer segments. This segmentation will help in the process of customizing plans and pricing for the user in context. The model will be capable of generating 2 types of segments based on customers' personal information and financial history.

Personalized Messaging and Recommendations LLM

This model will generate a personalized message to customers upon request fulfillment and give provider recommendations based on location, preference, and provider ratings.

Application services

1. **Orchestration layer:** Policy Generator and Policy Fulfillment form an application orchestration layer that connects the front end LLM to backend application services. These services serve the function of collating the responses from application services
2. **Backend Application services:** The application has several microservices that perform the tasks required to complete the business function. Plans service will take the user data and retrieve the customer segment. The segment information is then used to calculate plan coverage and pricing. Lead service is responsible for retrieving any available active leads for the user or creating a new one when requested by the policy composer. Payment Gateway is responsible for validating and authorizing the payment method. It must be capable of supporting various

payment methods like credit/debit cards, DDA accounts, Wallets, and online payment platforms like PayPal. It also needs to have the capability to support installment options.

The Consent service needs to capture the consent decision of the customer along with the terms and conditions that were accepted. This is required to provide post-purchase support to customers. The final service in the system will be the fulfillment service that creates the plan against the user in the XYZ insurance system and generates the final policy documents.

Infrastructure

The application can be served on any public cloud service like AWS or Azure, an on-prem distributed system, or a hybrid system based on the data privacy requirements of the micro app. Since OpenAI operations are hosted on Azure, it makes Azure the best option for seamlessly running inference for ChatGPT.

Key Performance Metrics

Transaction Per Second (TPS): This is the total number of requests being submitted to the LLM per second across all users. The supported TPS capacity depends on the available network bandwidth and latency between backend systems.

Latency: This is calculated as the time between the first user query submitted and the first LLM response to them. In the case of a full-flow fulfillment system, the latency for initial inquiry queries should be calculated separately from the subsequent fulfillment request. This is because of the number of backend systems involved in the plan option generation and fulfillment process.

Memory Requirements: LLMs require huge memory to seamlessly infer and serve the response to a user query. This makes the usage of a High-end GPU for LLM non-negotiable.

Scalability: Building the LLM on a cloud provider like AWS or Azure ensures that it can scale up to support rising traffic and scale down during low traffic hours to save costs.

Cost: The cost of running an LLM-based application is dependent on the servers being used and the number of nodes. Though the above metrics can be improved by using servers with large capacity and superior hardware, analysis must be performed to find a balance between cost and performance.

For example, let us assume at peak usage, there are 100 active users in the system each submitting 2 requests per second. This puts the TPS of the system at 200. XYZ insurance could impose a threshold of 50 ms to respond to every user query and 100 ms to fulfill insurance purchase requests.

The LLM supports up to 5 million parameters. Memory required to support this number of parameters can be calculated as (Number of parameters) * (bytes per param) /1024. Memory required = (5 million parameters) * (2 bytes/parameter) / 1024 = 9.76 GB.

Diving further we need to account for the batch size and any additional overhead. Thus, Final memory requirements = (Number of parameters) * (bytes per param) * Batch size * Overhead.

It is important to note that the hardware being used to serve the LLM plays a key role in determining the batch size and supported overhead.

Enterprise Support Chatbot

LLM models can be used to develop powerful and intuitive chatbots that can analyze internal and external datasets to present the user with concise and pertinent responses. The models available today are customizable to support various functions, user groups, and business organizations. They can be scaled and fine-tuned if necessary. In this paper, we will analyze the design of an enterprise chatbot that provides the employees of an IT company with support with day-to-day issues and queries (Figure 4). Traditional chatbots were built on static rule-based interpretation of user queries delivering predetermined responses based on keywords. These applications use pattern recognition to match the keywords in user queries to relevant responses in their dataset. Conventional chatbots are often menu-driven and able to perform only a limited number of functionalities like checking order status or providing flight information. These chatbots are severely restricted in their capability to understand user input and rely on prompting the user to use a set terminology to ask their queries.

Infrastructure Requirements

The chat application requires various components to function as expected and they can be grouped as below:

Frontend: The application will require a Chat UI to accept user inputs and a Prompt Optimizer to process and optimize the query using a natural language process.

Backend: For backend processing, the application will need to provision an LLM API to which the optimized query can be fed. This API will coordinate the communication between the services below and send the query results back to the UI:

- Cache to store or retrieve frequently accessed query results.
- Data filter that ensures that the LLM is not processing any unauthorized data like personally identifiable data or payment information.
- Content filter that will ensure that the query results do not contain any offensive or harmful information.
- Repetition filter to ensure that there is no duplicity in the query results.
- Embeddings Model that queries the Vector DB and retrieves the datasets relevant to preparing the result set for query in context.

Figure 4. Architecture diagram for Enterprise Chatbot

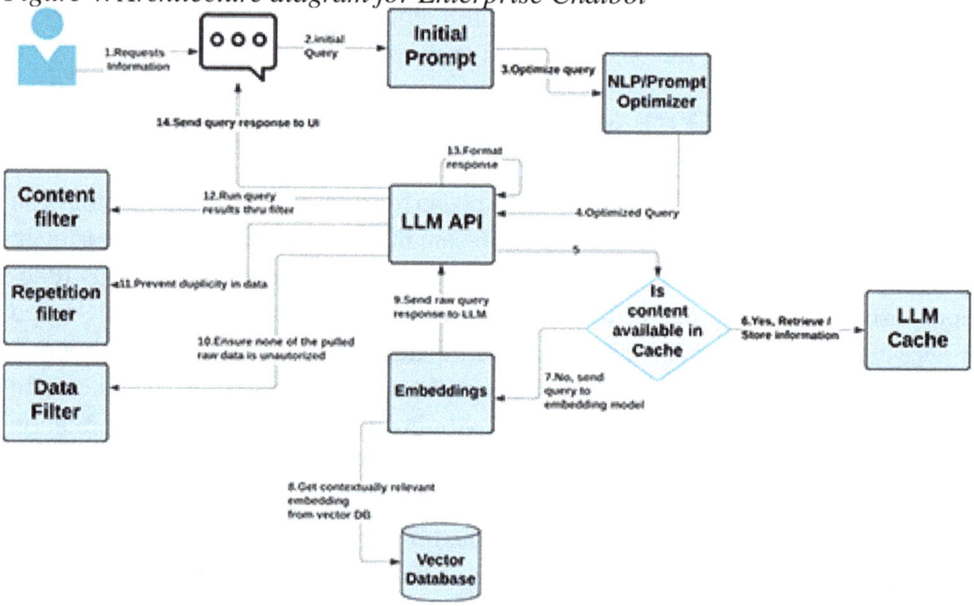

OpenAI's ChatGPT can provide the platform for building the chatbot with access to extensive LLM models. We should look at using Retrieval Augmented Generation using tools (e.g.: LangChain, LangGraph) to ensure that only relevant chunks of data are returned. This technique can also help us implement the required filters described above. OpenAI also provides 2 powerful version-3 embedding models (text-embedding-3-small and text-embedding-3-large) which can be used to optimize the search.

Key Performance Metrics

Transaction Per Second (TPS): This is the total number of requests submitted to the ChatGPT per second for all user's queries. The supported TPS capacity depends on the available TPM (transaction per minute) limit in OpenAI and various backend systems that will provide the supporting services.

Latency: This is calculated as the time between the first user query submitted and the first LLM response to them. In the case of an enterprise chatbot, the latency should be calculated as the time taken to understand the user query and detect the intent.

Memory Requirements: LLMs require substantial GPU memory to seamlessly infer and serve the response to a user query. However, since we are planning to use ChatGPT in this case, the overall graphical processing memory (GPU) should be lower. In case we need to run embedding models, then most of them can be run in consumer hardware with 8 to 16GB of GPU memory.

Scalability: Building the LLM on a cloud provider ensures that it can scale up. Also, there should be some backup plan for ChatGPT downtime. ChatGPT subscription to multiple regions is essential. The Enterprise team should check any provider that supports OpenAI services in different regions and use them.

Cost: The cost of running an LLM-based application is dependent on the backend servers being used and the number of embedding model servers. Backend systems can be repurposed if those are already being used hence, we can ignore those costs from this calculation.

FUTURE TRENDS

According to Reuters (2024), ChatGPT weekly users have grown to 200 million and are growing rapidly. Enterprise solutions using ChatGPT can use this huge growth and familiarity of ChatGPT to their advantage. More customers will demand this kind of publicly available functionality in their enterprise software. Getting ahead of the demand is essential for an enterprise to stay competitive. Moreover, research and investment in LLM and Generative AI are exponentially growing. Advanced models with multimodal capabilities such as GPT-4o and GPT-4o-mini are already available for enterprise use. Enterprises should capitalize on this and expand beyond text-only systems. For example- voice, image, and video-based enterprise systems can delight customers and enhance productivity. Voice agents can be helpful for massive-scale personalization and can be used in various sectors such as Sales and Marketing.

On the other hand, many frontier labs provide access to reasoning models. In contrast to GPT-like models, reasoning models provide a chain of thought. This is crucial for adapting ChatGPT-enabled solutions in some of the privacy-first enterprise solutions. For example, in the case of a medical claim, it is essential to provide the reasoning for the outcome. Simply providing an answer is not enough. Reasoning models can provide citations, step by step chain of thought, and explain the reason for the response. Along with an expert human, this enhanced system can cut down the time for adjudication. Some of the reasoning models that are available now are OpenAI o1, o1-mini, and o3-mini. These models can be used in ChatGPT solutions to enhance the capabilities of enterprise systems beyond traditional non-reasoning use cases. Although ChatGPT and relevant technologies experienced explosive growth recently, challenges such as hallucination, privacy, and security remain a concern. Rapid encryption of the data and multiple layers of guardrail systems that can be integrated seamlessly with ChatGPT is one of the key trends that is being explored by multiple vendors - both large-scale and startups are producing various solutions. For example- AWS bedrock now provides guardrail as a service to safeguard LLMs. As the adoption grows, the demand for privacy and security will grow even higher. Enterprises should have a plan for that and pivot to those solutions as fast as possible to maintain their edge.

CONCLUSION

Enterprise solutions are inherently complex. These systems need to balance traditional approaches to maintain trust with customers and cutting-edge technology to enhance the usefulness of the system. ChatGPT is a disruptive technology that not only changes the course of the Business-to-customer system(B2C), but it is also changing business-to-business (B2B) systems as well. This is different from other disruptive technologies such as Cloud computing. For example, even with the rapid growth of the cloud, many enterprises still host their services in traditional self-hosted data centers. However, as the OpenAI API is a third-party hosted offering, the barrier to entry for adapting ChatGPT solutions is lowered. Enterprises are also getting comfortable with harnessing the power of this technology provided they have robust data security practices in place.

In this chapter, we have explored the main pillars of scalable architectures and how ChatGPT can be used in the context of enterprise systems. We have provided details about how different sectors are using this technology or how they can use it soon. Since using LLMs is different from using standard services where the responses are deterministic, we have provided special consideration where we discussed how utilizing distributed systems along with microservice and middleware integration along with a streamlined data workflow strategy is necessary for successful implementation. Managing cost and speed is also paramount for the long-term success of any enterprise system. To that end, we have discussed how to utilize state-of-the-art model optimization techniques such as using prompt optimization, fine-tuning to align and expand the model beyond its basic capability, and distillation to reduce the latency and cost by enhancing a smaller model to perform similarly to a larger model. As highlighted in the chapter many times, we have stressed again the significance of data security. We have explained and provided a checklist for enterprises to ensure the data security framework is robust for ChatGPT solutions. Compliance is also a key factor for enterprise systems, and we have highlighted how the solutions should be architected to ensure ongoing compliance. We have also compared how DevOps patterns can be used in this new paradigm. Efficient DevOps practices are essential for the continued growth of any enterprise systems, both traditional and ChatGPT powered solutions. We have specifically provided details about how these practices should be augmented such as using the shift-left approach, continuous learning for the model, and LLM observability. We have provided two case studies so that the practitioner can use them as a blueprint and apply the learnings in their next GenAI-powered systems. Finally, future trends are discussed so that businesses should be aware of how to stay ahead in this rapidly changing landscape.

The evidence for using ChatGPT in enterprise solutions is clear. This disruptive technology is here and using it in a safe and scalable manner is essential. If used correctly, businesses and customers can both gain immense productivity. However, customer trust is also one of the key currencies for enterprise, and rushing a solution without understanding the limitations of ChatGPT can result in catastrophic financial and reputational loss. In this chapter, we have provided a detailed analysis of how an enterprise can build ChatGPT-powered solutions in a safe and scalable manner. Using the best practices and techniques mentioned in this chapter and along with understanding the key performance indicators, enterprises should be able to build the solutions for their use cases.

REFERENCES

Bing, Y. (2023). *Application and research of ChatGPT in accounting technology*. Atlantis Press., DOI: 10.2991/978-94-6463-262-0_48

Bushong, V., Abdelfattah, A. S., Maruf, A. A., Das, D., Lehman, A., Jaroszewski, E., Coffey, M., Cerný, T., Frajták, K., Tisnovsky, P., & Bures, M. (2021). On microservice analysis and architecture evolution: A systematic mapping study. *Applied Sciences (Basel, Switzerland)*, *11*(17), 7856. DOI: 10.3390/app11177856

Camarena, F., Gonzalez-Mendoza, M., & Chang, L. (2024). Knowledge distillation in video-based Human Action Recognition: An intuitive approach to efficient and flexible model training. *Journal of Imaging*, *10*(4), 85. DOI: 10.3390/jimaging10040085 PMID: 38667983

Celik, B., & Vanschoren, J. (2021). Adaptation Strategies for Automated Machine Learning on Evolving Data. *IEEE Transactions on Pattern Analysis and Machine Intelligence*, *43*(9), 3067–3078. DOI: 10.1109/TPAMI.2021.3062900 PMID: 33651683

Chui, M., Roberts, R., & Yee, L. (2022, December 20). *Generative AI is here: How tools like CHATGPT could change your business*. McKinsey & Company. https://www.mckinsey.com/capabilities/quantumblack/our-insights/generative-ai-is-here-how-tools-like-chatgpt-could-change-your-business

Cui, L. (2023). Exploring growth strategies of European small and medium-sized enterprises in the service sector using chatgpt. *European Integration Studies*, *1*(17), 175–198. DOI: 10.5755/j01.eis.1.17.33726

De Angeli, K., Gao, S., Blanchard, A., Durbin, E. B., Wu, X.-C., Stroup, A., Doherty, J., Schwartz, S. M., Wiggins, C., Coyle, L., Penberthy, L., Tourassi, G., & Yoon, H.-J. (2022). Using ensembles and distillation to optimize the deployment of deep learning models for the classification of Electronic Cancer Pathology reports. *JAMIA Open*, *5*(3), ooac075. Advance online publication. DOI: 10.1093/jamiaopen/ooac075 PMID: 36110150

De Mauro, A., Sestino, A., & Bacconi, A. (2022). Machine learning and artificial intelligence use in marketing: A general taxonomy. *Italian Journal of Marketing*, *2022*(4), 439–457. DOI: 10.1007/s43039-022-00057-w

Fowler, M. (2020, April 22). *Bliki: Domain driven design*. martinfowler.com. https://martinfowler.com/bliki/DomainDrivenDesign.html

Gao, L. (2023). The impact of ChatGPT on enterprise competitive intelligence systems. *Information Systems and Economics*, *4*(4), 62–69. DOI: 10.23977/infse.2023.040909

Gong, T., Lyu, C., Zhang, S., Wang, Y., Zheng, M., Zhao, Q., Liu, K., Zhang, W., Luo, P., & Chen, K. (2023, June 13). *Multimodal-GPT: A vision and language model for dialogue with humans*. arXiv.org. https://arxiv.org/abs/2305.04790

Górski, T. (2022). UML profile for messaging patterns in service-oriented architecture, microservices, and internet of things. *Applied Sciences (Basel, Switzerland)*, *12*(24), 12790. DOI: 10.3390/app122412790

Janamala, V., Ram, I. S., & Daram, S. B. (2023). Realization of green 5G cellular network role in medical applications: Use of CHATGPT-ai. *Annals of Biomedical Engineering*, *51*(11), 2337–2339. DOI: 10.1007/s10439-023-03257-3 PMID: 37261590

Ji, Z., Lee, N., Frieske, R., Yu, T., Su, D., Xu, Y., Ishii, E., Bang, Y. J., Madotto, A., & Fung, P. (2023). Survey of hallucination in natural language generation. *ACM Computing Surveys*, *55*(12), 1–38. DOI: 10.1145/3571730

Krstic, D., Petrovic, N., Suljovic, S., & Al-Azzoni, I. (2023). AI-Enabled Framework for mobile network experimentation leveraging chatgpt: Case study of channel capacity calculation for η-μ fading and co-channel interference. *Electronics (Basel)*, *12*(19), 4088. DOI: 10.3390/electronics12194088

Lee, I., & Shin, Y. J. (2020). Machine learning for enterprises: Applications, algorithm selection, and challenges. *Business Horizons*, *63*(2), 157–170. DOI: 10.1016/j.bushor.2019.10.005

Lewis, P., Perez, E., Piktus, A., Petroni, F., Karpukhin, V., Goyal, N., Küttler, H., Lewis, M., Yih, W., Rocktäschel, T., Riedel, S., & Kiela, D. (2021, April 12). *Retrieval-augmented generation for knowledge-intensive NLP tasks*. arXiv.org. https://arxiv.org/abs/2005.11401

Liu, Y., Deng, G., Xu, Z., Li, Y., Zheng, Y., Zhang, Y., Zhao, L., Zhang, T., & Wang, K. (2024). A hitchhiker's guide to jailbreaking CHATGPT via prompt engineering. *Proceedings of the 4th International Workshop on Software Engineering and AI for Data Quality in Cyber-Physical Systems/Internet of Things*, 12–21. DOI: 10.1145/3663530.3665021

Mariani, M. M., Machado, I., & Nambisan, S. (2023). Types of innovation and Artificial Intelligence: A systematic quantitative literature review and research agenda. *Journal of Business Research*, *155*, 113364. DOI: 10.1016/j.jbusres.2022.113364

McCarthy, J., Minsky, M. L., Rochester, N., & Shannon, C. E. (1955). A proposal for the Dartmouth summer research project on artificial intelligence, August 31, 1955. *AI Magazine*, *27*(4), 12. DOI: 10.1609/aimag.v27i4.1904

Orzoł, M., & Szopik-Depczyńska, K. (2023). ChatGPT as an innovative tool for increasing sales in online stores. *Procedia Computer Science, 225*, 3450–3459. DOI: 10.1016/j.procs.2023.10.340

Radford, A., Wu, J., Child, R., Luan, D., Amodei, D., & Sutskever, I. (2019). Language Models are Unsupervised Multitask Learners. https://github.com/openai/gpt-2

Raj, R., Singh, A., Kumar, V., & Verma, P. (2023). Analyzing the potential benefits and use cases of chatgpt as a tool for improving the efficiency and effectiveness of business operations. *BenchCouncil Transactions on Benchmarks. Standards and Evaluations, 3*(3), 100140. DOI: 10.1016/j.tbench.2023.100140

Reuters. (2024, August 29). OpenAI says ChatGPT's weekly users have grown to 200 million. Reuters. https://www.reuters.com/technology/artificial-intelligence/openai-says-chatgpts-weekly-users-have-grown-200-million-2024-08-29

Söylemez, M., Tekinerdogan, B., & Kolukısa Tarhan, A. (2022). Challenges and solution directions of microservice architectures: A systematic literature review. *Applied Sciences (Basel, Switzerland), 12*(11), 5507. DOI: 10.3390/app12115507

Sudirjo, F., Diantoro, K., Al-Gasawneh, J. A., Azzaakiyyah, H. K., & Ausat, A. M. A. (2023). Application of ChatGPT in improving customer sentiment analysis for businesses. *Jurnal Teknologi Dan Sistem Informasi Bisnis, 5*(3), 283–288. DOI: 10.47233/jteksis.v5i3.871

Surameery, N. M., & Shakor, M. Y. (2023). Use ChatGPT to solve programming bugs. *International Journal of Information Technology and Computer Engineering.*

Tariq, M. U. (2025). Innovative Business Models: Integrating Social, Economic, and Environmental Goals in Rural Manufacturing. In Prabhakar, A., Yu, P., & Erokhin, V. (Eds.), *Rural Social Entrepreneurship Development: Network-Based Manufacturing System Model* (pp. 147–174). IGI Global Scientific Publishing., DOI: 10.4018/979-8-3693-7515-0.ch005

Tariq, M. U. (2025). Revolutionizing Communication: EEG-Based Brain-Computer Interface for Speech and Mood Detection. In Prabhakar, A., Yu, P., & Erokhin, V. (Eds.), *Rural Social Entrepreneurship Development: Network-Based Manufacturing System Model* (pp. 237–264). IGI Global Scientific Publishing., DOI: 10.4018/979-8-3693-7515-0.ch008

Tariq, M. U. (2025). AI and Work-Life Balance: Transforming Employee Wellbeing in the Modern Workplace. In Ahmed, E., Babar, A., Samad, A., Ahmed, R., & Beydoun, G. (Eds.), *Strengthening Human Relations in Organizations With AI* (pp. 85–110). IGI Global Scientific Publishing., DOI: 10.4018/979-8-3693-6507-6.ch004

Tariq, M. U. (2025). AI and the Ethical Crossroads: Navigating Privacy, Personhood, and Autonomy in the Digital Age. In Chakraborty, S. (Ed.), *Human Values, Ethics, and Dignity in the Age of Artificial Intelligence* (pp. 49–72). IGI Global Scientific Publishing., DOI: 10.4018/979-8-3693-9035-1.ch003

Tariq, M. U. (2025). AI-Powered Business Process Automation: Revolutionizing Firm Management. In Derbali, A. (Ed.), *AI, Economic Perspectives, and Firm Business Management* (pp. 199–224). IGI Global Scientific Publishing., DOI: 10.4018/979-8-3693-7357-6.ch010

Troncoso, C., Isaakidis, M., Danezis, G., & Halpin, H. (2017). Systematizing decentralization and privacy: Lessons from 15 years of research and deployments. *Proceedings on Privacy Enhancing Technologies. Privacy Enhancing Technologies Symposium, 2017*(4), 404–426. DOI: 10.1515/popets-2017-0056

Vaswani, A., Shazeer, N., Parmar, N., Uszkoreit, J., Jones, L., Gomez, A. N., Kaiser, Ł., & Polosukhin, I. (2017). Attention is all you need. In *Proceedings of the 31st International Conference on Neural Information Processing Systems* (pp. 6000–6010). https://doi.org/DOI: 10.5555/3295222.3295349

Zhuang, X., & Wu, Y. (2024). ChatGPT: How it can support corporate social responsibility. *The Journal of Business Strategy*, *45*(6), 386–395. DOI: 10.1108/JBS-05-2023-0089

KEY TERMS AND DEFINITIONS

GPT: GPT is the short form of Generative Pre-trained Transformer. Transformer is a special type of machine learning model architecture that is mainly designed for machine translation and natural language processing tasks. This architecture was then modified for generating text resulting in the rise of GPT.

LLM: Large language models are defined as machine learning models that are trained in massive data (often internet-scale data) and can understand and provide answers in natural language. In general, from an end user's perspective, no special pre- or post-processing format is required for an LLM, unlike traditional machine learning models.

Scalable Architecture: A system is said to be scalable when it can handle increasing user load without significant re-architecting of the underlying components. A software or enterprise system architected in such a way is called a scalable system.

DevOps: DevOps or Development operations is a framework that breaks down the silo between development and support teams. As a result, it enables rapid software delivery, robust monitoring to detect issues, and quick remediation of any issue by using automated solutions.

Prompt Optimization: For large language models (LLMs) such as ChatGPT, input is often provided as natural language. This input is also known as prompt. Prompt optimization means enhancing these natural language inputs with extra context, examples, and relevant details so that LLMs can provide better answers.

Model Alignment: Since the responses from LLM are not always the same, there is always a possibility that it can generate a wrong, harmful, or an answer that is not aligned with the enterprise's value. Model alignment is a technique where the models are either fine-tuned or post-processed to ensure it aligned with their intended use in an enterprise context.

Chapter 8
The Evolution of Chatbots:
From Rule-Based to GPT Models

Aishwarya S
https://orcid.org/0009-0001-3731-2062
Sri Eshwar College of Engineering, India

Selvamurugan C
https://orcid.org/0000-0003-3447-1970
Dhaanish Ahmed Institute of Technology, India

Parthiban K G
Dhaanish Ahmed Institute of Technology, India

J Manoj Prabhakar
Dhaanish Ahmed Institute of Technology, India

J Tharik Raja
Dhaanish Ahmed Institute of Technology, India

Amrutha V J
CMS College of Engineering and Technology, India

ABSTRACT

The convergence of artificial intelligence and natural language processing has spurred a revolution in human-computer interaction, with chatbots emerging as a pivotal technology. From rudimentary rule-based systems like ELIZA to sophisticated generative models such as GPT-4, chatbots have undergone a dramatic evolution. This chapter explores this trajectory, dissecting the core architectures of retrieval-based, generative-based, and hybrid chatbots. We analyze the strengths and limitations of each approach, highlighting key advancements like Transformer networks and Retrieval-Augmented Generation (RAG). By tracing the evolution of chatbots, this chapter provides insights into the current state-of-the-art and future directions for conversational AI, a field poised to redefine how humans interact with machines.

DOI: 10.4018/979-8-3693-9841-8.ch008

INTRODUCTION

In the early days of the internet, finding information often meant relying on clunky search engines that returned a list of barely relevant links.Now, imagine instead being able to ask a question in plain English and receive a concise, helpful response in real-time. That is the promise of the modern chatbot, a technology that has evolved from simple keyword-matching programs to sophisticated AI-powered conversational agents. This chapter will guide you through that remarkable transformation, exploring how chatbots have moved from being a technological curiosity to an increasingly indispensable part of our digital lives. We will delve into the core architectures of retrieval-based, generative-based, and hybrid chatbots, illustrating their capabilities with examples ranging from early systems like ELIZA and A.L.I.C.E to innovative models such as ChatGPT and Google's Gemini. We will examine how each generation of chatbots has built upon its predecessors, overcoming limitations and pushing the boundaries of what is possible in human-computer interaction. By understanding this evolutionary journey, we can better appreciate the current state-of-the-art and the exciting possibilities that lie ahead for conversational AI.

CHATBOTS

Chatbots give us a fresh way to converse with computers. To get answers to our questions by a computer, we either use a search engine or fill out a form, whereas a chatbot allows us to simply ask questions in the same manner that we would ask a human, i.e., a chatbot is a program that mimics human conversation using Artificial Intelligence (AI). A chatbot is devised to be the ideal virtual assistant, helping one to complete different tasks such as answering questions, getting driving directions, turning up the thermostat in smart homes, to playing one's favourite tunes etc. Chatbots recently have gained a lot of popularity in the field of human-computer interaction. They are being used extensively in all sorts of applications like customer support, personal assistant, advising, sales, marketing etc. The technologies at the core of the rise of the chatbot are Machine Learning (ML) and Natural Language Processing (NLP). However, these chatbots lack one or more functionalities such as not being able to maintain a persona, unable to give personalized responses depending on the user or preventing faulty responses to unknown questions. (Aslam F, 2023).

The chatbots are categorized into three types based on their response generation mechanism (Sumit Pandey et al, 2023):

1. **Retrieval-Based Chatbots** – Select responses from a predefined database.

2. **Generative-Based Chatbots** – Generate responses dynamically using deep learning models.
3. **Hybrid Chatbots (Retrieval-Augmented Generation - RAG)** – Combine retrieval and generation to enhance accuracy and creativity.

Retrieval-Based Chatbots

Retrieval-based chatbots select responses from a predefined database using query processing, retrieval, and ranking. Early rule-based systems like ELIZA in 1966 and A.L.I.C.E in 1995 used pattern-matching and AIML, while later models incorporated statistical techniques like TF-IDF, LSA, and SVMs. Modern retrieval-based approaches leverage deep learning, such as dual-encoder models and BERT-based ranking, for improved accuracy. The chatbot preprocesses user queries, retrieves candidate responses using similarity-based techniques like cosine similarity, and ranks them using models like SBERT or ColBERT. While effective for FAQs and customer support, these chatbots struggle with open-ended conversations as they cannot generate novel responses. (Sumit Pandey et al., 2023)

Generative-Based Chatbots

Generative-based chatbots dynamically generate responses using deep learning models rather than relying on predefined replies. They use deep learning models like transformers to understand context and produce coherent, human-like responses. Early Seq2Seq models (Sutskever I et al., 2021) with RNNs and LSTMs, like Google's Neural Conversational Model (2015) and Facebook's HRED in 2016, improved conversational coherence but struggled with repetitive responses. The introduction of Transformer models in 2017 revolutionized generative chatbots, with GPT-2 in 2019 and GPT-3 in 2020 enabling more context-aware conversations. Modern models like ChatGPT, Claude, and Google Gemini (Team G et al., 2023) integrate instruction tuning, RLHF, and multimodal processing for enhanced performance. While excelling in open-domain chats, generative chatbots may produce hallucinations due to their probabilistic nature.

Hybrid Chatbots (Retrieval-Augmented Generation - RAG)

Hybrid chatbots blend retrieval-based and generative approaches to balance accuracy and creativity. A key advancement is Retrieval-Augmented Generation (RAG) (Lewis P et al., 2020), introduced by Facebook AI in 2020, enabling chatbots to retrieve real-time information from external sources for more reliable responses in knowledge-intensive domains like legal, medical, and academic fields. The workflow involves retrievalusing BM25, DPR, or FAISS-based vector search (Karpukhin V et al., 2020) (Nakano R et al., 2021) and generation, where a transformer model conditions response on retrieved data for factual accuracy. Recent developments, including OpenAI's WebGPT, Perplexity AI's search-augmented models, and Google's Gemini, have enhanced real-time retrieval capabilities, making hybrid models essential for enterprise AI applications.

EVOLUTION OF CHATBOTS

First Generation

- **Rule-based systems**: These chatbots use predefined rules to answer specific questions with fixed replies.
- **Pattern matching**: This involves matching incoming strings (customer text) with pre-defined patterns using regular expressions to classify the text into different blocks of resolution. This approach is suitable for narrow domains.
- **AIML (Artificial Intelligence Markup Language)**: AIML is used to create chatbots using pattern matching.
- **RiveScript**: RiveScript is a scripting language for creating chatbots, focusing on simplicity and ease of use for building conversational interfaces.

Second Generation

- **Statistical methods**: These methods employ techniques like NLP (Natural Language Processing) and NLU (Natural Language Understanding).
- **Hidden Markov Models (HMM)**: HMM is a statistical Markov model in which the system being modelled is assumed to be a Markov process with unobserved (hidden) states.
- **Support Vector Machines (SVM)**: SVM is a supervised machine learning model that can be used for classification and regression tasks.
- **Naive Bayes**: Naive Bayes is a probabilistic classifier based on applying Bayes' theorem with strong independence assumptions between the features.
- **Machine learning**: Machine learning algorithms such as SVM, decision trees, and random forests enable chatbots to learn and adapt from previous conversations.

Third Generation

- **Deep Learning**: This involves using neural networks to process input and understand intention in a broader context.
- **Recurrent Neural Networks (RNN)**: RNNs are a class of neural networks designed for processing sequential data, making them suitable for natural language tasks.
- **Long Short-Term Memory (LSTM)**: LSTMs are a type of RNN architecture capable of learning long-term dependencies, addressing the vanishing gradient problem in traditional RNNs.
- **Transformers**: Transformer networks rely on self-attention mechanisms to weigh the importance of various parts of the input sequence (Tariq M.U, 2025a).
- **BERT (Bidirectional Encoder Representations from Transformers)**: BERT is designed to pre-train deep bidirectional representations from unlabeled text by jointly conditioning on both left and right context in all layers.
- **GPT (Generative Pre-trained Transformer)**: GPT models use the transformer architecture to generate human-like text, excelling in various natural language tasks.
- **T5 (Text-to-Text Transfer Transformer)**: T5 frames all text-based language problems into a text-to-text format, using a transformer architecture to generate text from a given input text.

RULE-BASED CHATBOT

Rules are considered as one of the most natural ways to represent human knowledge. The origins of computer programs based on rules that were supposed to model human intelligence are related to the work of Newell and Simon on the early Logic Theorist system and the later General Problem Solver (GPS). This system aimed to mimic human problem-solving by breaking down complex problems into simpler sub-problems.

Rule-based systems are a foundational type of artificial intelligence that utilize predefined rules to make decisions and solve problems.

A rule-based system is an AI model that applies a set of human-defined rules to process data and derive conclusions. These rules are typically expressed in the form of "IF-THEN" statements, where the "IF" part specifies a condition and the "THEN" part outlines the action or conclusion that follows if the condition is met.

The rule-based systems are categorized into several types: Expert systems which mimic human expertise in specific domains (e.g. MYCIN), production systems, Decision Support Systems, Fuzzy logic systems, Frame based systems, hybrid systems, chatbots.

Rule-based chatbots operate by following a predetermined set of rules and criteria to interact with users, allowing them to provide specific responses based on recognized patterns in user input i.e., they are deterministic in nature, having a predictable and rigid responses. They cannot handle new scenarios, can only handle /respond effectively to the specific scenarios and questions they have been programmed for.

Figure 1. Rule based system structure

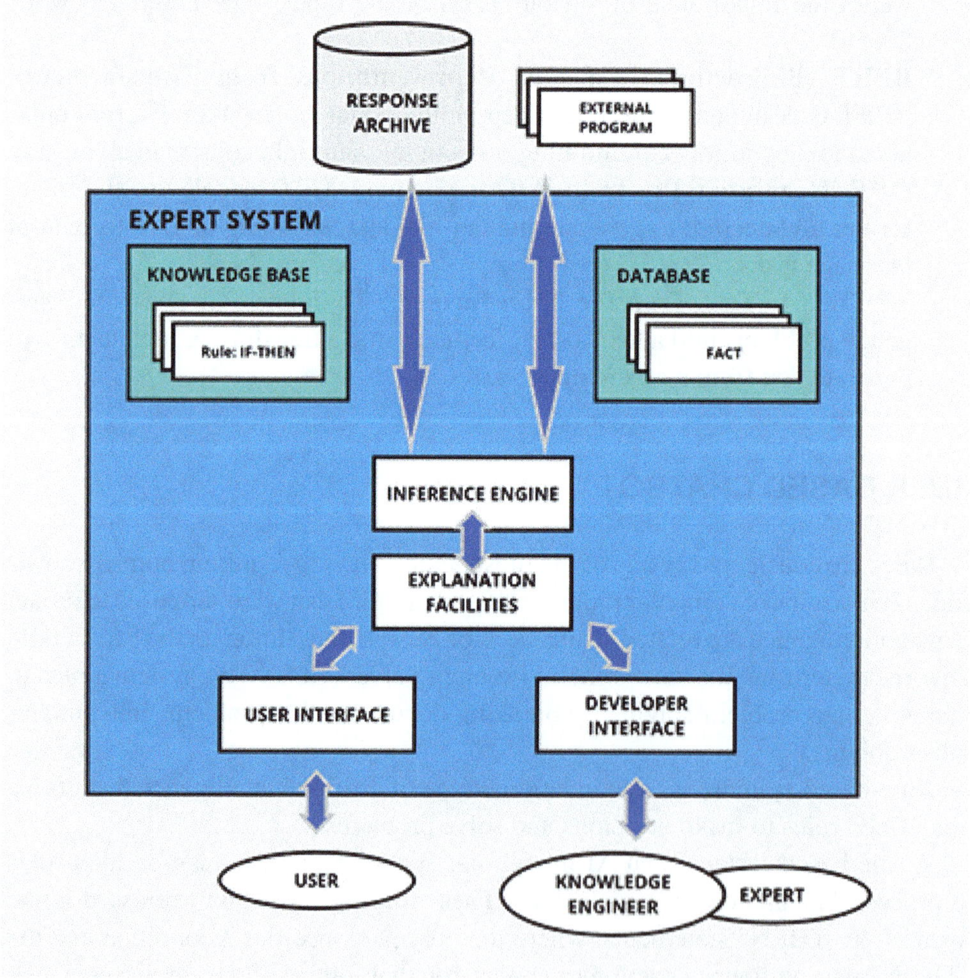

Consider a Medical Expert System Chatbot that helps doctors and patients diagnose diseases based on symptoms and medical history. It follows rule-based logic, combining stored facts and IF-THEN rules to suggest possible conditions. The Figure 1 shows the structure of rule based chatbots.

The Knowledge Base contains predefined medical rules, such as "IF fever + cough + breathing issues → THEN pneumonia." These rules help infer diagnoses based on user inputs.

The Database stores patient records, past diagnoses, and test results. When a user reports symptom, the system checks stored facts to refine its suggestions.

The Inference Engine processes user input by matching it with rules in the knowledge base. It retrieves facts from the database and applies logical reasoning to generate a diagnosis.

The Explanation Facility justifies its recommendations. For example, if a user reports fever and joint pain, the system explains that these are common dengue symptoms and suggests a blood test.

The User Interface allows patients and doctors to interact with the chatbot. Patients enter symptoms, while doctor's access detailed reports and recommendations.

The Developer Interface enables knowledge engineers to update rules, add new diseases, and improve system accuracy. Experts verify medical rules before they are added.

The system integrates External Data Sources, such as hospital databases and lab test results, ensuring accurate and up-to-date recommendations.

Rule-based chatbots are particularly useful in well-defined domains where user inquiries are predictable. Common applications include customer service for FAQs, basic troubleshooting, and guiding users through processes like booking appointments or making purchases.

In the early 2000s, SmarterChild revolutionized instant messaging with scripted responses for weather, stocks, and sports, offering instant accuracy but lacking open-ended conversation. Clippy, Microsoft's Office Assistant, used rule-based logic to anticipate user needs but was often seen as intrusive. Meanwhile, WeChat Official Account Bots automated customer service using keyword recognition, making them efficient for businesses.

Despite their limitations, rule-based chatbots were fast, reliable, and ideal for structured tasks. Today, popular rule-based chatbots include SalesTown Chatbot (CRM integration), Chatfuel (social media automation), and Tidio (e-commerce support). Others like ManyChat, Landbot, and Zendesk continue to provide structured automation solutions.

Current Rule-Based Chatbots

- **SalesTown Chatbot** This chatbot integrates with SalesTown CRM and allows users to create customizable workflows. It is suitable for businesses of all sizes and offers analytics to track customer interactions.
- **Chatfuel** Chatfuel helps businesses create rule-based bots for Facebook Messenger and other social platforms using a drag-and-drop interface. It is useful for automating customer support and marketing on social media.
- **Tidio** Tidio offers a rule-based chatbot solution designed for e-commerce and customer service applications. It enables businesses to automate answers to common customer questions and deliver quick responses using predefined rules. It provides multi-channel support, including chat, email, and Messenger.

Other rule-based chatbots include ManyChat, MobileMonkey, Landbot, Botsify, Flow XO, SnatchBot, and Zendesk Chatbot.

Pattern Matching

Pattern matching in chatbots is a technique where the system recognizes specific structures or sequences in user input to generate responses. It involves identifying patterns, and in early chatbots, this method determined responses by matching input to a known pattern. For instance, if a user enters "How are you?", the chatbot might respond with "I'm just a bot, but I'm functioning as expected!". Pattern matching offers more flexibility than purely rule-based bots by handling variations in phrasing and sentence structure without needing exact keyword matches. However, it still lacks the contextual awareness and learning capabilities of more advanced chatbots.

The flowchart in Figure 2 represents a pattern-matching-based chatbot that processes user input through a structured sequence of steps. First, the chatbot normalizes the input by converting it to uppercase and removing unnecessary variations. It then partitions the input into separate sentences for better matching. Each sentence is compared against predefined patterns using a lookup-based or rule-based approach. If an exact or approximate match is found, the chatbot selects a response randomly from a predefined list. For instance, "HELLO" is matched with greetings like "HELLO THERE!" or "HI THERE, CAN I TALK TO YOU?". Similarly, "HOW ARE YOU DOING TODAY?" is matched with responses like "NOT BAD" or "SO SO". Finally, the selected responses from different sentence matches are combined to form the final chatbot output. This approach ensures structured responses while maintaining slight variations, making the chatbot appear more interactive despite its simplicity (Tariq M.U, 2025b).

Figure 2. Pattern matching tree structure

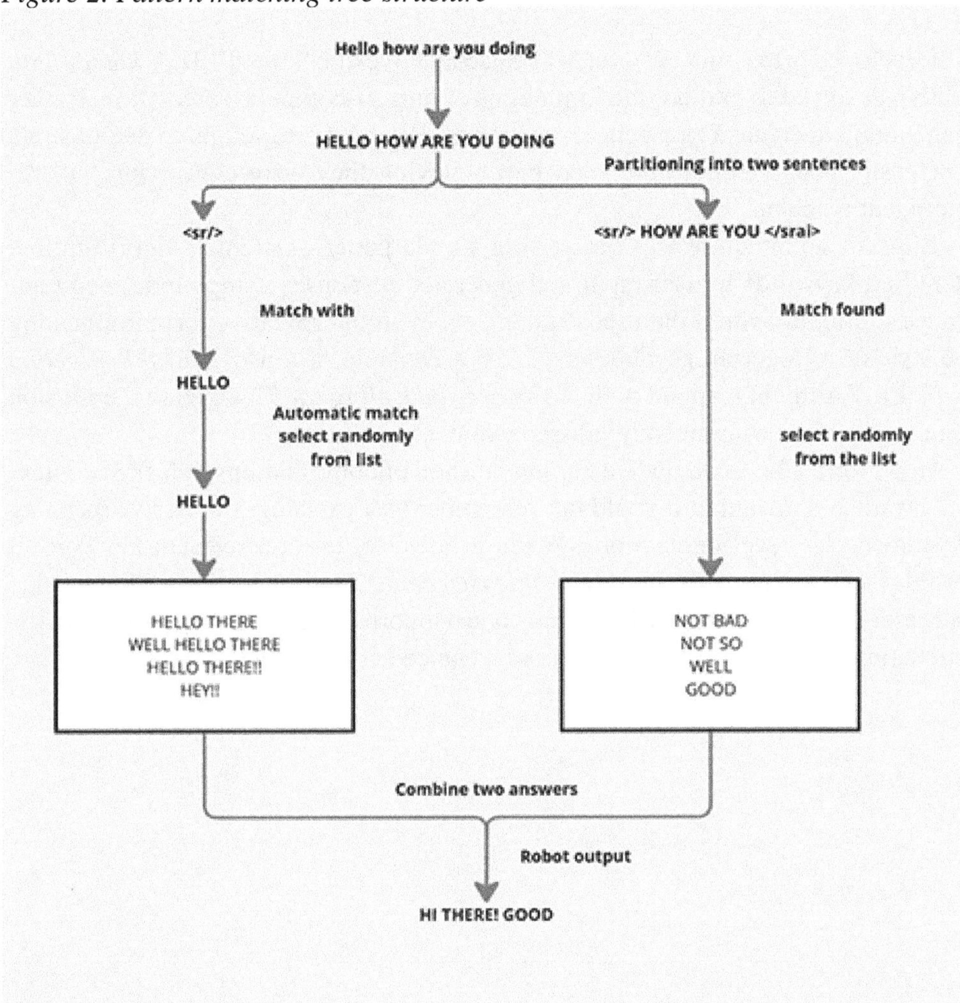

Pattern matching is a technique in computer science used to identify specific sequences or structures within data. It involves checking if a given sequence of tokens is present within a larger data set, and the match typically needs to be exact.

Pattern matching algorithms work with regular expressions to define the pattern to look for in testing data. This technique is fundamental in various applications, including data validation, syntax analysis, search algorithms, and artificial intelligence.

Pattern matching helps retrieve information from complex datasets and is used in machine learning for developing predictive models.

ELIZA

Developed in the mid-1960s at MIT by Joseph Weizenbaum, ELIZA was an early chatbot designed to explore the limitations of human-computer interaction. Rather than aiming to create a true conversational AI, Weizenbaum sought to demonstrate how easily people could be misled into believing they were conversing with an intelligent machine.

ELIZA's architecture was based on a simple pattern-matching algorithm that identified keywords in user input and generated responses using predefined templates. It often mirrored the user's statements in an interrogative form, mimicking the style of a Rogerian psychotherapist. For example, if a user said, *"I'm feeling sad,"* ELIZA might respond with *"Why are you feeling sad?"*—giving the illusion of understanding without truly grasping context.

However, ELIZA had no real comprehension of conversations. It lacked contextual awareness, meaning it could not remember past exchanges or derive meaning beyond surface-level interactions. When it failed to detect a relevant keyword, it would resort to generic prompts like *"Please go on."* Despite its limited knowledge and rigid response system, ELIZA was a groundbreaking experiment that laid the foundation for the development of more advanced conversational AI systems.

Figure 3. ELIZA basic logic flow

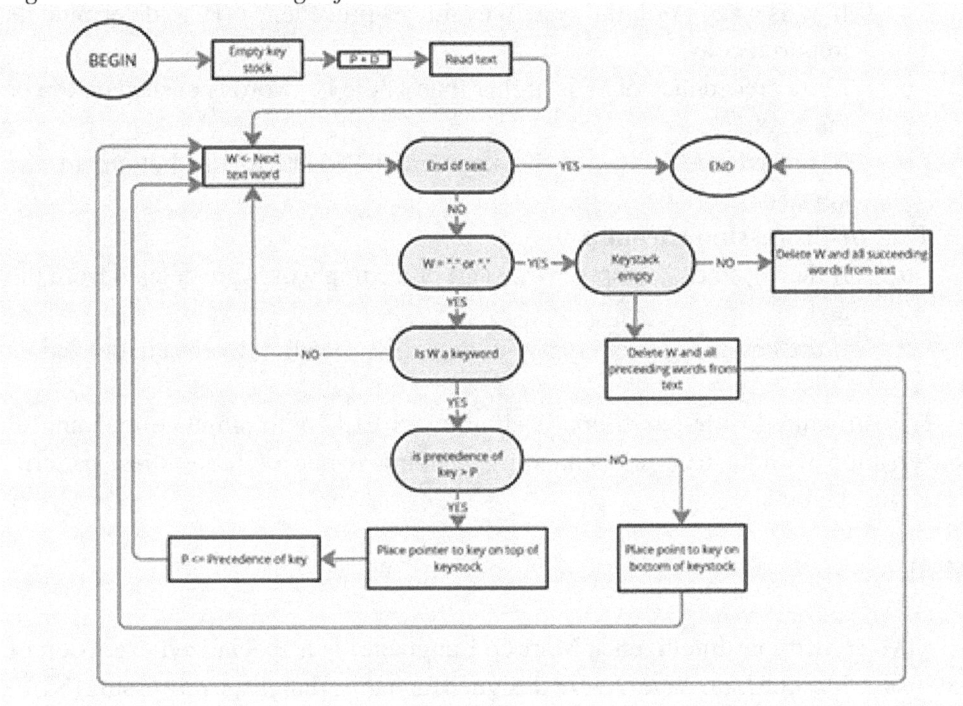

This flowchart in Figure 3 from the original ELIZA paper represents the keyword detection process, which is fundamental to ELIZA's rule-based conversation model. Below is a step-by-step breakdown of the flow:

1. **Initialization**
    - o The process begins with an empty keystack (used for keyword storage).
    - o A pointer P is initialized with a default value (P = 0).
    - o The system reads the input text.
2. **Processing Each Word**
    - o The system extracts the next word (W) from the input text.
3. **End of Text Check**
    - o If the end of the text is reached, the process terminates (END).
4. **Punctuation Handling**
    - o If W is a punctuation mark (.,,), it is ignored, and the next word is processed.
5. **Keyword Identification**
    - o The system checks if W is a keyword (a word relevant for forming responses).

6. **Precedence Handling**
   - If W is a keyword, the system evaluates precedence (P) to determine its importance.
   - If the precedence of W is higher than P, the keyword is pushed on top of the keystack.
   - If precedence is lower, the keyword is added to the bottom of the keystack.
7. **End-of-Processing Cleanup**
   - If the keystack is empty, W and all preceding words are deleted from the text.
   - If the keystack is not empty, W and all succeeding words are deleted.

This structured, rule-based approach allowed ELIZA to simulate meaningful conversation without true understanding, making it one of the earliest pattern-matching chatbots.

AIML

AIML (Artificial Intelligence Markup Language) is a specialized extension of Extensible Markup Language (XML) designed for natural language processing (NLP) and conversational AI applications, particularly chatbots. It provides a structured framework for defining patterns and responses, enabling machines to identify user inputs and generate either predefined or dynamic replies.

Figure 4. AIML tree structure

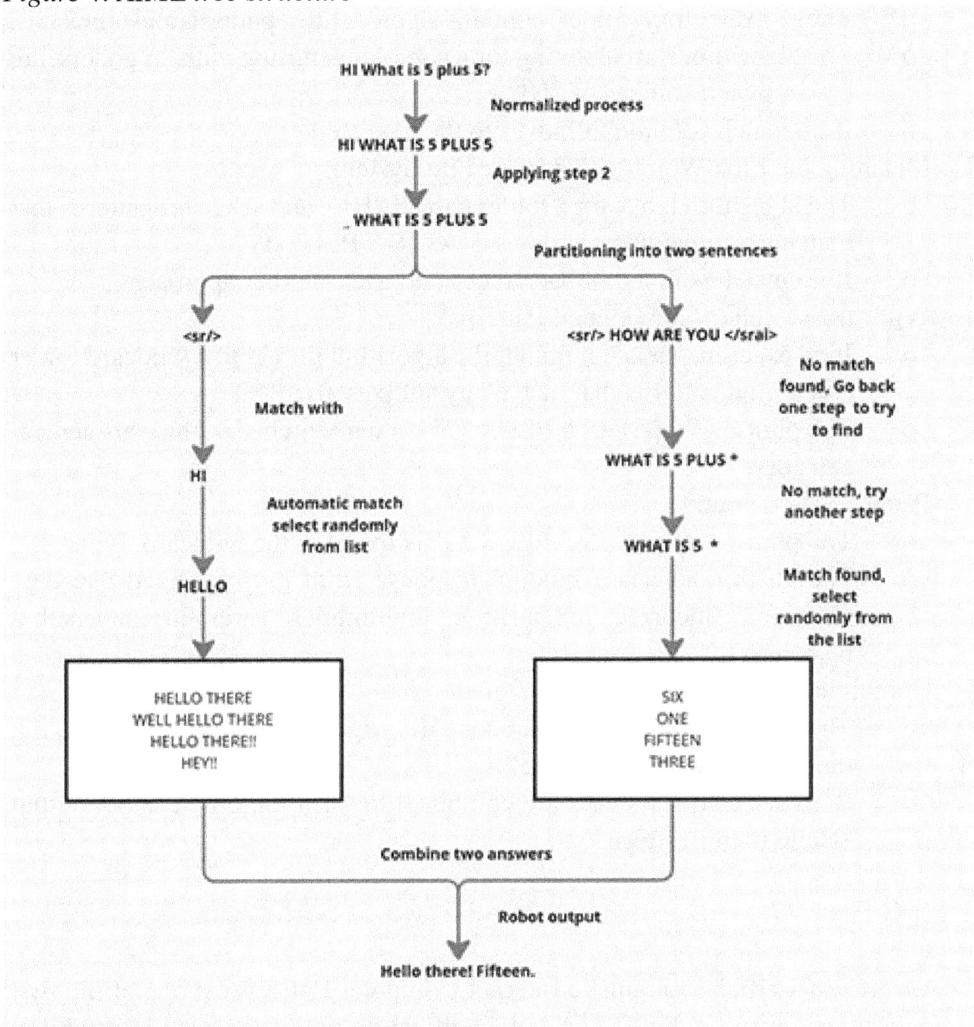

Flow of Pattern Matching Algorithm (Figure 4).

When a user inputs a query, the chatbot follows a structured process to identify the appropriate response. The steps are as follows:

1. Normalization:
   - o Convert the input to uppercase: “HI WHAT IS 5 PLUS 5?”, considering the user input to be “HiWhat is 5 plus 5?”

2. Searching for Patterns in the File System:
    - o The root directory (folder) contains all predefined patterns and templates.
    - o The algorithm starts looking for a subfolder starting with an underscore (_/) to match suffixes of "HI."
    - o If no match is found, it moves to the next step.
3. Matching the First Word ("HI") in the File System:
    - o The algorithm looks for a folder named "HI/" and scans for patterns that match the remaining words "WHAT IS 5 PLUS 5?"
    - o If no match is found, it backtracks and tries another approach.
4. Wildcard Search (*/ for General Patterns):
    - o If an exact match is not found, the algorithm moves to a wildcard folder (*/) to find patterns that match any suffixes after "HI."
    - o The phrase "WHAT IS 5 PLUS 5?" is then searched within this general category.
5. Pattern Match Found:
    - o The phrase "WHAT IS 5 PLUS 5?" is found in the wildcard folder.
    - o The chatbot selects a random response from its predefined list, e.g., "Fifteen." (incorrect on purpose, highlighting variability in chatbot responses).
6. Combining Responses:
    - o The system also finds a match for "HI" separately and selects a greeting randomly (e.g., "Hello there!").
    - o Both selected responses are combined to form the final chatbot output "Hello there! Fifteen."

A.L.I.C.E

A.L.I.C.E (Artificial Linguistic Internet Computer Entity) was one of the first online chatbots, inspired by ELIZA but significantly more advanced in its ability to simulate conversation. Unlike ELIZA, which relied on a small set of predefined rules, A.L.I.C.E was built using AIML (Artificial Intelligence Markup Language), allowing for a more structured and expandable dialogue system.

A.L.I.C.E operated purely on pattern matching without truly understanding the conversation, meaning it could recognize keywords and respond accordingly but lacked actual intelligence or context awareness. Despite this limitation, it was considered one of the most human-like chatbots of its time, winning the Loebner Prize multiple times for its conversational abilities.

A.L.I.C.E had a large knowledge base consisting of 41,000 templates and related patterns, compared to ELIZA's mere two hundred keywords and rules. However, it still fell short of true artificial intelligence, as it could not express emotions, infer meaning, or adapt dynamically to user interactions. Nevertheless, A.L.I.C.E laid the foundation for modern conversational AI by demonstrating the potential of structured chatbot frameworks.

Latent Semantic Analysis (LSA)

LSA can be integrated with AIML in chatbot development to identify similarities between words through vector representation. AIML handles template-based queries, such as greetings and general questions, while LSA is utilized to generate responses for unanswered queries. (Gang Wei Yun et al., 2016)

ChatScript: The Successor of AIML

ChatScript is an advanced chatbot framework that succeeded AIML, introducing a more structured and rule-based approach to chatbot design. Unlike AIML, which relied purely on pattern matching, ChatScript organizes responses into topics and rules, allowing for better context management. One of its key innovations is long-term memory, which enables chatbots to store and recall user-specific data such as names, ages, or preferences using $ variables. Additionally, ChatScript is case-sensitive, meaning it can interpret uppercase text as an indicator of emphasis, thereby enhancing conversational dynamics. As an open-source scripting language and engine, it is widely used for developing intelligent conversational agents with structured dialogues and contextual awareness. (Ramesh K et al., 2017)

RiveScript: A Lightweight Scripting Language for Chatbots

RiveScript is a simplified, text-based chatbot scripting language designed for ease of use and flexibility. Unlike AIML and ChatScript, which focus on structured rule-based responses, RiveScript uses a plain text, line-based approach, making chatbot development more accessible for beginners. It supports multiple programming languages, including Go, Java, JavaScript, Perl, and Python, allowing developers to integrate it seamlessly into different applications. While it lacks advanced features like memory and deep contextual understanding, RiveScript is a lightweight and efficient choice for building quick chatbot prototypes that require straightforward responses and minimal processing overhead (Adamopoulou et al., 2020).

Jabberwacky- 1998: The First AI-Driven Chatbot

Jabberwacky, developed in 1988, was one of the first chatbots to incorporate artificial intelligence in an attempt to pass the Turing Test. Unlike rule-based chatbots like ELIZA and ALICE, which relied on predefined responses, Jabberwacky aimed to mimic human conversation dynamically. It was built using CleverScript, a spreadsheet-based scripting language that allowed it to respond contextually based on previous interactions. While revolutionary at the time, Jabberwacky struggled with scalability and response speed, limiting its ability to handle multiple users efficiently. Despite these challenges, it was a pioneering step toward AI-driven chatbots, laying the groundwork for modern machine learning-based conversational agents (Tariq, 2025b).

Statistical NLP Models (Pre-Deeplearning Era)

Rule-based chatbots, while foundational in conversational AI, were limited by their reliance on predefined patterns, making them ineffective for handling dynamic conversations. They struggled with ambiguity, lacked contextual understanding, and could not adapt beyond their programmed responses.

The statistical era marked a shift towards data-driven approaches, leveraging large text corpora and computational power to analyze linguistic patterns. Techniques like Hidden Markov Models (HMMs) for speech recognition, n-gram models for language prediction, and machine learning algorithms enabled chatbots to learn and improve from experience. This transition laid the groundwork for more sophisticated natural language processing (NLP) systems, paving the way for future advancements.

NLU

During the statistical NLP era, Natural Language Understanding (NLU) revolutionized text processing by enabling systems to extract meaning and intent beyond simple keyword matching. As a subfield of NLP, NLU facilitated sentence analysis, disambiguation, and intent recognition, improving search engines, sentiment analysis, text categorization, and summarization. It introduced mapping language to vector representations, influencing early NLP tools like spellcheckers.

NLU primarily focuses on transforming unstructured text into structured data through two key tasks: intent detection, which classifies sentences based on user intent, and entity extraction (slot-filling), which tags relevant parts of a sentence with domain-specific labels. These advancements significantly enhanced the accuracy and sophistication of statistical NLP models. (Sangkeun Jung et al., 2018)

For example, when someone says, "Book a flight to New York," an NLU system must recognize "book" as an action, "flight" as the object, and "New York" as the destination.

Traditional Probabilistic Models

Hidden Markov Models (HMMs) for Chatbots

HMMs play a crucial role in chatbot development by enabling sequence-based language processing for tasks like Named Entity Recognition (NER) and Part-of-Speech (POS) tagging. These models help chatbots understand user input, extract relevant information, and generate structured responses.

How HMMs Work in Chatbots.

- **Hidden States & Observations** – In NER, words in a sentence are the observations, while hidden states represent entity tags like "PERSON", "LOCATION", or "O" (other). For instance, in *"Barack Obama was the President of the USA"*, HMM assigns tags such as PERSON and ORGANIZATION to relevant words.
- **Probability Estimations** – HMMs rely on:
  - **Transition Probabilities** – The likelihood of one entity type following another (e.g., "Barack" → "Obama" both being PERSON).
  - **Emission Probabilities** – The likelihood of a word belonging to a specific entity class (e.g., "Obama" being labeled as PERSON).
- **Training & Learning** – HMMs learn these probabilities from labeled datasets, using algorithms like Baum-Welch.
- **Decoding & Prediction** – When processing new text, chatbots use the Viterbi algorithm to determine the most probable sequence of named entity tags.

Why HMMs Matter for Chatbots.

- **Better Context Understanding** – Helps identify usernames, locations, dates, and product names.
- **Improved Responses** – Enhances chatbot accuracy by structuring responses based on recognized entities.
- **Language Flexibility** – HMM-based models can be adapted to different languages and domains.

By integrating HMMs, chatbots can efficiently interpret, categorize, and respond to user inputs, improving conversational flow and user engagement.

Naïve Bayes

Naïve Bayes is a simple yet effective algorithm that helps chatbots classify and understand user messages based on probability. It works by analyzing words in a sentence and determining the most likely category or intent. For instance, if a user says *"Hello"* or *"Good morning,"* the chatbot can recognize it as a greeting. Similarly, words like *"order," "delivery,"* or *"status"* may indicate a customer service request. By using probability calculations, the chatbot can predict the most appropriate response, improving the user experience.

This method is particularly useful for intent recognition, sentiment analysis, and filtering spam messages in chatbot interactions. Since Naïve Bayes assumes that each word contributes independently to the meaning of a sentence, it simplifies computation while still providing reliable results. This makes it an efficient choice for chatbots that need to quickly classify messages and generate relevant responses without requiring complex processing.

How it Works.

1. **Data Preparation:** Training data consists of labeled examples (e.g., emails classified as "spam" or "not spam").
2. **Probability Calculation:** The algorithm calculates the prior probabilities of each class (e.g., the probability of an email being spam) and the class-conditional probabilities (e.g., the probability of a specific word appearing in a spam email).
3. **Classification:** For a new, unseen data point, the algorithm calculates the posterior probability for each class and assigns the data point to the class with the highest posterior probability.

Naïve Bayes Formula

$$P(AB) = P(BA)*P(A)P(B)$$

Where:

- $P(AB)$is the posterior probability of class A (target) given predictor B (attribute).
- $P(BA)$is the likelihood which is the probability of predictor B given class A.
- $P(A)$is the prior probability of class A (target).
- $P(B)$is the prior probability of predictor B (attribute).

Conditional Random Fields (CRFs) in Chatbots

Conditional Random Fields (CRFs), while not explicitly mentioned in the initial search results, play a significant role in enhancing the natural language understanding capabilities of chatbots, particularly in sequence labelling tasks. CRFs excel at Named Entity Recognition (NER), identifying and classifying key entities within user input, such as names, organizations, and locations, thus enabling the chatbot to extract and utilize specific information from user queries.

MACHINE LEARNING-BASED APPROACHES

Machine learning overcame traditional statistical approaches by offering the ability to automatically learn patterns from large, complex datasets without relying on predefined assumptions. It also excels in handling high-dimensional and non-linear relationships, making it more flexible and accurate in real-world applications.

Decision Trees and Random Forest

Decision trees are supervised learning algorithms used for both classification and regression tasks. They create a tree-like structure to model decisions based on input data. The tree starts at a root node, which asks a question about the data, leading to branches that represent potential answers. These branches connect to decision (internal) nodes, which ask further questions, generating more branches and outcomes until the data reaches a terminal (leaf) node, where a prediction is made. Decision trees mimic human decision-making, are easy to understand, and provide a visual representation of possibilities.

How Decision Trees are Used in Chatbots

While decision trees are not the most common approach in chatbot development, their ability to classify and predict outcomes makes them useful for several chatbot functions:

- **Intent Recognition:** Decision trees can categorize user input to identify intent by using words and phrases as features to navigate the tree and determine the most likely intent.
- **Dialogue Management:** They can manage conversation flow by selecting the next appropriate response based on the user's previous input and the current state of the conversation.

- **Task Completion:** Decision trees can guide users through step-by-step processes, such as booking a flight or ordering a product, by presenting options and determining the next step based on user responses.
- **Classification:** They classify data or predict what will come next, making them useful for both classification and regression tasks in chatbot applications.

While decision trees offer simplicity and interpretability, modern chatbot development often favours more advanced techniques, such as neural networks, which can better handle nuanced language understanding and generate more natural responses.

SVM

SVMs are valuable tools in chatbot development, primarily for classification tasks that enable more accurate and contextually relevant interactions. By training on labelled examples, SVMs can effectively classify user intents, allowing chatbots to understand the purpose behind a user's message and provide appropriate responses. This capability enhances the chatbot's ability to offer personalized assistance, particularly in areas like medical or banking chatbots, where accurate intent classification is crucial for delivering targeted and helpful information.

Mitsuku (2005)

Mitsuku, also known as Kuki, is an award-winning chatbot developed by Steve Worswick using AIML and rule-based processing, enhanced with statistical NLP methods for improved conversational quality. Launched in 2005 on the Pandorabots platform, Mitsuku has won the Loebner Prize five times, demonstrating its ability to simulate human-like conversations. By combining AIML with NLP, it can interpret user inputs effectively and generate contextually relevant responses across diverse topics.

A study by Hill, Ford, and Farreras -2015 compared Mitsuku with other conversational agents, finding its accuracy comparable to human responses in problem-solving tasks. While Mitsuku excels in engaging dialogue, it may still struggle with complex queries, a common limitation in AI chatbots. However, its success highlights the potential of combining rule-based and statistical NLP techniques to enhance chatbot interactions.

DEEP LEARNING

Deep learning has revolutionized chatbot technology by automating feature extraction, handling unstructured data, and achieving higher accuracy with large datasets. Unlike traditional machine learning, which relies on manual feature engineering and structured data, deep learning models, particularly recurrent and transformer-based architectures, learn features directly from raw data, enabling them to understand context and generate human-like responses.

These models improve independently with minimal manual tuning, detecting patterns and inferring user intent with high precision by analysing historical interactions. While traditional machine learning works well for structured tasks, deep learning excels in complex scenarios requiring the interpretation of unstructured data, making it ideal for advanced chatbot development.

RNN

Recurrent Neural Networks (RNNs) are a class of artificial neural networks designed for processing sequential data. Unlike traditional feedforward networks, RNNs maintain a memory of past inputs through their hidden state, making them well-suited for natural language processing (NLP) tasks such as chatbot development. A chatbot needs to process and understand conversational input while generating a coherent response, which requires handling sequences of text dynamically. In chatbot applications, RNNs can function as both an encoder and a decoder in a Sequence-to-Sequence (Seq2Seq) architecture. This enables the chatbot to interpret a user's message, encode its meaning into a representation, and then generate an appropriate response based on this representation. (Sherstinsky A., 2018).

A chatbot using RNNs follows a Seq2Seq model, consisting of an encoder and a decoder. The encoder RNN processes the input sentence sequentially, updating its hidden state at each step to retain contextual information. The final hidden state acts as a context vector, summarizing the entire input.

The decoder RNN takes this context vector and generates a response word by word. It starts with a special start-of-sequence (SOS) token and continues predicting words until reaching an end-of-sequence (EOS) token. This structure enables chatbots to transform user inputs into meaningful responses, making them effective for conversational AI.

To illustrate how an RNN-based chatbot functions, consider a user input such as "What is your name?". During the encoding phase, the chatbot processes each word sequentially. First, "What" is encoded into a hidden state, followed by "is," "your," and finally "name?" The encoder accumulates context through these steps, producing a final hidden state that serves as the context vector.

In the decoding phase, the decoder takes this context vector and generates a response one word at a time. It starts by predicting the first word, which might be "My," then continues to generate "name," followed by "is," and finally "ChatGPT." The process stops when the <EOS> token is generated, signaling that the chatbot has completed its response. The final conversation output is "My name is ChatGPT." This demonstrates how RNNs can be used to structure chatbot responses by encoding and decoding conversational sequences.

Challenges with RNN-Based Chatbots

- Fixed-Length Context Vector – Standard RNN encoders condense input into a single hidden state, making it hard to retain details in long sentences. Solution: The Attention Mechanism enables the decoder to focus on relevant parts of the input dynamically.
- Vanishing Gradient Problem – Gradients shrink during backpropagation, limiting the model's ability to learn long-term dependencies. Solution: LSTM and GRU networks use gating mechanisms to retain valuable information over long sequences, improving response accuracy.

LSTM

Long Short-Term Memory (LSTM) networks are a specialized type of Recurrent Neural Networks (RNNs) designed to overcome the limitations of traditional RNNs, particularly the vanishing gradient problem. (Aishwarya Selvamurugan et al., 2025) Standard RNNs struggle with remembering long-term dependencies, which is a crucial requirement in chatbot applications where conversations often rely on context from previous exchanges. LSTMs introduce a gating mechanism that allows the network to selectively retain or forget information, enabling more effective learning from long sequences of text. This makes LSTMs highly suitable for chatbots that require meaningful and contextually aware conversations. A chatbot using LSTMs follows a Seq2Seq architecture, consisting of an encoder LSTM and a decoder LSTM. Unlike standard RNNs, LSTMs efficiently capture long-term dependencies using cell states and gates (forget, input, and output gates) to regulate information flow, ensuring relevant details are retained while discarding unnecessary ones.

The encoder LSTM processes the input sentence word by word, updating both its hidden state and cell state, which serve as a context vector summarizing the input. The decoder LSTM then generates a response iteratively, using the context vector, past hidden states, and previously generated words. The response generation continues until an end-of-sequence (EOS) token is reached, ensuring coherent

Consider a user input like "Tell me a joke." The encoder LSTM processes each word sequentially, storing relevant contextual information in its hidden state and cell state. Once the final state is obtained, it is passed to the decoder, which begins generating the chatbot's response. The decoder might start with a start-of-sequence (<SOS>) token, then produce words like "Why," "did," "the," "chicken," and finally "cross the road?" The process stops when the <EOS> token is generated, resulting in the chatbot's full response: "Why did the chicken cross the road?".

This example highlights how LSTMs improve upon standard RNNs by effectively handling long-range dependencies, ensuring the chatbot maintains coherence across different conversational contexts.

Advantages of LSTM in Chatbots

- **Long-Term Memory:** Overcomes RNN limitations by retaining user preferences and long-form inputs.
- **Better Context Handling:** Gating mechanisms help process noisy or incomplete inputs, improving response accuracy.

Challenges & Solutions.

- **High Computational Cost:** LSTMs require more memory and longer training times. Solution: Optimize models or use efficient architectures for deployment.
- **Handling Long Conversations:** Struggles with extremely long sequences. Solution: Attention Mechanism enhances context retention and response quality.

Transformers

Transformers revolutionized natural language processing (NLP) by overcoming the limitations of traditional sequential models like Recurrent Neural Networks (RNNs) and Long Short-Term Memory (LSTM) networks. Introduced in the paper *"Attention Is All You Need"* by Vaswani et al. (2017) (Vaswani A et al., 2018), transformers rely entirely on self-attention mechanisms to process input sequences in parallel, making them highly efficient and scalable for large datasets (Aishwarya S et al., 2024).

Table 1. Comparison with Previous Models

Feature	Rule-Based Chatbots	Statistical & ML-Based Models	RNNs & LSTMs	Transformers
Learning Approach	Predefined rules	Machine-learned patterns	Sequential processing	Self-attention mechanism
Context Retention	Limited	Moderate	Short-term memory (via recurrence)	Long-range context understanding
Scalability	Poor	Moderate	Struggles with long texts	Highly scalable
Parallelization	N/A	Low	Low (due to sequential nature)	High (processes entire input at once)
Training Efficiency	Fast but inflexible	Moderate	Computationally expensive	Efficient for large data

Why Transformers?

Unlike RNNs and LSTMs, which process text sequentially, transformers analyze all words in parallel while assigning importance using *self-attention*. This enables them to capture long-range dependencies and nuanced meanings in text, making them ideal for modern AI applications, including advanced chatbots like GPT.

Consider the sentence,

"Despite the heavy rain, the match continued as the players adapted to the wet conditions."

This sentence contains multiple dependencies:

- "Despite the heavy rain" introduces contrast.
- "The match continued" is the main action.
- "As the players adapted" explains why the match continued.
- "Wet conditions" refers back to "rain."

A sequential model like an RNN or LSTM would process this word by word (or in both directions for a Bi-LSTM), but a Transformer can analyze all words at once, capturing relationships more effectively and efficiently.

Step 1: Tokenization & Embedding

First, the sentence is broken into tokens, each representing a word or sub word. These tokens are then converted into embeddings, numerical vectors capturing semantic meaning.

For example, the words:

Table 2. Embedding

Word	Token	Embedding (simplified)
Despite	1	[0.1, 0.3, 0.2]
heavy	2	[0.5, 0.4, 0.6]
rain	3	[0.7, 0.6, 0.8]
match	4	[0.9, 0.7, 0.5]

Each embedding is a set of numerical values that represent word meaning in a high-dimensional space. At this stage, however, the model does not yet know the order of the words in the sentence.

Step 2: Positional Encoding

Unlike RNNs or LSTMs, Transformers do not process words sequentially. To help the model retain word order, positional encodings are added to the embeddings. These encodings are mathematical patterns that provide the model with information about where a word appears in the sentence.

For instance:

Table 3. Positional Encoding

Word	Embedding	Positional Encoding	Final Input Vector
Despite	[0.1, 0.3, 0.2]	[0.05, 0.02, 0.03]	[0.15, 0.32, 0.23]
rain	[0.7, 0.6, 0.8]	[0.01, 0.03, 0.02]	[0.71, 0.63, 0.82]

Now, the model knows both the meaning of the word (from embeddings) and its position in the sentence (from positional encoding).

Step 3: Self-Attention (Understanding Word Relationships)

At this stage, the Transformer calculates attention scores between all words in the sentence. Each word determines how much focus it should place on every other word.

For example:

- "Rain" is strongly related to "wet conditions".
- "Players adapted" is closely linked to "match continued".
- "Despite" changes the meaning of "continued" by introducing contrast.

To compute these relationships, each word generates three vectors:

1. **Query (Q)** – What this word is looking for in others.
2. **Key (K)** – How relevant other words are to this word.
3. **Value (V)** – The actual word meaning to pass along.

The attention score between two words is calculated as:

$$Attention\ Score = \frac{Q.K^T}{\sqrt{d_k}}$$

(where d_k is a scaling factor to prevent extreme values).
For our example, some computed attention scores might be:

Table 4. Attention Score

Word 1	*Word 2*	*Attention Score*
rain	wet conditions	0.95
players	adapted	0.92
despite	continued	0.85
match	continued	0.75

Words that are more contextually connected get higher attention scores, allowing the model to focus on the most relevant parts of the sentence.

Step 4: Multi-Head Attention (Analyzing Multiple Meanings Simultaneously)

Instead of relying on a single attention mechanism, Transformers use multiple attention heads, allowing the model to analyze various aspects of the text simultaneously.

For example:

- **Head 1** focuses on subject-verb relationships ("match" → "continued").
- **Head 2** looks at cause-effect ("players adapted" → "match continued").
- **Head 3** tracks conditions ("rain" → "wet conditions").

Each head produces separate attention scores, which are then combined to form a richer word representation.

Step 5: Feedforward Network & Normalization

Once attention scores are applied, each word representation is passed through a fully connected neural network. This network helps refine the representation further by introducing non-linearity and making it more expressive.

Additionally, layer normalization is used to keep values stable, and dropout is applied to prevent overfitting.

Step 6: Output Processing (Final Understanding and Response Generation)

At the end, the refined word representations are passed to the final output layer, depending on the task:

For translation: Convert to another language.

For chatbots: Generate the next response.

For text generation (GPT models): Predict the next word.

For our example, if we use GPT to predict the next sentence, the output might be:

"The officials decided not to stop the game unless the conditions worsened."

This output is context-aware, meaning the Transformer understood:

- The contrast introduced by "despite".
- The cause-and-effect relationship between adaptation and continuation.
- The importance of "rain" leading to "wet conditions".

GPT Models

GPT, introduced by OpenAI, revolutionized NLP with its Transformer-based decoder architecture, enabling scalable and context-aware language generation. Unlike its predecessors, GPT does not process language sequentially but rather attends to all previous words in parallel, making it significantly faster and more accurate in generating coherent and contextually relevant responses. The introduction of self-attention, masked attention, and large-scale pretraining made GPT one of the most influential AI advancements in text-based AI systems.

Evolution of GPT Models: From GPT-1 to GPT-4

The Generative Pre-trained Transformer (GPT) models have evolved significantly, introducing major advancements in language understanding, text generation, and efficiency. Each iteration has improved scaling, reasoning, and multimodal capabilities.

GPT-1 (2018) – Foundation of Generative Pre-Training

GPT-1 introduced the transformer-based architecture to natural language processing. It featured a decoder-only Transformer with twelve layers, twelve attention heads, and 117M parameters. Trained on BooksCorpus (~7,000 books), it learned language representations using unsupervised learning. Though it performed well in NLP tasks like sentiment analysis, it struggled with long-range dependencies and generalization. (Yenduri G et al., 2023)

GPT-2 (2019) – Scaling and Zero-Shot Learning

GPT-2 marked a breakthrough in zero-shot learning, allowing it to perform tasks without explicit fine-tuning. With 1.5B parameters trained on eight million web pages, it generated more coherent and contextually relevant text. The model improved self-attention mechanisms, enhancing long-range text dependencies. However, it raised concerns due to bias propagation and misinformation risks, along with increased computational demands. (Hanna M et al., 2023)

GPT-3 (2020) – Few-Shot Learning & Massive Scaling

GPT-3 dramatically scaled up to 175B parameters, improving few-shot learning—enabling it to learn new tasks with minimal examples. Trained on diverse datasets (books, Wikipedia, internet text), it exhibited adaptive text generation, producing high-quality essays, poetry, and even programming code (Codex). Despite its advancements in zero-shot and few-shot learning, it suffered from hallucinations and high computational costs. (Brown T. B et al., 2020)

GPT-3.5 (2022) – Optimized Performance

GPT-3.5 powered ChatGPT, optimizing real-time conversational AI. It introduced faster response times, lower latency, and improved fine-tuning via RLHF (Reinforcement Learning from Human Feedback). This led to more coherent and aligned responses, making it more practical for applications like chatbots. However, it still faced limitations in reasoning and long-context recall.

GPT-4 (2023) – Multimodal AI & Enhanced Reasoning

GPT-4 introduced multimodal capabilities, allowing it to process both text and images. With a larger, undisclosed number of parameters, it featured enhanced attention mechanisms for improved coherence and memory. GPT-4 significantly improved factual accuracy, reduced hallucinations, and extended context understanding. Trained with RLHF, it became safer and more aligned, though challenges like bias and high computational requirementspersist. (OpenAI, et al., 2023)

Deep Research (2025)

As of February 2025, OpenAI's most advanced model is Deep Research, launched in early February 2025. This model represents a significant leap in artificial intelligence capabilities, performing complex tasks that were traditionally the domain of human experts.

- **Advanced Task Handling:** Deep Research can manage intricate tasks such as financial analysis and generating comprehensive reports, roles typically handled by consultants.
- **Economic Integration:** Within nine days of its release, Deep Research was already performing 5% of all economic tasks, indicating its rapid adoption and effectiveness.
- **Anticipation of AGI:** OpenAI's CEO, Sam Altman, has suggested that with advancements like Deep Research, Artificial General Intelligence (AGI) could emerge within the current presidential term, set to end in 2028.

How it is different from Standard Transformers

GPT-4 is an evolution of the transformer-based language models, improving upon previous versions like GPT-3. While the fundamental transformer architecture remains the same, several key enhancements have been introduced:

Increased Model Depth: More transformer layers and attention heads enhance pattern recognition.

Optimized Attention: Improved mechanisms like Sparse Attention or MoE for better long-context processing.

Multimodal Support: Can process both text and images with an additional visual embedding layer.

Advanced Activation Functions: Likely uses SwiGLU for better training efficiency and convergence.

Enhanced Regularization: Improved dropout and layer normalization for stable deep-network training.

Efficient Training: Uses supervised fine-tuning and RLHF for better alignment and reasoning.

Longer Context Handling: Supports extended input lengths for improved comprehension of lengthy content.

Chatbot Applications Powered by ChatGPT

1. **ChatSupport (Customer Service):** Automates customer interactions, handling FAQs, troubleshooting, and order tracking with human-like responses.
2. **LearnBot (Education Assistant):** Provides interactive tutoring, personalized learning paths, and real-time problem-solving for students.
3. **LegalAI (Legal Chatbot):** Assists in legal research, document drafting, and compliance checks with contextual understanding of legal texts.
4. **MediBot (Healthcare Assistant):** Helps with symptom analysis, medical advice, and patient history summarization while ensuring HIPAA compliance.
5. **CodeMate (Developer Assistant):** Enhances coding productivity by offering debugging support, code suggestions, and real-time explanations within IDEs.

Llama Models

Llama (Large Language Model Meta AI), developed by Meta, represents a family of transformer-based language models optimized for efficiency and deployment flexibility. Unlike traditional large-scale models, Llama is designed to provide high performance with lower computational requirements, making it more accessible for research and real-world applications. Its architecture follows a decoder-only transformer framework, similar to GPT, but focuses on optimization techniques that enhance inference speed, energy efficiency, and accessibility.

Evolution of Llama Models: From Llama 1 to Llama 3

Llama models have evolved with improvements in scaling, efficiency, and adaptability, enhancing chatbot and AI applications.

- **Llama 1 (2023):** Open-source, efficient transformer model with 7B–65B parameters, optimized for research with lower resource usage than GPT-3. (Touvron H et al., 2023)
- **Llama 2 (2023):** Improved scalability, RLHF fine-tuning, reduced biases, and open-source for commercial use, outperforming GPT-3.5 in benchmarks. (Touvron, H et al., 2023)
- **Llama 3 (2024):** Exceeded 400B parameters, enhanced reasoning, long-context understanding, and domain-specific fine-tuned variants for tasks like customer support and coding. (Grattafiori A et al. 2024).

Table 5. Llama vs. GPT in Chatbots

Feature	Llama	GPT
Model Size	Compact, fewer parameters	Large, resource-intensive
Inference Speed	Faster with GQA	Slower due to multi-head attention
Hardware Needs	Runs on local GPUs	Requires cloud-based enterprise GPUs
Training Data	Filtered, high-quality	Broad, includes more noise
Cost	Free & self-hostable	Paid API access
Context Handling	Efficient memory optimization	Good but costly

Chatbot Applications Powered by Llama

1. **AssistAI (Customer Support):** Built with Llama 2 13B, AssistAI automates e-commerce customer support, handling inquiries, order tracking, and recommendations with cost-efficient, context-aware responses.
2. **EduBot (Virtual Tutor):** Powered by Llama 3, EduBot provides personalized STEM tutoring, tracking learning progress and adapting explanations for interactive problem-solving.
3. **LexAI (Legal Assistant):** A legal chatbot leveraging Llama models to summarize case laws, draft contracts, and ensure privacy-focused deployment for law firms.
4. **MediAI (Healthcare Assistant):** Built on Llama 3, MediAI aids doctors with symptom analysis, medical history summarization, and treatment recommendations while ensuring data privacy.
5. **DevHelper (Code Assistant):** Llama 2 13B-based DevHelper assists developers with debugging, code suggestions, and refactoring, integrating seamlessly into IDEs for offline support.

Table 6. Transformer models comparison table

Model Name	Developer	Model Size (Parameters)	Architecture	Training Data Source	Context Length	Fine-tuning Capability	Safety & Bias Control
GPT-4	OpenAI	Undisclosed (~1T est.)	Standard Transformer	Broad web + curated	128K tokens	Limited	Strong (RLHF)
GPT-3.5	OpenAI	175B	Standard Transformer	Broad web	16K tokens	Limited	Medium
Llama 3 (70B)	Meta	70B	Transformer with GQA	High-quality, filtered	8K tokens	LoRA, Full fine-tuning	Strong (RLHF)
Llama 3 (8B)	Meta	8B	Transformer with GQA	High-quality, filtered	8K tokens	LoRA	Medium
Claude 2	Anthropic	~100B (est.)	Transformer	Broad web + constitutional AI	100K tokens	Limited	Strong (RLHF + Constitutional AI)
Claude 1	Anthropic	~50B (est.)	Transformer	Broad web	100K tokens	Limited	Medium
Mistral 7B	Mistral AI	7B	Transformer (Dense)	Open web + curated	8K tokens	LoRA, Full fine-tuning	Medium
Mistral 8x22B (MoE)	Mistral AI	176B (8 experts)	Mixture of Experts (MoE)	Open web + curated	32K tokens	LoRA, Full fine-tuning	Medium
Falcon 180B	TII	180B	Standard Transformer	Large-scale web data	8K tokens	LoRA	Medium
Falcon 7B	TII	7B	Standard Transformer	High-quality filtered	8K tokens	LoRA	Medium

Limitations of Transformer-Based Chatbots

Transformer-based language models, while achieving remarkable fluency and coherence, suffer from a critical limitation: hallucination, where the models generate outputs that are syntactically correct but factually inaccurate (Maynez et al., 2020). Studies show that hallucination rates in large-scale models like GPT-3 can reach up to 60% in knowledge-intensive tasks (Ji et al., 2023).

Retrieval-Augmented Generation (RAG) mitigates this problem by explicitly integrating external knowledge during inference. Instead of relying on static memories, RAG systems dynamically retrieve relevant documents and condition the generation process on retrieved evidence (Lewis et al., 2020). Empirical studies have demonstrated that grounding model outputs in retrieved documents reduces hallucination rates significantly — for example, OpenAI's WebGPT achieved a

25% improvement in factual consistency compared to GPT-3 on open-domain QA benchmarks (Nakano et al., 2021).

Recent advances in retrieval-augmented systems further improve performance. Techniques like Fusion-in-Decoder (Izacard G et al, 2021), which integrate multiple retrieved documents during decoding, and Open-RAG in 2024, which enables open-source RAG pipelines over dynamic knowledge bases, illustrate how hybrid architectures continue to evolve.

FACTORS DRIVING CHATBOT GROWTH

Advancements in AI and NLP

Natural Language Processing (NLP) and machine learning are the brains behind chatbots. As these technologies improve, chatbots become more sophisticated in understanding and responding to human language, leading to more natural and effective conversations.

Growing Customer Service Demands

Businesses are constantly seeking ways to improve customer service efficiency and reduce costs. Chatbots offer 24/7 availability, instant responses, and the ability to handle a large volume of inquiries simultaneously, making them an attractive solution.

Increased Adoption of Messaging Platforms

The widespread use of messaging apps like WhatsApp, Facebook Messenger, and Slack has created a natural environment for chatbot deployment. Users are already comfortable interacting with these platforms, making it easier to adopt chatbot interactions.

E-Commerce Boom

Online shopping continues to grow, and chatbots play a crucial role in assisting customers with product information, order tracking, and purchase support, driving chatbot adoption in the e-commerce sector.

Personalization and Data-Driven Insights

Chatbots can collect and analyze vast amounts of data about customer preferences and behaviour. This data can be used to personalize interactions, improve chatbot performance, and gain valuable business insights.

Voice Assistant Integration

The increasing popularity of voice assistants like Alexa and Google Assistant has opened new avenues for chatbot integration, enabling users to interact with chatbots using voice commands.

KEY TRENDS SHAPING THE FUTURE OF CHATBOTS

Hyper-Personalization: Chatbots will become even better at understanding individual user preferences and tailoring interactions accordingly. This includes personalized recommendations, proactive support, and customized content.

AI-Powered Empathy: Expect advancements in "emotional AI" that allow chatbots to detect and respond to user emotions, creating more empathetic and human-like conversations.

Multimodal Chatbots: Chatbots will increasingly integrate with other modalities like images, videos, and augmented reality to provide richer and more engaging experiences. For example, a chatbot could show you a product image or guide you through a task using an AR overlay.

No-Code/Low-Code Chatbot Platforms: These platforms are making it easier for businesses to build and deploy chatbots without extensive coding knowledge, democratizing access to chatbot technology.

Specialized Chatbots: We will see more chatbots designed for specific industries and use cases, such as healthcare, finance, and education. These specialized chatbots will have deep domain expertise and be able to handle complex tasks.

Proactive Chatbots: Instead of just responding to user queries, chatbots will become more proactive in anticipating needs and helping before being asked.

Seamless Handoff to Humans: Chatbots will get better at recognizing when a human agent is needed and seamlessly transferring the conversation to a live agent, ensuring a positive customer experience.

Enhanced Security and Privacy: With increasing concerns about data privacy, chatbot platforms will need to prioritize security and data protection measures.

POTENTIAL CHALLENGES

Lack of Natural Language Understanding: While NLP has made considerable progress, chatbots still struggle with complex language, sarcasm, and nuanced expressions. Improving NLP capabilities is crucial for creating more effective chatbots.

Data Privacy and Security Concerns: As chatbots collect and process sensitive data, ensuring data privacy and security is paramount. Data breaches and privacy violations could erode trust and hinder adoption.

Integration Complexity: Integrating chatbots with existing systems and workflows can be complex and time-consuming. Simplifying integration processes is essential for wider adoption.

User Adoption and Acceptance: Some users may be hesitant to interact with chatbots, preferring human interaction. Building trust and demonstrating the value of chatbots is key to driving user adoption.

Ethical Considerations: As chatbots become more sophisticated, ethical considerations such as bias, transparency, and accountability need to be addressed.

ETHICAL AND SOCIETAL CHALLENGES IN CHATBOTS

AI Bias and Fairness: Large language models often inherit gender, racial, and cultural biases from training data. These biases can marginalize users in sensitive areas like recruitment, healthcare, and customer service. Developers must apply bias detection, mitigation, and fairness audits to ensure equitable AI systems.

Misinformation and Hallucination Risks: Generative models like GPT-3 and GPT-4 frequently hallucinate — producing plausible but false information. In customer-facing roles, this can cause legal risks, reputational damage, and loss of user trust. Research into Retrieval-Augmented Generation (RAG) and post-generation verification aims to reduce misinformation.

Privacy and Data Security: Chatbots handle sensitive data, requiring compliance with regulations like GDPR, the EU AI Act, and the U.S. Executive Order 14110. Organizations must enforce consent, data minimization, and user rights protections to avoid breaches, fines, and erosion of customer trust.

MARKET PROJECTIONS

Many market research firms predict substantial growth in the chatbot market. Here are some general estimates (note that these can vary depending on the source and specific market segment):

- **Overall Market Size:** The global chatbot market is projected to reach billions of dollars in the next few years, with a significant compound annual growth rate (CAGR).
- **Key Growth Sectors:** Customer service, e-commerce, healthcare, and finance are expected to be key growth sectors for chatbot adoption.
- **Regional Growth:** North America, Europe, and Asia-Pacific are expected to be major markets for chatbots, with Asia-Pacific showing particularly robust growth due to the high adoption of messaging platforms and mobile technologies.

CONCLUSION

This chapter has charted the remarkable evolution of chatbots, from their nascent stages as rule-based systems to the sophisticated AI-driven conversational agents of today. We have seen how the limitations of early chatbots, such as their inability to handle complex queries and their lack of adaptability, paved the way for the development of more advanced techniques like deep learning and Transformer networks. The emergence of generative models like GPT-3 and hybrid approaches like RAG has pushed the boundaries of what is possible, enabling chatbots to engage in more natural, context-aware, and informative conversations. As we look to the future, it is clear that chatbots will continue to play an increasingly key role in our lives, transforming the way we interact with technology and access information. However, challenges remain, including addressing issues of bias, ensuring factual accuracy, and maintaining user privacy. By understanding the past, we can better navigate the future and harness the full potential of chatbots to create more intuitive, efficient, and human-centred interactions.

REFERENCES

Adamopoulou, L. M., & Moussiades, L. (2020). Chatbots: History, technology, and applications. *Machine Learning with Applications*, *2*, 100006. DOI: 10.1016/j.mlwa.2020.100006

Aishwarya S, Selvamurugan C, Parthiban K G, Nathan B, Manoj Prabhakar J, Mohamed Noordeen A (2024). Generative AI in focus : A comprehensive review of leading models across modalities. IEEE, 1–9. DOI: 10.1109/ICUIS64676.2024.10867014

Aslam, F. (2023). The Impact of Artificial Intelligence on Chatbot Technology: A Study on the Current Advancements and Leading Innovations. *European Journal of Technology*, *7*(3), 62–72. DOI: 10.47672/ejt.1561

Brown, T. B., Mann, B., Ryder, N., Subbiah, M., Kaplan, J., Dhariwal, P., Neelakantan, A., Shyam, P., Sastry, G., Askell, A., & Agarwal, S. J., Winter, C. (2020). Language Models are Few-Shot Learners. arXiv.org. https://arxiv.org/abs/2005.14165

Gang, W. Y. (2016). "An e-business chatbot using AIML and LSA." *2016 International Conference on Advances in Computing, Communications and Informatics (ICACCI),* 2740-2742.DOI: DOI: 10.1109/ICACCI.2016.7732476

Grattafiori, A., Dubey, A., Jauhri, A., Pandey, A., Kadian, A., Al-Dahle, A., Letman, A., Mathur, A., Schelten, A., & Vaughan, A. Hinsvark, A. (2024). The Llama 3 herd of models. arXiv.org. https://arxiv.org/abs/2407.21783

Hanna, M., Liu, O., & Variengien, A. (2023). How does GPT-2 compute greater-than?: Interpreting mathematical abilities in a pre-trained language model. arXiv.org. https://arxiv.org/abs/2305.00586

Izacard, G., & Grave, E. (2020). Leveraging Passage Retrieval with Generative Models for Open Domain Question Answering. *arXiv (Cornell University)*. https://doi.org//arxiv.2007.01282DOI: 10.48550

Ji, Z., Lee, N., Frieske, R., Yu, T., Su, D., Xu, Y., Ishii, E., Bang, Y. J., Madotto, A., & Fung, P. (2022). Survey of Hallucination in Natural Language Generation. *ACM Computing Surveys*, *55*(12), 1–38. DOI: 10.1145/3571730

Jung, S. (2019). Semantic vector learning for natural language understanding. *Computer Speech & Language*, *56*, 130–145. DOI: 10.1016/j.csl.2018.12.008

Karpukhin, V., Oğuz, B., Min, S., Lewis, P., Wu, L., Edunov, S., Chen, D., & Yih, W. (2020). Dense passage retrieval for Open-Domain question answering. arXiv.org. https://arxiv.org/abs/2004.04906 DOI: 10.18653/v1/2020.emnlp-main.550

Lewis, P., Perez, E., Piktus, A., Petroni, F., Karpukhin, V., Goyal, N., Küttler, H., Lewis, M., Yih, W., Rocktäschel, T., Riedel, S., & Kiela, D. (2020). Retrieval-Augmented Generation for Knowledge-Intensive NLP tasks. arXiv.org. https://arxiv.org/abs/2005.11401

Maynez, J., Narayan, S., Bohnet, B., & McDonald, R. (2020). On faithfulness and factuality in abstractive summarization. *arXiv*. /arxiv.2005.00661DOI: 10.18653/v1/2020.acl-main.173

Nakano, R., Hilton, J., Balaji, S., Wu, J., Ouyang, L., Kim, C., Hesse, C., Jain, S., Kosaraju, V., Saunders, W., Jiang, X., Cobbe, K., Eloundou, T., Krueger, G., Button, K., Knight, M., Chess, B., & Schulman, J. (2021). WebGPT: Browser-assisted question-answering with human feedback. arXiv.org. https://arxiv.org/abs/2112.09332

Open, A. I., Achiam, J., Adler, S., Agarwal, S., Ahmad, L., Akkaya, I., Aleman, F. L., Almeida, D., Altenschmidt, J., Altman, S., Anadkat, S., Avila, R., Babuschkin, I., Balaji, S., Balcom, V., Baltescu, P., Bao, H., Bavarian, M., & Belgum, J. (2023). GPT-4 Technical Report. https://arxiv.org/abs/2303.08774

Pandey, S., & Sharma, S. (2023). A comparative study of retrieval-based and generative-based chatbots using Deep Learning and Machine Learning. *Healthcare Analytics*, *3*, 100198. DOI: 10.1016/j.health.2023.100198

Ramesh, K., Ravishankaran, S., Joshi, A., & Chandrasekaran, K. (2017). A Survey of Design Techniques for Conversational Agents. *Communications in Computer and Information Science*, *750*, 336–350. Advance online publication. DOI: 10.1007/978-981-10-6544-6_31

Selvamurugan, A., Ganesan, P. K., & Shashank, S. (2024, November 26). Nayak, Arockiaraj Simiyon, and Thirunavukkarasu Indiran. (2025). CNN-LSTM-Based Nonlinear Model Predictive Controller for Temperature Trajectory Tracking in a Batch Reactorhttps. *ACS Omega*, *9*(47), 47203–47212. Advance online publication. DOI: 10.1021/acsomega.4c07893 PMID: 39619559

Sherstinsky, A. (2018). Fundamentals of Recurrent Neural Network (RNN) and Long Short-Term Memory (LSTM) Network. *ArXiv, abs/1808.03314*.

Sutskever, I., Vinyals, O., & Le, Q. V. (2014). Sequence to Sequence Learning with Neural Networks. arXiv.org. https://arxiv.org/abs/1409.3215

Tariq, M. U. (2025a). AI and the Ethical Crossroads: Navigating Privacy, Personhood, and Autonomy in the Digital Age. In Chakraborty, S. (Ed.), *Human Values, Ethics, and Dignity in the Age of Artificial Intelligence* (pp. 49–72). IGI Global Scientific Publishing., DOI: 10.4018/979-8-3693-9035-1.ch003

Tariq, M. U. (2025b). AI-Powered Business Process Automation: Revolutionizing Firm Management. In Derbali, A. (Ed.), *AI, Economic Perspectives, and Firm Business Management* (pp. 199–224). IGI Global Scientific Publishing., DOI: 10.4018/979-8-3693-7357-6.ch010

Team, G., Anil, R., Borgeaud, S., Alayrac, J., Yu, J., Soricut, R., Schalkwyk, J., Dai, A. M., Hauth, A., Millican, K., Silver, D., Johnson, M., Antonoglou, I., & Schrittwieser, J. Vinyals, O. (2023). Gemini: a family of highly capable multimodal models. arXiv.org. https://arxiv.org/abs/2312.11805

Touvron, H., Lavril, T., Izacard, G., Martinet, X., Lachaux, M., Lacroix, T., Rozière, B., Goyal, N., Hambro, E., Azhar, F., Rodriguez, A., Joulin, A., Grave, E., & Lample, G. (2023). LLAMA: Open and Efficient Foundation Language Models. arXiv.org. https://arxiv.org/abs/2302.13971

Touvron, H., Martin, L., Stone, K., Albert, P., Almahairi, A., Babaei, Y., Bashlykov, N., Batra, S., Bhargava, P., Bhosale, S., Bikel, D., Blecher, L., Ferrer, C. C., Chen, M., Cucurull, G., Esiobu, D., Fernandes, J., Fu, J., & Fu, W. (2023). Llama 2: Open foundation and Fine-Tuned chat models. arXiv.org. https://arxiv.org/abs/2307.09288

Vaswani, A., Shazeer, N., Parmar, N., Uszkoreit, J., Jones, L., Gomez, A. N., Kaiser, L., & Polosukhin, I. (2017). Attention is all you need. arXiv.org. https://arxiv.org/abs/1706.03762

Yenduri, G. M, R., G, C. S., Y, S., Srivastava, G., Maddikunta, P. K. R., G, D. R., Jhaveri, R. H., B, P., Wang, W., Vasilakos, A., V., &Gadekallu, T. R. (2023). Generative Pre-trained Transformer: a comprehensive review on enabling technologies, potential applications, emerging challenges, and future directions. arXiv.org. https://arxiv.org/abs/2305.10435

Chapter 9

Transforming Marketing With Generative AI and ChatGPT: Insights From Literature and Real-World Companies

Moez Bellaaj
https://orcid.org/0000-0001-7149-5109
Higher Institute of Business Administration - ISAAS, University of Sfax, Tunisia

ABSTRACT

In recent years, the rapid advancement of generative artificial intelligence (AI) in marketing has been fueled by increasing data availability, significant breakthroughs in deep learning, and evolving computational power. Generative AI tools such as ChatGPT offer businesses transformative opportunities, including the generation of novel data, personalized content creation, and innovative marketing strategies. However, these advancements also bring challenges that need to be addressed to harness their potential. This chapter investigates the current literature and analyzes real-world companies to uncover the opportunities and obstacles associated with generative AI in marketing. It provides insights into the future trajectory of these technologies and offers practical guidance for professionals seeking to leverage generative AI effectively.

DOI: 10.4018/979-8-3693-9841-8.ch009

INTRODUCTION

Artificial intelligence (AI) enables machines to perform tasks that typically require human intervention and execution (Chintalapati & Pandey, 2022; Lee, 2024; Mehta et al., 2022; Volkmar et al., 2022). This intelligence is based on algorithms and computer programs that use data for learning to improve the performance of specific tasks. Traditional algorithms and programs were designed to process structured data like numbers or tables. However, with the increase in data storage capabilities and computing power, researchers have begun to explore the possibility of processing unstructured data, such as images, videos, sound, and raw text (De Bruyn et al., 2020; Volkmar et al., 2022). This technological development in computer science has led to the rise of generative AI, which aims to create new data and content rather than classify existing ones. Unlike traditional algorithms that analyze and treat existing data (e.g., decision trees, Bayesian networks), recent advancements in computer science in the domain of machine learning (ML) and deep learning (DL) have led to the creation of powerful AI systems capable of autonomously generating new information and creating novel content from training data (De Bruyn et al., 2020).

Businesses have begun exploring the possibilities offered by generative AI to enhance their marketing program, product offerings, and operational processes. For example, Adobe launched a tool called "Adobe Sensei" that uses generative AI to help designers create innovative and creative designs from simple descriptions. This tool can save designers time and improve productivity by automating repetitive tasks and offering design suggestions based on current trends. Similarly, IBM has introduced a platform called "Watson," which uses generative AI to help businesses automate processes and optimize employee time.

Recently, OpenAI developed a new virtual assistant called ChatGPT, capable of more natural and fluid dialogues and discussions with humans (Deng & Lin, 2022; Dwivedi et al., 2023). This chatbot represents a significant advancement compared to previous conversational agents, which were limited in their ability to understand and coherently respond to user queries. Released in November 2022, ChatGPT has pushed the boundaries of chatbots by employing a generative natural language model called "Generative Pre-trained Transformer" (GPT). GPT models are based on a transformer architecture pre-trained on large amounts of textual data through unsupervised learning. This technology can be adapted to various natural language processing (NLP) tasks such as text generation, translation, and classification (Dwivedi et al., 2023).

The global success of ChatGPT demonstrates its ability to have a significant impact as a generative artificial intelligence across many fields. These fields may include software development, banking services, tourism, education, health care, and publishing (Dwivedi et al., 2023; Hongladarom & Sakprasert, 2024; Tariq, 2025).

Furthermore, in the marketing domain, generative AI could open new horizons in communication, advertising, and content creation, offering promising opportunities for digital creation and personalization, web advertising, and online assistance (De Bruyn et al., 2020; Huang & Rust, 2021).

On the other hand, the growth of AI and its rapid progress raises concerns for businesses, decision-makers, and marketing professionals (De Bruyn et al., 2020). With the constant improvement of generative AI algorithms, reduced costs, and ease of implementation, marketers may face undeniable benefits but also have to anticipate many challenges (Davenport et al., 2020; Hermann, 2022; Volkmar et al., 2022). New issues and problems such as the quality and accuracy of information provided, data privacy and protection, and algorithmic biases are challenges that enterprises and managers will need to address in the few upcoming months (Anayat & Rasool, 2022; Davenport et al., 2020; De Bruyn et al., 2020; Dwivedi et al., 2023; Joshi, 2024).

This chapter aims to analyze the opportunities and challenges associated with using generative AI tools like ChatGPT in marketing and business activities through the lens of theoretical background and by analyzing various real-world companies. By exploring this topic, we aim to better understand the advantages and limits of these technologies in the marketing domain and to help professionals and managers use Gen AI efficiently in their practices and strategies. We will also provide at the end of this chapter some research avenues to guide future academic studies that could provide in the future more informed answers on the use of generative AI and its potential to improve the effectiveness and success of the firm's digital strategies.

GENERATIVE AI AND MARKETING COMMUNICATION

Generative Artificial Intelligence (Gen AI) is fundamentally transforming various aspects of marketing including marketing communication. As a technology, it is reshaping how brands and businesses engage with their audiences. This transformation influences all the marketing communication levels (Mehta et al., 2022; Kopalle et al., 2022; Malthouse & Copulsky, 2023). Indeed, AI empowers machines to undertake communication tasks that traditionally required human skills and has progressed from handling structured data (customers, markets, trends, etc.) to managing unstructured data, including images, videos, audio files, and raw text (De Bruyn et al., 2020; Ben Saad & Choura, 2022; Volkmar et al., 2022). Recent advancements in machine learning and deep learning, particularly the emergence of generative AI, have expanded AI's capabilities, introducing different types of intelligence (mechanical, cognitive, and emotional). Mechanical AI automates repetitive communication tasks, cognitive AI processes data to generate insights and make communication decisions, and emotional AI analyzes human interactions to understand and respond with appropriate communication to emotions (Anayat et al., 2022; Dwivedi et al., 2023; Huang & Rust, 2018).

The strategic communication cycle encompassing communication research, communication strategy, and communication actions provides a theoretical framework for evaluating the contributions of these three types of AI (Huang & Rust, 2021). Each type of AI significantly enhances each phase of this cycle. All of them (mechanical, cognitive, and emotional AI) may refine data collection, help in marketing research, guide strategy development (through advanced analytics), and improve digital advertising by automation and personalization. Despite extensive research on AI's technical aspects and its potential opportunities and challenges (Chintalapati & Pandey, 2022; Davenport et al., 2020; De Bruyn et al., 2020), there is a more need to understand how the diverse facets of AI address marketing communication challenges from a strategic perspective.

The Marketing Communication Cycle

The "Research - Strategy - Action" cycle, as shown in Figure 1, serves as a conceptual framework for analyzing marketing communication from a strategic perspective (Huang & Rust, 2021).

Figure 1. The Strategic Communication Cycle (adapted from Huang & Rust, 2021)

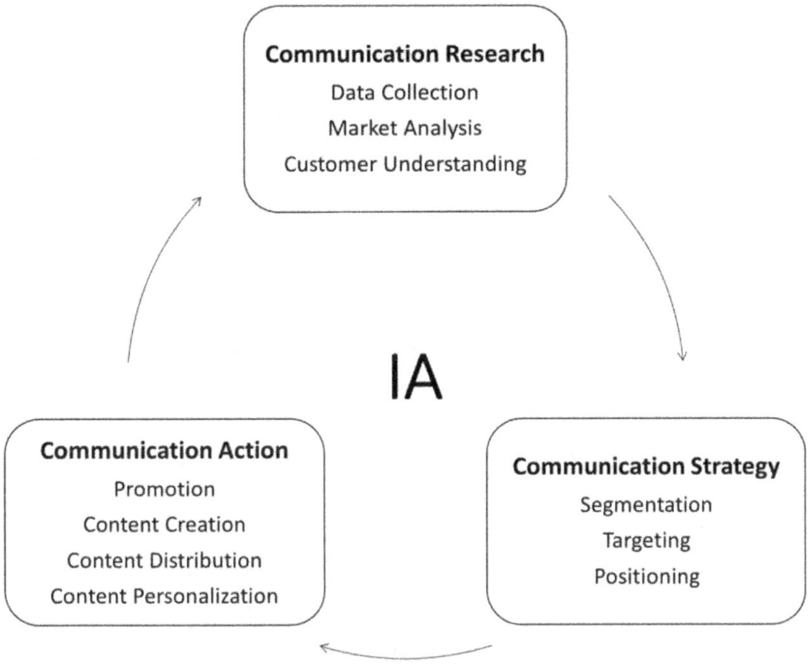

The marketing communication process starts with comprehensive market research. This step is crucial for understanding the competitive landscape, customer behaviors, and needs, providing the foundation for all subsequent actions. Next, in the strategy phase, segmentation, targeting, and positioning are developed. Using insights from the research, marketers define their target audience, identify key market segments, and position their offerings to meet the specific needs of these groups. The third phase involves executing the communication program. This stage ensures that the brand's message is delivered clearly and consistently across all communication channels, engaging customers and reinforcing the brand's position in the market.

Importantly, this process is not a one-time effort but an ongoing cycle. Feedback from the market continuously informs the process, allowing for continuous improvement. This iterative approach ensures that the communication strategy remains relevant and effective as market conditions and customer expectations evolve.

The Marketing Communication Cycle and AI

In the communication research phase, AI could be a powerful tool. It uses advanced systems like intelligent web crawlers and chatbots to automatically gather, organize, and analyze information from online platforms and social networks. Machine learning algorithms then dive deeper into this data, uncovering trends in consumer behavior and markets (Davenport et al., 2020; Gao & Liu, 2022). For example, GenAI could execute an extensive analysis of the reactions of millions of customers to help marketers understand the emotions customers express with their online comments made on social media. During the communication strategy phase, AI could detect patterns in what customers want and how they behave. By analyzing purchase histories for example, Gen AI can identify specific preferences and needs and then suggest which segments of customers to target (Cheng & Jiang, 2021; De Bruyn et al., 2020; Huang & Rust, 2021). Furthermore, Advanced tools like neural networks can even adjust these segments continually as customer behaviors change, ensuring that communication strategies stay relevant at any time.

In the communication action phase, AI ensures that communication efforts align with the strategies set in the previous stages. For instance, AI can automatically tailor advertising content on social media to fit the targeted audience and brand positioning. Additionally, AI-powered chatbots provide personalized customer service, enhancing the overall user experience by offering tailored responses and support.

Table 1 below shows how GenAI influences each stage of the marketing communication cycle. At each stage, AI plays a specific role in supporting marketing tasks. For example, at the stage of marketing research, GenAI supports three main tasks: data collection, market analysis, and customer understanding. Some examples are then presented to explain how AI influences marketing communication in real-world companies.

Table 1. AI and the Marketing Communication Cycle

Stage	Task	AI's Role
Marketing research	Data Collection	Continuously monitoring and gathering market and customer data using automated tools.
	Market Analysis	Using data analysis to understand the perceptions of competitors and partners and compare products.
	Customer Understanding	Analyzing customer emotions and behaviors during interactions to fine-tune marketing strategies.

continued on following page

Table 1. Continued

Stage	Task	AI's Role
Communication Strategy	Segmentation	Identifying new patterns in customer preferences with AI.
	Targeting	Recommending the most profitable customer segments based on past purchase data.
	Positioning	Refining marketing messages to create an emotionally engaging brand position by analyzing customer data.
Communication action	Automating Customer Interaction	Using AI chatbots to deliver targeted messages and provide real-time customer support.
	Personalizing Promotional Content	Tailoring promotions to individual preferences with AI-driven content personalization systems.
	Adapting Communication in Real-Time	Adjusting communication style and tone based on real-time analysis of customer emotional feedback.

EXAMPLES FROM REAL-WORLD COMPANIES

To illustrate the strategic impact of artificial intelligence on marketing communication, we will present different experiences of real-world companies. These companies were chosen based on their relevance and diversity, with data primarily collected from reliable Internet sources. These examples show how various companies have integrated AI into their marketing strategies and communication practices. Through comparative analysis, these examples offer empirical evidence that complements and deepens the theoretical discussion previously presented.

Coca-Cola

Coca-Cola uses AI to make its marketing more personal and engaging. By analyzing customer data, AI helps the company understand what people like in different regions. This allows Coca-Cola to create customized ads and product labels that connect better with consumers. From updating the communication campaign to using AI for content creation and chatbots, the company shows how AI can improve every step of marketing communication, from research to execution. This approach helps Coca-Cola better understand and meet the needs of its global audience.

Starbucks

Starbucks uses AI in its mobile app to make the customer experience more personalized and engaging. AI analyzes past purchases and preferences to suggest drinks and special offers that match each customer's tastes. This helps the app provide useful recommendations, making ordering easier and more enjoyable. Features like customized drink suggestions, targeted promotions, and a smoother ordering process all come from AI-powered insights. By tailoring its approach to individual customers, Starbucks strengthens customer loyalty and improves communication.

Netflix

Netflix uses AI to make marketing more effective by predicting what users will enjoy. First, AI analyzes viewing habits and interactions to understand user preferences. Then, this data helps create personalized content recommendations. Finally, these recommendations are shown to users, keeping them engaged and reducing cancellations. This strategy shows how AI can improve communication by anticipating and adapting to user behavior.

Amazon

Amazon uses AI to enhance both its supply chain and customer experience. First, AI analyzes sales data to predict which products will be in demand, helping Amazon stock inventory efficiently. Next, this data is used to personalize product recommendations based on customer preferences. Finally, these AI-driven strategies are put into action, improving order fulfillment and making shopping more convenient. By integrating AI into both logistics and customer interactions, Amazon creates a seamless experience that boosts efficiency and strengthens communication with its customers.

Sephora: Augmenting Reality with AI

Sephora uses AI to enhance online makeup shopping by making it more personal and interactive. First, the AI scans your facial features and remembers your makeup preferences. Based on this information, it suggests products that would look good on you. Using your phone's camera, you can then try the makeup on virtually in real-time, like a magic mirror. This allows you to see how the makeup will look before you buy it, making the shopping experience more enjoyable and helping you feel more confident in your purchase. In short, Sephora's AI makes online shopping fun and easier by letting you virtually try on products.

Nike

Nike uses AI to transform its content creation and marketing strategies, as shown in the "Nike Epic React" campaign. By analyzing social media interactions and user data, AI identifies specific audience preferences. This information is then used to create personalized video content that speaks directly to different customer groups. As a result, Nike can deliver targeted advertisements that boost engagement. Nike's use of AI in this way helps optimize communication by ensuring content is relevant and tailored to each consumer, highlighting how powerful AI can be in modern marketing.

BMW

BMW, like many modern companies, uses AI-driven chatbots to handle customer inquiries, helping to streamline their customer service. AI analyzes common customer questions to identify patterns, allowing BMW to refine chatbot responses and improve interactions. This results in faster response times, boosting service efficiency and customer satisfaction. By automating routine inquiries, BMW can free up human agents to focus on more complex issues, further enhancing the overall service experience. In summary, this approach accurately reflects how BMW leverages AI chatbots to improve customer service and communication.

H&M

H&M strategically integrates AI into its supply chain to improve operational communication and responsiveness. By analyzing real-time sales data, AI predicts demand trends, allowing H&M to adjust inventory levels proactively. This data-driven approach helps minimize both stock shortages and overstock, ensuring product availability and optimizing resource allocation. As a result, H&M enhances its communication cycle, streamlining operations to better align with consumer demand. This efficiency is crucial in the fast-paced fashion industry, where staying ahead of trends and managing complexities is key to success.

Marketing Research

AI revolutionizes data collection and analysis in the initial phase of marketing communication. For example, Coca-Cola uses AI to personalize content by analyzing large amounts of data, which helps monitor market trends and consumer behavior in real time. Similarly, Starbucks leverages AI to analyze purchase histories, gaining insights into customer preferences. Additionally, AI enhances market analysis through sentiment analysis and emotional data interpretation, allowing companies to refine their strategies with deeper consumer insights. However, the extensive data collection needed for AI raises concerns about privacy and security, making it essential to implement strong measures to protect consumer information and address potential privacy issues.

Communication Strategy

In this phase, AI is essential for developing and improving marketing strategies. For example, Netflix uses AI to analyze viewing habits and tailor content recommendations, which helps them target specific audience segments with personalized content. Similarly, H&M uses AI to adjust inventory in real-time, allowing for more effective segmentation and targeting. AI also helps refine how brands position themselves by analyzing customer emotions and preferences, as seen with Nike's personalized video ads and Sephora's augmented reality tool. However, there are risks with AI-driven segmentation, including potential biases in algorithms and the creation of filter bubbles, which could limit people's exposure to diverse content and ideas.

Communication Action

AI plays a key role in automating and personalizing communication. For example, BMW uses AI-driven chatbots to automate customer interactions, providing instant responses and efficiently handling various inquiries. Similarly, AI enhances engagement by personalizing promotional content, as seen in Amazon's recommendation engine and Starbucks' app, tailoring messages to individual preferences. AI also supports content creation, as demonstrated by Nike's targeted ads, which are highly relevant and engaging. However, it's important to manage this automation carefully to avoid over-reliance and maintain authentic brand messaging. Moreover, while AI allows for real-time adjustments to communication strategies, it requires constant monitoring to ensure it aligns with changing consumer expectations and maintains a balance between personalization and privacy.

AI and Customer Understanding

AI enhances firms' understanding of connected customers by collecting, processing, and analyzing vast amounts of data. Through advanced data analysis, AI tools provide detailed insights into customer behaviors and preferences (Gao & Liu, 2022; Malthouse & Copulsky, 2023; Volkmar et al., 2022). These insights enable businesses to tailor marketing messages and campaigns to local preferences while crafting emotionally resonant communications.

For instance, Starbucks leverages AI in its mobile app to analyze customer purchase histories and preferences, delivering personalized marketing messages that strengthen customer engagement (Cheng & Jiang, 2021). Similarly, AI-powered tools monitor social media activity, gather sentiment data, and track visitor behaviors, allowing firms to refine their marketing strategies (Davenport et al., 2020; Dwivedi et al., 2023). A case in point is Google Analytics, which uses real-time data analysis to predict future customer preferences based on past behavior, facilitating the creation of highly targeted marketing messages (Huang & Rust, 2021).

AI Guides Communication Strategies

AI plays a crucial role in shaping communication strategies by refining segmentation, targeting, and positioning decisions (Ameen et al., 2022; Huang & Rust, 2021; Huang et al., 2019; Mehta et al., 2022). By analyzing complex consumer data patterns, AI enables firms to identify and target specific customer segments with greater precision.

For instance, AI-powered recommendation engines suggest products tailored to individual preferences, optimizing marketing strategies and enhancing customer engagement. Similarly, AI-driven content recommendations leverage predictive analytics to refine marketing messages based on user behavior. Additionally, real-time sentiment analysis tools allow brands to monitor customer reactions and adjust their marketing positioning dynamically, ensuring that communication strategies remain relevant and impactful.

AI Facilitates Executing Communication Strategy

AI streamlines the execution of communication campaigns by automating content creation, distribution, and performance evaluation (Ameen et al., 2022; Huang & Rust, 2021; Malthouse & Copulsky, 2023). For content creation, AI tools like GPT-4 efficiently generate marketing copy, product descriptions, and social media posts on scale. Businesses can also leverage AI to produce personalized video ads, enhancing audience engagement.

For content distribution, AI-driven platforms such as Hootsuite automate scheduling and posting based on user activity, ensuring marketing messages reach the right audience at optimal times.

Finally, AI-powered analytics tools, including Google Analytics, track campaign performance through engagement metrics such as clicks, likes, and shares. This data-driven approach enables firms to refine their marketing strategies in real time, optimizing campaign effectiveness (Chintalapati & Pandey, 2022; Dwivedi et al., 2023; Kshetri et al., 2023).

GENERATIVE AI AND MARKETING DOMAIN

Marketing Service

AI-powered virtual assistants like ChatGPT could play an important role in service management. By leveraging generative AI, businesses can offer automated services that are more relevant to users, cost-effective for clients, and easy to deploy, ultimately enhancing service quality and customer relationships (Cheng & Jiang, 2021; Davenport et al., 2020; De Bruyn et al., 2020; Huang & Rust, 2021). AI chatbots improve customer service by using natural language processing (NLP) to provide intelligent, precise, and personalized responses before and after a purchase (Dwivedi et al., 2023). For instance, an online retailer can integrate ChatGPT into its e-commerce platform to assist customers throughout the purchase cycle. Before a purchase, ChatGPT helps users find suitable products by understanding their preferences and budget, offering tailored recommendations. After the purchase, it manages after-sales support, addressing inquiries related to order tracking, returns, warranties, and exchanges. By delivering accurate, real-time responses, ChatGPT enhances customer experience and service efficiency.

Marketing Automation

Generative AI transforms how businesses produce and deliver services by streamlining, simplifying, and automating processes before, during, and after purchase, often without human intervention (Bezuidenhout et al., 2022; De Bruyn et al., 2020; Huang & Rust, 2021; Volkmar et al., 2022).

For example, an AI-powered online travel agency can deploy an automated recommendation system using deep learning algorithms to analyze customer preferences, booking history, and real-time interactions. This enables the system to generate tailored travel offers dynamically, eliminating the need for human advisors. Such automated, personalized services are likely to become standard across industries like financial services, healthcare, and education, given their low marginal costs and significant productivity gains from process automation (Davenport et al., 2020; Dwivedi et al., 2023).

Customer Journey

Customer experience encompasses a customer's entire journey with a company, spanning multiple touchpoints from pre-purchase to post-purchase interactions. This dynamic process integrates past experiences and external factors at each stage (Lemon & Verhoef, 2016).

Generative AI could reshape the customer journey by enabling companies to innovate and enhance customer interactions (Cheng & Jiang, 2021; Gao & Liu, 2022; Huang & Rust, 2021). For instance, future hair salons could use AI-powered smart mirrors to analyze a customer's hair and suggest hairstyles tailored to their face shape, with haircutting robots executing the chosen style. Similarly, in retail, smart mirrors equipped with augmented reality could allow customers to virtually try on clothes, offering a more interactive and personalized shopping experience.

Marketing Performance

The growing adoption of generative AI is enhancing marketing performance by automating decisions, services, and processes (Dwivedi et al., 2023). In the future, customers may no longer distinguish between AI-driven and human-provided services, as this distinction will likely become insignificant to them (Davenport et al., 2020; Dwivedi et al., 2023).

With continuous advancements in AI and deep learning, customers will prioritize 24/7 service availability and multilingual communication over traditional call centers with fixed hours. Businesses will increasingly rely on conversational agents like ChatGPT to engage customers and provide personalized solutions, reducing costs and optimizing productivity without compromising service quality (Deng & Lin, 2022; Dowling & Lucey, 2023).

Marketing Advertising

Generative AI influences marketing advertising by transforming content creation and producing images, videos, texts, and even music (Dwivedi et al., 2023). This technology reshapes advertising and marketing practices, enabling professionals to generate content more efficiently and develop highly targeted, personalized messages (Chintalapati & Pandey, 2022; Malthouse & Copulsky, 2023; Mehta et al., 2022).

A key application of generative AI in advertising is using text generation algorithms to craft individualized messages and product descriptions tailored to specific audiences. These algorithms use customer data to highlight product features and benefits that are most relevant to each user. This allows brands to create highly personalized websites and social media content more efficiently and automatically (Dumitriu & Popescu, 2020).

Marketing Processes

AI enhances marketing processes by optimizing customer engagement, conversion rates, and campaign effectiveness (Anayat & Rasool, 2022; De Bruyn et al., 2020; Huang & Rust, 2021; Volkmar et al., 2022). Machine learning algorithms can provide data-driven recommendations to improve conversion rates, identify weaknesses in the customer journey, and refine advertising strategies. Additionally, advanced AI systems can optimize product pricing by analyzing market trends, costs, and consumer preferences. AI also plays a crucial role in cybersecurity, using anomaly detection algorithms and deep learning techniques to identify and prevent malicious online activities (Dwivedi et al., 2023). Table 2 summarizes the various ways generative AI impacts different marketing areas. However, these effects will continue to evolve as AI technology advances.

Table 2. Use of GenAI in Marketing

Area	Impact of Generative AI
Customer Service	Improving service by automating responses through AI-powered chatbots available 24/7. Proactively resolving issues using predictive analysis to identify and address potential problems before they affect many customers.
Customer Experience	Enhancing online experiences with personalized recommendations based on previous preferences and purchase history. Personalizing in-store experiences with facial recognition and augmented reality for a more interactive and immersive experience.
Consumer Behavior	Analyzing marketing data in real time to identify trends and consumer expectations. Using statistical modeling and neural networks to understand online and offline behavior, anticipate cross-channel trends, and better meet customer needs.
Content Creation	Generating personalized content, including images and videos, using machine learning and natural language processing algorithms. Creating creative ideas and automatically testing online advertising content.
Process Optimization	Providing recommendations to improve conversion rates, identifying critical points in the customer journey, and optimizing advertising effectiveness using machine learning algorithms. Adjusting product pricing based on market data, costs, and preferences using advanced AI systems. Detecting fraud and malicious activities through AI anomaly detection algorithms and deep learning techniques.

GENERATIVE AI AND NEW CHALLENGES

New Skills

Generative artificial intelligence is reshaping the skills needed for success in the digital age. AI-powered tools, such as virtual assistants and advanced algorithms, are not only automating routine marketing tasks but also redefining the expertise required in the field (Chintalapati & Pandey, 2022; De Bruyn et al., 2020; Huang & Rust, 2021; Mehta et al., 2022).

For instance, sophisticated chatbots like ChatGPT can replace traditional customer service roles and automate content creation, potentially diminishing the need for human in advertising and customer management.

As companies integrate generative AI into their marketing operations, they increasingly require professionals who can manage and leverage AI-generated data effectively. These specialists must possess the skills to interpret AI-driven insights and apply them strategically to enhance marketing performance (Davenport et al., 2020; De Bruyn et al., 2020; Dwivedi et al., 2023).

While AI transforms existing roles, it also creates demand for new capabilities. Adapting to this shift is essential for both companies and marketers, who must learn to collaborate with AI tools to fully harness their potential and maximize their benefits.

Appropriate Use

The adoption of AI tools and generative AI (GenAI) algorithms in marketing raises important concerns regarding their appropriate and ethical use (Cheng & Jiang, 2021; De Bruyn et al., 2020; Kopalle et al., 2022; Volkmar et al., 2022). Effectively leveraging these technologies is not a simple task, it requires both knowledge and expertise to maximize their benefits.

For instance, AI-powered chatbots can generate a wide range of marketing content, from advertisements to product descriptions. However, if not properly managed, they may produce content that fails to accurately reflect customer interests and preferences. Additionally, the improper use of AI-generated content can result in messaging that misaligns with a company's brand image or positioning, potentially harming its reputation (Dwivedi et al., 2023).

Transparency

Generative AI can create different types of content, such as text, images, and videos. However, generating large amounts of information comes with challenges, especially in transparency and understanding how AI works (Anayat & Rasool, 2022; De Bruyn et al., 2020; Dwivedi et al., 2023; Hermann, 2022).

AI tools and algorithms are often seen as "black boxes" meaning it is hard for non-experts to understand how they produce results. For example, marketing professionals using ChatGPT may not know exactly how it generates text, images, or videos. Additionally, AI-generated content can be affected by biases or errors in the training data, which may reduce its quality and reliability (Dwivedi et al., 2023).

Cybersecurity

Using generative AI in marketing also comes with cybersecurity risks. For example, companies that use chatbots or virtual assistants can be targeted by hackers (De Bruyn et al., 2020; Dwivedi et al., 2023; Hermann, 2022). Cybercriminals may pretend to be company representatives, give false information, or try to steal private details like banking information. If a chatbot or virtual assistant is hacked, attackers could access sensitive company data, such as customer names, addresses, phone numbers, and financial records. Table 3 below shows the main challenges of using AI in marketing.

Table 3. Generative AI and New Challenges

Challenges	Description
Skills Evolution	Generative AI transforms marketing skills, making some obsolete and creating new ones. Companies and employees must adapt to maximize the benefits of AI tools.
Misuse of AI	Incorrect use of AI tools like ChatGPT can lead to issues such as inappropriate advertisements and content misalignment with brand image. Proper implementation is essential to avoid negative impacts.
Transparency and Explainability	Generative AI tools pose challenges in terms of understanding their output mechanisms. Professionals must be aware of potential biases and inconsistencies in training data.
Cybersecurity	The use of AI in marketing increases the risk of cyberattacks. Cybercriminals could exploit vulnerabilities to impersonate company representatives or access sensitive information.

CHALLENGES OF USING AI IN MARKETING: INSIGHTS FROM REAL-WORLD COMPANIES

Many companies are using generative AI in marketing to improve customer engagement, boost sales, and optimize operations. However, AI also comes with challenges such as data security risks, bias in content creation, and the need for human oversight. Below are some real-world examples of AI in marketing, along with their benefits and challenges.

Adobe Sensei – AI for Design

- Benefit: Adobe Sensei helps designers create images and layouts automatically, saving time and effort.
- Challenge: AI-generated designs may lack originality and creativity, requiring human adjustments.

Coca-Cola – AI-Powered Customer Chatbots

- Benefit: AI chatbots answer customer questions, recommend products, and personalize interactions.
- Challenge: If not well-trained, chatbots may provide incorrect responses, harming the brand's reputation.

Sephora Virtual Artist – AI for Beauty

- Benefit: Customers can try on makeup virtually, making online shopping easier.
- Challenge: AI-generated recommendations may not always match real-life results, leading to customer dissatisfaction.

IBM Watson – AI in Finance

- Benefit: AI helps banks detect fraud, assist customers, and analyze financial trends.
- Challenge: AI systems require large amounts of sensitive data, increasing cybersecurity risks.

H&M – AI for Inventory Management

- Benefit: AI predicts fashion trends and manages stock to reduce waste and meet demand.
- Challenge: AI predictions may not always be accurate, leading to overstock or shortages.

Amazon – AI for Product Recommendations

- Benefit: AI suggests products based on customer behavior, increasing sales.
- Challenge: AI may over-recommend certain products, limiting variety for customers.

BMW – AI for Customer Assistance

- Benefit: BMW's AI assistant helps drivers with voice commands and car settings.
- Challenge: AI assistants can misunderstand voice inputs, leading to frustration.

Spotify – AI for Personalized Playlists

- Benefit: AI creates custom playlists based on listening habits, improving user experience.
- Challenge: AI recommendations can become repetitive if not properly updated.

Nike – AI for Personalized Marketing

- Benefit: AI helps Nike create custom shoes and marketing campaigns based on customer preferences.
- Challenge: AI-driven customization may lead to production delays if not well-managed.

Unilever – AI for Content Creation

- Benefit: AI automates social media posts and ads, making marketing faster and more efficient.
- Challenge: AI-generated content may lack human creativity and emotional appeal.

GEN AI AND NEW PRACTICES

AI-Powered Personalization

AI is becoming popular in marketing because it helps personalize content. For example, Amazon's recommendation system and Spotify's personalized playlists suggest products or music based on what customers like. These AI systems get better over time by learning from customer choices, making their suggestions more accurate. This is important for customer engagement. By giving customers what they want, AI helps build stronger relationships and makes them more loyal. Nike is a good example. It lets customers design their own shoes using AI, making the product feel more personal. This leads to stronger connections with the brand and more purchases.

AI-Powered Automation

AI helps automate routine tasks which offer valuable benefits for companies. For example, Adobe Sensei and H&M use AI to make their processes more efficient. These AI systems save time by handling repetitive tasks, which lowers costs and lets employees focus on more important, creative work. Adobe Sensei, for example, helps designers by automating design tasks, so they can focus on being more creative. H&M uses AI in its supply chain to improve inventory accuracy and quickly respond to market trends, reducing waste and boosting efficiency.

These improvements give companies a competitive position by helping them operate more efficiently and adapt quickly to changes in the market. AI also helps with complex decisions like setting prices and predicting trends, allowing businesses to adjust their marketing strategies.

AI-Powered Services

AI has transformed customer service, especially through AI-powered chatbots and virtual assistants. BMW's Intelligent Personal Assistant and Coca-Cola's AI chatbots show how AI can provide 24/7 support, offering quick and accurate answers to customer questions. This improves customer satisfaction by reducing wait times and ensuring consistent service quality. AI also helps customer service teams scale up their operations. For example, ChatGPT can handle complex questions in multiple languages, making it useful for global companies that want to offer excellent service in many markets. However, there are still challenges, like finding the right balance between automation and human interaction, which is important for handling more complex customer issues.

AI-Powered Content Creation

Generative AI is changing how content is created in marketing. For example, Unilever uses AI to automate content for its brands, which helps keep creativity high while staying consistent across different marketing channels. AI can create text, images, and videos that follow brand guidelines and quickly adjust to trends and customer preferences.

AI also helps improve marketing campaigns. Amazon's recommendation system shows how AI can analyze customer behavior to suggest products, which leads to more sales and higher conversion rates. AI tools also give valuable insights into how campaigns are performing, helping marketers adjust their strategies for better results.

AI-Powered Security

While AI offers many benefits across various marketing practices, it also presents several challenges and ethical considerations that need to be addressed. A key concern is the potential misuse of AI, such as generating content that does not align with a brand's identity. Moreover, ensuring the transparency and explainability of AI systems is essential for maintaining fairness and minimizing bias in AI-driven decisions. Cybersecurity also remains a significant issue, as AI systems can become prime targets for cyberattacks. Therefore, companies must implement robust security measures to safeguard sensitive customer data from breaches. Table 4 summarizes the impact of Generative AI on marketing practices.

Table 4. Gen AI and New Practices

Practice	AI Applications	Examples	Key Insights
Customer Personalization	Personalized recommendations, targeted advertising	Amazon (Recommendations), Spotify (Playlists)	Enhances customer engagement and loyalty through tailored experiences.
Operational Efficiency	Supply chain optimization, generative design	H&M (Supply Chain), Adobe Sensei (Design Automation)	Reduces costs and improves operational agility by automating routine tasks.
Customer Service	AI-powered chatbots, virtual assistants	BMW (Personal Assistant), Coca-Cola (Chatbots)	Provides scalable, 24/7 customer support, improving service quality and consistency.

continued on following page

Table 4. Continued

Practice	AI Applications	Examples	Key Insights
Content Creation	Automated content generation, creative AI tools	Unilever (Content Creation), Nike (Customization)	Facilitates high-volume, personalized content production, driving brand consistency.
Marketing Optimization	Predictive analytics, dynamic pricing	Amazon (Recommendation System), H&M (Market Response)	Optimizes marketing strategies in real-time based on data-driven insights.
Ethical and Security Challenges	Transparency, bias in AI models, cybersecurity risks	General Industry Concerns	Requires careful management to prevent misuse and ensure ethical AI deployment.

STRATEGIES FOR SUCCESSFUL ADOPTION AND USE OF AI

Successfully adopting AI and integrating it with human service requires a clear strategy and careful planning, especially in today's digital environment. Marketers can adopt AI not only to improve efficiency but also to strengthen customer relationships and provide personalized experiences.

Key Practices

To maximize AI's use in marketing, businesses should focus on the following key strategic practices:

- Define Clear Objectives and Needs: Identify the marketing processes that can be automated through AI (e.g., customer segmentation, content personalization, predictive analytics) while recognizing areas where human interaction remains essential (e.g., building emotional connections, high-level decision-making).
- Select the Right AI Tools: Choose AI technologies tailored to specific marketing needs. For example, generative AI can be leveraged to create personalized content, while chatbots or virtual assistants can improve customer engagement and reduce response times.
- Train and Support Employees: Equip marketing teams with the skills to effectively use AI tools, and ensure smooth collaboration between AI systems and human service providers. A hybrid model in which employees work alongside AI will maximize operational efficiency and customer satisfaction.

- Measure and Optimize: Establish key performance indicators (KPIs) to assess the impact of AI and human service integration. Metrics such as customer satisfaction, brand loyalty, conversion rates, and the time it takes to resolve customer queries will help marketers adjust strategies and refine the use of AI.
- Ethics and Transparency: Communicate clearly with customers about the role of AI in their interactions with the brand. Ensuring transparency, especially regarding data usage, builds trust and helps customers feel more comfortable engaging with AI-driven marketing channels.

Determinants of AI Adoption and Use

Generative AI gives businesses a powerful way to improve customer engagement and satisfaction. For successful adoption, marketers need to consider key factors such as AI capabilities, customer needs, and service delivery methods. Understanding these factors helps companies ensure AI is accepted and valued by users. The main factors influencing AI adoption and use include: system characteristics, customer characteristics, and service characteristics. System characteristics deal with how AI is designed and its ability to meet customer expectations. They play a critical role in its adoption. For example, a personalized generative AI content tool that creates product recommendations based on customer behavior is more likely to be embraced than a one-size-fits-all solution. Customer characteristics are about customers' familiarity with technology, age, gender, cultural background, and personality traits. They affect how they perceive and use AI. Younger, tech-savvy generations may be more receptive to AI-driven marketing experiences like chatbots or personalized email campaigns. However, older customers might prefer a more human-centered approach or require additional support when interacting with AI-powered services. Service characteristics determine the way AI interacts with customers. The nature of the service and the level of interaction required are key to determining AI's role in the customer journey. For instance, AI can automate routine tasks such as answering FAQs or processing transactions, but for more complex queries or emotionally driven services (like customer complaints or high-stakes purchases), human interaction remains vital.

System Characteristics

- Design: Intuitive AI interfaces, such as personalized recommendation engines or generative AI tools that create content based on customer profiles, will be better received. Human-like interactions, including the use of conversational

AI with natural language processing, can make the customer experience more engaging and relatable.

- Notification: Transparent communication about AI usage is critical for fostering trust. For example, informing customers when they are interacting with a generative AI system for personalized content creation will ensure customers understand the role AI plays in their journey.
- Proactivity: AI that anticipates customers' needs—such as sending personalized offers or content recommendations—based on previous interactions or data trends, will enhance engagement. Marketers can use generative AI to create tailored marketing messages that are proactive rather than reactive.
- Affect: AI that displays empathy or emotional intelligence can enhance customer experiences. A generative AI tool, for example, can create content or interactions that resonate emotionally with customers by considering tone, sentiment, and personalization. This is especially useful for brands trying to create lasting emotional connections with their audience.

Customer Characteristics

- Technological Readiness: The more familiar customers are with technology, the more likely they are to embrace AI-driven marketing. Marketers can use generative AI to create personalized experiences for more tech-savvy segments, but they must also ensure that simpler options are available for less familiar customers.
- Cultural Influence: AI adoption can vary significantly across cultures. For instance, in some regions, AI is perceived as a valuable tool, while in others, there may be concerns about privacy or trust. Marketers must adapt their AI tools to meet cultural expectations and preferences.
- Personality and Engagement: Customers who exhibit traits like curiosity or openness to new experiences are more likely to adopt AI-driven marketing tools. Marketers can design engaging, interactive experiences that allow customers to experiment with AI features, increasing their engagement with the brand.

Service Characteristics

- Information Delivery: The clarity, relevance, and personalization of AI-generated content can significantly impact customer perceptions. Generative AI models can create tailored product recommendations, advertisements, and content that speak directly to the customer's interests and behaviors.

- Level of Involvement: The degree to which customers are involved in AI decisions can enhance their experience. For example, an AI-driven platform that allows customers to customize their preferences for product recommendations or marketing messages will make customers feel more engaged and valued.
- Problem Resolution: AI's ability to handle complaints and resolve issues effectively can influence its acceptance. When generative AI tools are employed to provide quick and relevant responses to customer queries, they contribute to an enhanced customer experience, improving customer loyalty.

Adoption of AI with Human Service

The integration of generative AI with human service presents a unique opportunity for marketers to create exceptional customer experiences. By combining AI's ability to deliver personalized, efficient solutions with human empathy and judgment for more complex interactions, brands can enhance customer satisfaction and foster loyalty. AI should not be seen as a replacement for human service but as a tool that amplifies it, allowing humans to focus on high-touch, emotionally intelligent aspects of customer interaction. As AI continues to evolve, its integration into marketing practices will only grow, offering marketers more innovative ways to engage with customers and build lasting relationships.

TRENDS OF AI IN MARKETING

Artificial Intelligence is profoundly reshaping the service sector in a transformative and far-reaching manner. Comparable to past industrial and digital revolutions, this technological shift not only alters how services are delivered but also redefines consumer interactions. AI holds the potential to revolutionize traditional service paradigms; however, this transition also presents complex challenges and raises critical ethical concerns. This chapter explores current AI trends in services and identifies the key challenges that must be addressed to optimize its adoption and effectiveness.

Increased Automation

AI is being implemented across various service sectors, driving significant transformations in service delivery methods and customer perceptions. Automation is one of the most prominent aspects of AI in services, drastically changing how tasks are performed. While automation enhances efficiency, it also raises concerns about the quality of human interactions.

For example, in the banking sector, AI-powered chatbots, such as those deployed by Ally Bank, have revolutionized loan application processing and financial advising. These automated systems handle a high volume of requests simultaneously, reducing operational costs and improving service speed. However, automation may also lead to depersonalization, particularly in cases requiring personalized attention, such as complex or sensitive financial inquiries.

Similarly, in the hospitality industry, virtual assistants used by Marriott International leverage natural language processing to provide personalized recommendations and respond to customer inquiries. While these assistants enhance customer satisfaction by offering quick and tailored responses, they may lack the emotional nuance that human interactions provide.

Enhanced Personalization

AI enables advanced service personalization by analyzing vast datasets to tailor offerings to individual consumer needs. While this level of customization is advantageous, it also presents significant challenges.

E-commerce giants like Amazon use sophisticated algorithms to recommend products based on users' purchase histories and preferences. This ability to provide personalized recommendations can increase sales and customer loyalty. However, collecting and analyzing personal data raises privacy and security concerns, requiring careful data management to maintain consumer trust.

Platforms such as Mint utilize AI to analyze users' spending habits and offer personalized financial advice. While this approach helps consumers better manage their finances, an overreliance on automated recommendations may limit users' ability to make independent financial decisions and understand underlying financial principles.

Improved Efficiency

AI enhances accuracy and speed across various service sectors, though its growing reliance requires careful monitoring to mitigate associated risks.

For instance, IBM Watson employs AI to analyze medical images and detect anomalies, such as tumors, with accuracy comparable to that of human experts. This technology enables faster and more precise diagnostics, which is critical for patient care. However, excessive dependence on AI systems could reduce healthcare professionals' involvement in case evaluations, potentially impacting the quality of care.

Similarly, companies like DHL use AI to optimize delivery routes, reducing costs and transit times through real-time predictive analytics. Despite these benefits, over-optimization could overlook human factors, such as the need for flexibility in unforeseen circumstances.

Productivity Enhancement

AI facilitates large-scale task management, but this increased efficiency should not overshadow potential challenges related to automation.

For example, chatbots developed by companies like Intercom handle numerous customer inquiries simultaneously, providing 24/7 support without fatigue. This reduces costs and improves response times. However, excessive automation may result in a loss of personal touch in customer service, making interactions feel less human.

Tools like UiPath automate repetitive processes such as data entry and invoice processing, freeing employees to focus on higher-value activities. However, excessive automation may lead to skill loss among employees and increased dependency on technology.

Service Employees and Service Robots

The service sector is undergoing significant transformation due to the rising influence of AI and robotics. While human employees require ongoing training and incur high hiring costs, service robots though expensive initially offer long-term cost savings through scalability and reduced labor expenses. Furthermore, their ability to provide standardized services ensures consistent productivity. Service robots and human employees will likely coexist, each contributing unique advantages to enhancing customer experiences (Table 5). Organizations must adopt strategic approaches to integrating these technologies while maintaining the human aspect of service.

Table 5. Service Employees and Service Robots

Dimension	Service Employees	Service Robots
Training and Learning	Requires initial and ongoing training	Systematic updates and unlimited data access
Customer Experience	Varied experience, subject to biases	Consistent and scalable personalization
Additional Costs	High costs for new hires	High initial costs, but significant economies of scale

Integrating Emotional Intelligence

Developing emotionally intelligent AI systems remains a significant challenge with important implications for service design and interactions. Technologies developed by companies like Affectiva aim to detect human emotions by analyzing facial expressions and vocal tones. While these systems are improving in emotional recognition, they still struggle to capture the complexity of human emotions and their impact on interactions.

Service robots, such as Pepper by SoftBank Robotics, are designed to establish emotional connections with users. However, ensuring that these interactions feel natural rather than artificial is crucial for maintaining a positive user experience. AI systems must also strike a careful balance in their level of proactivity to avoid being perceived as intrusive. Users generally prefer proactive assistance only when it is clearly beneficial and expected, requiring thoughtful design of AI behaviors.

Impact of AI on Employment

The impact of AI on employment is a complex issue that requires in-depth analysis of its social and economic effects.

While AI can automate many tasks, certain sectors, such as elderly care, still require human interaction that cannot be entirely replaced by robots. AI should be designed to complement, rather than replace, human interactions. Customers often prefer human interactions in contexts where empathy and understanding are crucial, such as healthcare and education. It is essential to develop AI systems that enhance service quality without eliminating essential human interactions.

Ethics and Governance

Establishing a robust ethical and governance framework for AI is essential to ensuring its responsible use. Privacy concerns are at the heart of AI debates, requiring clear regulations to protect user data while enabling innovation. Researchers must explore governance models that balance innovation with data protection.

Ensuring transparency in AI algorithms is crucial to building user trust and preventing systemic biases. Future research should focus on developing methods to make AI decision-making processes more explainable and accessible.

FUTURE RESEARCH ON AI

The application of AI in services presents numerous research opportunities, particularly regarding its impact on customer experience, employment, and ethics. Several key areas require further exploration to optimize AI integration while meeting user and business expectations. First, AI design poses significant challenges, particularly in integrating emotions and empathy into interactions and balancing autonomy with service personalization. It is also critical to determine whether AI can truly replace certain human jobs or if a collaborative approach between employees and AI systems would be more effective in enhancing efficiency and customer satisfaction.

Furthermore, AI-driven customer experiences warrant careful study to identify the most valuable touchpoints in the customer journey and how AI interactions create value.

Finally, ethical concerns surrounding AI in services must be addressed, including issues of accountability in case of failure and the social and psychological consequences of AI deployment. These research directions offer valuable insights for a more ethical and effective application of AI in service industries. Table 6 below summarizes the future research on AI specially on the service domain.

Table 6. Future Research on AI Application in Services (Adapted from Flavián & Casaló, 2021)

Themes	Questions	Research Topics
AI Design Challenges	How should emotions/affects be integrated into AI-based services?	• Ability to identify emotions • Robot personality design • Appropriate level of robot proactivity • Adaptation to customers • Possible differences due to individual characteristics or service context.
	What additional elements should be integrated into AI to add value?	• Analysis of the optimal level of anthropomorphism • Exploration of additional physical capabilities • Appropriate level of empowerment • Study of potential differences due to individual characteristics or service context.
AI and Employment	Should companies replace employees with AI initiatives?	• Identifying services that still require human intervention (e.g., childcare) • Analyzing the consequences of government regulations and laws.
	Do customers prefer employee-AI collaboration over replacement?	• Identifying task-level differences • Deepening the understanding of the strengths and limitations of both systems.

continued on following page

Table 6. Continued

Themes	Questions	Research Topics
Customer Experience with AI	At what points in the customer journey should AI interactions occur?	• Identifying customer segments: should companies let customers choose? • Understanding customer preferences for AI services: Why and which customers prefer these services?
		• Analyzing customer responses to AI services at different moments (e.g., post-service sales, complaint management). • Identifying the preferred moments for AI interactions.
	How can AI initiatives create value for customers?	• Gaining deeper insights into key factors (e.g., customer-centric, service-related, or technological) influencing value creation through AI services. • Analyzing the value of AI services for existing and potential customers.
		• Comparing whether AI is more effective in retaining existing customers or attracting new ones. • Studying AI initiatives in B2C and B2B contexts. • Addressing concerns related to AI-driven customer data analysis.
Ethics	Who is responsible in case of AI failure?	• Analyzing liability assigned to the company (owner), developer, government, the robot itself, society, or customers. • Assessing the perceived severity of failure. • Identifying differences depending on the tasks involved.
	What could be the negative consequences of implementing AI services?	• Identifying not only physical harm but also potential psychological damage (e.g., loneliness, feeling of incompetence). • Analyzing potential inequalities (e.g., job losses, robots preferred over humans).
		• Examining the consequences of possible dehumanization. • Identifying other unforeseen consequences.

Future research on AI applications in services will focus on four key themes: AI design, employment impact, customer experience, and ethical considerations. First, AI design research should explore how to integrate emotions effectively, optimize anthropomorphism, and tailor AI interactions to individual customer needs. Second, the employment dimension examines whether AI should replace or complement human workers, considering task-specific requirements and regulatory implications. Third, customer experience research focuses on determining the optimal points for AI interactions in the service journey and assessing AI's effectiveness in enhancing customer engagement and retention. Finally, ethical concerns address responsibility in cases of AI failure and potential negative consequences, such as job displacement, psychological effects, and dehumanization. Together, these themes provide a comprehensive framework for understanding and advancing AI-driven service innovation.

CONCLUSION

Artificial Intelligence (AI) has revolutionized marketing communications by streamlining operations, enhancing customer insights, and enabling more effective decision-making. By automating repetitive tasks, processing vast amounts of data, and analyzing customer sentiments, AI empowers businesses to craft data-driven marketing strategies and optimize digital communication execution. While AI offers remarkable benefits, businesses must also navigate challenges such as maintaining a human touch in customer interactions and ensuring ethical AI deployment.

To fully leverage AI's capabilities while addressing these challenges, companies should adopt strategic approaches that include investing in AI expertise, aligning AI with marketing strategies, balancing automation with personalization, ensuring data privacy and security, and continuously evaluating AI's impact. Recruiting and training professionals with AI competencies can enhance content creation, campaign management, and personalization while maintaining human oversight to ensure authenticity and brand consistency. AI should complement rather than replace traditional marketing methods, serving as a strategic enabler within broader communication initiatives to enhance engagement and efficiency. Automation improves content creation, distribution, and performance tracking, but businesses must also implement personalization strategies to foster meaningful customer interactions. Transparency in AI-driven data handling and adherence to privacy regulations are critical for maintaining customer trust, requiring robust cybersecurity measures to protect sensitive information. AI-driven strategies must also be regularly assessed based on key performance indicators (KPIs) such as customer satisfaction, return on investment (ROI), and engagement metrics to refine approaches and mitigate unintended consequences.

Future research should focus on key areas that enhance AI's role in marketing communication. Cross-platform data integration can help synthesize data from various sources, such as social media, websites, and mobile apps, creating a unified customer view and improving understanding of customer behavior across multiple touchpoints. Advanced emotional AI mechanisms can refine content personalization by accurately interpreting and responding to emotional cues, significantly improving engagement and optimizing communication strategies. Financial implications and ROI should be analyzed to assess the profitability, productivity, and cost-effectiveness of AI-powered tools in content creation, distribution, and performance measurement. Ethical and regulatory frameworks must be developed to ensure responsible

AI deployment in marketing, addressing data transparency, algorithmic biases, and ethical AI-driven customer interactions. Additionally, best practices for human-AI interaction should be examined to integrate AI-driven efficiencies while maintaining a personal touch in marketing communications, fostering trust and engagement.

The advent of generative AI tools, such as ChatGPT, presents new opportunities for innovation in marketing communication. These tools offer immense potential for content creation, data-driven insights, and customer engagement but also introduce challenges related to brand consistency, security, and ethical considerations. Strategies for maximizing generative AI in marketing include developing an AI-proficient workforce, leveraging AI for data-driven insights, ensuring brand consistency, optimizing efficiency and security, and adapting marketing strategies dynamically. Training employees in AI-related skills can help integrate generative AI seamlessly across online and offline customer experiences. AI-powered analytics can extract deep customer insights and optimize cross-channel marketing strategies. Establishing clear content guidelines ensures that AI-generated material aligns with the brand's identity, values, and positioning. Designing AI-powered marketing frameworks can enhance operational efficiency while incorporating robust security measures to mitigate cyber threats and prevent misinformation. AI-driven marketing strategies must also be continuously refined to maximize benefits and address emerging challenges in consumer behavior and technological advancements.

To fully explore the transformative potential of generative AI, future research should investigate its impact on content creation, customer interaction enhancements, brand management, and ethical considerations in AI deployment. Research should assess how generative AI influences brand storytelling, content strategy, and audience engagement. The role of AI-powered conversational agents in reshaping customer communication and overall brand experience should also be examined. AI's role in brand management should be explored in relation to brand image development, online reputation monitoring, and risk mitigation. Ethical considerations should be a focus to ensure responsible AI use in marketing, particularly in content personalization and customer engagement, aligning with ethical guidelines.

By addressing these key areas, businesses and researchers can gain valuable insights into the effective utilization of AI in marketing communications. When implemented strategically and responsibly, AI has the potential to redefine marketing strategies, drive customer engagement, and optimize business performance. As AI technology continues to evolve, companies must remain adaptive and proactive in leveraging its capabilities to sustain competitive advantage in the ever-changing digital marketing landscape.

REFERENCES

Ameen, N., Sharma, G. D., Tarba, S., Rao, A., & Chopra, R. (2022). Toward advancing theory on creativity in marketing and artificial intelligence. *Psychology and Marketing*, *39*(9), 1802–1825. DOI: 10.1002/mar.21699

Anayat, S., & Rasool, G. (2022). Artificial intelligence marketing (AIM): Connecting-the-dots using bibliometrics. *Journal of Marketing Theory and Practice*. Advance online publication. DOI: 10.1080/10696679.2022.2103435

Ben Saad, S., & Choura, F. (2022). Online shopping during the Covid-19 crisis: The impact of anthropomorphic virtual agents on consumers' psychological states. *International Journal of Technology Marketing*, *16*(1/2), 27–49. DOI: 10.1504/IJTMKT.2022.122450

Bezuidenhout, C., Heffernan, T., Abbas, R., & Mehmet, M. (2022). The impact of Artificial Intelligence on the marketing practices of Professional Services Firms. *Journal of Marketing Theory and Practice*, *0*(0), 1–22. DOI: 10.1080/10696679.2022.2090005

Cheng, Y., & Jiang, H. (2021). Customer–brand relationship in the era of artificial intelligence: Understanding the role of chatbot marketing efforts. *Journal of Product and Brand Management*, *31*(2), 252–264. DOI: 10.1108/JPBM-05-2020-2907

Chintalapati, S., & Pandey, S. K. (2022). Artificial intelligence in marketing: A systematic literature review. *International Journal of Market Research*, *64*(1), 38–68. DOI: 10.1177/14707853211018428

Davenport, T., Guha, A., Grewal, D., & Bressgott, T. (2020). How artificial intelligence will change the future of marketing. *Journal of the Academy of Marketing Science*, *48*(1), 24–42. DOI: 10.1007/s11747-019-00696-0

De Bruyn, A., Viswanathan, V., Beh, Y. S., Brock, J. K.-U., & von Wangenheim, F. (2020). Artificial intelligence and marketing: Pitfalls and opportunities. *Journal of Interactive Marketing*, *51*(1), 91–105. DOI: 10.1016/j.intmar.2020.04.007

Deng, J., & Lin, Y. (2022). The benefits and challenges of ChatGPT: An overview. *Frontiers in Computing and Intelligent Systems*, *2*(2), 2. Advance online publication. DOI: 10.54097/fcis.v2i2.4465

Dowling, M., & Lucey, B. (2023). ChatGPT for (finance) research: The Bananarama conjecture. *Finance Research Letters*, *53*, 103662. DOI: 10.1016/j.frl.2023.103662

Dumitriu, D., & Popescu, M. A.-M. (2020). Artificial intelligence solutions for digital marketing. *Procedia Manufacturing*, *46*, 630–636. DOI: 10.1016/j.promfg.2020.03.090

Dwivedi, Y. K., Kshetri, N., Hughes, L., Slade, E. L., Jeyaraj, A., Kar, A. K., Baabdullah, A. M., Koohang, A., Raghavan, V., Ahuja, M., Albanna, H., Albashrawi, M. A., Al-Busaidi, A. S., Balakrishnan, J., Barlette, Y., Basu, S., Bose, I., Brooks, L., Buhalis, D., & Wright, R. (2023). "So what if ChatGPT wrote it?" Multidisciplinary perspectives on opportunities, challenges and implications of generative conversational AI for research, practice and policy. *International Journal of Information Management*, *71*, 102642. DOI: 10.1016/j.ijinfomgt.2023.102642

Flavián, C., & Casaló, L. V. (2021). Artificial intelligence in services: Current trends, benefits and challenges. *Service Industries Journal*, *41*(13–14), 853–859. DOI: 10.1080/02642069.2021.1989177

Gao, Y., & Liu, H. (2022). Artificial intelligence-enabled personalization in interactive marketing: A customer journey perspective. *Journal of Research in Interactive Marketing, ahead-of-print*, 1–18. https://doi.org/DOI: 10.1108/JRIM-01-2022-0023

Hermann, E. (2022). Leveraging artificial intelligence in marketing for social good—An ethical perspective. *Journal of Business Ethics*, *179*(1), 43–61. DOI: 10.1007/s10551-021-04843-y PMID: 34054170

Hongladarom, S., & Sakprasert, S. (2024). Ethical implications of Thai ChatGPT public discourses. *Communication Research and Practice*, 1–12. https://doi.org/DOI: 10.1080/22041451.2024.2346429

Huang, M.-H., & Rust, R. (2021). A strategic framework for artificial intelligence in marketing. *Journal of the Academy of Marketing Science*, *49*(1), 30–50. DOI: 10.1007/s11747-020-00749-9

Huang, M.-H., Rust, R., & Maksimovic, V. (2019). The feeling economy: Managing in the next generation of artificial intelligence (AI). *California Management Review*, *61*(4), 43–65. DOI: 10.1177/0008125619863436

Huang, M.-H., & Rust, R. T. (2018). Artificial intelligence in service. *Journal of Service Research*, *21*(2), 155–172. DOI: 10.1177/1094670517752459

Joshi, D. (2024). *AI governance in India – law, policy and political economy*. Communication Research and Practice., DOI: 10.1080/22041451.2024.2346428

Kopalle, P. K., Gangwar, M., Kaplan, A., Ramachandran, D., Reinartz, W., & Rindfleisch, A. (2022). Examining artificial intelligence (AI) technologies in marketing via a global lens: Current trends and future research opportunities. *International Journal of Research in Marketing*, *39*(2), 522–540. DOI: 10.1016/j.ijresmar.2021.11.002

Kshetri, N., Dwivedi, Y. K., Davenport, T. H., & Panteli, N. (2023). Generative artificial intelligence in marketing: Applications, opportunities, challenges, and research agenda. *International Journal of Information Management*. Advance online publication. DOI: 10.1016/j.ijinfomgt.2023.102716

Lee, T. (2024). Artificial intelligence: Governing Singapore's smart digital journey. *Communication Research and Practice*, 1–9. https://doi.org/DOI: 10.1080/22041451.2024.2346430

Lemon, K. N., & Verhoef, P. C. (2016). Understanding customer experience throughout the customer journey. *Journal of Marketing*, *80*(6), 69–96. DOI: 10.1509/jm.15.0420

Malthouse, E., & Copulsky, J. (2023). Artificial intelligence ecosystems for marketing communications. *International Journal of Advertising*, *42*(1), 128–140. DOI: 10.1080/02650487.2022.2122249

Mehta, P., Jebarajakirthy, C., Maseeh, H. I., Anubha, A., Saha, R., & Dhanda, K. (2022). Artificial intelligence in marketing: A meta-analytic review. *Psychology and Marketing*, *39*(11), 2013–2038. DOI: 10.1002/mar.21716

Tariq, M. U. (2025). Empowering patients with AI-ethical digital tools for health data management and decision. In Pesqueira, A., & de Bem Machado, A. (Eds.), *Navigating privacy, innovation, and patient empowerment through ethical healthcare technology* (pp. 197–216). IGI Global., DOI: 10.4018/979-8-3693-7630-0.ch008

Volkmar, G., Fischer, P. M., & Reinecke, S. (2022). Artificial intelligence and machine learning: Exploring drivers, barriers, and future developments in marketing management. *Journal of Business Research*, *149*, 599–614. DOI: 10.1016/j.jbusres.2022.04.007

Compilation of References

Abbas, M., Jam, F. A., & Khan, T. I. (2024). Is it harmful or helpful? Examining the causes and consequences of generative AI usage among university students. *International Journal of Educational Technology in Higher Education*, *21*(1), 10. DOI: 10.1186/s41239-024-00444-7

Adamopoulou, E., & Moussiades, L. (2020). An overview of chatbot technology. In *IFIP international conference on artificial intelligence applications and innovations* (pp. 373–383). Springer.

Adamopoulou, E., & Moussiades, L. (2020). Chatbots: History, technology, and applications. *Machine Learning with Applications*, *2*, 100006. DOI: 10.1016/j.mlwa.2020.100006

Aishwarya S, Selvamurugan C, Parthiban K G, Nathan B, Manoj Prabhakar J, Mohamed Noordeen A (2024). Generative AI in focus : A comprehensive review of leading models across modalities. IEEE, 1–9. DOI: 10.1109/ICUIS64676.2024.10867014

Ajagekar, A., & You, F. (2023). Molecular design with automated quantum computing-based deep learning and optimization. *npj Computational Materials*, *9*(1), 143. https://doi.org/DOI: 10.1038/s41524-023-01099-0

Akhtar, Z. B. (2024). Unveiling the evolution of generative AI (GAI): A comprehensive and investigative analysis toward LLM models (2021–2024) and beyond. *Journal of Electrical Systems and Information Technology*, *11*(1), 22. DOI: 10.1186/s43067-024-00145-1

Alsentzer, E., Murphy, J., Boag, W., Weng, W.-H., Jindi, D., Naumann, T., & McDermott, M. (2019). *Publicly available clinical. Proceedings of the 2nd Clinical Natural Language Processing Workshop*. https://doi.org/DOI: 10.18653/v1/W19-1909

Ameen, N., Sharma, G. D., Tarba, S., Rao, A., & Chopra, R. (2022). Toward advancing theory on creativity in marketing and artificial intelligence. *Psychology and Marketing*, *39*(9), 1802–1825. DOI: 10.1002/mar.21699

Anayat, S., & Rasool, G. (2022). Artificial intelligence marketing (AIM): Connecting-the-dots using bibliometrics. *Journal of Marketing Theory and Practice*. Advance online publication. DOI: 10.1080/10696679.2022.2103435

An, P., Liang, J., Hong, X., Quan, S., Ma, T., Chen, Y., Wang, L., & Ma, J. (2023). Leveraging self-paced semi-supervised learning with prior knowledge for 3D object detection on a LiDAR-camera system. *Remote Sensing (Basel)*, *15*(3), 627. DOI: 10.3390/rs15030627

Arora, A., Arora, A., & McIntyre, J. (2023). Developing chatbots for cyber security: Assessing threats through sentiment analysis on social media. *Sustainability (Basel)*, *15*(17), 13178. DOI: 10.3390/su151713178

Ashikullah, M. (2024). Investigating the pros and cons of Artificial Intelligence (AI)-Based Systems: A case study on the use of ChaTGPT in higher education in the northern region of Bangladesh. *International Journal on Studies in English Language and Literature*, *12*(6), 1–8. DOI: 10.20431/2347-3134.1206001

Askr, H., Elgeldawi, E., Aboul Ella, H., Elshaier, Y. A. M. M., Gomaa, M. M., & Hassanien, A. E. (2023). Deep learning in drug discovery: An integrative review and future challenges. *Artificial Intelligence Review*, *56*(7), 5975–6037. DOI: 10.1007/s10462-022-10306-1 PMID: 36415536

Aslam, F. (2023). The impact of artificial intelligence on chatbot technology: A study on the current advancements and leading innovations. *European Journal of Technology*, *7*(3), 62–72. DOI: 10.47672/ejt.1561

Awal, M. R., & Asaduzzaman, . (2024). Curse or blessing? Students' experience from ChatGPT with an application of Colaizzi's phenomenological descriptive method of enquiry and content analysis. *Higher Education. Skills and Work-Based Learning*, *14*(6), 1299–1313. DOI: 10.1108/HESWBL-09-2023-0249

Ayinde, L., Wibowo, M. P., Ravuri, B., & Emdad, F. B. (2023). ChatGPT as an important tool in organizational management: A review of the literature. *Business Information Review*, *40*(3), 137–149. DOI: 10.1177/02663821231187991

Baek, C., Tate, T., & Warschauer, M. (2024). "ChatGPT seems too good to be true": College students' use and perceptions of generative AI. *Computers and Education Artificial Intelligence*, *100294*, 100294. Advance online publication. DOI: 10.1016/j.caeai.2024.100294

Balasubramaniam, S., Kadry, S., Prasanth, A., & Dhanaraj, R. K. (2024). *Generative AI and LLMs: Natural Language Processing and Generative Adversarial Networks*. Walter de Gruyter GmbH & Co KG. DOI: 10.1515/9783111425078

Balderas, A., García-Mena, R. F., Huerta, M., Mora, N., & Dodero, J. M. (2023). Chatbot for communicating with university students in emergency situation. *Heliyon*, *9*(9), e19517. DOI: 10.1016/j.heliyon.2023.e19517 PMID: 37809667

Baltrusaitis, T., Ahuja, C., & Morency, L.-P. (2019). Multimodal machine learning: A survey and taxonomy. *IEEE Transactions on Pattern Analysis and Machine Intelligence*, *41*(2), 423–443. DOI: 10.1109/TPAMI.2018.2798607 PMID: 29994351

Banerjee, B. (2021). Smart student guide case of HUGI, a chatbot for education.

Banerjee, S., Agarwal, A., & Bar, A. K. (2024). Securing Well-Being: Exploring Security Protocols and Mitigating Risks in AI-Driven Mental Health Chatbots for Employees. *American Journal of Computer Science and Technology*, *7*(1), 1–8. DOI: 10.11648/j.ajcst.20240701.11

Belen-Saglam, R., Nurse, J. R., & Hodges, D. (2022). An investigation into the sensitivity of personal information and implications for disclosure: A UK perspective. *Frontiers of Computer Science*, *4*, 908245. DOI: 10.3389/fcomp.2022.908245

Belikov, O., & Schunn, C. D. (2020). Ethics in educational technology: Considerations for AI tools. *AI & Society*, *35*(3), 575–586.

Beltagy, I., Lo, K., & Cohan, A. (2019). *SciBERT: A pretrained language model for scientific text. Proceedings of the 2019 Conference on Empirical Methods in Natural Language Processing and the 9th International Joint Conference on Natural Language Processing (EMNLP-IJCNLP)*. https://doi.org/DOI: 10.18653/v1/D19-1371

Ben Saad, S., & Choura, F. (2022). Online shopping during the Covid-19 crisis: The impact of anthropomorphic virtual agents on consumers' psychological states. *International Journal of Technology Marketing*, *16*(1/2), 27–49. DOI: 10.1504/IJTMKT.2022.122450

Bengesi, S., El-Sayed, H., Sarker, M. K., Houkpati, Y., Irungu, J., & Oladunni, T. (2024). Advancements in Generative AI: A Comprehensive Review of GANs, GPT, Autoencoders, Diffusion Model, and Transformers. *IEEE Access : Practical Innovations, Open Solutions*, *12*, 69812–69837. DOI: 10.1109/ACCESS.2024.3397775

Bezuidenhout, C., Heffernan, T., Abbas, R., & Mehmet, M. (2022). The impact of Artificial Intelligence on the marketing practices of Professional Services Firms. *Journal of Marketing Theory and Practice*, *0*(0), 1–22. DOI: 10.1080/10696679.2022.2090005

Bing, Y. (2023). *Application and research of ChatGPT in accounting technology*. Atlantis Press., DOI: 10.2991/978-94-6463-262-0_48

Borah, A. R., Nischith, T., & Gupta, S. (2024). *Improved learning based on GenAI.* Paper presented at the 2024 2nd International Conference on Intelligent Data Communication Technologies and Internet of Things (IDCIoT). DOI: 10.1109/IDCIoT59759.2024.10467943

Bozkurt, A., Junhong, X., Lambert, S., Pazurek, A., Crompton, H., Koseoglu, S., & Honeychurch, S. (2023). Speculative futures on ChatGPT and generative artificial intelligence (AI): A collective reflection from the educational landscape. *Asian Journal of Distance Education, 18*(1), 53–130.

Brown, T. B., Mann, B., Ryder, N., Subbiah, M., Kaplan, J., Dhariwal, P., Neelakantan, A., Shyam, P., Sastry, G., Askell, A., & Agarwal, S. J., Winter, C. (2020). Language Models are Few-Shot Learners. arXiv.org. https://arxiv.org/abs/2005.14165

Brown, N., Fiscato, M., Segler, M. H., & Vaucher, A. C. (2019). GuacaMol: Benchmarking models for de novo molecular design. *Journal of Chemical Information and Modeling, 59*(4), 1096–1108. DOI: 10.1021/acs.jcim.8b00839 PMID: 30887799

Brüggemeier, B., & Lalone, P. (2022). Perceptions and reactions to conversational privacy initiated by a conversational user interface. *Computer Speech & Language, 71*, 101269. DOI: 10.1016/j.csl.2021.101269

Bui, N. M., & Barrot, J. S. (2024). ChatGPT as an automated essay scoring tool in the writing classrooms: How it compares with human scoring. *Education and Information Technologies*, •••, 1–18.

Bunmi, E. E., Esegbona-Isikeh, O. M., Oriakhi, V. N., Akiotu, C. A., Emakporuena, D., & Matthew, U. O. (2024). STEM application in education: Implication of STEM computational paradigm on employment prospects. *HAFED POLY Journal of Science. Management and Technology, 6*(1), 131–148.

Bushong, V., Abdelfattah, A. S., Maruf, A. A., Das, D., Lehman, A., Jaroszewski, E., Coffey, M., Cerný, T., Frajták, K., Tisnovsky, P., & Bures, M. (2021). On microservice analysis and architecture evolution: A systematic mapping study. *Applied Sciences (Basel, Switzerland), 11*(17), 7856. DOI: 10.3390/app11177856

Camarena, F., Gonzalez-Mendoza, M., & Chang, L. (2024). Knowledge distillation in video-based Human Action Recognition: An intuitive approach to efficient and flexible model training. *Journal of Imaging, 10*(4), 85. DOI: 10.3390/jimaging10040085 PMID: 38667983

Cao, H., Liu, Z., Lu, X., Yao, Y., & Li, Y. (2025). InstructMol: Multi-modal integration for building a versatile and reliable molecular assistant in drug discovery. In *Proceedings of the 31st International Conference on Computational Linguistics* (pp. 354–379). Association for Computational Linguistics.

Castagna, F., Kökciyan, N., Sassoon, I., Parsons, S., & Sklar, E. (2024). Computational argumentation-based chatbots: A survey. *Journal of Artificial Intelligence Research*, *80*, 1271–1310. DOI: 10.1613/jair.1.15407

Celik, B., & Vanschoren, J. (2021). Adaptation Strategies for Automated Machine Learning on Evolving Data. *IEEE Transactions on Pattern Analysis and Machine Intelligence*, *43*(9), 3067–3078. DOI: 10.1109/TPAMI.2021.3062900 PMID: 33651683

Chalkidis, I., Fergadiotis, E., Malakasiotis, P., Aletras, N., & Androutsopoulos, I. (2019). *Extreme multi-label legal text classification: A case study in. Proceedings of the Natural Legal Language Processing Workshop 2019*. https://doi.org/DOI: 10.18653/v1/W19-2209

Chaudhry, I. S., Sarwary, S. A. M., El Refae, G. A., & Chabchoub, H. (2023). Time to revisit existing student's performance evaluation approach in higher education sector in a new era of ChatGPT—A case study. *Cogent Education*, *10*(1), 2210461. DOI: 10.1080/2331186X.2023.2210461

Cheng, Y., & Jiang, H. (2021). Customer–brand relationship in the era of artificial intelligence: Understanding the role of chatbot marketing efforts. *Journal of Product and Brand Management*, *31*(2), 252–264. DOI: 10.1108/JPBM-05-2020-2907

Chen, M. X., Firat, O., Bapna, A., Johnson, M., Macherey, W., Foster, G., Jones, L., Schuster, M., Shazeer, N., Parmar, N., Vaswani, A., Uszkoreit, J., Kaiser, L., Chen, Z., Wu, Y., & Hughes, M. (2018). *The best of both worlds: Combining recent advances in neural machine translation. Proceedings of the 56th Annual Meeting of the Association for Computational Linguistics* (Volume 1: Long Papers). https://doi.org/DOI: 10.18653/v1/P18-1008

Chintalapati, S., & Pandey, S. K. (2022). Artificial intelligence in marketing: A systematic literature review. *International Journal of Market Research*, *64*(1), 38–68. DOI: 10.1177/14707853211018428

Chiu, T. K. (2023). Future research recommendations for transforming higher education with generative AI. *Computers and Education Artificial Intelligence*, *6*, 100197. DOI: 10.1016/j.caeai.2023.100197

Cho, H. (2023). Analyzing ChatGPT's Judgments on Nativelikeness of Sentences Written by English Native Speakers and Korean EFL Learners. *Multimedia-Assisted Language Learning, 26*(2).

Choedak, K. (2020). The effect of chatbots response latency on users' trust (Doctoral dissertation, Ph. D. Dissertation. University of Oklahoma).

Chui, M., Roberts, R., & Yee, L. (2022, December 20). *Generative AI is here: How tools like CHATGPT could change your business*. McKinsey & Company. https://www.mckinsey.com/capabilities/quantumblack/our-insights/generative-ai-is-here-how-tools-like-chatgpt-could-change-your-business

Collobert, R., & Weston, J. (2008). *A unified architecture for natural language processing*. Proceedings of the 25th International Conference on Machine Learning - ICML '08, 160–167. https://doi.org/DOI: 10.1145/1390156.1390177

Conneau, A., Rinott, R., Lample, G., Williams, A., Bowman, S., Schwenk, H., & Stoyanov, V. (2018). *XNLI: Evaluating cross-lingual sentence representations. Proceedings of the 2018 Conference on Empirical Methods in Natural Language Processing*. https://doi.org/DOI: 10.18653/v1/D18-1269

Cui, L. (2023). Exploring growth strategies of European small and medium-sized enterprises in the service sector using chatgpt. *European Integration Studies, 1*(17), 175–198. DOI: 10.5755/j01.eis.1.17.33726

Dai, Z., Yang, Z., Yang, Y., Carbonell, J., Le, Q., & Salakhutdinov, R. (2019). *Transformer-XL: Attentive language models beyond a fixed-length context. Proceedings of the 57th Annual Meeting of the Association for Computational Linguistics*. https://doi.org/DOI: 10.18653/v1/P19-1285

Dalalah, D., & Dalalah, O. M. (2023). The false positives and false negatives of generative AI detection tools in education and academic research: The case of ChatGPT. *International Journal of Management Education, 21*(2), 100822. DOI: 10.1016/j.ijme.2023.100822

Daniel, K., Msambwa, M. M., & Wen, Z. (2025). Can Generative AI Revolutionise Academic Skills Development in Higher Education? A Systematic Literature Review. *European Journal of Education, 60*(1), e70036. DOI: 10.1111/ejed.70036

Davenport, T., Guha, A., Grewal, D., & Bressgott, T. (2020). How artificial intelligence will change the future of marketing. *Journal of the Academy of Marketing Science, 48*(1), 24–42. DOI: 10.1007/s11747-019-00696-0

De Angeli, K., Gao, S., Blanchard, A., Durbin, E. B., Wu, X.-C., Stroup, A., Doherty, J., Schwartz, S. M., Wiggins, C., Coyle, L., Penberthy, L., Tourassi, G., & Yoon, H.-J. (2022). Using ensembles and distillation to optimize the deployment of deep learning models for the classification of Electronic Cancer Pathology reports. *JAMIA Open*, *5*(3), ooac075. Advance online publication. DOI: 10.1093/jamiaopen/ooac075 PMID: 36110150

De Bruyn, A., Viswanathan, V., Beh, Y. S., Brock, J. K.-U., & von Wangenheim, F. (2020). Artificial intelligence and marketing: Pitfalls and opportunities. *Journal of Interactive Marketing*, *51*(1), 91–105. DOI: 10.1016/j.intmar.2020.04.007

De Mauro, A., Sestino, A., & Bacconi, A. (2022). Machine learning and artificial intelligence use in marketing: A general taxonomy. *Italian Journal of Marketing*, *2022*(4), 439–457. DOI: 10.1007/s43039-022-00057-w

De Schryver, G.-M. (2023). Generative AI and lexicography: The current state of the art using ChatGPT. *International Journal of Lexicography*, *36*(4), 355–387. DOI: 10.1093/ijl/ecad021

Deng, J., & Lin, Y. (2022). The benefits and challenges of ChatGPT: An overview. *Frontiers in Computing and Intelligent Systems*, *2*(2), 2. Advance online publication. DOI: 10.54097/fcis.v2i2.4465

Devlin, J., Chang, M.-W., Lee, K., & Toutanova, K. (2019). *BERT: Pre-training of deep bidirectional transformers for language understanding*. *Proceedings of the 2019 Conference of the North American Chapter of the Association for Computational Linguistics*. https://doi.org/DOI: 10.18653/v1/N19-1423

Dhinagaran, D. A., Martinengo, L., Ho, M. H. R., Joty, S., Kowatsch, T., Atun, R., & Tudor Car, L. (2022). Designing, developing, evaluating, and implementing a smartphone-delivered, rule-based conversational agent (DISCOVER): Development of a conceptual framework. *JMIR mHealth and uHealth*, *10*(10), e38740. DOI: 10.2196/38740 PMID: 36194462

Doe, J., & Smith, J. (2024). AI Chatbots in Healthcare: Deployment and Impact Analysis. *Journal of Health Care Technology*.

Dop, T. (2020). [*Build smart, AI-driven linguistic applications using deep learning and NLP techniques*: Packt Publishing Ltd.]. *Hands-On Natural Language Processing with PyTorch*, *1*, x.

Dowling, M., & Lucey, B. (2023). ChatGPT for (finance) research: The Bananarama conjecture. *Finance Research Letters*, *53*, 103662. DOI: 10.1016/j.frl.2023.103662

Dumitriu, D., & Popescu, M. A.-M. (2020). Artificial intelligence solutions for digital marketing. *Procedia Manufacturing*, *46*, 630–636. DOI: 10.1016/j.promfg.2020.03.090

Dwivedi, Y. K., Kshetri, N., Hughes, L., Slade, E. L., Jeyaraj, A., Kar, A. K., Baabdullah, A. M., Koohang, A., Raghavan, V., Ahuja, M., Albanna, H., Albashrawi, M. A., Al-Busaidi, A. S., Balakrishnan, J., Barlette, Y., Basu, S., Bose, I., Brooks, L., Buhalis, D., & Wright, R. (2023). "So what if ChatGPT wrote it?" Multidisciplinary perspectives on opportunities, challenges and implications of generative conversational AI for research, practice and policy. *International Journal of Information Management*, *71*, 102642. DOI: 10.1016/j.ijinfomgt.2023.102642

Dwivedi, Y. K., Malik, T., Hughes, L., & Albashrawi, M. A. (2024). Scholarly Discourse on GenAI's Impact on Academic Publishing. *Journal of Computer Information Systems*, •••, 1–16. DOI: 10.1080/08874417.2024.2435386

Ebong, G. N., Matthew, U. O., Olofin, B., Andrew-Vitalis, N., Fatai, L. O., Waliu, A. O., & Oladipupo, M. A. (2024). *Multimedia Cloud Data Warehouse Design for Knowledge Sharing in the University Environment: A Proposed Digital Solution Implementing Interactive Learning Strategies in Higher Education*. IGI Global. DOI: 10.4018/979-8-3693-3559-8.ch010

Farhi, F., Jeljeli, R., Aburezeq, I., Dweikat, F. F., Al-Shami, S. A., & Slamene, R. (2023). Analyzing the students' views, concerns, and perceived ethics about chat GPT usage. *Computers and Education Artificial Intelligence*, *5*, 100180. DOI: 10.1016/j.caeai.2023.100180

Feng, D. (2003). *Cooperative model-based language understanding in dialogue*. Proceedings of the 2003 Conference of the North American Chapter of the Association for Computational Linguistics on Human Language Technology: Proceedings of the HLT-NAACL 2003 Student Research Workshop - NAACL '03, 3, 1–6. https://doi.org/DOI: 10.3115/1073416.1073426

Firat, M. (2023). What ChatGPT means for universities: Perceptions of scholars and students. *Journal of Applied Learning & Teaching*, *6*(1). Advance online publication. DOI: 10.37074/jalt.2023.6.1.22

Flavián, C., & Casaló, L. V. (2021). Artificial intelligence in services: Current trends, benefits and challenges. *Service Industries Journal*, *41*(13–14), 853–859. DOI: 10.1080/02642069.2021.1989177

Fowler, M. (2020, April 22). *Bliki: Domain driven design*. martinfowler.com. https://martinfowler.com/bliki/DomainDrivenDesign.html

Gang, W. Y. (2016). "An e-business chatbot using AIML and LSA." *2016 International Conference on Advances in Computing, Communications and Informatics (ICACCI),* 2740-2742.DOI: DOI: 10.1109/ICACCI.2016.7732476

Gao, Y., & Liu, H. (2022). Artificial intelligence-enabled personalization in interactive marketing: A customer journey perspective. *Journal of Research in Interactive Marketing, ahead-of-print*, 1–18. https://doi.org/DOI: 10.1108/JRIM-01-2022-0023

Gao, L. (2023). The impact of ChatGPT on enterprise competitive intelligence systems. *Information Systems and Economics*, *4*(4), 62–69. DOI: 10.23977/infse.2023.040909

Gill, S. S., Xu, M., Patros, P., Wu, H., Kaur, R., Kaur, K., & Parlikad, A. K. (2024). Transformative effects of ChatGPT on modern education: Emerging Era of AI Chatbots. *Internet of Things and Cyber-Physical Systems*, *4*, 19–23. DOI: 10.1016/j.iotcps.2023.06.002

Giovanola, B., & Granata, P. (2024). *Ethics for human-centered education in the age of AI Entrepreneurship and Digital Humanities*. Edward Elgar Publishing.

Gong, T., Lyu, C., Zhang, S., Wang, Y., Zheng, M., Zhao, Q., Liu, K., Zhang, W., Luo, P., & Chen, K. (2023, June 13). *Multimodal-GPT: A vision and language model for dialogue with humans*. arXiv.org. https://arxiv.org/abs/2305.04790

Goodfellow, I., Pouget-Abadie, J., Mirza, M., Xu, B., Warde-Farley, D., Ozair, S., Courville, A., & Bengio, Y. (2020). Generative adversarial networks. *Communications of the ACM*, *63*(11), 139–144. DOI: 10.1145/3422622

Górski, T. (2022). UML profile for messaging patterns in service-oriented architecture, microservices, and internet of things. *Applied Sciences (Basel, Switzerland)*, *12*(24), 12790. DOI: 10.3390/app122412790

Grassini, S. (2023). Shaping the future of education: Exploring the potential and consequences of AI and ChatGPT in educational settings. *Education Sciences*, *13*(7), 692. DOI: 10.3390/educsci13070692

Grattafiori, A., Dubey, A., Jauhri, A., Pandey, A., Kadian, A., Al-Dahle, A., Letman, A., Mathur, A., Schelten, A., & Vaughan, A. Hinsvark, A. (2024). The Llama 3 herd of models. arXiv.org. https://arxiv.org/abs/2407.21783

Gumel, A. A., & Abdullahi, A. B., & O, U. M. (2019). *The Need for a Multimodal Means of Effective Digital Learning through Data Mining and Institutional Knowledge Repository: A Proposed System for Polytechnics in Northern Nigeria.* Paper presented at the Proceedings of the 2019 5th International Conference on Computer and Technology Applications. DOI: 10.1145/3323933.3324068

Gupta, M., Akiri, C., Aryal, K., Parker, E., & Praharaj, L. (2023). From chatgpt to threatgpt: Impact of generative ai in cybersecurity and privacy. *IEEE Access : Practical Innovations, Open Solutions, 11*, 80218–80245. DOI: 10.1109/ACCESS.2023.3300381

Gupta, R., Nair, K., Mishra, M., Ibrahim, B., & Bhardwaj, S. (2024). Adoption and impacts of generative artificial intelligence: Theoretical underpinnings and research agenda. *International Journal of Information Management Data Insights, 4*(1), 100232. DOI: 10.1016/j.jjimei.2024.100232

Gupta, R., & Patel, J. (2022). Investigating the impact of ChatGPT on language proficiency and academic support. *Journal of Linguistics and Education, 23*(1), 45–59.

Gururangan, S., Marasović, A., Swayamdipta, S., Lo, K., Beltagy, I., Downey, D., & Smith, N. A. (2020). *Don't stop pretraining: Adapt language models to domains and tasks. Proceedings of the 58th Annual Meeting of the Association for Computational Linguistics.* https://doi.org/DOI: 10.18653/v1/2020.acl-main.740

Hanna, M., Liu, O., & Variengien, A. (2023). How does GPT-2 compute greater-than?: Interpreting mathematical abilities in a pre-trained language model. arXiv.org. https://arxiv.org/abs/2305.00586

Hasal, M., Nowaková, J., Ahmed Saghair, K., Abdulla, H., Snášel, V., & Ogiela, L. (2021). Chatbots: Security, privacy, data protection, and social aspects. *Concurrency and Computation, 33*(19), e6426. DOI: 10.1002/cpe.6426

Hassija, V., Chakrabarti, A., Singh, A., Chamola, V., & Sikdar, B. (2023). Unleashing the potential of conversational AI: Amplifying Chat-GPT's capabilities and tackling technical hurdles. *IEEE Access : Practical Innovations, Open Solutions, 11*, 143657–143682. DOI: 10.1109/ACCESS.2023.3339553

He, J., Nittinger, E., Tyrchan, C., Czechtizky, W., Patronov, A., Bjerrum, E. J., & Engkvist, O. (2022). Transformer-based molecular optimization beyond matched molecular pairs. *Journal of Cheminformatics, 14*(1), 18. DOI: 10.1186/s13321-022-00599-3 PMID: 35346368

Hermann, E. (2022). Leveraging artificial intelligence in marketing for social good—An ethical perspective. *Journal of Business Ethics, 179*(1), 43–61. DOI: 10.1007/s10551-021-04843-y PMID: 34054170

Holmes, W., & Miao, F. (2023). *Guidance for generative AI in education and research.* UNESCO Publishing.

Holtzman, A., Buys, J., Forbes, M., Bosselut, A., Golub, D., & Choi, Y. (2018). *Learning to write with cooperative discriminators. Proceedings of the 56th Annual Meeting of the Association for Computational Linguistics* (Volume 1: Long Papers). https://doi.org/DOI: 10.18653/v1/P18-1152

Hongladarom, S., & Sakprasert, S. (2024). Ethical implications of Thai ChatGPT public discourses. *Communication Research and Practice*, 1–12. https://doi.org/DOI: 10.1080/22041451.2024.2346429

Hooda, M., Rana, C., Dahiya, O., Rizwan, A., & Hossain, M. S. (2022). Artificial intelligence for assessment and feedback to enhance student success in higher education. *Mathematical Problems in Engineering*, *2022*(1), 5215722. DOI: 10.1155/2022/5215722

Howard, J., & Ruder, S. (2018). *Universal language model fine-tuning for text classification. Proceedings of the 56th Annual Meeting of the Association for Computational Linguistics* (Volume 1: Long Papers). https://doi.org/DOI: 10.18653/v1/P18-1031

Huang, M.-H., & Rust, R. (2021). A strategic framework for artificial intelligence in marketing. *Journal of the Academy of Marketing Science*, *49*(1), 30–50. DOI: 10.1007/s11747-020-00749-9

Huang, M.-H., & Rust, R. T. (2018). Artificial intelligence in service. *Journal of Service Research*, *21*(2), 155–172. DOI: 10.1177/1094670517752459

Huang, M.-H., Rust, R., & Maksimovic, V. (2019). The feeling economy: Managing in the next generation of artificial intelligence (AI). *California Management Review*, *61*(4), 43–65. DOI: 10.1177/0008125619863436

Huang, Z., Shi, J., Gao, Y., Cui, C., Zhang, S., Li, J., Zhou, Y., & Cui, Q. (2019). HMDD v3.0: A database for experimentally supported human microRNA-disease associations. *Nucleic Acids Research*, *47*(D1), D1013–D1017. DOI: 10.1093/nar/gky1010 PMID: 30364956

IEEE Transactions on Neural Networks and Learning Systems Publication Information. (2021). IEEE TRANSACTIONS ON NEURAL NETWORKS AND LEARNING SYSTEMS Publication Information. *IEEE Transactions on Neural Networks and Learning Systems*, *32*(6), C2–C2. DOI: 10.1109/TNNLS.2021.3078592

Ionu -Alexandru, C. (2021). Challenges and Ethical Solutions in Using the Chatbot. Database Systems Journal, 12.

Jalali, N. A., & Hongsong, C. (2024). Comprehensive framework for implementing blockchain-enabled federated learning and full homomorphic encryption for chatbot security system. *Cluster Computing*, *27*(8), 1–24. DOI: 10.1007/s10586-024-04515-2

Janamala, V., Ram, I. S., & Daram, S. B. (2023). Realization of green 5G cellular network role in medical applications: Use of CHATGPT-ai. *Annals of Biomedical Engineering*, *51*(11), 2337–2339. DOI: 10.1007/s10439-023-03257-3 PMID: 37261590

Jensen, J. H. (2019). A graph-based genetic algorithm and generative model/Monte Carlo tree search for the exploration of chemical space. *Chemical Science (Cambridge)*, *10*(15), 3567–3572. DOI: 10.1039/C8SC05372C PMID: 30996948

Ji, Z., Lee, N., Frieske, R., Yu, T., Su, D., Xu, Y., Ishii, E., Bang, Y. J., Madotto, A., & Fung, P. (2023). Survey of hallucination in natural language generation. *ACM Computing Surveys*, *55*(12), 1–38. DOI: 10.1145/3571730

Joshi, D. (2024). *AI governance in India – law, policy and political economy*. Communication Research and Practice., DOI: 10.1080/22041451.2024.2346428

Joshi, S., & Roy, A. (2021). The effect of AI tools like ChatGPT on student motivation and academic performance. *Indian Journal of Higher Education*, *17*(3), 66–79.

Jung, S. (2019). Semantic vector learning for natural language understanding. *Computer Speech & Language*, *56*, 130–145. DOI: 10.1016/j.csl.2018.12.008

Kadiyala, L. A., Mermer, O., Samuel, D. J., Sermet, Y., & Demir, I. (2024). The Implementation of Multimodal Large Language Models for Hydrological Applications: A Comparative Study of GPT-4 Vision, Gemini, LLaVa, and Multimodal-GPT. *Hydrology*, *11*(9), 148. DOI: 10.3390/hydrology11090148

Kangwa, M. (2023). Prevention of personally identifiable information leakage in ecommerce using offline data minimization and online pseudonymisation (Doctoral dissertation, The University of Zambia).

Karpukhin, V., Oğuz, B., Min, S., Lewis, P., Wu, L., Edunov, S., Chen, D., & Yih, W. (2020). Dense passage retrieval for Open-Domain question answering. arXiv. org. https://arxiv.org/abs/2004.04906 DOI: 10.18653/v1/2020.emnlp-main.550

Khan, I., Chohan, I., & Malik, S. I. (2024). *Leveraging ChatGPT-4 for Enhanced Education: Personalized Problem-Solving and Consistent Learning*. Paper presented at the 2024 2nd International Conference on Computing and Data Analytics (ICCDA). DOI: 10.1109/ICCDA64887.2024.10867340

Khan, N., Khan, Z., Koubaa, A., Khan, M. K., & Salleh, R. B. (2024). Global insights and the impact of generative AI-ChatGPT on multidisciplinary: A systematic review and bibliometric analysis. *Connection Science*, *36*(1), 2353630. DOI: 10.1080/09540091.2024.2353630

Khan, N., & Sabahat, N. (2024). Role of AI chatbots in revolutionizing gaming experiences – a survey. *VFAST Transactions on Software Engineering*, *12*(1), 93–104. DOI: 10.21015/vtse.v12i1.1725

Kim, H., Kim, E., Lee, I., Bae, B., Park, M., & Nam, H. (2020). Artificial intelligence in drug discovery: A comprehensive review of data-driven and machine learning approaches. *Biotechnology and Bioprocess Engineering; BBE*, *25*(6), 895–930. DOI: 10.1007/s12257-020-0049-y PMID: 33437151

Kopalle, P. K., Gangwar, M., Kaplan, A., Ramachandran, D., Reinartz, W., & Rindfleisch, A. (2022). Examining artificial intelligence (AI) technologies in marketing via a global lens: Current trends and future research opportunities. *International Journal of Research in Marketing*, *39*(2), 522–540. DOI: 10.1016/j.ijresmar.2021.11.002

Krstic, D., Petrovic, N., Suljovic, S., & Al-Azzoni, I. (2023). AI-Enabled Framework for mobile network experimentation leveraging chatgpt: Case study of channel capacity calculation for η-μ fading and co-channel interference. *Electronics (Basel)*, *12*(19), 4088. DOI: 10.3390/electronics12194088

Kshetri, N. (2024). The academic industry's response to generative artificial intelligence: An institutional analysis of large language models. *Telecommunications Policy*, *48*(5), 102760. DOI: 10.1016/j.telpol.2024.102760

Kshetri, N., Dwivedi, Y. K., Davenport, T. H., & Panteli, N. (2023). Generative artificial intelligence in marketing: Applications, opportunities, challenges, and research agenda. *International Journal of Information Management*. Advance online publication. DOI: 10.1016/j.ijinfomgt.2023.102716

Kumar, P., & Deshmukh, M. (2020). Enhancing collaboration and communication in group projects with AI tools. *Journal of Indian Educational Technology*, *11*(2), 122–134.

Kwon, Y., & Lee, J. (2021). MolFinder: An evolutionary algorithm for the global optimization of molecular properties and the extensive exploration of chemical space using SMILES. *Journal of Cheminformatics*, *13*(1), 24. DOI: 10.1186/s13321-021-00501-7 PMID: 33736687

Law, M. (2023). Sensitive data like passwords and PII shared to AI chatbots. https://cybermagazine.com/articles/sensitive-data-like-passwords-and-pii-shared-to-ai-chatbots

Lee, T. (2024). Artificial intelligence: Governing Singapore's smart digital journey. *Communication Research and Practice*, 1–9. https://doi.org/DOI: 10.1080/22041451.2024.2346430

Lee, I., & Shin, Y. J. (2020). Machine learning for enterprises: Applications, algorithm selection, and challenges. *Business Horizons*, *63*(2), 157–170. DOI: 10.1016/j.bushor.2019.10.005

Lee, J., Yoon, W., Kim, S., Kim, D., Kim, S., So, C. H., & Kang, J. (2019). BioBERT: A pre-trained biomedical language representation model for biomedical text mining. *Bioinformatics (Oxford, England)*, *36*(4), 1234–1240. DOI: 10.1093/bioinformatics/btz682 PMID: 31501885

Lemon, K. N., & Verhoef, P. C. (2016). Understanding customer experience throughout the customer journey. *Journal of Marketing*, *80*(6), 69–96. DOI: 10.1509/jm.15.0420

Lewis, P., Perez, E., Piktus, A., Petroni, F., Karpukhin, V., Goyal, N., Küttler, H., Lewis, M., Yih, W., Rocktäschel, T., Riedel, S., & Kiela, D. (2020). Retrieval-Augmented Generation for Knowledge-Intensive NLP tasks. arXiv.org. https://arxiv.org/abs/2005.11401

Lewis, P., Perez, E., Piktus, A., Petroni, F., Karpukhin, V., Goyal, N., Küttler, H., Lewis, M., Yih, W., Rocktäschel, T., Riedel, S., & Kiela, D. (2021, April 12). *Retrieval-augmented generation for knowledge-intensive NLP tasks*. arXiv.org. https://arxiv.org/abs/2005.11401

Li, C., Gan, Z., Yang, Z., Yang, J., Li, L., Wang, L., & Gao, J. (2024). Multimodal foundation models: From specialists to general-purpose assistants. *Foundations and Trends® in Computer Graphics and Vision, 16*(1-2), 1-214.

Likhosherstov, V., Choromanski, K., & Weller, A. (2023). On the expressive flexibility of self-attention matrices. *Proceedings of the AAAI Conference on Artificial Intelligence*, *37*(7), 8773–8781. DOI: 10.1609/aaai.v37i7.26055

Limna, P., Kraiwanit, T., Jangjarat, K., Klayklung, P., & Chocksathaporn, P. (2023). The use of ChatGPT in the digital era: Perspectives on chatbot implementation. *Journal of Applied Learning & Teaching*, *6*(1). Advance online publication. DOI: 10.37074/jalt.2023.6.1.32

Liu, S., Wang, J., Yang, Y., Wang, C., Liu, L., Guo, H., & Xiao, C. (2023). ChatGPT-powered conversational drug editing using retrieval and domain feedback. *arXiv*. https://doi.org//arXiv.2305.18090DOI: 10.48550

Liu, K., Sun, X., Jia, L., Ma, J., Xing, H., Wu, J., Gao, H., Sun, Y., Boulnois, F., & Fan, J. (2019). Chemi-Net: A molecular graph convolutional network for accurate drug property prediction. *International Journal of Molecular Sciences*, *20*(14), 3389. DOI: 10.3390/ijms20143389 PMID: 31295892

Liu, Y., Deng, G., Xu, Z., Li, Y., Zheng, Y., Zhang, Y., Zhao, L., Zhang, T., & Wang, K. (2024). A hitchhiker's guide to jailbreaking CHATGPT via prompt engineering. *Proceedings of the 4th International Workshop on Software Engineering and AI for Data Quality in Cyber-Physical Systems/Internet of Things*, 12–21. DOI: 10.1145/3663530.3665021

Lui, C., Ibraimova, A., White, D. C., Survase, R. P., Chihani, B., & Pham, T. K. (2024). OPTIMIZING LLM-BASED QUERIES AND RESPONSES USING SECURE, PORTABLE, AND PERSONALIZED ENCODED USER PROFILE.

Madaan, A., Zhou, S., Alon, U., Yang, Y., & Neubig, G. (2022). *Language models of code are few-shot commonsense learners. Proceedings of the 2022 Conference on Empirical Methods in Natural Language Processing*. https://doi.org/DOI: 10.18653/v1/2022.emnlp-main.90

Madotto, A., Ishii, E., Lin, Z., Dathathri, S., & Fung, P. (2020). Plug-and-play conversational models. *Findings of the Association for Computational Linguistics: EMNLP, 2020*, 2422–2433. DOI: 10.18653/v1/2020.findings-emnlp.219

Mahmood, O., Mansimov, E., Bonneau, R., & Cho, K. (2021). Masked graph modeling for molecule generation. *Nature Communications*, *12*(1), 3156. DOI: 10.1038/s41467-021-23415-2 PMID: 34039973

Malthouse, E., & Copulsky, J. (2023). Artificial intelligence ecosystems for marketing communications. *International Journal of Advertising*, *42*(1), 128–140. DOI: 10.1080/02650487.2022.2122249

Mamoshina, P., Volosnikova, M., Ozerov, I. V., Putin, E., Skibina, E., Cortese, F., & Zhavoronkov, A. (2018). Machine learning on human muscle transcriptomic data for biomarker discovery and tissue-specific drug target identification. *Frontiers in Genetics*, *9*, 242. DOI: 10.3389/fgene.2018.00242 PMID: 30050560

Mariani, M. M., Machado, I., & Nambisan, S. (2023). Types of innovation and Artificial Intelligence: A systematic quantitative literature review and research agenda. *Journal of Business Research*, *155*, 113364. DOI: 10.1016/j.jbusres.2022.113364

Marzuki, M. J., & Nurpahmi, S. (2019). Using video blog in teaching speaking. *English Language Teaching for EFL Learners*, *1*(1), 13. DOI: 10.24252/elties.v1i1.7422

Matthew, U. O., Kazaure, J. S., Kazaure, A. S., Onyedibe, O. N., & Okafor, A. N. (2022). The Twenty First Century E-Learning Education Management & Implication for Media Technology Adoption in the Period of Pandemic. *EAI Endorsed Transactions on e-Learning*, *8*(1).

Matthew, U. O., Bakare, K. M., Ebong, G. N., Ndukwu, C. C., & Nwanakwaugwu, A. C.Ugochukwu Okwudili MatthewKafayat Motomori BakareGodwin Nse EbongCharles Chukwuebuka NdukwuAndrew Chinonso Nwanakwaugwu. (2023). Generative Artificial Intelligence (AI) Educational Pedagogy Development: Conversational AI with User-Centric ChatGPT4. *Journal of Trends in Computer Science and Smart Technology*, *5*(4), 401–418. DOI: 10.36548/jtcsst.2023.4.003

Matthew, U. O., Kazaure, A. S., Kazaure, J. S., Hassan, I. M., Nwanakwaugwu, A. C., & Okafor, N. U.Ugochukwu Okwudili MatthewAdo Saleh KazaureJazuli Sanusi KazaureIbrahim Muhammad HassanAndrew Chinonso NwanakwaugwuNwamaka U. Okafor. (2022). Educational Technology Adaptation & Implication for Media Technology Adoption in the Period of COVID-19. *Journal of Trends in Computer Science and Smart Technology*, *4*(4), 226–245. DOI: 10.36548/jtcsst.2022.4.002

Matthew, U. O., & Kazaure, J. S. (2020). Multimedia e-learning education in nigeria and developing countries of Africa for achieving SDG4. [IJICTHD]. *International Journal of Information Communication Technologies and Human Development*, *12*(1), 40–62. DOI: 10.4018/IJICTHD.2020010103

Matthew, U. O., Kazaure, J. S., & Haruna, K. (2020). Multimedia information system (MIS) for knowledge generation and ICT policy framework in education: Innovative sustainable educational investment. [IJICTHD]. *International Journal of Information Communication Technologies and Human Development*, *12*(3), 28–58. DOI: 10.4018/IJICTHD.2020070102

Matthew, U. O., Kazaure, J. S., & Okafor, N. U. (2021). Contemporary development in E-Learning education, cloud computing technology & internet of things. *EAI Endorsed Transactions on Cloud Systems*, *7*(20), e3–e3.

Matthew, U. O., Oyekunle, D. O., Akpan, E. E., Oladipupo, M. A., Chukwuebuka, E. S., Adekunle, T. S., & Onumaku, V. C. (2024). *Generative Artificial Intelligence (AI) on Sustainable Development Goal 4 for Tertiary Education: Conversational AI With User-Centric ChatGPT-4 Impacts of Generative AI on Creativity in Higher Education*. IGI Global. DOI: 10.4018/979-8-3693-2418-9.ch010

Maynez, J., Narayan, S., Bohnet, B., & McDonald, R. (2020). On faithfulness and factuality in abstractive summarization. *arXiv*. /arxiv.2005.00661DOI: 10.18653/v1/2020.acl-main.173

McCarthy, J., Minsky, M. L., Rochester, N., & Shannon, C. E. (1955). A proposal for the Dartmouth summer research project on artificial intelligence, August 31, 1955. *AI Magazine*, *27*(4), 12. DOI: 10.1609/aimag.v27i4.1904

Mehta, P., Jebarajakirthy, C., Maseeh, H. I., Anubha, A., Saha, R., & Dhanda, K. (2022). Artificial intelligence in marketing: A meta-analytic review. *Psychology and Marketing*, *39*(11), 2013–2038. DOI: 10.1002/mar.21716

Mehta, P., & Sharma, A. (2022). Impact of AI on personalized learning support in Indian universities. *Journal of Innovation in Education*, *18*(2), 75–88.

Meyers, R. M., Bryan, J. G., McFarland, J. M., Weir, B. A., Sizemore, A. E., Xu, H., Dharia, N. V., Montgomery, P. G., Cowley, G. S., Pantel, S., Goodale, A., Lee, Y., Ali, L. D., Jiang, G., Lubonja, R., Harrington, W. F., Strickland, M., Wu, T., Hawes, D. C., & Tsherniak, A. (2017). Computational correction of copy number effect improves specificity of CRISPR-Cas9 essentiality screens in cancer cells. *Nature Genetics*, *49*(12), 1779–1784. DOI: 10.1038/ng.3984 PMID: 29083409

Mina, M., Rodríguez, C., Gonzalez Agirre, A., & Villegas, M. (2024). Extending off-the-shelf NER Systems to Personal Information Detection in Dialogues with a Virtual Agent: Findings from a Real-Life Use Case. In In Proceedings of the Workshop on Computational Approaches to Language Data Pseudonymization (CALD-pseudo 2024): St. Julian's, Malta: 21-22 March, 2024 (pp. 44-53). Association for Computational Linguistics.

Mitra, S., & Gopalakrishnan, V. (2022). AI and stress reduction in education: A study on ChatGPT's role in academic assistance. *Indian Psychological Review*, *44*(1), 37–49.

Mogavi, R. H., Deng, C., Kim, J. J., Zhou, P., Kwon, Y. D., Metwally, A. H. S., Tlili, A., Bassanelli, S., Bucchiarone, A., Gujar, S., Nacke, L. E., & Hui, P. (2023). ChatGPT in education: A blessing or a curse? A qualitative study exploring early adopters' utilization and perceptions. *Computers in Human Behavior Artificial Humans*, *2*(1), 100027. DOI: 10.1016/j.chbah.2023.100027

Nair, R., & Bhargava, A. (2020). Ethical considerations in using AI tools in Indian educational contexts. *AI and Society in India*, *15*(3), 54–62.

Nakano, R., Hilton, J., Balaji, S., Wu, J., Ouyang, L., Kim, C., Hesse, C., Jain, S., Kosaraju, V., Saunders, W., Jiang, X., Cobbe, K., Eloundou, T., Krueger, G., Button, K., Knight, M., Chess, B., & Schulman, J. (2021). WebGPT: Browser-assisted question-answering with human feedback. arXiv.org. https://arxiv.org/abs/2112.09332

Nemkul, K. (2024). Use of Bidirectional Encoder Representations from Transformers (BERT) and Robustly Optimized BERT Pretraining Approach (RoBERTa) for Nepali news classification. *Tribhuvan University Journal*, *39*(1), 124–137. DOI: 10.3126/tuj.v39i1.66679

Ngo, T. T. A. (2023). The perception by university students of the use of CHATGPT in education. [iJET]. *International Journal of Emerging Technologies in Learning, 18*(17), 4–19. DOI: 10.3991/ijet.v18i17.39019

Nikolic, S., Sandison, C., Haque, R., Daniel, S., Grundy, S., Belkina, M., Lyden, S., Hassan, G. M., & Neal, P. (2024). ChatGPT, Copilot, Gemini, SciSpace and Wolfram versus higher education assessments: An updated multi-institutional study of the academic integrity impacts of Generative Artificial Intelligence (GenAI) on assessment, teaching and learning in engineering. *Australasian Journal of Engineering Education, 29*(2), 126–153. DOI: 10.1080/22054952.2024.2372154

Noroozi, O., Soleimani, S., Farrokhnia, M., & Banihashem, S. K. (2024). Generative AI in Education: Pedagogical, Theoretical, and Methodological Perspectives. *International Journal of Technology in Education, 7*(3), 373–385. DOI: 10.46328/ijte.845

Ong, J., Hariprasad, S. M., & Chhablani, J. (2023). ChatGPT and GPT-4 in ophthalmology: Applications of large language model artificial intelligence in retina. *Ophthalmic Surgery, Lasers & Imaging Retina, 54*(10), 557–562. DOI: 10.3928/23258160-20230926-01 PMID: 37847163

Open, A. I., Achiam, J., Adler, S., Agarwal, S., Ahmad, L., Akkaya, I., Aleman, F. L., Almeida, D., Altenschmidt, J., Altman, S., Anadkat, S., Avila, R., Babuschkin, I., Balaji, S., Balcom, V., Baltescu, P., Bao, H., Bavarian, M., & Belgum, J. (2023). GPT-4 Technical Report. https://arxiv.org/abs/2303.08774

Oriakhi, V. N., Esegbona-Isikeh, O. M., Esseme, B., Claude, A., Emakporuena, D., Nwanakwaugwu, A. C., & Matthew, U. O. (2024). Generative artificial intelligence in education: ChatGPT-4 experiences to anticipated ChatGPT-5. *HAFED POLY Journal of Science. Management and Technology, 6*(1), 149–169.

Orzoł, M., & Szopik-Depczyńska, K. (2023). ChatGPT as an innovative tool for increasing sales in online stores. *Procedia Computer Science, 225*, 3450–3459. DOI: 10.1016/j.procs.2023.10.340

Oyekunle, D. O. T., Okwudili Matthew, U., Preston, D., & Boohene, D. (2024). Trust beyond Technology Algorithms: A Theoretical Exploration of Consumer Trust and Behavior in Technological Consumption and AI Projects. *Journal of Computer and Communications, 12*(06), 10.4236.

Oyekunle, D., Claude, B. E. A., Waliu, A. O., Adekunle, T. S., & Matthew, U. O. (2024). Cloud based adaptive learning system: virtual reality and augmented reality assisted educational pedagogy development on clinical simulation. *Journal of Digital Health*, 49-62.

Oyekunle, D. O., Esseme, A. C. B., Oladipupo, M. A., Oseni, V. E., Adebola, N. T., Nwaiku, M., & Matthew, U. O. (2025). *Artificial Neural Network Algorithm in Nutritional Assessment: Implication for Machine Learning Prediction in Nutritional Assessments Precision Health in the Digital Age: Harnessing AI for Personalized Care*. IGI Global Scientific Publishing.

Oyekunle, D. O., Nwaiku, M., Matthew, U. O., Ogechukwu, O. N., Nwanakwaugwu, A. C., Adebola, N. T., & Olawoyin, O. O. (2025). *Transition to Sustainable Human-Centric Education in Emerging Artificial Intelligence Industry 5.0: Conversational AI With User-Centric ChatGPT-5 Higher Education and Quality Assurance Practices*. IGI Global Scientific Publishing.

Oyekunle, D., Matthew, U., Waliu, A., & Fatai, L. (2024). Healthcare applications of Augmented Reality (AR) and Virtual Real-ity (VR) simulation in clinical ceducation. *Journal of Clinical Images and Medical Case Reports*, *5*(6), 3141.

Pandey, S., & Sharma, S. (2023). A comparative study of retrieval-based and generative-based chatbots using Deep Learning and Machine Learning. *Healthcare Analytics*, *3*, 100198. DOI: 10.1016/j.health.2023.100198

Pareek, R., & Pandey, R. K. (2025). *Integrating STEM Education With Sustainable Development Goals: A Framework for Innovation and Inclusive Learning in India Transformative Approaches to STEAM Integration in Modern Education*. IGI Global Scientific Publishing. DOI: 10.4018/979-8-3693-7408-5.ch013

Pasupuleti, R., Vadapalli, R., & Mader, C. (2023, November). Cyber Security Issues and Challenges Related to Generative AI and ChatGPT. In *2023 Tenth International Conference on Social Networks Analysis, Management and Security (SNAMS)* (pp. 1-5). IEEE. DOI: 10.1109/SNAMS60348.2023.10375472

Petroni, F., Piktus, A., Fan, A., Lewis, P., Yazdani, M., De Cao, N., Thorne, J., Jernite, Y., Karpukhin, V., Maillard, J., Plachouras, V., Rocktäschel, T., & Riedel, S. (2021). *KILT: A benchmark for knowledge intensive language tasks. Proceedings of the 2021 Conference of the North American Chapter of the Association for Computational Linguistics: Human Language Technologies*. https://doi.org/DOI: 10.18653/v1/2021.naacl-main.200

Petyuk, V. A., Chang, R., Ramirez-Restrepo, M., Beckmann, N. D., Henrion, M. Y. R., Piehowski, P. D., Zhu, K., Wang, S., Clarke, J., Huentelman, M. J., Xie, F., Andreev, V., Engel, A., Guettoche, T., Navarro, L., De Jager, P., Schneider, J. A., Morris, C. M., McKeith, I. G., & Myers, A. J. (2018). The human brainome: Network analysis identifies HSPA2 as a novel Alzheimer's disease target. *Brain*, *141*(10), 2721–2739. DOI: 10.1093/brain/awy215 PMID: 30137212

Piñero, J., Ramírez-Anguita, J. M., Saüch-Pitarch, J., Ronzano, F., Centeno, E., Sanz, F., & Furlong, L. I. (2020). The DisGeNET knowledge platform for disease genomics: 2019 update. *Nucleic Acids Research, 48*(D1), D845–D855. PMID: 31680165

Planas, E., Martínez, S., Brambilla, M., & Cabot, J. (2023). Modeling and enforcing access control policies in conversational user interfaces. *Software & Systems Modeling, 22*(6), 1925–1944. DOI: 10.1007/s10270-023-01131-3

Poddar, R. Securing Generative AI in the Enterprise.

Pranaya, D., & Venugopal, K. (2023, August). Impact of mother tongue on students' speaking abilities in English language at rural places. In *English Language Competence in Rural Youth: Improving Job Readiness* (pp. 143–157). Current Publications. ISBN 978-81-19255-30-6.

Prien, T., & Goldhammer, K. (2024). Artificial Intelligence in the Media Economy: A Systematic Review of Use Cases, Application Potentials, and Challenges of Generative Language Models. *Handbook of Media and Communication Economics: A European Perspective*, 1-69.

Radford, A., Wu, J., Child, R., Luan, D., Amodei, D., & Sutskever, I. (2019). Language Models are Unsupervised Multitask Learners. https://github.com/openai/gpt-2

Rahman, M. M., & Watanobe, Y. (2023). ChatGPT for education and research: Opportunities, threats, and strategies. *Applied Sciences (Basel, Switzerland), 13*(9), 5783. DOI: 10.3390/app13095783

Rajpurkar, P., Zhang, J., Lopyrev, K., & Liang, P. (2016). *SQuAD: Machine comprehension of text. Proceedings of the 2016 Conference on Empirical Methods in Natural Language Processing*. https://doi.org/DOI: 10.18653/v1/D16-1264

Raj, R., Singh, A., Kumar, V., & Verma, P. (2023). Analyzing the potential benefits and use cases of chatgpt as a tool for improving the efficiency and effectiveness of business operations. *BenchCouncil Transactions on Benchmarks. Standards and Evaluations, 3*(3), 100140. DOI: 10.1016/j.tbench.2023.100140

Ramesh, K., Ravishankaran, S., Joshi, A., & Chandrasekaran, K. (2017). A Survey of Design Techniques for Conversational Agents. *Communications in Computer and Information Science, 750*, 336–350. Advance online publication. DOI: 10.1007/978-981-10-6544-6_31

Rasul, T., Nair, S., Kalendra, D., Robin, M., De Oliveira Santini, F., Ladeira, W. J., Sun, M., Day, I., Rather, R. A., & Heathcote, L. (2023). The role of ChatGPT in higher education: Benefits, challenges, and future research directions. *Journal of Applied Learning & Teaching*, *6*(1). Advance online publication. DOI: 10.37074/jalt.2023.6.1.29

Ray, P. P. (2023). ChatGPT: A comprehensive review on background, applications, key challenges, bias, ethics, limitations and future scope. *Internet of Things and Cyber-Physical Systems*, *3*, 121–154. DOI: 10.1016/j.iotcps.2023.04.003

Reuters. (2024, August 29). OpenAI says ChatGPT's weekly users have grown to 200 million. Reuters. https://www.reuters.com/technology/artificial-intelligence/openai-says-chatgpts-weekly-users-have-grown-200-million-2024-08-29

Richardson, P., Griffin, I., Tucker, C., Smith, D., Oechsle, O., Phelan, A., Rawling, M., Savory, E., & Stebbing, J. (2020). Baricitinib as potential treatment for 2019-nCoV acute respiratory disease. *Lancet*, *395*(10223), e30–e31. DOI: 10.1016/S0140-6736(20)30304-4 PMID: 32032529

Rolfe, V. (2020). Sustainability in education: Why it matters and how AI can help. *Journal of Educational Technology*, *21*(2), 135–148.

Rouf, N., Amin, F., & Franzon, P. D. (2024). *Can Low-Rank Knowledge Distillation in LLMs be Useful for Microelectronic Reasoning?* Paper presented at the 2024 IEEE LLM Aided Design Workshop (LAD). DOI: 10.1109/LAD62341.2024.10691755

Rowland, D. R. (2023). Two frameworks to guide discussions around levels of acceptable use of generative AI in student academic research and writing. *Journal of Academic Language and Learning*, *17*(1), T31–T69.

Roy, P., Podder, A., & Roy, S. (2023). A voting classification approach for sentiment extraction from Bengali text. *International Journal (Toronto, Ont.)*, *11*(5).

Sahoo, T., Mondal, A., Roy, P., & Podder, A. (2024). *Artificial intelligence and its application in engineering: A comprehensive review.* Emerging Engineering Technologies and Industrial Applications, 1–20.

Sanchez, S., & Franco, M. (2020). An intent-aware chatbot for cybersecurity recommendation. https://files.ifi.uzh.ch/CSG/staff/franco/extern/theses/MA-S-Sanchez.pdf

Sarker, I. H. (2022). AI-based modeling: Techniques, applications and research issues towards automation, intelligent and smart systems. *SN Computer Science*, *3*(2), 158. DOI: 10.1007/s42979-022-01043-x PMID: 35194580

Selvamurugan, A., Ganesan, P. K., & Shashank, S. (2024, November 26). Nayak, Arockiaraj Simiyon, and Thirunavukkarasu Indiran. (2025). CNN-LSTM-Based Nonlinear Model Predictive Controller for Temperature Trajectory Tracking in a Batch Reactorhttps. *ACS Omega, 9*(47), 47203–47212. Advance online publication. DOI: 10.1021/acsomega.4c07893 PMID: 39619559

Sharma, S., Singh, G., Islam, N., & Dhir, A. (2022). Why do SMEs adopt artificial intelligence-based chatbots? *IEEE Transactions on Engineering Management, 71*, 1773–1786. DOI: 10.1109/TEM.2022.3203469

Sheng, E., Chang, K.-W., Natarajan, P., & Peng, N. (2019). *The woman worked as a babysitter: On biases in language generation. Proceedings of the 2019 Conference on Empirical Methods in Natural Language Processing and the 9th International Joint Conference on Natural Language Processing (EMNLP-IJCNLP).* https://doi.org/DOI: 10.18653/v1/D19-1339

Sherstinsky, A. (2018). Fundamentals of Recurrent Neural Network (RNN) and Long Short-Term Memory (LSTM) Network. *ArXiv, abs/1808.03314.*

Shi-An, S. L., Er, K. Y. X., Thesman, R. N., & Nin, T. L. (2022). *AI-Driven Data Analytics Assessing Methods to Localize Preexisting Natural Language-Processing Data.* Paper presented at the IRC-SET 2021: Proceedings of the 7th IRC Conference on Science, Engineering and Technology, August 2021, Singapore. DOI: 10.1007/978-981-16-9869-9_15

Silva, G. R. S., & Canedo, E. D. (2024). Towards user-centric guidelines for chatbot conversational design. *International Journal of Human-Computer Interaction, 40*(2), 98–120. DOI: 10.1080/10447318.2022.2118244

Silva, P., Gonçalves, C., Antunes, N., Curado, M., & Walek, B. (2022). Privacy risk assessment and privacy-preserving data monitoring. *Expert Systems with Applications, 200*, 116867. DOI: 10.1016/j.eswa.2022.116867

Somanadh, K. V., & Venugopal, K. (2024). Impact of children's engagement in traditional sports on the fitness: A descriptive study in Andhra Pradesh. In *Reviving Indian Sport's Heritage to Regain Health, Harmony, Glory and Legacy: Reclaiming the Past, Shaping the Future* (pp. 197–204). ISBN: 978-81-970389-8-3.

Söylemez, M., Tekinerdogan, B., & Kolukısa Tarhan, A. (2022). Challenges and solution directions of microservice architectures: A systematic literature review. *Applied Sciences (Basel, Switzerland), 12*(11), 5507. DOI: 10.3390/app12115507

Stahl, B. C., & Eke, D. (2023). The ethics of ChatGPT – Exploring the ethical issues of an emerging technology. *International Journal of Information Management*, *74*, 102700. DOI: 10.1016/j.ijinfomgt.2023.102700

Sublime, J. (2024). The AI Race: Why Current Neural Network-based Architectures are a Poor Basis for Artificial General Intelligence. *Journal of Artificial Intelligence Research*, *79*, 41–67. DOI: 10.1613/jair.1.15315

Sudirjo, F., Diantoro, K., Al-Gasawneh, J. A., Azzaakiyyah, H. K., & Ausat, A. M. A. (2023). Application of ChatGPT in improving customer sentiment analysis for businesses. *Jurnal Teknologi Dan Sistem Informasi Bisnis*, *5*(3), 283–288. DOI: 10.47233/jteksis.v5i3.871

Suglia, A., Konstas, I., & Lemon, O. (2024). Visually Grounded Language Learning: A review of language games, datasets, tasks, and models. *Journal of Artificial Intelligence Research*, *79*, 173–239. DOI: 10.1613/jair.1.15185

Surameery, N. M., & Shakor, M. Y. (2023). Use ChatGPT to solve programming bugs. *International Journal of Information Technology and Computer Engineering*.

Sutskever, I., Vinyals, O., & Le, Q. V. (2014). Sequence to Sequence Learning with Neural Networks. arXiv.org. https://arxiv.org/abs/1409.3215

Su, Y., Wang, X., Ye, Y., Xie, Y., Xu, Y., Jiang, Y., & Wang, C. (2024). Automation and machine learning augmented by large language models in a catalysis study. *Chemical Science (Cambridge)*, *15*(31), 12200–12233. DOI: 10.1039/D3SC07012C PMID: 39118602

Tariq, M. U. (2025). AI-Driven Personalized Learning-Enhancing Student Engagement and Outcomes. In H. Mamede & A. Santos (Eds.), *AI and Learning Analytics in Distance Learning* (pp. 151-178). IGI Global Scientific Publishing. https://doi.org/DOI: 10.4018/979-8-3693-7195-4.ch007

Tariq, M. U., & Sergio, R. (Eds.). (2025). *Cases on AI-Driven Solutions to Environmental Challenges*. IGI Global, 2025. https://doi.org/DOI: 10.4018/979-8-3693-7483-2

Tariq, M. U. (2025). AI and the Ethical Crossroads: Navigating Privacy, Personhood, and Autonomy in the Digital Age. In Chakraborty, S. (Ed.), *Human Values, Ethics, and Dignity in the Age of Artificial Intelligence* (pp. 49–72). IGI Global Scientific Publishing., DOI: 10.4018/979-8-3693-9035-1.ch003

Tariq, M. U. (2025). AI and Work-Life Balance: Transforming Employee Wellbeing in the Modern Workplace. In Ahmed, E., Babar, A., Samad, A., Ahmed, R., & Beydoun, G. (Eds.), *Strengthening Human Relations in Organizations With AI* (pp. 85–110). IGI Global Scientific Publishing., DOI: 10.4018/979-8-3693-6507-6.ch004

Tariq, M. U. (2025). AI-Driven Innovations: Transforming Healthcare, Agriculture, and Environmental Science. In Emara, T., Hassan, E., Trinh, T., Li, G., & Saber, A. (Eds.), *The Role of Artificial Intelligence in Advancing Applied Life Sciences* (pp. 87–118). IGI Global Scientific Publishing., DOI: 10.4018/979-8-3693-9208-9.ch003

Tariq, M. U. (2025). *AI-Driven Learning and Engagement in Higher Education*. IGI Global., DOI: 10.4018/979-8-3693-4074-5

Tariq, M. U. (2025). AI-Driven Pedagogy for the Cyber Nomad Generation-Redefining Learning in the Third Millennium. In Babulak, E. (Ed.), *Educational AI Humanoid Computing Devices for Cyber Nomads* (pp. 15–40). IGI Global Scientific Publishing., DOI: 10.4018/979-8-3693-8985-0.ch002

Tariq, M. U. (2025). AI-Driven Personalized Learning: Revolutionizing Student Engagement and Teacher Efficiency in Education 5.0. In Mobo, F. (Ed.), *AI and Emerging Technologies for Emergency Response and Smart Cities* (pp. 75–96). IGI Global Scientific Publishing., DOI: 10.4018/979-8-3693-9770-1.ch004

Tariq, M. U. (2025). AI-Powered Business Process Automation: Revolutionizing Firm Management. In Derbali, A. (Ed.), *AI, Economic Perspectives, and Firm Business Management* (pp. 199–224). IGI Global Scientific Publishing., DOI: 10.4018/979-8-3693-7357-6.ch010

Tariq, M. U. (2025). AI-Powered Cybersecurity: Defending Green IT Systems With Intelligent Solutions. In Gupta, B., Pramod, D., & Moslehpour, M. (Eds.), *Sustainable Information Security in the Age of AI and Green Computing* (pp. 141–156). IGI Global Scientific Publishing., DOI: 10.4018/979-8-3693-8034-5.ch007

Tariq, M. U. (2025). Balancing Flexibility and Precarity: Ethical Implications and Sustainable Practices in Global Gig Economies. In Doon, R. (Ed.), *Sustainability and Adaptability of Gig Economies in Global Business* (pp. 323–346). IGI Global Scientific Publishing., DOI: 10.4018/979-8-3693-9385-7.ch012

Tariq, M. U. (2025). Bridging Cultures and Languages: Innovative Literacy Strategies for Inclusive and Engaged Classrooms. In Tussey, J., & Haas, L. (Eds.), *Supporting Cultural Differences Through Literacy Education* (pp. 257–282). IGI Global Scientific Publishing., DOI: 10.4018/979-8-3693-9271-3.ch010

Tariq, M. U. (2025). Bridging Home and Classroom: Harnessing Cultural and Ecological Wisdom in Teacher Education. In Liu, L., Mohamed, N., Lin, C., Bauler, C., & Kapur, K. (Eds.), *Funds of Knowledge in Teacher Education: Sustaining Local Diversity Amidst Global Standards* (pp. 405–424). IGI Global Scientific Publishing., DOI: 10.4018/979-8-3693-8094-9.ch018

Tariq, M. U. (2025). Co-Living With Augmented Digital Beings-Navigating the Intersection of AI and Everyday Life. In Moutinho, L., & Martins, L. (Eds.), *Impacts of Sensetech on Society* (pp. 187–206). IGI Global Scientific Publishing., DOI: 10.4018/979-8-3693-7147-3.ch009

Tariq, M. U. (2025). Community-Led Tourism and Social Equity: A Regenerative Approach to Sustainable Development. In Sousa, B., Arantes, L., & Bhartiya, S. (Eds.), *Regenerative Tourism for Social Development* (pp. 339–360). IGI Global Scientific Publishing., DOI: 10.4018/979-8-3373-0235-5.ch014

Tariq, M. U. (2025). Developing a Model for Sustainable Entrepreneurship Competencies: Strategic Decision-Making for a Green Future. In Duháček Šebestová, J., & Popescu, C. (Eds.), *Building a Green Future Through Essential Decision-Making Competencies* (pp. 137–158). IGI Global Scientific Publishing., DOI: 10.4018/979-8-3373-0189-1.ch006

Tariq, M. U. (2025). Empathy-Driven Development: Integrating Design Thinking Into Next-Gen Software Engineering. In Aguilar-Calderón, J., & Tripp-Barba, C. (Eds.), *Innovative Design Thinking Approaches in Software Engineering* (pp. 85–110). IGI Global Scientific Publishing., DOI: 10.4018/979-8-3693-9531-8.ch004

Tariq, M. U. (2025). Empowering patients with AI-ethical digital tools for health data management and decision. In Pesqueira, A., & de Bem Machado, A. (Eds.), *Navigating privacy, innovation, and patient empowerment through ethical healthcare technology* (pp. 197–216). IGI Global., DOI: 10.4018/979-8-3693-7630-0.ch008

Tariq, M. U. (2025). Empowering Women Entrepreneurs: Innovative Crowdfunding and Alternative Financing Models for Sustainable Business Growth. In Katper, N. (Ed.), *Crowdfunding and Alternative Financing Models for Women Entrepreneurs* (pp. 1–34). IGI Global Scientific Publishing., DOI: 10.4018/979-8-3693-9193-8.ch001

Tariq, M. U. (2025). Enhancing Cyber Resilience in Software Development: Integrating Secure Coding Practices and Cybersecurity Frameworks. In Shah, I., & Jhanjhi, N. (Eds.), *Navigating Cyber Threats and Cybersecurity in the Software Industry* (pp. 35–64). IGI Global Scientific Publishing., DOI: 10.4018/979-8-3693-6250-1.ch003

Tariq, M. U. (2025). Enhancing Security and Surveillance With AI-Driven Drones. In Ali Shah, I., & Jhanjhi, N. (Eds.), *Computer Vision and Edge Computing Technologies for the Drone Industry* (pp. 105–128). IGI Global Scientific Publishing., DOI: 10.4018/979-8-3693-8497-8.ch005

Tariq, M. U. (2025). Harnessing 4IR Technologies: Innovating the Digital Preservation of Indigenous Knowledge. In Masenya, T., & Bhuda, M. (Eds.), *Revaluation and Preservation of Indigenous Knowledge Systems in Modern Society* (pp. 321–342). IGI Global Scientific Publishing., DOI: 10.4018/979-8-3693-7964-6.ch016

Tariq, M. U. (2025). Harnessing Life Cycle Assessment for Sustainable Success in Industry 5.0: Integrating AI and Digital Transformation. In Wongmahesak, K., Karim, F., & Wongchestha, N. (Eds.), *Sustainable Futures With Life Cycle Assessment in Industry 5.0* (pp. 21–40). IGI Global Scientific Publishing., DOI: 10.4018/979-8-3693-9346-8.ch002

Tariq, M. U. (2025). Harnessing Technology to Combat Bias: Innovative Tools and Techniques in HR. In Kanwal, S. (Ed.), *Navigating Bias in Human Resource Management* (pp. 155–184). IGI Global Scientific Publishing., DOI: 10.4018/979-8-3693-7132-9.ch006

Tariq, M. U. (2025). Harnessing the Power of GANs and Meta-Learning for Few-Shot Image Generation. In Simaiya, S., Lilhore, U., Sharma, Y., & Kumar, S. (Eds.), *Exploring Generative Adversarial Networks and Meta-Learning Synergies* (pp. 301–324). IGI Global Scientific Publishing., DOI: 10.4018/979-8-3693-7575-4.ch012

Tariq, M. U. (2025). Innovative Business Models: Integrating Social, Economic, and Environmental Goals in Rural Manufacturing. In Prabhakar, A., Yu, P., & Erokhin, V. (Eds.), *Rural Social Entrepreneurship Development: Network-Based Manufacturing System Model* (pp. 147–174). IGI Global Scientific Publishing., DOI: 10.4018/979-8-3693-7515-0.ch005

Tariq, M. U. (2025). Innovative Mentoring Programs: Strategies for Success in Post-COVID-19 Education. In Putnam, J., VanValkenburgh Banks, J., & Brown, S. K. (Eds.), *Mentoring Students and Instructors for Retention and Success* (pp. 123–158). IGI Global Scientific Publishing., DOI: 10.4018/979-8-3693-7590-7.ch005

Tariq, M. U. (2025). Integrating Advanced Technologies for Multi-Stakeholder Collaboration: Driving Sustainability in Supply Chains Through Industry 4.0. In Frichi, Y., & Jawab, F. (Eds.), *Multi-Stakeholder Collaboration for Sustainable Supply Chain* (pp. 313–334). IGI Global Scientific Publishing., DOI: 10.4018/979-8-3693-8925-6.ch014

Tariq, M. U. (2025). Leveraging Data Analytics for Predictive Consumer Behavior Modelling. In Miguélez-Juan, B., & Rebollo-Bueno, S. (Eds.), *AI Impacts on Branded Entertainment and Advertising* (pp. 207–224). IGI Global Scientific Publishing., DOI: 10.4018/979-8-3693-3799-8.ch011

Tariq, M. U. (2025). Navigating Cancer Care: The Crucial Role of Educators and Healthcare Providers in Supporting Patients of Color. In Clarke, K., & Moffett, N. (Eds.), *Cancer Diagnosis, Treatment and Care: Reflections for the Education of Survivors and Healthcare Providers* (pp. 405–424). IGI Global Scientific Publishing., DOI: 10.4018/979-8-3693-5400-1.ch021

Tariq, M. U. (2025). Navigating the Intersection of Diversity and Innovation: Transformative Leadership in Global Workplaces. In Harriott, S. (Ed.), *Innovative Approaches to Managing Conflict and Change in Diverse Work Environments* (pp. 21–48). IGI Global Scientific Publishing., DOI: 10.4018/979-8-3693-9556-1.ch002

Tariq, M. U. (2025). Revitalizing Pedagogy: Integrating Indigenous Knowledge and Practices Into Higher Education Disciplines. In Kgari-Masondo, M. (Ed.), *Indigenous Teaching Disciplines and Perspectives for Higher Education* (pp. 379–400). IGI Global Scientific Publishing., DOI: 10.4018/979-8-3693-9296-6.ch018

Tariq, M. U. (2025). Revolutionizing Urban Congestion: Smart Traffic Management Systems for a Seamless Commute. In Bellam, K., Nagappan, K., Sankaran, N., Chowdhury, S., & Perakovic, D. (Eds.), *Urban Mobility and Challenges of Intelligent Transportation Systems* (pp. 1–16). IGI Global Scientific Publishing., DOI: 10.4018/979-8-3693-7984-4.ch001

Tariq, M. U. (2025). Smart Forecasting With AI: Revolutionizing Energy Consumption and Storage. In Derbali, A. (Ed.), *Integrating Artificial Intelligence Into the Energy Sector* (pp. 165–184). IGI Global Scientific Publishing., DOI: 10.4018/979-8-3693-7112-1.ch009

Tariq, M. U. (2025). The Challenge of Artificial Intelligence in Environmental Sustainability: Opportunities, Risks, and Policy Implications. In Ahmadi, A., & Mna, A. (Eds.), *Nexus of Environmental Quality and Technology Innovation* (pp. 267–292). IGI Global Scientific Publishing., DOI: 10.4018/979-8-3373-1822-6.ch012

Tariq, M. U. (2025). The Social Media Wildfire: Examining Twitter, Facebook, and TikTok's Role in Spreading Supply Chain Misinformation. In Bukhari, S., & Zafar, I. (Eds.), *Mass Media and Impact of Fake News on Supply Chains* (pp. 91–120). IGI Global Scientific Publishing., DOI: 10.4018/979-8-3373-2175-2.ch004

Tariq, M. U. (2025). Unveiling Consumer Insights: The Power of Qualitative Research in Market Analysis. In Segura, L., Vasconcelos, A., & Slomski, V. (Eds.), *Exploring Qualitative Research in Business: Approaches, Strategies, And Methods* (pp. 127–154). IGI Global Scientific Publishing., DOI: 10.4018/979-8-3693-7698-0.ch005

Tauseef, M., Jana, S., Gouda, A. R., Mishra, A., & Srivastava, U. R. (2024). Building a Secure and Transparent Online Conversation Platform: A Blockchain-Based Website With Integrated Virtual Assistant. In *AI and Blockchain Applications in Industrial Robotics* (pp. 276–299). IGI Global.

Team, G., Anil, R., Borgeaud, S., Alayrac, J., Yu, J., Soricut, R., Schalkwyk, J., Dai, A. M., Hauth, A., Millican, K., Silver, D., Johnson, M., Antonoglou, I., & Schrittwieser, J. Vinyals, O. (2023). Gemini: a family of highly capable multimodal models. arXiv.org. https://arxiv.org/abs/2312.11805

Thomas, A., Duggal, H. K., Khatri, P., & Corvello, V. (2024). ChatGPT appropriation: A catalyst for creative performance, innovation orientation, and agile leadership. *Technology in Society*, *78*, 102619. DOI: 10.1016/j.techsoc.2024.102619

Thurzo, A., Strunga, M., Urban, R., Surovková, J., & Afrashtehfar, K. I. (2023). Impact of artificial intelligence on dental education: A review and guide for curriculum update. *Education Sciences*, *13*(2), 150. DOI: 10.3390/educsci13020150

Touvron, H., Lavril, T., Izacard, G., Martinet, X., Lachaux, M., Lacroix, T., Rozière, B., Goyal, N., Hambro, E., Azhar, F., Rodriguez, A., Joulin, A., Grave, E., & Lample, G. (2023). LLAMA: Open and Efficient Foundation Language Models. arXiv.org. https://arxiv.org/abs/2302.13971

Touvron, H., Martin, L., Stone, K., Albert, P., Almahairi, A., Babaei, Y., Bashlykov, N., Batra, S., Bhargava, P., Bhosale, S., Bikel, D., Blecher, L., Ferrer, C. C., Chen, M., Cucurull, G., Esiobu, D., Fernandes, J., Fu, J., & Fu, W. (2023). Llama 2: Open foundation and Fine-Tuned chat models. arXiv.org. https://arxiv.org/abs/2307.09288

TRIALOPA, E. F. (2022). Optimizing The Customer Service Performance With Using Chatbot By Utilizing Bot Accuracy, Journey Completion Rate, And Customer Satisfaction Score (CSAT)(Case Study: PT YAI).

Troncoso, C., Isaakidis, M., Danezis, G., & Halpin, H. (2017). Systematizing decentralization and privacy: Lessons from 15 years of research and deployments. *Proceedings on Privacy Enhancing Technologies. Privacy Enhancing Technologies Symposium*, *2017*(4), 404–426. DOI: 10.1515/popets-2017-0056

Tsherniak, A., Vazquez, F., Montgomery, P. G., Weir, B. A., Kryukov, G., Cowley, G. S., Gill, S., Harrington, W. F., Pantel, S., Krill-Burger, J. M., Meyers, R. M., Ali, L., Goodale, A., Lee, Y., Jiang, G., Hsiao, J., Gerath, W. F. J., Howell, S., Merkel, E., & Hahn, W. C. (2017). Defining a cancer dependency map. *Cell*, *170*(3), 564–576. e16. DOI: 10.1016/j.cell.2017.06.010 PMID: 28753430

Uğraş, M. (2024). *Evaluation of CHATGPT usage in preschool education: Teacher perspectives*. Eğitim ve İnsani Bilimler Dergisi Teori ve Uygulama., DOI: 10.58689/eibd.1537337

UNESCO. (2021). *Artificial intelligence and education: Guidance for policymakers*. UNESCO.

United Nations. (2015). *Transforming our world: The 2030 agenda for sustainable development*. Retrieved from https://sdgs.un.org/goals

Vakamullu Gopalakrishna, & Venugopal, K. (2023, August). Assessment on the intricacies of English speaking abilities by rural students in India. In *English Language Competence in Rural Youth: Improving Job Readiness* (pp. 114–126). Current Publications. ISBN 978-81-19255-30-6.

Valeri, F., Nilsson, P., & Cederqvist, A. (2024). Exploring students' experience of CHATGPT in STEM education. *Computers and Education Artificial Intelligence, 100360*. Advance online publication. DOI: 10.1016/j.caeai.2024.100360

van Dam, S., Võsa, U., van der Graaf, A., Franke, L., & de Magalhães, J. P. (2018). Gene co-expression analysis for functional classification and gene-disease predictions. *Briefings in Bioinformatics, 19*(4), 575–592. PMID: 28077403

Vaswani, A., Shazeer, N., Parmar, N., Uszkoreit, J., Jones, L., Gomez, A. N., Kaiser, L., & Polosukhin, I. (2017). Attention is all you need. arXiv.org. https://arxiv.org/abs/1706.03762

Vaswani, A., Shazeer, N., Parmar, N., Uszkoreit, J., Jones, L., Gomez, A. N., Kaiser, Ł., & Polosukhin, I. (2017). Attention is all you need. In *Proceedings of the 31st International Conference on Neural Information Processing Systems* (pp. 6000–6010). https://doi.org/DOI: 10.5555/3295222.3295349

Venugopal, K., & Saumendra Das. (2023, September). Prediction analysis of Gen Zers' attitudes on ecological consciousness. In *Sustainable Science and Intelligent Technologies for Societal Development* (pp. 242–257). IGI Global.

Venugopal, K. (2024). Exploring Gen Z perspectives toward ChatGPT in academic contexts. In Bansal, R., Chakir, A., Hafaz Ngah, A., Rabby, F., & Jain, A. (Eds.), *AI algorithms and ChatGPT for student engagement in online learning* (pp. 51–69). IGI Global., DOI: 10.4018/979-8-3693-4268-8.ch004

Venugopal, K., & Jagadeesh, B. (2024). Theoretical insights into user security and privacy in social media environments. In Kumar, R., Srivastava, S., & Elngar, A. (Eds.), *Human impact on security and privacy: Network and human security, social media, and devices* (pp. 289–312). IGI Global., DOI: 10.4018/979-8-3693-9235-5.ch015

Venugopal, K., & Somanadh, K. V. (2024). Smart library systems: Integrating IoT for enhanced user experience. In *Libraries as Wisdom Hubs* (pp. 196–205). Interdisciplinary Insights for the Future.

Virshup, A. M., Contreras-García, J., Wipf, P., Yang, W., & Beratan, D. N. (2013). Stochastic voyages into uncharted chemical space produce a representative library of all possible drug-like compounds. *Journal of the American Chemical Society, 135*(19), 7296–7303. DOI: 10.1021/ja401184g PMID: 23548177

Volkmar, G., Fischer, P. M., & Reinecke, S. (2022). Artificial intelligence and machine learning: Exploring drivers, barriers, and future developments in marketing management. *Journal of Business Research, 149*, 599–614. DOI: 10.1016/j.jbusres.2022.04.007

Waheed, N., Ikram, M., Hashmi, S. S., He, X., & Nanda, P. (2022, October). An empirical assessment of security and privacy risks of web-based chatbots. In *International Conference on Web Information Systems Engineering* (pp. 325-339). Cham: Springer International Publishing. DOI: 10.1007/978-3-031-20891-1_23

Waliu, A. O., Muojekwu, E. E., Matthew, U. O., Kazaure, J. S., Oseni, V. E., Ononiwu, C. C., & Haruna, K. (2025). *Clinical Simulation in nursing education: Immersive Educational Tech for nurses and midwives Creating Immersive Learning Experiences Through Virtual Reality (VR)*. IGI Global.

Wang, T., & Zhu, Q. (2024). *ChatGPT–Technical Research Model, Capability Analysis, and Application Prospects.* Paper presented at the 2024 IEEE 7th Advanced Information Technology, Electronic and Automation Control Conference (IAEAC). DOI: 10.1109/IAEAC59436.2024.10503756

Wang, J., Hu, H., Wang, Z., Yan, S., Sheng, Y., & He, D. (2024). Evaluating large language models on academic literature understanding and review: An empirical study among early-stage scholars. In *Conference on Human Factors in Computing Systems (CHI)* (pp. 1–18). https://doi.org/DOI: 10.1145/3613904.3641917

Weeks, C., Cheruvu, A., Abdullah, S. M., Kanchi, S., Yao, D., & Viswanath, B. (2023, December). A first look at toxicity injection attacks on open-domain chatbots. In *Proceedings of the 39th Annual Computer Security Applications Conference* (pp. 521-534). DOI: 10.1145/3627106.3627122

Wu, T. Y., Yang, L., Luo, J. N., & Wu, M.-T. (2021). J. (2021). A Provably Secure Authentication and Key Agreement Protocol in Cloud-Based Smart Healthcare Environments. *Security and Communication Networks*, (1), 2299632.

Yenduri, G. M, R., G, C. S., Y, S., Srivastava, G., Maddikunta, P. K. R., G, D. R., Jhaveri, R. H., B, P., Wang, W., Vasilakos, A., V., &Gadekallu, T. R. (2023). Generative Pre-trained Transformer: a comprehensive review on enabling technologies, potential applications, emerging challenges, and future directions. arXiv.org. https://arxiv.org/abs/2305.10435

Yenduri, G., Ramalingam, M., Selvi, G. C., Supriya, Y., Srivastava, G., Maddikunta, P. K. R., & Wang, W. (2024). Gpt (generative pre-trained transformer)–a comprehensive review on enabling technologies, potential applications, emerging challenges, and future directions. *IEEE Access : Practical Innovations, Open Solutions*, *12*, 54608–54649. DOI: 10.1109/ACCESS.2024.3389497

Yigci, D., Eryilmaz, M., Yetisen, A. K., Tasoglu, S., & Ozcan, A. (2024). Large Language Model-Based Chatbots in Higher Education. *Advanced Intelligent Systems*, •••, 2400429.

Zawacki-Richter, O.. (2019). The impact of AI in higher education: A review of trends and developments. *International Journal of Educational Technology in Higher Education*, *16*(1), 39. DOI: 10.1186/s41239-019-0171-0

Zellers, R., Holtzman, A., Bisk, Y., Farhadi, A., & Choi, Y. (2019). HellaSwag: Can a machine really finish your sentence? *Proceedings of the 57th Annual Meeting of the Association for Computational Linguistics*. https://doi.org/DOI: 10.18653/v1/P19-1472

Zhang, W., Zhang, Q., Cai, M., Wang, D., & Zheng, Y. (2024). *Navigating the Application Challenges of ChatGPT in Education: Promoting Responsible Use and Minimizing Mental Risks*. Paper presented at the Proceedings of the 2024 9th International Conference on Distance Education and Learning. DOI: 10.1145/3675812.3675843

Zhuang, X., & Wu, Y. (2024). ChatGPT: How it can support corporate social responsibility. *The Journal of Business Strategy*, *45*(6), 386–395. DOI: 10.1108/JBS-05-2023-0089

About the Contributors

Muhammad Usman Tariq has more than 16+ year's experience in industry and academia. He has authored more than 200+ research articles, 110+ case studies, 150+ book chapters and several books other than 4 patents. He is founder and CEO of The Case HQ, a unique repository for courses, narrative and video case studies. He has been working as a consultant and trainer for industries representing six sigma, quality, health and safety, environmental systems, project management, and information security standards. His work has encompassed sectors in aviation, manufacturing, food, hospitality, education, finance, research, software and transportation. He has diverse and significant experience working with accreditation agencies of ABET, ACBSP, AACSB, WASC, CAA, EFQM and NCEAC. Additionally, Dr. Tariq has operational experience in incubators, research labs, government research projects, private sector startups, program creation and management at various industrial and academic levels. He is Certified Higher Education Teacher from Harvard University, USA, Certified Online Educator from HMBSU, Certified Six Sigma Master Black Belt and has been awarded PFHEA, SFSEDA, SMIEEE, and CMBE.

***

Oyedemi Oluyemisi Adenike is a lectuer in the Department of Computer Science/Cybersecurity, University of Ilesa, Ilesa, Osun State, Nigeria. She is currently on postdoctoral study in the Department of Computer Science, Federal University of Lavras, Brazil. Her research interest is in the area of Machine learning, IoT context and Cybersecurity. In the area of Machine learning, she has worked on intelligent system to detect Cyberthreat. She is currently exploring the world of connected devices and the intricacies of sensor networks in IoT platforms.

Monojit Banerjee is an accomplished leader in the AI platform and DevOps space. He oversees the development and management of a robust platform that powers a wide range of AI applications, widely adopted across multiple industries. Monojit's expertise spans AI/ML, DevOps, cloud computing, and Generative AI, making him a versatile and influential figure. A passionate contributor to the AI and DevOps community, Monojit serves as a technical reviewer for renowned publishers like Packt and Manning. He is also a journal reviewer for Transactions on Machine Learning Research (TMLR) and actively participates in various conferences by contributing to technical program committees. Additionally, he is the owner of EinsteinPlayground, an open-source tool for building natural language and vision models, which is widely utilized by organizations around the globe. Monojit is an IEEE Senior Member and a dedicated mentor in the Adplist program, where he supports the growth of professionals and newcomers in AI, DevOps, and STEM fields. His commitment to advancing the community and fostering innovation has made him a respected thought leader.

Eboesomi Esther Bunmi is dynamic and professional with extensive expertise in travel management, project coordination, and client engagement. As the founder of Round D Globe Travels and Tours Limited in Nigeria, I achieved 196% year-over-year growth by delivering tailored travel solutions for clients across four continents. Currently, I serve as Operations Team Lead with Dwelling At Ease, where I leverage GDS platforms like Amadeus to lead high-performing teams and implement strategic initiatives aimed at optimizing operations and enhancing client experiences. Additionally, I act as a Training Lead with Stutern, focusing on skills development. Core Competencies Travel Consultation & Operations Leadership & Team Management Strategic Planning & Execution Project Coordination Client Relationship Management Education & Certifications M.Sc. in Management with Tourism & Hospitality University of Huddersfield IATA Management Certification International Air Transport Association Certified South African Specialist

Daniel Emakporuena is a skilled Data Scientist/Analyst focused on creating impactful data solutions and generating insights to drive business decision-making. His research area is centered on implementing AI and Data Science in driving business and sustainability solutions, using his advanced analytical techniques to solve complex problems. Daniel gained his Bachelor's degree in Mathematics and further developed his skills in Computation and quantitative analysis gaining a Master's degree in Data Science and Big Data Analytics. Daniel is proficient in a range of data science tools and software, including Excel, PowerBI, Python, SQL, and various machine learning frameworks, to extract meaningful insights from data. His expertise in AI allows him to develop predictive models, Analytical dashboard and intelligent systems that optimize business operations and support sustainable practices. Throughout his career, Daniel has led numerous projects that have driven significant improvements in operational efficiency, resource management, and strategic planning. His ability to merge data science with AI applications positions him as a leader in the evolving fields of business intelligence and sustainable technology. Daniel remains committed to continuous learning and staying at the forefront of technological advancements. His dedication to excellence is evident in his work, mentorship, and contributions to industry publications and forums, where he actively shares his knowledge and ideas.

Ogheneruona Maria Esegbona-Isikeh is a Data Journalist with years of experience in uncovering compelling stories through data analysis and visualization. She specializes in using Python, R, and SQL to mine large datasets and distill complex information into clear, engaging narratives. Ogheneruona's work often explores social justice, economic trends, and public policy, with a particular focus on making data accessible to a broad audience. Her investigative reporting has been featured in leading publications such as News agency of Nigeria (NAN), The Guardian, UrbanKapital Magazine agmonst others. She has written multiple health data stories. Ogheneruona holds a Master's degree in Data Journalism from Birmingham City University(BCU), United Kingdom and a Bachelor's degree in Mass Communication from Delta State University, Abraka in Nigeria.When she's not crunching numbers, Ogheneruona enjoys mentoring aspiring data journalists and speaking at technology conferences about the importance of transparency in data storytelling.

Sanchita Ghosh is a highly driven worker who holds a Master of Computer Applications degree. Her current position as a Technical Assistant at Brainware University allows her to specialize on IoT,NLP, AI, networking, cybersecurity, and cloud computing. Sanchita is passionate about using technology to solve complicated challenges, and she actively participates in projects and activities that promote innovation and progress the digital transformation. Her diversified skill set and dedication to continual learning make her an invaluable asset in the ever-changing field of information technology.

Antonio D. Juan has a degree in English Studies from the University of Murcia and a PhD from the National University of Distance Education (UNED) with the positive accreditation by the ANECA body, being given the Extraordinary Doctorate Award. He is currently working as a professor at the University of Granada. He has been awarded a scholarship by University College (Cork, Ireland), the Franklin Institute (University of Alcala de Henares, Spain) and the Radcliffe

Institute for Advanced Study (Harvard University, USA), where he conducted a pre-doctoral research visit in the year 2012. He is currently a member of the scientific committee of several national and international journals as well as a member of the editorial board of several international journals. He also belongs to the organizing and scientific committee of several conferences organized by the Athens Institute for Education and Research (Greece). Among his main lines of research we can emphasize the following aspects: cultural studies in the United States; gender issues associated with the role of women in the Anglo-American literature; or the teaching practice and process of English.

Madhavi Kappagantula is an associate Professor and Head for the department of MBA in Acharya Graduate studies has an immense interest in research and community services . She has published good quality papers and conducted many research activities and management events for the students as well as faculty.

Kazi Kutubuddin Sayyad Liyakat has completed his B.E., M.E., and Ph.D. in E&TC Engineering and is nowadays working as a Professor & Head of Department, E&TC Engineering Department and was Dean R&D. He is Post-Doctoral Fellow working on IoT in Healthcare Applications. His area of Interest is IoT, IoRT, IoBT, AI, ML, and AIIoT. He has published more than 160+ papers, including Book chapters with various renowned publishers like IGI Global, CRC, NOVA publishers. Also he had received various 42 Patents from Indian Patent House (Utility, Design and Copyright), UK Design Grant Patents, South African Design Grant Patents and Canadian Copyright Patents. He received funds for various projects on IoT applications. He published 22 books under different National and International publishers. He worked as Editor for 1 book. He worked as a Reviewer for Scopus Conferences and Journal and for IGI Global. Also, he work as Editorial Board Member for 6 Journals. He got 3 Best Researcher Awards, 1 Best Faculty Award, a appreciation letter form Nextwave, 1 Best HoD Award and 2-Appreciation Letter from MoE's Innovation Cell, Government of India.

Ugochukwu O. Matthew, presently is an Academic scholar with Hussaini Adamu Federal Polytechnic, Nigeria, in the Department of Computer Science with specialty in AI, Big Data Science, Cloud Computing, Internet of Things, Data Mining, Multimedia and E-Learning Education. A Member of Nigeria Computer Society (NCS), Nigeria Institute of Management (NIM), International Association of Computer Science & Information Technology (IACSIT), European Alliance for Innovation(EAI) and also a member of Teaching & Education Research Association (TERA). Ugochukwu O. Matthew hold Masters in Computer Applications from Bayero University Kano, Nigeria. Ugochukwu O. Matthew had reviewed several

Journals and a member of Review Board Committee of Journals Indexed by Scopus and Web of Science including IEEE Access, SN Computer Science (Springer), International Journal of Information Communication Technologies & Human Development(IJICTHD), International Journal of Business Data Communications and Networking (IJBDCN), International Journal of Cloud Applications and Computing (IJCAC). Ugochukwu O. Matthew is a cofounder of U&J Digital Consult Limited, an IT and Educational Consulting Firm in Nigeria.

Anshit Mukherjee is presently pursuing Bachelor of Technology (Hons.) in Computer Science and Engineering from the Abacus Institute of Engineering and Management, which is affiliated with Maulana Abul Kalam Azad University of Technology, and is presently in final year. He was the zonal topper of the AMBIKA KALNA zone in I.C.S.E. 2019 (10 TH STANDARD) and the second zonal topper in I.S.C. 2021 (12 TH STANDARD). He is also awarded with NPTEL Discipline Star in July–December 2023 and Motivated Learner in January-June 2024.

Morgan Nwaiku is a dedicated cybersecurity professional with a strong foundation in software development and a background in computer engineering. With a focus on building and monitoring systems that utilize anomaly detection and artificial intelligence, Morgan ensures that software products are both secure and user-friendly, balancing the critical aspects of security and usability. His passion for technology extends beyond his professional work, as he actively mentors aspiring tech enthusiasts and contributes to the tech community through volunteering and knowledge sharing. Morgan's expertise spans across various tools and technologies, including Azure cloud services, SQL and NoSQL databases, Python programming, application testing, and API. By integrating AI into their anomaly detection systems, Morgan stays at the cutting edge of cybersecurity innovation. This diverse skill set, coupled with a commitment to staying at the forefront of technological advancements, positions Morgan as a valuable asset in the technology space.

Victor Oluwasegun Omoboye is a result-driven Data Scientist and Thought Leader specialising in Artificial Intelligence, Machine Learning, Predictive Analytics and AI-powered automation. He has developed and deployed scalable AI solutions that drive efficiency and business growth across various industries, including healthcare, e-commerce, and finance. Omoboye is proficient in Python, TensorFlow, SQL, and NLP, with hands-on experience in building recommender systems, dynamic pricing models, and real-time risk prediction tools. His academic foundation includes an MSc in Data Science from the University of Roehampton London, United Kingdom and certifications in Full Stack Data Science. Omoboye has contributed to the innovation of digital technology via his recently built AI-driven application for early detection of COPD, bridging the gap between cutting-edge AI advancements and practical learning methodologies.

Tulika Paul is a highly driven worker who holds a Master of Computer Applications degree. Her current position as a Technical Assistant at Brainware University allows her to specialize on IoT, AI, networking, cybersecurity. Tulika is passionate about using technology to solve complicated challenges, and she actively participates in projects and activities that promote innovation and progress the digital transformation. Her diversified skill set and dedication to continual learning make her an invaluable asset in the ever-changing field of information technology.

B. Govindarajulu is an assistant Professor in The department of Civil Engineering for 15 years has contributed significant research and community service activities such as publications, Consultancies, Seminars, FDPs and training programmes. He is interested in researching on social aspects and contextual issues

Bitan Roy is a highly driven worker who holds a Master of Computer Applications degree. His current position as a Technical Assistant at Brainware University allows his to specialize on IoT, AI, networking, cybersecurity. Bitan is passionate about using technology to solve complicated challenges, and he actively participates in projects and activities that promote innovation and progress the digital transformation. His diversified skill set and dedication to continual learning make him an invaluable asset in the ever-changing field of information technology.

Piyal Roy is an accomplished academician in the field of Computer Science & Engineering. He has completed his BSc in Computer Science, MSc in Computer Science and MTech in Computer Science & Engineering. Currently, he is working as an Assistant Professor at Computer Science & Engineering department at Brainware University, India.

Aditya Singh is an Independent Researcher, Editorial Review Board Member in 5 American International Journals (IJSSMET, IJSDS, IJPAEI, IJESGT, IJDSST), Reviewer in 8 American, 3 Singaporean & 1 Indonesian International Journals (IJUPSC, IJCVIP, IRMJ, JTA, IJRLEDM, IJAIBM, IJCEWM, JITR, JDSIS, AAES, JCCE, & IJEECS) & Ex-Alumni Mentor (LPU) at present. He had completed his regular B. Tech degree in Civil Engineering from Lovely Professional University, India, in 2020. He is currently affiliated with Amrita Vishwa Vidyapeetham, Coimbatore, India. He has 24 publications under his name, in which he is a single author in 17 of them, whereas in 5 of them he is the main author. Most of his publications are Indexed in Scopus. He had also worked as a Reviewer/Editorial Review Board Member for 138 times in the evaluation of manuscripts so far in international conferences, international books and international journals. He had also won 2 International Awards((Thailand) & (Cambodia)) as a Reviewer in 2023. He had worked on 44 positions in International Journals, International Conferences & International Research Books so far in his professional career internationally.

Koppala Venugopal, a professor in Management Studies at Aditya Institute of Technology and Management at Srikakulam, A.P. has had an adroit experience of academic, Research and community service. He has contributed 5 Projects, 2 patents, 10 books, 70 publications, 48 paper presentations, 56 resource talks and 12 memberships. He is guiding 4 scholars from various universities. His exceptional interest industry interface has made his efforts dexterous.

Williams Ugbomeh is a seasoned Data scientist, Business Analyst and Scrum Master with a proven track record of leveraging agile methodologies to drive efficiency, foster collaboration, and deliver strategic value. With extensive experience in requirement gathering, stakeholder management, and data analysis, he excels at transforming complex business challenges into actionable insights that optimize productivity and performance. A dynamic leader, Williams is adept at managing change expectations, mitigating risks, and minimizing inefficiencies by seamlessly integrating data-driven insights into business frameworks. His expertise extends beyond process improvement—he is a strong advocate for team resilience, organizational agility, and a culture of continuous improvement. Passionate about technology and innovation, Williams actively mentors aspiring tech professionals and contributes to the tech community through volunteering, knowledge-sharing, and professional development initiatives. His technical proficiency spans a wide range of tools and technologies, including: Data Visualization: Tableau, Power BI, Qlik Sense Databases: SQL, NoSQL Machine Learning: Alteryx, Python Productivity & Collaboration: Microsoft Office Suite Committed to staying at the forefront of technological advancements, Williams integrates AI-driven anomaly detection systems into business operations, ensuring organizations remain competitive, data-driven, and future-ready. His blend of analytical expertise, technical acumen, and leadership skills makes him an invaluable asset in the ever-evolving technology landscape.

Index

A

B

C

D

E

F

G

H

I

K

L

M

N

P

R

S

T

U

www.ingramcontent.com/pod-product-compliance
Lightning Source LLC
LaVergne TN
LVHW081531300926
849161LV00006B/1376